Holiday Magazine Award Cookbook

Introduction by Robert Lawrence Balzer

ILLUSTRATIONS BY LUCIAN LUPINSKI

HOLIDAY MAGAZINE AWARD COOKBOOK

Famous Recipes from the HOLIDAY
Award Winning Restaurants

Selected and Edited by
Charlotte Turgeon

THE CURTIS PUBLISHING COMPANY
Indianapolis, Indiana

THE CURTIS PUBLISHING COMPANY
Beurt SerVaas, *Chairman and Publisher*
Cory SerVaas, *Co-Chairman and Publisher*

HOLIDAY MAGAZINE AWARD COOKBOOK
Charlotte Turgeon, *Editor-in-Chief*
Jean White, *Editor*
Starkey Flythe, Jr., *Managing Editor*
Sandra Strother, *Art Director and Designer*
John Bayliss, *Text Editor*
St. Leger "Monty" Joynes, *Business Manager*
Jack Merritt, *Manager, Book Division*
David M. Price, *Production Manager*

Staff for this Book
Anna Lyon Baker, Marie Caldwell, Louise Fortson,
Astrid Henkels, Kathryn Klassen, Lynne McPherson, Steve Miller,
Gary Moore, John Rea, Lynn Troup, Geri Watson

*Special thanks to Maryanne Casey, The Kitchen Door,
Indianapolis, for the loan of cooking untensils.*

Contents

Foreword

One new and exciting recipe is worth the price of a whole new cookbook (which seldom costs as much as one good restaurant meal). When a book gives over two hundred recipes gleaned from the foremost chefs in Continental North America whose restaurants have received the Holiday Award, that is more than a bargain—it's a steal.

Here are revealed the mysteries of the very best of French, Italian, Mexican, Canadian and honest-to-goodness American food in terms that every lay cook, man or woman, can understand. These are not everyday recipes. They are dishes to be served on special occasions, dishes that the home cook who wants to cook nobly can achieve.

There are beautiful, beautiful soups; magnificent creations with shellfish of all varieties; broiled ocean fish graced with *beurre blanc*, that subtle sauce left usually to accomplished men who wear the *toque blanche*, but within every patient cook's ability. Wonderful dishes of beef, veal, lamb, pork, poultry and game; vegetables treated with culinary appreciation, and marvelous salads; all preludes to extravagant and lovely desserts that delight the eye and complete a perfect meal.

But this is not only a cookbook; it is a passport to extraordinary restaurants all over the country and beyond. A traveler would do well to tuck the royal purple volume under his arm and make his way from restaurant to restaurant. He'll be welcomed as an old friend. If travel is not in your particular set of stars, follow the recipes and be both chef and guest. Bon Appétit.

Charlotte Turgeon

Amherst, Massachusetts
June 1976

Introduction

This book is an avenue to the pleasure kingdom of food. The guides are the many chefs whose originality and understanding of the culinary arts make possible this domestic adventuring.

Our world is still relatively young. The first restaurant was a new idea in Paris in 1765, when a soup vendor named Boulanger broke a tradition of centuries in offering a choice of dishes to any who might enjoy them. He called his nourishing soups *restaurants* because he believed they were restoratives! With significant wit, he embellished his outdoor sign with a Latin pun: *"Venite ad me, vos qui stomacho laboratis et ego restaurabo vos."* In brief: "If you're hungry, I'll restore you." His promise was an instant success. Even imitators flourished. Tavern hosts and *traiteurs* (caterers who by French law could sell only whole roasts) were finished as the sole purveyors of food. Parliament decreed in favor of Boulanger, and the restaurant trade was born. An eloquent customer, Jean Anthelme Brillat-Savarin, recognized this answer to a common need, and, as the cheerful idea began to spread, wrote that it brought to each, "according to his purse or according to his appetite, copious or delicate meals, which formerly were the perquisite of the very rich."

In this last quarter of the 20th Century, only a little more than two hundred years after the idea of the restaurant was born, a book of recipes from the fine restaurants of the world is a reality. Two thousand years ago, in Imperial Rome, a handful of recipes were of enough value to turn a slave into a freedman . . . through artful performance in the kitchen. Such arts were almost akin to sorcery, and culinary formulas quickly became secrets. The first cookbook, out of Rome, was subject to plagiarism for centuries once Johann Gutenberg came up with movable type. The Bible was Gutenberg's most famous printed work, but I think his heart was in Platina's *De Honesta Voluptate ac Valetudine*, the world's first printed cookery book.

Worry not about "veils of secrecy" making any of these recipes less than a direct route to your achievement of gastronomic supremacy. And bear in mind that the Stradivarius does not play itself but needs a Yehudi Menuhin before glorious music can come from the inanimate wood and catgut strings. In the common egg is the yolk which, when combined with butter and lemon, judicious salt, and grains of cayenne, produces the yellow, velvet Hollandaise sauce. The whites, whipped to airy froth, become the white clouds of meringue for *vacherin* . . . or the light magic of quenelles.

You are the "third dimension" of this cookery book. It *can* work joyous triumphs for you. As students of the masters, we are here only given our lessons, the musical notes or the colors for the palette. The rest is up to us.

Robert Lawrence Balzer

Santa Ana, California
July 5, 1976

*The discovery of a new dish
does more for the happiness of mankind
than the discovery of a star.*

Brillat-Savarin

The East

The Eastern region of our nation was firstest with the mostest. Sea, mountain, river, lake and woods poured down upon early diners a plethora of fish and fowl, wild berry and Indian maize. But the food of this wonderful part of America never turned into a pompous national table. It is a lively, serendipitous mix of native invention where freshness is all, and seasoning depends more on the original than on any imported herbs or spices. A lobster boiled moments from its trap (pot) is tenderer than the melted butter which should be its only adornment. A cranberry tart, sharp and somehow misty, obliterates the memory of over-sweet Thanksgiving versions of the bog berry. And chowder, corn or clam, warms and soothes as no other soup can, short of the ubiquitous chicken broth of every mama's stock and trade.

Below (geographically, only) New England is New York, the melting pot of a thousand foreign dishes, and today, the city of the world where all nations convene, a sort of gastronomical peace plan in microcosm (at the UN) and macrocosm in the city itself where squabbles cease at lunchtime. Then you have a choice. The best restaurants are French, the language of the kitchen. Expensive, chic, an intense concentration of the world's glamour and personality where the show never outdoes the food. Or, sometimes just next door or across the street, a sandwich, dubbed hero or submarine or poorboy containing the world. Soft savory beef, translucent onions, inquisitive peppers, mushrooms, cheeses and a thousand other fluctuations and modifications on Lord Sandwich's universally adored structure.

Around the corner, China and Italy and Japan and Hungary and Germany and England and Spain and Morocco and the Middle East and India are spreading their perpetual picnics. One wonders there aren't more rotund northerners, that Manhattan doesn't sink into the sea from the weight of its pleasures; but this is also the working capital of the world where good food is merely the just desert of hard work and persistent endeavor. The competition is keen here, among restaurants and among men. To succeed one has to be the very best.

Anthony's Pier 4

What can provide a better memory than "the unusual touch"? At Anthony's Pier 4 restaurant, clients not only have a magnificent view of Boston Harbor from the end of a converted pier but when a vessel of exceptional significance passes by, a brass bell is sounded and the ship's name, home port, destination and a description of the cargo are announced. President of the company Anthony Athanas is out to please because it aids his great desire to make Boston a showplace for living. An added attraction in the harbor is the four-decked former Hudson River dayliner, the SS *Peter Stuyvesant* that Anthony has exquisitely redecorated and berthed alongside the restaurant, where it serves as a facility for cocktail parties and special functions. Anthony is proud of Boston—and he has served the city in many ways. He was chairman of the International Institute of Boston's 1975 International Fair which celebrated the ethnic heritage of the city. In 1972, that institute awarded him its prestigious Golden Door Award as one of the leading Americans of foreign birth who have made distinguished contributions to American life and culture.

A host of diners enjoy the best seafood in an Old Salt atmosphere of figureheads, scrimshaw, lamps, casks and nameplates. Appetites are whetted by the enticing display of fish at the entrance. Once inside, the feast begins, with freshly shucked oysters, steaming chowders, broiled Boston scrod. It's the greatest happening since the Boston Tea Party.

140 NORTHERN AVENUE, BOSTON

New England Clam Chowder

¼ pound salt pork
3-4 potatoes
½ cup clam juice

1. Cut the salt pork into small cubes and cook over moderate heat until the cubes are crisp. Drain off the fat and reserve.

2. Peel and dice the potatoes. Rinse in cold water. Drain well.

3. Put the potatoes in a heavy pot or

3 cups minced clams
with juice
1 teaspoon salt
¼ teaspoon white pepper
¾ teaspoon Worcestershire
sauce
½ teaspoon Tabasco
2 teaspoons chicken base
(or 2 chicken bouillon
cubes)
4 tablespoons butter
½ cup flour
2½ cups whole milk
2½ cups light cream

kettle. Add the clam juice, minced clams, salt and pepper, Worcestershire sauce, Tabasco and chicken base. Cover and simmer, stirring occasionally, for 30 minutes. If moisture evaporates, add more clam juice.

4. Sauté the onions in the pork fat just until tender, then add onions and pork fat to the potato-clam mixture.

5. Melt the butter and stir in the flour to make a paste. Add half of this to the potatoes and clams and boil hard for 10 minutes. If the mixture seems too thin, add more of the butter-flour paste.

6. Scald the milk and cream but do not let it boil. Add to the clam mixture. Keep on very low heat for about 30 minutes. The mixture will thicken gradually.

7. Serve very hot.

MAKES 8 1-CUP SERVINGS

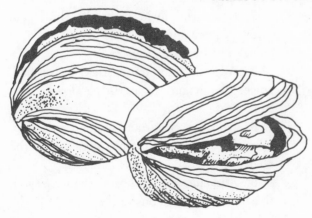

Café Budapest

An American dowager may be seen hobnobbing with a Hungarian gypsy—in sedate Boston. Saints alive! The dowager is the 62-year-old Copley Square Hotel recently restored to its former charm under the capable direction of Roger A. Saunders, hotel owner. Then came the gypsy, in the form of Mrs. Edith Ban's Café Budapest, and ensconced herself in the lower lobby of the hotel. The aromas that come from the kitchen are so enticing that not only the hotel guests but all Boston makes tracks to Café Budapest.

In bright surroundings of cut flowers, red carpet and napkins, the menu performs its Hungarian rhapsody of specialties: baked chicken paprikas, veal goulache served with cucumber-onion salad; Rice Pilaf à la Baron and Szekely Goulache. With a deft sweetness, the desserts present themselves: Gundel pancake with almond-orange cream filling, Hungarian strudels with 5 types of coffee for the final curtsy. Bravos . . .

90 EXETER STREET, BOSTON

Chilled Cherry Soup à la Budapest

3 1-pound cans pitted
  tart cherries
Water
1 2-inch piece of
  cinnamon stick
6 cloves
6 whole allspice
1 slice lemon
½ cup sugar
1 pinch salt

1. Put 2 cans of cherries with their juice in a large saucepan.
2. Drain the juice from the third can. Pour the juice only into the pan.
3. Add 1 canful of water.
4. Add the cinnamon stick, cloves, allspice, lemon and sugar. Bring slowly to a boil.
5. Whisk the flour and cream together in a bowl until completely blended. Add to the cherries.
6. Add the wine and bring the soup again to a boil, whisking constantly.

1 tablespoon flour
1 pint medium cream
Half bottle of dry red French
    Médoc wine
Whipped cream

7. Remove from the heat and let cool. Chill in the refrigerator.

8. Serve the soup in individual cups or small bowls. Garnish each serving with a little whipped cream. A single cherry on the whipped cream and a dusting of finely chopped parsley may also be added if desired. This refreshing soup makes a pleasant beginning to a meal, winter or summer. It can be made in advance. It will keep in the refrigerator for at least 2 weeks.

SERVES 12

Dodin-Bouffant

Many successful restaurateurs are inheritors of tradition who began to absorb the secrets of haute cuisine if not with their mother's milk, at least with their first sit-up-at-the-table dinners. Not so Karen and Robert Pritsker, moving spirits behind Dodin-Bouffant. Neither one grew up in the restaurant business. She was a journalist, he a lawyer accountant. Their involvement with fine food began as a hobby; they liked to eat well, so they learned to cook well. Soon friends were asking them to cater small dinner parties, then large ones, and a growing confidence engendered their own restaurant. The Dodin-Bouffant opened downtown, near Copley Square; and upstairs, via a very special elevator with shiny brass folding gate.

The unusual name for the establishment was inspired by a fictional character, a gastronome, created by French novelist Marcel Rouff. The menu would be much to Monsieur's liking, for the specialties change daily.

384 BOYLSTON STREET, BOSTON

Charlotte aux Abricots
(Apricot Charlotte)

Genoise cake:

- 4 tablespoons clarified butter (page 420)
- 6 eggs
- 1 cup sugar
- 1 cup sifted cake flour
- 1 teaspoon vanilla

- 1 pound dried apricots
- 2 cups sugar
- 1 cup water
- 1 package gelatin
- 4 tablespoons kirsch

1. Prepare clarified butter and let it cool slightly.

2. Let the eggs stand in very warm water for 5 to 10 minutes. Rinse out the electric mixer bowl in very hot water.

3. Break the eggs into the heated bowl and start beating. When foamy, gradually add the sugar and continue beating until the mixture is almost stiff.

4. Preheat the oven to 350 degrees F.

5. Grease a 9-inch round cake pan. Place a round of wax paper in the bottom and grease the paper.

6. Fold the flour and the vanilla into the egg mixture, using a rubber spatula. Fold in the clarified butter, a little at a time.

2-3 teaspoons lemon juice
  2 cups heavy cream
Whipped cream and custard
    sauce (page 420)

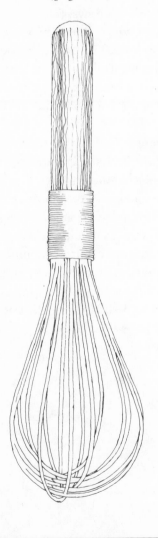

7. Pour the batter into the pan and bake on the middle rack of the oven for 40 to 45 minutes. Turn the cake onto a cooling rack and let stand at least 8 hours before frosting or filling. Cut into 3 layers horizontally.

8. Reserve 3 or 4 dried apricots for decoration and soak the rest in warm water just until soft. Bring the sugar and water to a boil in a saucepan and cook the softened apricots in the syrup until very tender.

9. Butter a 2-quart soufflé mold or other deep straight-sided dish. Place a layer of cake in the bottom and line the side with strips cut from one of the layers.

10. Soften the gelatin in ¼ cup cold water.

11. Puree the apricots and syrup in a blender or food processor. Add the gelatin. Pour the mixture into a bowl and stir over ice until cool.

12. Beat the cream until thick but not stiff and fold it into the puree. Add the kirsch and lemon juice according to taste.

13. Pour the mixture into the dish and cover with the third cake layer. Chill for at least 6 hours in the refrigerator.

14. Unmold onto a round dessert platter. Garnish with whipped cream and decorate with designs cut from the dried apricots. Serve with custard sauce.

SERVES 10

Hugo's Lighthouse

You look for something different at Cohasset Harbor, just south of Boston, and you find it. For over fifty years, Hugo's Lighthouse has catered to the nautical palate of its clients, including royalty and Hollywood celebrities. The appointments in the dining rooms cruise with the yachts scudding in the charming bay outside the panoramic windows. But uniquely nautical are the indoor ocean lobster pools from which diners may make their choice and have it prepared in any classic presentation: baked, broiled, thermidor, Newburg—or simply the white tender meat drenched in butter. Oysters and clams, living in the ocean water up to the moment of selection, are also prepared to individual taste. Steaks and chops are broiled in front of a gourmet audience.

Historically, Cohasset Harbor is likewise different. There's that thoroughly New England landmark, Minot's Lighthouse (1860), lying 2½ miles out to sea. But more interestingly, the bay was the site of a landing by Captain John Smith in 1614. This ardent explorer, with a penchant for annoying his friends, had led a topsy-turvy existence which included engaging in single combat with three notable Turkish warriors and being sold into slavery to a Turkish Pasha's wife—an interesting fate. London merchants sent him to New England's shores in search of whales and gold—but independent Smith returned instead with a valuable cargo of fish and furs. In his *Description of New England* (1616), he noted the good fishing to be had there. He would have mentioned the good dining if he had arrived somewhat later.

44 BORDER STREET, COHASSET HARBOR

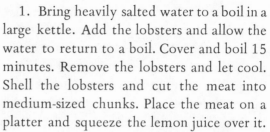

Lobster Newburg,
à la Hugo

2 2-pound (or 5 1-pound)
   live lobsters
Juice of ½ fresh lemon
½ cup melted butter
1 teaspoon paprika
½ cup sherry
4 egg yolks
3 cups light cream
Salt
Toast points or patty shells

1. Bring heavily salted water to a boil in a large kettle. Add the lobsters and allow the water to return to a boil. Cover and boil 15 minutes. Remove the lobsters and let cool. Shell the lobsters and cut the meat into medium-sized chunks. Place the meat on a platter and squeeze the lemon juice over it.

2. Heat the butter in a large, heavy saucepan. Add the lobster meat and sprinkle with paprika. Sauté for 3 or 4 minutes, being careful not to burn the paprika.

3. Add half the sherry and light with a match.

4. In a mixing bowl beat the egg yolks with the cream until well blended. Gradually add the egg-cream mixture to the lobster, stirring gently and continually with a wooden spoon until smooth and bubbling. Continue to cook over low heat, stirring continually, just until the mixture thickens. Add the remaining sherry and season to taste.

5. To serve: Place in a serving dish and garnish with toast points or serve in patty shells.

SERVES 6

The Manor

"**B**edazzling" was the term used by one reporter to describe The Manor, certainly one of the most resplendent restaurants in America. The interior is lavishly decorated with chandeliers costing over $8,000 each, and wall mirrors adorned with 24-carat gold inlays. The red brick building looks opulent in its white wood trim. But the final touch to this palatial setting is afforded by the 20 acres of manicured lawns, perfectly tended formal gardens, walkways, patios, fountains, and a waterfall that cascades in tiers over European-style gargoyles. Everything is on a grand scale. The staff of 350 includes a photographer, florist and music director—to ease the young couples in their chase for the perfect wedding. Owner Harry Knowles, Jr., is aware that such an opulent dream is, for a restaurant, the result of hard work. "We give a lot of attention to detail," he says. "You may not notice that the fish fork is Continental style, or that we use fresh flowers, but overall you know you are someplace special."

More importantly, the service and cuisine will be fit for a king. In the giant kitchen (133 feet long by 45 feet wide) there are signs like the following: "If a plate can be picked up from this station without the use of a napkin or glove, it is considered cold." From out of the kitchen stream wonderful Filets of Beef Wellington, Boneless Breast of Squab, Scallops Stuffed with Lobster Mousse—the à la carte menu is 15 pages long. And if your request for wine is a regal one, there will be a bottle of Château Pétrus, 1966.

111 PROSPECT AVENUE, WEST ORANGE

Les Coquilles Farcies à la Mousse de Homard (*Scallops Stuffed with Lobster Mousse*)

1 pound (20) scallops

1. Prepare the lobster mousse: Chop the lobster meat very finely with a knife or spin it in a blender or food processor. Gradually add the egg whites, blending continuously. Slowly add the cream and season well with salt and pepper.

New Jersey

1¼ cups uncooked lobster
    mousse
4 5-ounce molds lobster
    mousse, cooked
4 cups glaze sauce
Flour
Salt and pepper
Clarified butter (page 420)
Fresh dill

Lobster mousse:
1 pound cooked lobster
    meat
3 egg whites
2½ cups heavy cream
1 tablespoon salt
    teaspoon white pepper

Glaze sauce:
4 cups fish stock (or
    2 cups clam broth and
    2 cups chicken broth)
½ tablespoon soft butter
½ tablespoon flour
1 cup heavy cream
½ cup Hollandaise sauce
    (page 424)
½ cup heavy cream,
    whipped

2. Fill small round greased molds (5 ounce). Bake 20 minutes in a pan of hot water at 300 degrees F. Reserve the rest of the mixture.

3. Prepare the glaze sauce: Heat the fish stock and boil it down to half its original quantity. Work the butter and flour together and drop it into the stock in small bits. Whisk until the sauce thickens. Add the cream and remove from the heat to cool completely. Mix in the Hollandaise and whipped cream.

4. Using a pastry bag fitted with a small plain tube, pipe the uncooked mousse into the scallops. Sprinkle the scallops with salt and pepper and dredge them with flour.

5. Heat 4 tablespoons of clarified butter in a skillet and sauté the scallops over moderately low heat for 10 to 15 minutes.

6. To serve: Unmold a tin of cooked lobster mousse onto a heated plate. Surround with the stuffed scallops. Cover the scallops with the glaze sauce and brown under a preheated broiler. Garnish with fresh dill. If preferred, all the lobster mousses and the scallops can be glazed and served on one platter.

SERVES 4

Barbetta

Most Italian restaurants remind the diner of the grandeur that was Rome, while Barbetta's tries, and succeeds, to remind one of the fresh presence that *is* Piedmont. It isn't just a matter of a wine bottle in a wicker basket. The Maioglios came from Piedmont and opened their restaurant way back in 1906. Enrico Caruso, Arturo Toscanini, Ezio Pinza came to sing arias or to wave batons of praise over the excellent northern Italian menu. The owners grew older and in 1960 it seemed that a tradition would be lost to the city. But their daughter Laura, who had spent every summer in Piedmont since being a toddler and who had received her degree in art history magna cum laude from Bryn Mawr, put all her knowledge and background into reopening Barbetta's in 1962. She festooned the restaurant with authentic antiques gleaned from the refulgent Savoy era in Piedmont. Little had to be changed in the intimate summer garden that continued to bloom with wisteria and dogwoods and which offered shade under its grape arbor.

Back in northern Italy, the family had continuously maintained a 17th-Century house, a farm and vineyards, and from these sources Laura was able to augment the restaurant offerings with Gattinara, Barolo and Barbaresco wines, with truffles hunted by the Maioglios' own hounds and flown in fresh three times a week in season. Laura herself often travels to Italy to seek out new recipes to add even more diversity to a menu including such favorites as Squab alla Piemontese, Vitel Tonne and Fonduta con Tartufi.

321 WEST 46TH STREET, NEW YORK CITY

New York

Squab in Casserole alla Piemontese

6 1¼-pound fresh domestic or wild squab, cleaned
4 celery stalks, diced
2 medium leeks, white part only, diced
4 medium onions, diced
4 medium carrots, diced
2 tablespoons olive oil
2 tablespoons butter
1 cup white wine
½ teaspoon rosemary leaves
6 sage leaves
1 cup stock or consommé
Salt and pepper

1. Wash and wipe the squab dry. Cut off the wings, rub the interior with salt and truss for roasting.

2. Prepare the vegetables.

3. Place the squabs together with the wings in a heavy pan and brown for 3 minutes in the oil and butter over high heat. Add the vegetables and brown 5 minutes more.

4. Add the white wine and the herbs. Bring to a boil and cook, uncovered, until the liquid is reduced by half.

5. Add half the stock or consommé and bring again to a boil, then cover the pan and place in a 350-degree oven. Cook for 45 minutes, basting occasionally with the remaining stock or consommé.

6. To serve: Remove the wings from the pan and discard them. Place the squabs on a heated platter and remove the trussing twine. Using a slotted spoon, lift the vegetables from the pan and place them on the platter, surrounding the squabs. Spoon off any excess fat from the top of the sauce and pour the remaining sauce over the squabs.

SERVES 6

The Box Tree

An 18th-Century world of charm and personal attention lies just 40 minutes from New York City at Purdy Station. The Box Tree, located in the Early American home of the original Purdy, shows as much care and detail in the creation of the proper atmosphere as it does in the preparation of its fine French cuisine. Owner-chef Augustin V. Paeges describes the food served in the spacious, high-ceilinged dining rooms as "French inspired, but really American," and he adds his special touch to favorites such as Coulibriacs de Saumon, Croustade de Crevettes and that rarity of French desserts, the vacherin.

Those reluctant to leave this peaceful oasis are in luck, for shortly The Box Tree will open three guest suites that will provide the ultimate in sumptuous accommodations. Each suite will include a private dining room for groups up to twelve, and overnight guests will awake to a superb breakfast that features quail and other game served on Haviland china.

PURDY STATION, WESTCHESTER COUNTY

Hazelnut Vacherin with Raspberries

5 egg whites
⅔ cup sugar
½ cup shelled, toasted hazelnuts, finely ground
3 cups heavy cream
2 teaspoons sugar
1 teaspoon vanilla extract
1 tablespoon Grand Marnier

1. Four to five hours before you intend to serve this dessert, preheat oven to 200 degrees F.

2. Outline three 9-inch circles on parchment paper (see note), using an inverted 9-inch pie plate as your pattern. For most home ovens, it will be necessary to use three baking levels at once. (You can improvise a third level by setting two bricks on the bottom of your oven.)

3. Beat the egg whites until they form soft peaks. Add the ⅔ cup sugar and con-

1 pint fresh raspberries
   or hulled fresh
   strawberries
Confectioners' sugar

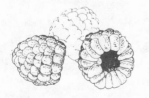

tinue beating until the whites form peaks that are stiff but not dry.

4. Fold the hazelnuts into the meringue very gently.

5. Spread a third of the meringue with a spatula onto each of the three circles.

6. Bake on cookie sheets for 60 minutes. Then turn off oven and leave meringue in the closed oven for one or more hours.

7. A half hour before serving, start whipping the heavy cream. When it begins to form peaks, add sugar, vanilla and Grand Marnier. Continue whipping until stiff.

8. Set out the meringue layers, putting one of them on the serving platter you intend to use. Spread that layer and another layer with the raspberries or strawberries.

9. Then, working carefully with a spatula, cover the fruit with the whipped cream. Use about a third of the cream for each of the two layers. Smooth off the top of the cream on both layers and stack them on the serving platter. Put the third layer on top of the two stacked layers.

10. Spread the remaining whipped cream evenly around the side of the cake.

11. Dust the top of the *vacherin* with confectioners' sugar. To serve, use a sharp, long serrated knife and a gentle sawing motion.

SERVES 12

Brussels

The Brussels is the kind of restaurant one must know about not only for impeccable dining *en famille* but to send inquiring visitors to "the best." Actually its pedigree preceded the World's Fair of 1939. Legend has it that when Fair officials asked the Belgian Government for some priceless Vermeers to display at their national pavilion, *les Belgiques* sheepishly were compelled to refer the officials to the Brussels Restaurant in Manhattan for the finest existing originals.

Today, the restaurant is ensconced in one of the city's finer townhouses, originally the residence of a Vanderhof, on 54th Street, north side, just east of Park, then as now an impeccable address—and presently that of the current owner Albert Giambelli, whose service and menu in the sumptuous dining room (graced as you enter by one of the most ethereal spiral staircases you have ever viewed) are a challenge to the taste and sophistication of the diner. Signor Giambelli, a dashing and confident host, is willing to recommend and hover discreetly in the search for perfection. It is frequently achieved, by reference to a regal wine list (braced by rare purchases from the cellar of one of America's greatest financial names) and the semi-religious dedication of a chef who dares to dream the impossible soufflé in the Escoffier tradition.

Where else Saumon à L'Oseille, Chateaubriand Maison en Paillotte or Soufflé de Turbotin Brillat-Savarin? An exquisitely private bar for your cocktails and/or after-dinner liqueur.

115 EAST 54TH STREET, NEW YORK CITY

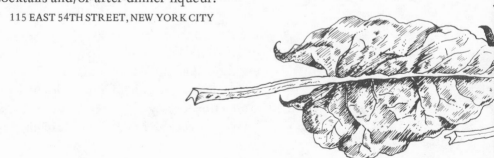

New York

Saumon à L'Oseille
(Salmon with Sorrel Sauce)

8 small new potatoes
1½ pounds fresh salmon
   fillets, cut ¼ inch thick
½ cup flour
½ teaspoon salt
⅛ teaspoon white pepper
5 tablespoons sweet
   butter
1 teaspoon finely
   chopped shallots
½ cup Chablis wine
½ cup heavy cream
4 tablespoons chopped
   fresh sorrel
1 teaspoon sweet butter
¼ teaspoon sugar
Salt and white pepper

1. Peel potatoes if desired, or scrub well, rinse in several waters and cook with skins. Boil in just enough salted water to cover 15 to 25 minutes, depending on size. Drain well and keep warm.

2. Place the flour on a plate and add the salt and pepper. Lightly coat each salmon fillet in the mixture. Heat 5 tablespoons of butter in a skillet and sauté the fillets 2 minutes on each side. Transfer the salmon to a heated platter and keep warm.

3. Using the same skillet, sauté the shallots until soft. Add the wine and boil down to a syrupy consistency. Add the cream and sorrel. Simmer the sauce for several minutes, stirring well. Add the butter and sugar and season to taste.

4. To serve: Pour the sauce over the fish and surround with the boiled potatoes.

SERVES 2 FOR DINNER OR 4 AS AN APPETIZER

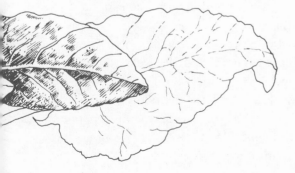

Café Argenteuil

If the Greeks, who made Bacchus their god of wine, were still busily god-making, they would declare Bocuse their god of cuisine. Paul Bocuse is one of that small group of outstanding French chefs who have promoted *la nouvelle cuisine*—and two of his good friends and devotees are Andre Maulhan and Claude Uson, partners in the French Provincial rendezvous of Café Argenteuil. In their approach to cooking, the trio relies on a directness that will not stifle original tastes with a variety of garnishings. Consequently, there is a sure touch in the Quiche Lorraine, in the Bouillabaisse, and in the Champignons à la Grecque. The Bass en Croûte seems to have come straight from the water and not to be emerging with a last gasp from a plateful of sauces, the Rouget Soufflé is as delicate as a baby's hand waving at a butterfly, and La Crème de Moules Maxime is the crowning achievement of a restaurant where the meats always come well prepared.

253 EAST 52ND STREET, NEW YORK CITY

La Crème
de Moules Maxime
(Cream of Mussel Soup)

2 pounds mussels,
    bearded and scrubbed
½ cup minced shallots
Salt and freshly ground
    pepper
1¼ cups dry white wine
2 cups chopped leeks
1 cup minced onions
½ stalk celery, diced

1. Heat 6 tablespoons of butter in a saucepan. Add the cleaned mussels, shallots, 1 teaspoon of salt, ⅛ teaspoon of freshly ground pepper and the white wine. Cover and bring to a boil, lower the heat and simmer 25 minutes.

2. In another saucepan, melt 6 tablespoons of butter, add the leeks, onion and celery. Sauté gently until the onions are transparent. Add the bouillon or water, ½ teaspoon of salt and ⅛ teaspoon of pepper. Simmer gently for 1 hour.

3. Add the potatoes and cook 25 minutes

1 quart beef bouillon
   or water
2 large potatoes, peeled
   and diced
⅔ cup heavy cream

longer or until the potatoes are tender. Force
this mixture through a food mill, return to
the saucepan, and set aside.

4. Use a slotted spoon to lift the mussels
from the cooking liquid and place them in a
deep dish or bowl. Add the cooking liquid,
straining it through several thicknesses of
cheesecloth to remove any possible sand.
Force the mussels and broth through a food
mill or puree in a blender or food processor.

5. Combine the mussel mixture with the
potato soup and add the heavy cream. Bring
to a simmer over low heat. Add the remaining butter and season to taste, then force the
soup through a heavy sieve, pressing firmly
with the back of a soup ladle.

6. Serve immediately or cool, refrigerate,
and reheat when needed.

SERVES 8

Chez Raymond Café St. Denis

Some leading restaurants, or in this case bistros, have blood lines that read like those of racehorses. Formerly the Café St. Denis, a door or so from the old Stork Club, this eating place relocated near Lincoln Center in the late '60s under the name Chez Raymond. Owner Raymond Guiheneuf graduated from the Central Hotel in Nantes, and went on to the Plaza Athénée Hotel in Paris, California Palace, Cannes, the Café Royal, London—to become the youngest maître d'hôtel on the fabled liner S.S. *Normandie.* And so to glittering New York, to work at La Crémaillère, Le Veau d'Or, to co-own La Potinière du Soir for 14 years. And now to the fountained world of Lincoln Center, where he is today ably assisted by his chef of 20 years, Geau De Lu.

Born of such backgrounds, Chez Raymond easily catches the international flavor: tables covered with red cloths topped with small white ones on the bias, fresh flowers, golden baskets of large half loaves of French bread, bowls of radishes with green stems—and on the pale walls trompe l'oeil pictures of New York, Paris, Cannes. Peeping from among the wine barrels is the freshness of displayed hors d'oeuvres: mussels, mushrooms, Ratatouille, Eggs Mayonnaise and vine-ripened tomatoes.

240 WEST 56TH STREET, NEW YORK CITY

Crab Meat Crêpes

Savory Crêpe Batter:
- 6 tablespoons flour
- ¼ teaspoon salt
- 3 eggs, slightly beaten
- 2 cups milk
- 1 teaspoon melted butter

1. Combine all the ingredients for the crêpes and beat until smooth. Let stand for at least 30 minutes.

2. Heat the butter in a saucepan and sauté the shallots and onion until transparent. Add the wine, tomato puree, 8 tablespoons of the Béchamel sauce, the crab meat, and the cream. Bring to a boil and simmer for 5 minutes. Set aside while making the crêpes.

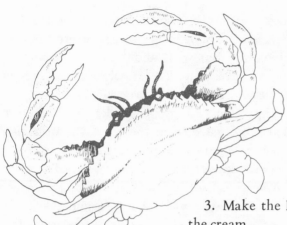

Filling:
- 2 tablespoons butter
- 3 shallots, minced
- 1 tablespoon chopped onion
- 1 cup dry white wine
- 1 cup tomato puree
- 1½ cups Béchamel sauce (page 416)
- ¾ pound crab meat
- 2 cups heavy cream

Salt and pepper
- ½ cup Hollandaise sauce (page 424)
- ½ cup heavy cream, whipped

3. Make the Hollandaise sauce and whip the cream.

4. Heat a 5-inch crêpe pan or a small skillet. Butter lightly and ladle in a spoonful of batter. The bottom of the pan should be thinly coated. Cook over moderately high heat until the batter has set. Flip the crêpe over and lightly brown on the other side. Turn upside down on a working surface and continue cooking the crêpes until you have 18.

5. Put a generous spoonful of the filling on each crêpe. Roll it up and place in a shallow, ovenproof serving dish or platter.

6. Preheat the broiler.

7. Combine 1 cup of the remaining Béchamel with Hollandaise and whipped cream. Pour over the crêpes and brown lightly under a broiler. Serve immediately.

SERVES 6

Le Cirque

Perhaps we understand more French than we are given credit for. The meanings of camaraderie, menagerie (dare we mention lingerie) are a cinch—maybe even coterie and chinoiserie. But what about the word *singerie*? There we are brought to a halt. It means a monkey house. All this to explain that the fascinating decor of this new restaurant is a true copy of the *singerie* at the Palace of Versailles. Top New York designer Ellen McClusky has drawn plaudits (from the Latin) of patrons for the murals of frolicking monkeys, based on 17th-Century caricatures that portrayed monkeys gowned and coiffed as courtiers. It was a way of making fun of VIP's of the time without becoming tangled in strict censorship laws. The mural design is accentuated by the trellis pattern on the walls, the predominating color scheme being shades of tan, beige, brown, with accents of tangerine. The light fixtures are made of toile orange trees modeled after a unique decoration discovered in France. If the atmosphere at Le Cirque is fit for a Sun King, so is the food, prepared by chef Jean Vergnes and guided to your table by maitre d' Sirio Maccioni, both men formerly of The Colony.

58 EAST 65TH STREET, NEW YORK CITY

Suprême de Volaille Gismonda *(Breast of Chicken with Mushrooms and Spinach)*

4 chicken breasts,
  boned and skinned
Salt
White pepper
Flour
1 egg
1 tablespoon water
4 tablespoons grated

1. Place the chicken breasts between sheets of wax paper and pound them gently with a mallet or rolling pin. Sprinkle each one with salt and pepper and dredge with flour.

2. Beat the egg slightly with the water and on a separate plate mix the cheese and bread crumbs. Dip each chicken breast first in the egg mixture and then in the bread crumbs.

3. Heat 2 tablespoons of butter in a skillet and brown the chicken, allowing 10 minutes to a side.

Parmesan cheese
¾ cup fine white bread
  crumbs
3 tablespoons butter
1 pound cooked spinach,
  fresh or frozen
½ pound mushrooms, sliced
2 tablespoons brown sauce
  (page 418)
Chopped fresh parsley

4. Spread a bed of coarsely chopped cooked spinach on a heated serving platter. Arrange the chicken breasts on top and keep hot.

5. To the skillet, add the remaining butter and sauté the mushrooms until tender. Spoon the mushrooms over the chicken and pour the hot brown sauce around the chicken. Sprinkle with chopped parsley.

SERVES 4

Broiled Flounder Cirque

2 large fillets flounder
1½ cups white bread crumbs
2 tablespoons vegetable
  oil
1½ tablespoons melted
  butter

Mustard-Hollandaise sauce:
1 cup Hollandaise
  (page 424)
2 teaspoons Dijon
  mustard
2 teaspoons chopped
  chives
Dash Tabasco
Salt and pepper to taste

1. Combine ingredients for the sauce and keep warm.

2. Preheat the broiler. Season the flounder fillets with salt, dip one side at a time into the oil and then in the crumbs. Place on a foil-lined baking sheet.

3. Broil 6 to 8 minutes on each side, about 3 inches from the broiler element, basting with the melted butter.

4. Serve the fish with boiled potatoes and the mustard-Hollandaise sauce. Garnish with lemon wedges and fresh parsley if desired.

SERVES 2

Clos Normand

The Normandy Invasion: June 6, 1944. The Allies, commanded by General Dwight D. Eisenhower, established assault beachheads, code-named Utah, Omaha, Gold, Juno and Sword. The reconquest of Europe had begun in earnest. Such endeavors form the stirring happenings of history. In peacetime, worthy events are not always so frenetic. Take, for example, the Normandy Invasion of New York. The Clos Normand restaurant, under the able command of Maurice Bertrand and Robert Treboux, opened its doors to the skyscraper folk of the city to promote a feel for the atmosphere and cuisine of this northern province of France. Gustatory beachheads were established with Filet de Bar Fecampoise, Rognons de Veau Rouennaise, Caneton aux Fugues, Sorbet au Cassis. Victory has been assured by the addition of a pleasant decor: tan plaster walls, beams, rough-hewn wooden pillars, rustic sconces, seating covered in rough red-wool upholstery—and evocative murals of the Norman countryside.

42 EAST 52ND STREET, NEW YORK CITY

Quiche de Clos Normand

¾ pound unsweetened puff pastry (store bought)
1 cup king crab meat
1 cup lobster meat, coarsely diced
Red pepper
7 eggs, beaten light
1 teaspoon Madras curry
1 pint milk
1 pint heavy cream
Salt and pepper

Preheat the oven to 350 degrees F.

1. Butter 2 shallow layer-cake tins or pie tins very lightly.

2. Roll out the pastry very thin (⅛ inch) and line the tins.

3. Cover the bottom of the pastry with a mixture of the crab and lobster meat.

4. Sprinkle liberally with red pepper.

5. Combine the beaten eggs with the curry, milk and cream and pour half into each tin. Bake 25 minutes.

SERVES 8

New York

Médaillons de Veau Normand (*Veal Clos Normand*)

2 pounds veal, cut in scallopini
Flour
4 tablespoons butter
½ pound mushrooms, sliced
Salt and pepper
1 pint heavy cream
2 tablespoons Calvados

1. Pound each piece of veal lightly between pieces of wax paper, using a mallet. Rub a little flour into each piece.

2. Heat the butter in a large skillet over a high flame. Put in the veal and reduce the heat to moderate. Brown the veal 5 minutes on each side. Add the mushrooms, sprinkle with salt and freshly ground white pepper. Cook for 10 minutes longer.

3. Transfer the veal to a heated platter and keep warm. To the mushrooms, add the cream and Calvados and stir with a wooden spoon gently until the sauce begins to thicken. Pour over the veal and serve.

SERVES 8

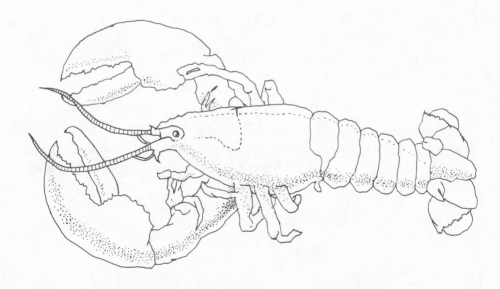

The Coach House

Greenwich Village—of book and print shops, of love beads and pop culture—catches its breath in the expanse of Washington Square. It's a mixture of the zany and sedate, a home for art and literary culture, the Off-Broadway theater, the ephemerally exotic. The mixture extends to the quaint cafés and traditional restaurants, such as The Coach House—a name born of those days when the Village was peopled by wealthy Colonial New Yorkers, when Henry James wrote *Washington Square*, when John Masefield scrubbed saloon floors there on his way to becoming the Poet Laureate of England.

At The Coach House, you dine in the excellence of the past, amid 19th-Century hunting scenes hung from glowing brick walls, and feast on Veal Chop à la Campagne or Fresh Smelts Savory, to end with dacquoise, a specialty dessert consisting of a delicate almond-and-egg pastry filled with flavored butter.

110 WAVERLY PLACE, NEW YORK CITY (JUST WEST OF WASHINGTON SQUARE)

Fresh Smelts Savory

24 smelts
Salt, pepper, flour
Olive oil
2 bay leaves
3 cloves garlic, minced
¾ cup wine vinegar
1 onion, sliced thin
1 tablespoon rosemary
1 tablespoon chopped
   parsley

1. Heat ½ cup oil in a heavy skillet and sauté the fish, a few at a time, until golden brown. Add more oil to the skillet as needed. As the fish are cooked, arrange them side by side in a baking dish.

2. When all fish have been cooked, add to the skillet all other ingredients except the parsley. Simmer 10 minutes, adding more oil if needed to make enough liquid to cover all the fish. Strain liquid over the fish. Cool, then cover and refrigerate at least 4 hours before serving.

3. Serve smelts cold, drained, sprinkled with the chopped parsley.

SERVES 6 TO 8 AS AN APPETIZER

New York

Cold Eggplant Salad

4 medium-sized unpeeled
   eggplants
1 onion, grated
3 cloves garlic, minced
2 large tomatoes, peeled
   and chopped
10 green olives stuffed with
    pimientos, chopped
½ cup olive oil
Dash of dry mustard
Juice of 1½ lemons
½ cup finely chopped
   parsley
Salt and freshly ground
    pepper to taste

1. Preheat oven to 375 degrees F. Rub the eggplant with a little olive oil. Pierce in several places to prevent from bursting and put in a greased pan. Roast until tender. Remove from the oven and cool.

2. Remove the skins from the eggplants and place the flesh in a colander to drain completely. You may refrigerate them for quick cooling. Chop the cooled eggplants very fine. Place in a large bowl and add the onion, garlic, tomatoes and olives. Mix well and pour in the olive oil gradually, stirring constantly. Add the mustard, lemon juice and parsley. Blend well and taste for seasoning. Chill for at least 2 hours.

3. Serve cold as an appetizer, with French bread or melba toast.

SERVES 8

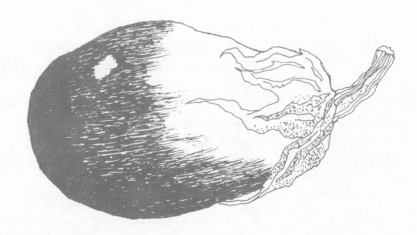

La Côte Basque

How, one wonders, can any New York restaurant hope to survive—much less flourish—without catering to metropolitan theater hordes? Such a feat, nigh impossible at best, becomes truly miraculous when you consider that for most New York glamour spots this late-night/early-morning traffic is lifeblood. But *most* is not *all*. Indeed, while the rest gear up for the après-Broadway throng, La Côte Basque is—if not already closed—then closing. Closing? At 10:30 p.m.? A good hour before the patrons of the arts descend? What sort of insanity is this?

The insanity is not insanity at all, but rather a tremendously assured, well-placed self-confidence. After all, when you have served presidents, princes and such for more than a decade, you need no longer worry about the night owls. You have arrived. So, with its reputation secure and inviolate, La Côte Basque closes at 10:30 p.m. Behind darkened doors rest elegant rooms of Spanish Andalusian decor, an unparalleled French cuisine, a superb and extensive wine selection—and yet another day of success. Ah, success. It comes in all shapes and sizes, but the kind that flourishes at La Côte Basque is surely the most attractive.

5 EAST 55TH STREET, NEW YORK

Striped Bass Duglere

1 striped bass (approximately 5 pounds)
¼ pound sweet butter
1 tablespoon chopped onion
5 fresh tomatoes

1. Ask the fish dealer to fillet the fish and to trim the two fillets evenly. Be sure that he gives you the head, tail, skin and bones.

2. Put all the fish trimmings in a pan of slightly salted water. Boil down until it measures 2 cups. Strain. This will make the basis for a fish velouté (page 423), which will be made while the fish is cooking.

3. At the same time melt 2 tablespoons of

1 tablespoon coarsely
   chopped parsley
Sprig of thyme
¼ bay leaf
⅛ teaspoon minced
   garlic
1½ cups dry white wine

butter in a skillet or other shallow pan large enough to accommodate the fillets. Add the onion and sauté just until tender.

4. Peel and halve the tomatoes and squeeze out the seeds. Chop coarsely and add to the onion.

5. Add the parsley, thyme, bay leaf and garlic.

6. Lay the fillets on this base and pour the wine over the fish. Season with salt and pepper. Bring to a boil and cover with a piece of buttered brown paper or a pan cover. Simmer 15 minutes.

7. Transfer the fish with 2 spatulas to a serving platter and keep warm.

8. Remove the bay leaf and thyme from the cooking liquid and add 2 tablespoons of fish velouté; or, if you prefer the sauce can be thickened with 1 tablespoon of beurre manié (page 417).

9. Boil down the sauce to half its original volume and whisk in 6 tablespoons of butter. Taste for seasoning before pouring over the fish. Serve with boiled potatoes or rice.

SERVES 6

L'Endroit

The spot, or as the French would say, *l'endroit*, is the place to visit. Opened in early 1974, L'Endroit has already earned a strong reputation for the quality of its cuisine. The decor is French Provincial, with stucco walls set off by antique cooking implements, exposed wooden beams, wrought-iron chandeliers; and for a splash of color, paintings by renowned South American painter Leandro Velasco. Yellow candle lamps glow upon the white tablecloths and hand-blown crystal. The menu is mainly French, a few favorite Italian dishes being added for good measure. Fish is highlighted with mushrooms and white wine; the veal is milk fed. The talk of Long Island is the Foie de Veau—and those succulent desserts: Manager Walter Arango's own creation: chocolate Gâteau Saint Honoré and chef Avelino de Sousa's pecan pie.

148 GLEN COVE ROAD, EAST HILLS

Foie de Veau Bercé
(Calves' Liver)

3 pounds calves' liver,
  sliced thin
Flour
Clarified butter (page 420)
3 tablespoons butter
3 tablespoons chopped
  shallots
½ cup white wine
2 cups brown sauce
  (page 418)
Juice of 1 lemon
Salt and pepper
Chopped parsley

1. Lightly flour the liver slices. Sauté in clarified butter as desired—medium, medium-rare, etc.

2. Remove liver slices to a heated platter and keep warm. Drain butter from the pan and discard. Add 3 tablespoons fresh butter to the pan. Add the shallots, wine and brown sauce. Simmer for 3 minutes.

3. Taste sauce for seasoning; add salt and pepper as desired. Stir in fresh chopped parsley and pour over meat. Serve immediately.

SERVES 6

L'Endroit Salad Dressing

- 1 teaspoon chopped shallots
- 1 teaspoon crushed garlic
- 1 teaspoon salt
- ½ teaspoon monosodium glutamate (Accent)
- 1 teaspoon sugar
- 1 teaspoon freshly ground black pepper
- ½ cup red or white wine vinegar
- 2 whole eggs
- ½ jar A-1 Sauce (2½ ounces)
- 4 tablespoons Dijon mustard
- 5 tablespoons Lea & Perrins
- 1 gallon salad oil
- ½ cup boiling water

Mix all ingredients except oil and water in an electric mixing bowl. Add the oil gradually, whipping it to a thick consistency. Finish by adding the water.

Serve on lettuce leaves garnished with chopped chives.

(This recipe can be halved or quartered but it will keep well in a bottle or jar in the refrigerator.)

MAKES 1 GALLON

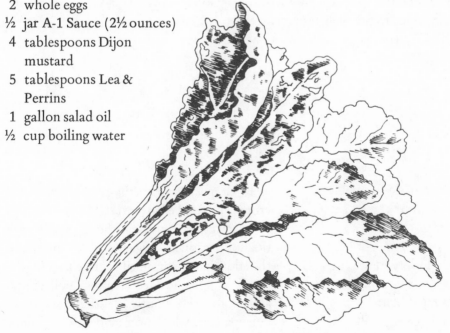

L'Epicure Restaurant

Any wife or husband returning panting from the local gourmet class can serve a Veal à l'Oscar or Fraises Romanoff-Millefeuilles, but Craig Claiborne, of the *New York Times*, will not be making a pilgrimage to their supper table. However, Claiborne will make reverent passage to East Greenbush, where at L'Epicure, chef Jean Roger prepares classic dishes divinely. Jean's domain consists of a Colonial building some 150 years old, set in acres of beautiful landscape—and, especially for the preparation of the best in French cuisine, a large vegetable garden. To use canned or frozen foods would be a desecration. Jean started his apprenticeship at fourteen years of age in Nice's Grand Hotel Ruhl and later worked in London, Switzerland and Belgium. In 1952 he came to New York to lend his talents at restaurants like the Four Seasons. Only then did he feel his ministry could begin in earnest, in a blissful spot six miles southeast of Albany. Today, his menu has burgeoned to thirty different entrees.

1547 COLUMBIA TURNPIKE, EAST GREENBUSH

Crêpes de Chef De L'Epicure *(Chef's Crêpes Epicure)*

12 dessert crêpes (page 421)

Pastry cream:
 5 large egg yolks

1. Crêpes: Prepare the recipe for dessert crêpes and let the batter rest.

2. Pastry cream: Beat the egg yolks with the confectioners' sugar until smooth. Add the flour and stir until blended. Add the vanilla and the scalded cream or milk gradually, beating constantly. Put the mixture in a saucepan and whisk over moderate heat until

¾ cup confectioners'
   sugar
½ cup minus 1 tablespoon
   sifted cake flour
1 teaspoon vanilla extract
2 cups half-and-half,
   cream or milk, scalded

Cream topping:
1½ cups whipping cream
 2 tablespoons kirsch,
   Grand Marnier or
   Benedictine

Praline:
1½ cups sliced almonds
 ½ cup sugar
 1 teaspoon vanilla extract

the mixture thickens. Pour into a bowl and cover with Saran wrap to prevent a crust from forming. Cool.

3. Cream topping: Mix the whipping cream with the liqueur of your choice.

4. Praline: Brown the almonds in a 300-degree oven. At the same time, cook the sugar with the vanilla in a small heavy skillet until the sugar turns brown. Add 1 cup of the browned almonds, stir and pour into a buttered pie tin. Let the mixture harden. Break into pieces and pulverize in a blender.

5. Cook 12 5-inch crêpes in a lightly buttered skillet or special crêpe pan. Turn the cooked crêpes onto a working surface. Spread each crêpe with the pastry cream and sprinkle with praline. Roll each crêpe up and place it in a chafing dish. When all the crêpes are in place, cover them with the cream topping. Heat the crêpes gently. Sprinkle with confectioners' sugar and brown quickly under a preheated broiler. Sprinkle with the remaining almonds and serve hot.

SERVES 3 TO 4

The Four Seasons

What do an 18th-Century Venetian girls' orphanage and a 20th-Century New York City restaurant have in common? They both enshrine a memorable celebration of the four seasons. Antonio Vivaldi, a priest who taught music at the Ospedale della Antonio Pieta for thirty-seven years, was one of the most influential creators of instrumental music during the late Baroque period. From the cloistered solemnity of the orphanage grew Vivaldi's celebrated work, "The Four Seasons." In the summer of 1959, a restaurant opened in the Seagram Building which in its own way was to epitomize the glory of the changing seasons. The appointments are keyed to the colors of trees in their seasonal colors. Menu items, plantings, graphics and certain appointments are changed as the calendar progresses. The decor is elegant and simple.

Like the studied quiet of Vivaldi's composing room, there is in the dining room a 20-foot-square pool of cool Italian white marble. Paintings by Picasso, sculptures by Richard Lippold are changed seasonally. Hither come the great and well known to celebrate not winters of discontent but the springs of success: King Hussein, Princess Lee Radziwill (to commemorate her first 1,000 published words), a party for Pearl Bailey, a gathering to launch a new Truman Capote work (honoring Italians: de Sica, Mastroianni, Fellini, Ponti). The Four Seasons is music for the eye and for the palate. There's a wine cellar stocked with 50,000 bottles of choice vintages—and sherbets lapped in fresh fruit, and the likes of whole striped bass set ablaze in burning fennel, then set to swim again in a house invention called sauce Gregoire.

99 EAST 52ND STREET, NEW YORK CITY

New York

Sautéed Calves' Liver with Avocado

2 pounds calves' liver
Flour
Salt and pepper
3 slightly under-ripe
   medium-size avocados
3 tablespoons oil
2 tablespoons butter
Few drops lemon juice
Chopped parsley

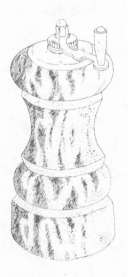

1. Order calves' liver cut ½ inch thick. Trim the filament around each slice.

2. Season the flour with a little salt and pepper and coat each slice on both sides with the mixture. Lay on a platter.

3. Peel the avocados. Split them and remove the seeds. Cut each half into thirds, cutting the avocados lengthwise.

4. Coat the avocado slices with the flour mixture.

5. Heat the oil and butter in a large skillet. Sauté both the liver and the avocado slices over high heat, allowing 1 minute to each side.

6. Place the sautéed liver and avocado slices alternately on a long heated serving platter, keeping the platter in a warm place until all the slices are cooked.

7. Pour a little water into the pan and quickly loosen the cooking juices from the bottom of the pan with a fork. Strain the pan gravy over the liver and avocado.

8. Sprinkle with salt and pepper and lemon juice.

9. Garnish with parsley and serve at once.
SERVES 6

35

Gage & Tollner

Where were you when the lights went out? Not at Gage & Tollner. There, gaslight continues to glow, even when a power failure plunges the rest of the city into blackness. The brass chandeliers have served nearly a century, since 1879 to be exact. This landmark dining room was opened when Brooklyn was still a separate city, when people were just beginning to savor a night out at Delmonico's or Rector's in Manhattan. So first families and flamboyant millionaires like Diamond Jim Brady trooped over to the suburb to dine at mahogany tables, sit in cane-backed chairs and twirl their mustaches before giant wall mirrors. The decor remains the same to this day—the mahogany by now mellowed—and the food is as wonderful as it was during La Belle Epoque.

The restaurant is noted for its seafood, especially the Soft Clam Bellies: Dewey Pan Roast (named after Admiral George Dewey), Duxbury Stew, Shell Roast, Baltimore Broil. There are also hearty steaks and chops and servings of real shredded cabbage. But above all is the tumble of the sea: oysters, shrimp, crab meat, lobster, surging through an old-fashioned eight-page menu. Meals to be washed down with good American wines from the Gage & Tollner wine cellar.

Waiters wear their fraternity pins of service: a gold eagle for 25 years, a gold star for five years, a gold bar for one year. Maybe it's anachronistic but so is the incredibly unfading excellence of Gage & Tollner.

372 FULTON STREET, BROOKLYN (NEAR BOROUGH HALL)

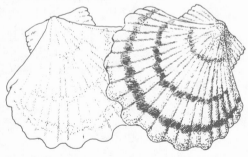

Soft Clam Belly Broil

4 dozen soft clams
  (steamers)
2 eggs
¼ cup milk
2 cups freshly ground
  cracker crumbs
½ cup melted butter
Toast points
Lemon wedges
Parsley

1. Preheat the broiler. Use only the small round bellies.
2. Beat the eggs with the milk in a small bowl.
3. Spread the cracker crumbs on a plate.
4. Dip each clam first in the egg mixture and then in the cracker crumbs. Place on a buttered baking sheet. Brush with melted butter.
5. Broil quickly under very high heat.
6. Serve on toast points, garnished with lemon wedges and parsley.

SERVES 4

Bay Scallops Newburg

2 cups tiny bay scallops,
  uncooked
4 tablespoons butter
4 tablespoons flour
Salt
Paprika
4 cups milk, warmed
¼ cup good sherry

In a heavy saucepan melt the butter, add the flour and cook, stirring, for 2 minutes. Add paprika to color and salt to taste.

Gradually stir in the warm milk, stirring constantly with a wooden spoon or beating with a wire whisk, and cook till moisture is thick and smooth.

Stir in the sherry and the scallops and cook gently 2 to 3 minutes. Serve on toast points.

SERVES 2

Gloucester House

New York City is living taken to great heights. You meet an executive in his suite on a 50th floor, and all the while you have that eerie, somewhat blasphemous notion that the Almighty must reside on the 75th. . . . But the city is also such a compound expression of life that you feel, in spite of the skyscrapers, that it's an oceanside community. At the Battery, water laps the investment notes, the Staten Island ferry continues to churn out its marine hayrides, a tugboat is as ordinary as a film crew outside Macy's. Accordingly, it is no surprise that New York City revels in the tang of fine seafood restaurants, notably the Gloucester House restaurant. If Gloucester, Massachusetts, is the quintessence of a seafaring town, Gloucester House is the epitome of seafaring dining. Here, seated in a captain's chair, with an eye cocked on a ship's model or a sailor's knot, you may enjoy a New England menu which crests in a long list of fish entrees—the morning's catch at the market. Bluefish, snapper, halibut, flounder. If you are not filled to the gills by the ample portions, there'll be room for desserts like the airy Gloucester House Special or the Blueberry Slump.

37 EAST 50TH STREET, NEW YORK CITY

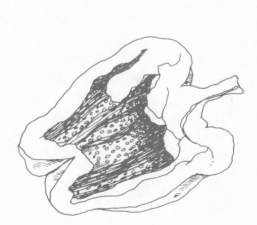

Manhattan Clam Chowder

24 chowder clams
 5 cups water
 3 slices bacon
 2 cups finely diced carrots
1¾ cups chopped celery
1¾ cups chopped onions
 ¾ cup chopped green
    pepper
 1 clove garlic, finely
    chopped
 1 teaspoon thyme
 1 cup fresh or canned
    tomatoes
 4 cups small potato cubes
Salt and freshly ground
    pepper

1. Wash the clams well, drain, rinse again and drain again. Place the clams in water in a kettle, cover, and simmer until the shells open.

2. Chop the bacon and prepare all the vegetables.

3. Put the bacon in a large kettle and cook gently until the bacon loses its fat. Add the carrots, celery, onions and green pepper. Simmer 5 minutes, stirring often. Add the garlic and thyme.

4. When the clams open, lift them out of the kettle and reserve. Strain the cooking liquid through a fine sieve to remove any sand.

5. Measure 12 cups of the clam liquid and add to the bacon mixture. (If there are not 12 cups of clam liquid, supplement it with water.)

6. Add the tomatoes and cook 15 minutes.

7. Remove the clams from the shells and chop the clam bodies quite fine. Add them and the potatoes to the kettle. Season with salt and pepper and cook 1 hour.

SERVES 10 TO 12

La Grenouille

As one food specialist noted, at La Grenouille you will find "some of the best food available in this country"—obviously the *grenouilles*, the frog legs, are superb; but so will be the Terrine de Campagne, the Bayonne Ham, the Clams Corsini and the succulent Soufflés. Faced with such excellent repasts and enjoying the bright atmosphere of fresh flowers set against apple green walls, one is reminded of those words of Brillat-Savarin, the great French connoisseur of dining: "Gourmandise is one of the greatest benefits of society. It is responsible for the gradual spread of that spirit of conviviality which every day brings together people of different social levels, welds them into a single whole, enlivens conversation and rubs off the corners of conventional social inequality. . . . When it is shared, it has the most important influence imaginable on the happiness of a marriage." You are not married, you say! Well, here is another piece of Gallic wisdom: "Gourmandise is the enemy of excess; every man who gives himself indigestion or gets drunk runs the risk of no longer being a true gourmand." Now to enjoy your dinner at La Grenouille.

3 EAST 52ND STREET, NEW YORK CITY

Chicken with Herbs

1 2½-pound chicken, cut in
   6 pieces
Butter
¼ medium-size onion,
   chopped
Pinch of rosemary
1 bay leaf
⅛ teaspoon powdered
   thyme

1. Preheat oven to 400 degrees F. Wash the chicken and wipe dry with paper towels.

2. Melt 2 tablespoons butter over high heat in an ovenproof skillet. Add the dark meat of the chicken, sprinkle with thyme, and sauté for 3 minutes.

3. Lower the heat and add the chicken breasts and onion. Brown for 5 minutes.

4. Transfer skillet to the oven and bake chicken for 20 minutes.

5. Using pincers, lift the pieces of chicken

1 clove garlic, pressed
5 tablespoons dry white
   wine
¼ cup water
1 tablespoon chopped
   parsley

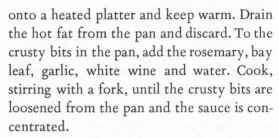

onto a heated platter and keep warm. Drain the hot fat from the pan and discard. To the crusty bits in the pan, add the rosemary, bay leaf, garlic, white wine and water. Cook, stirring with a fork, until the crusty bits are loosened from the pan and the sauce is concentrated.

6. Strain the sauce over the chicken, sprinkle with parsley and serve piping hot.

SERVES 2

Charles Masson's Bread and Butter Pudding

5 slices white bread
   ½-inch thick
3½ cups milk
½ vanilla bean or 1½
   teaspoons vanilla
   extract
5 egg yolks
½ cup sugar
Salt
½ cup raisins
¼ pound butter
Custard sauce (page 420)

Toast the bread lightly and remove crusts. Carefully split the slices horizontally, then cut in half. Preheat the oven to 350 degrees F. (moderate).

Mix together the milk, the seeds scraped from the vanilla bean, or the vanilla extract, the egg yolks, sugar and salt to taste. Pour this custard mixture into an oval baking dish about 12 inches long.

Add a layer of toast slices, sprinkle with the raisins and push toast down into the custard mixture. Top with the butter, cut into small bits. Bake about 40 minutes or until just set but not firm. Serve warm, with the custard sauce which may be flavored with a little brandy.

SERVES 4

Le Manoir

What better way to relax after strenuous endeavor in the executive suites and high-fashion salons of New York than to swoop into Le Manoir for a memorable meal?

Under the experienced management of Maurice Bertrand and Robert Treboux, this dining place offers its patrons fine French food in the Soulé tradition, in a luxurious setting, impressive and comfortable. No wonder it is a favorite of knowledgeable New Yorkers.

The food is well prepared and impeccably served. Surrounded by dark wood paneling and murals depicting French manor houses and bucolic pastures of an earlier time one might begin by tasting the liver mousse, the excellent crusty rolls and cold sweet butter. One might order a flaky quiche Lorraine, a perfectly poached artichoke, then plunge into a savory entree of Coq au Vinaigre. The repast nearly complete, one might add a final and crowning touch by requesting Les Crêpes de Normandie, splendid in a flaming sunshine of Calvados.

120 EAST 56TH STREET, NEW YORK CITY

Coq au Vinaigre
(Chicken in White Wine Vinegar)

1   2½-pound broiling chicken, cut in 6 pieces
4   tablespoons butter
2   tablespoons olive oil
½   pound fat bacon (in one piece)
10   small white onions
10   small mushrooms
Flour

1. Heat butter and olive oil together with the fat bacon cut in small cubes in a heat-proof deep casserole or Dutch oven. Stir, and when the bacon begins to turn golden, add the onions. Cook for 2 minutes and add the mushrooms. Sauté this mixture until the onions begin to turn transparent and the mushrooms to brown. Remove everything from casserole with a slotted spoon to another dish and keep warm.

2. Sprinkle the chicken pieces with ½ cup of flour seasoned with ½ teaspoon of salt and ⅛ teaspoon of pepper. Sauté the chicken in

Salt and freshly ground
   white pepper
2 cloves garlic,
   finely chopped
2 sprigs thyme
2 bay leaves
2 sprigs parsley
1 cup white wine vinegar
2 tablespoons butter
2 tablespoons finely
   chopped parsley

the same fat for 5 minutes. Using pincers, turn the chicken pieces over to brown on the other side. When they are well browned, add the vegetables and bacon to the chicken, sprinkle with salt and pepper. Add garlic, thyme, bay leaves and parsley. Cover the casserole and cook in a 375-degree oven for 30 minutes.

3. Remove the contents of the casserole to another dish and keep warm. Skim off excess fat from the juices in the casserole. Place the casserole over high heat and add the white wine vinegar. Boil down to half its original quantity. Thicken by dropping a mixture of 2 tablespoons each of butter and flour mixed together into the juices and stirring until well blended. Strain the sauce into a deep ovenproof serving dish. Place the chicken pieces, bacon, and vegetables in the dish. Cover and simmer in a 300-degree oven for 20 minutes or until ready to serve. Sprinkle with finely chopped parsley.

SERVES 4

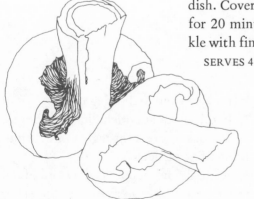

Lutèce

There was a time when any education worthy of the name included a study of Julius Caesar's *Gallic Wars*. Never mentioned was Caesar's real reason for casting a hungry eye upon that country: He was after the Gallic excellence in salting and preserving meats; the superb preparation of hams, sausages and foie gras. In this spirit, the proprietors of Lutèce called their restaurant after the Roman name for Paris and a legion of diners agree they are conquerors in gastronomy.

Lutèce has been singled out for the quality of its soups—a turtle soup, stolen from the English by the French (perhaps because turtle soup was considered an elixir), is brewed to perfection here, as are Crème St. Germain and Consommé de Volaille. But these form only the tip of the phalanx into dining pleasure. The assorted pâtés are Gallic masterpieces, with their aromas of pork forcemeat and goose liver, their trails of herbs, truffles and hazelnuts. And on to dishes marching to glory: Médaillon de Veau aux Morilles, Mignon de Boeuf en Croûte Lutèce, Carré de Pauillac Persillé.

In spite of the splendor of its offerings, the restaurant itself is unpretentious, preferring coziness to serried ranks of chairs in red velvet. Little rooms are squeezably endearing with flower painting, tapestry and mirrors, like an apartment overlooking the Bois.

249 EAST 50TH STREET, NEW YORK CITY

Mousse de Pigeon au Genièvre *(Squab with Juniper Berries)*

1 small squab (¾ pound)
½ pound chicken livers

1. Preheat oven to 250 degrees F.
2. Put the squab, including the bones, and the chicken livers through a meat grinder, using a fine blade.
3. Add salt and pepper and a third of the duck fat (reserved from roasting 2 ducks) or

¾ teaspoon salt
1 teaspoon freshly ground
   pepper
1 cup duck fat or lard
6 juniper berries
6 tablespoons of dry
   white wine

a third of the lard and the juniper berries. Mix until smooth with a wooden spoon or a food processor.

4. Put the squab mixture in a small ovenproof dish and set the dish in a shallow pan of water on the middle rack of the oven. Cook for 30 minutes.

5. Stir in the wine, blending well; and cook for another 15 minutes.

6. Push the cooked mousse through a strainer or puree it briefly in a food processor. Let it cool. Blend in the remaining duck fat or lard which has been heated until soft.

7. Pack the mousse in a small tureen and smear the top with a thin layer of softened lard. Store in the refrigerator.

8. Serve as an appetizer with melba toast.

SERVES 8 AS AN APPETIZER

Maxwell's Plum

It has been called the most eye-filling of New York's restaurants. Decorated to a fare-thee-well, it features an illuminated stained-glass ceiling vauled at $2.5 million, flickering gaslights, live shrubbery, statues, mirrors. Perhaps Maxwell's Plum would be better characterized as a ticker-tape celebration since it has been sold out day and night—1,200 meals per day—ever since it opened in 1966. The owners asked for it, and they got it—they touted the establishment not only as a restaurant and café but also as "a gathering place." All New York turned up: businessmen, models, performers, artists, politicians, newsmen. However, if you were advertising just a meeting place you might as well have erected a sign under a tree in Central Park. What has attracted the large clientele has been the high quality of the fare being offered. Atmosphere can soon wear thin in front of a dried-up hamburger. Here you can enjoy delicious smoked salmon, trout or sturgeon while the ceiling says grace for you—or sample red snapper grilled to perfection amid the bosky surroundings of the café. And since everyone else is having a fling, allow yourself to be tempted by the dessert tray. Its wares are likely to include Black Forest Cake or a sinfully rich pecan pie.

64TH AND FIRST AVENUE, NEW YORK CITY

Black Forest Cake

5 whole eggs
⅓ cup sugar
½ cup sifted cake flour
2 tablespoons cornstarch
2 tablespoons Baker's cocoa
2 tablespoons butter, melted

1. Preheat the oven to 350 degrees F. Butter a 10-inch cake pan and dust it with flour.

2. Break eggs into a stainless steel mixing bowl. Add the sugar and stir over low heat just until the mixture reaches body temperature (98 degrees F.) Test this with your finger. Remove from the heat and, using a rotary mixer or whisk, beat the mixture until it becomes thick and creamy.

Cream filling and coating:
- 1 pint heavy cream, whipped
- 4 tablespoons confectioners' sugar
- 6 ounces chocolate chips
- Kirsch
- Chocolate shavings and chocolate chips

3. Sift and mix together the flour, cornstarch and cocoa and stir this mixture into the eggs and sugar.

4. Still stirring, slowly add the hot butter.

5. Pour into the prepared cake pan and bake at 350 degrees F. for 30 to 35 minutes. Note: Let the cake set at least 8 hours before filling and frosting it.

To make the cream filling and coating:

1. Whip all the cream and stir in the confectioners' sugar.

2. Melt the chocolate in a double boiler. Add half the whipped cream to the melted chocolate and heat very slightly over a low flame, blending the mixture just until it is creamy. Stir constantly with a whisk.

3. Remove from the heat and gently fold in the remaining whipped cream.

4. Cut the cake horizontally in 3 even layers. Sprinkle 2 layers with kirsch and cover with the cream filling. Top with the third layer. Cover entire cake with the remaining mixture. Cover the top with shaved semi-sweet chocolate and the sides with chocolate chips.

SERVES 6 TO 8

Nanni il Valletto

It is disconcerting to hang out one's shingle and have to inscribe thereon: At the Sign of the Bulldozer. The situation arose for Luigi Nanni who came from Italy in 1968 to open Nanni's restaurant on East 46th Street in Manhattan. The building was an old brownstone and the threat of demolition hung over it. Accordingly, the operator attached a second string to his gastronomic bow and opened Il Valletto in 1974, in case the bulldozer caught him between the appetizer and the soup at Nanni's. Perhaps that's the reason for the new name—Nanni il Valletto means a running footman. Among those who have followed this flying footman are regulars Steve McQueen and theatrical producer David Merrick.

The decor at Il Valletto is Florentine, with settees upholstered in red velvet to contrast with the tones of the imported tile of the floor. Pink linen tablecloths add another dash of color. Otherwise, the dashes are in the food; the piquant presence of crushed garlic in the salad dressing, of tender little mussels in the seafood salad, of the same mussels baked with bass. Il Valletto means to stay.

133 EAST 61ST STREET, NEW YORK CITY

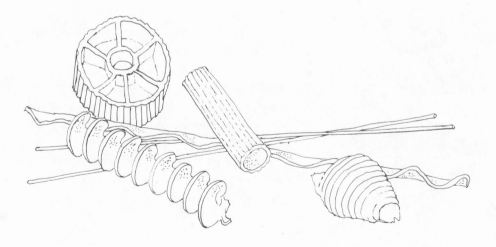

Capelli D'Angelo Primavera *(Springtime Noodles)*

¼ pound butter
2 tablespoons vegetable oil
2 shallots, minced
2 thin slices prosciutto
3 medium-size mushroom caps
3 tablespoons fresh green peas
1 medium-size zucchini
1 large tomato
3 tablespoons dry white wine
½ cup chicken broth
Salt and pepper
½ pound Capelli d'Angelo (a very fine imported noodle)
½ cup freshly grated Parmesan cheese

1. Prepare all the ingredients in advance but cook the noodles and sauce just before serving. Total cooking time should not exceed 15 minutes. In advance, cut the prosciutto into narrow strips. Slice thinly the zucchini and the mushroom caps. Halve the tomato, squeeze gently to remove seeds and liquid, then dice the solid part.

2. Heat 4 tablespoons of butter and the oil in a saucepan; sauté the shallots and the prosciutto over low heat for 2 minutes. Add the sliced mushrooms and then the peas. Cook 3 minutes and add the zucchini, tomato and the wine. Simmer 5 minutes, add the chicken broth and simmer for 5 minutes longer. Season to taste.

3. Meanwhile, bring a large saucepan of salted water to boil and cook the very thin noodles for 6 minutes or just until tender (*al dente*), drain thoroughly and put in a serving bowl. Add the remaining butter to the sauce, stir until melted and pour over the noodles. Sprinkle generously with Parmesan cheese.

SERVES 4

Orsini's

One is allowed to be pontifical about Orsini's restaurant—assert that it is the acme of gourmet dining—since the original Italian family of Orsini provided a long line of prince assistants to the papal throne, along with three popes: Celestine III, Nicholas III and Benedict XIII. The elegant Orsini touch may be felt upstairs, in an aery theater of windblown curtains and green foliage, where the contessas of moviedom and high fashion receive acclaims from the silent eyes of admirers. The sad thought is that these women must watch their willowy waistlines while seated before such cornucopias. Downstairs at Orsini's the lights are dim, the decor soft and romantic, the air conspiratorial—not for Guelf and Ghibelline but for the denizens of Wall Street. There are reminders of the days when the restaurant was starting out as a cozy, small coffee house.

Here is dining in style, to the lilting tunes of a "Roman Italian" menu—Fettuccine all'Alfredo, Osso Buco alla Milanese, Pollo alla Margarita Spaghettini alla Chiatarra—to the tinkling notes of a notable Chianti.

41 WEST 56TH STREET, NEW YORK CITY

Pollo alla Margarita
(Chicken Margarita)

4 individual boned breasts
  of chicken
Flour
1 egg
2 tablespoons water
Salt and pepper
Olive oil
3 tablespoons butter
4 tablespoons white wine

1. Beat the egg with the 2 tablespoons of water. Dip each chicken breast in flour and then in the beaten egg.

2. In a heavy skillet heat ½ inch of olive oil to 360 degrees F. or until the oil sizzles. Brown the chicken breasts well on both sides and drain on paper towels.

3. In a pan large enough to hold all 4 pieces of chicken, melt the butter, sprinkle with the salt and pepper, and add the wine and sherry. Cook over medium heat, stirring continually, till the sauce is concentrated.

4 tablespoons dry sherry
4 slices (3x3 inches)
   Mozzarella cheese

4. Place the 4 pieces of chicken in the pan and put a slice of mozzarella cheese on top of each piece. Cover the pan and cook over moderate heat just until the chicken is heated through and the cheese melted.

5. To serve: Place the chicken on a heated platter and pour the sauce around it.

SERVES 2

Rinaldo Morando's Fettuccine

1 pound egg noodles
6 tablespoons butter
4 tablespoons heavy cream
4 egg yolks
6 tablespoons Parmesan
   cheese
Salt and pepper to taste

Cook the noodles in salted water and drain.

In another large pan melt the butter and stir in the cream. Add the drained noodles and mix well with a fork, over moderate heat. Stir in the Parmesan cheese. At the last moment add the egg yolks and toss rapidly with the fork till just blended. Remove from heat and serve at once.

SERVES 4

The Palace

"**H**ow could it possibly succeed?" worried the cognoscenti when The Palace Restaurant opened in New York City, March 1975—with a prix fixe of $50 (later advanced to $60). And you would still have to pay for the wine, tax and tip. It was a flutter over an enormous gamble. But the gamble has paid off because the principle of "the best" was faithfully followed.

At the Palace you enter upon a dining experience that may last four hours. You will be successfully tempted by the nine courses prepared by chef Claude Baills (formerly of The Laurent, Lutèce and S.S. *France*) and served with style by maître d' Gabriel Hemery and his knowledgeable staff.

420 EAST 59TH STREET, NEW YORK CITY

Poulet Demi-Deuil
(Chicken in Half Mourning)

1   3-4 pound roasting
     chicken
2   medium truffles
Unsalted butter
4   tablespoons Madeira
     wine
1   large slice of fatback pork
Chicken broth or bouillon
2   cups heavy cream
3   egg yolks
Salt and pepper

1. Loosen the skin on the breast and thighs by inserting fingers under the skin.

2. Slice the truffles ⅛ inch thick. Sauté the slices in 2 tablespoons of butter for a few minutes, turning them carefully. Add the wine and cook gently until the wine has evaporated. Cool.

3. Insert the truffle slices under the breast and thigh skin, making the two sides look alike. Wrap the chicken in the fatback and tie it with kitchen twine.

4. Bring chicken broth (enough to cover the chicken) to a boil in a large kettle. Add the chicken, breast side down. Cover the chicken with a clean dish towel and cover the kettle. Poach over moderate heat 1½ hours.

5. Transfer the chicken to a shallow oven-

serving dish, breast side up so the black truffle slices show. Add a cupful of the chicken stock and keep warm.

6. Measure 2 cups of the chicken stock. Skim off any fat and boil until it is reduced to about 4 tablespoons. Add the heavy cream and simmer over gentle heat until the sauce is reduced to half its volume.

7. Beat the egg yolks slightly, adding the hot sauce gradually. Return to the heat and cook, stirring continuously, until the sauce is thick and smooth. Just before serving add 2 teaspoons of butter, pour a little over the chicken and serve the rest in a side dish.

Beurre Blanc Nantais

2 tablespoons dry
  white wine
2 tablespoons white
  wine vinegar
1 tablespoon shallots,
  finely chopped
⅛-¼ teaspoon freshly
  ground white pepper
1 cup fish stock
6 tablespoons very
  cold sweet butter
Salt

Combine the wine, vinegar, shallots and pepper in a small saucepan. Boil over high heat until the mixture measures about 1 tablespoonful. Cool.

In another saucepan boil down the fish stock until it measures 2 tablespoonfuls.

Combine the two liquids and heat over a low flame, whisking in the butter in small portions. Continue whisking until the sauce is light and foamy. Season to taste with salt. The amount of pepper used is a matter of preference. Pour the sauce over freshly broiled sea fish and serve immediately.

SERVES 2

Pearl's

No bright chandelier hanging from a ceiling of cherubs can enliven a blitzed blintz or a karated crêpe. For the diner, it's menus before murals. This is not to say that restaurant design should be buried as a useless corpse, or classed with a dusty bunch of plastic flowers tossed in farewell. Establishments such as Pearl's owe much of their success to the quality of their design. Hitherto, every Chinese restaurant had to have those opium-den little red lanterns, those screenloads of fat mandarins forever crossing trellis bridges, in search of maidens or butterflies. Not so at Pearl's.

This restaurant, completed in 1973, marked the first venture of the architectural firm of Charles Gwathmey and Robert Siegel into restaurant design. Pearl Wong, the proprietor, wanted the simplicity of modern design and not Cathay kitsch. Accordingly, she got a long white room, given life by the subtle details of mirrors, small touches of color and a ceiling that makes a quarter arc. The architects tried their darnedest to break all the earlier rules of restaurant design and they succeeded brilliantly. The rest was left to Pearl Wong—and she came through with the best cooked, most elegantly served Chinese cuisine in the city.

38 WEST 48TH STREET, NEW YORK CITY

Lee Lum's Lemon Chicken

4 whole chicken breasts, boned and skinned
2 tablespoons light soy sauce
¼ teaspoon sesame oil
1 teaspoon salt
1 tablespoon gin or vodka

1. Place the chicken in a shallow earthenware dish or bowl. Combine the soy sauce, sesame oil, salt and gin or vodka and pour over the chicken. Turn the chicken pieces to coat them on all sides and let stand for 30 minutes.

2. Prepare the vegetables by shredding the lettuce finely and cutting the carrots, pepper and scallions into thin one-inch strips.

¼ head iceberg lettuce
3 small carrots
½ large green pepper
3 scallions
3 egg whites
1 cup water chestnut flour
  (available at
  Chinese groceries)
Peanut or salad oil
1 lemon
¾ cup sugar
½ cup white vinegar
1 cup chicken broth
1 tablespoon cornstarch
2 tablespoons water
1 teaspoon monosodium
  glutamate (Accent)
½ cup shredded canned
  pineapple
2 tablespoons (1 ounce)
  lemon extract

3. Beat the egg whites until frothy and spread the water chestnut flour on a plate.

4. Drain the chicken and discard the marinade. Dip the chicken pieces in the beaten egg whites and coat with the water chestnut flour.

5. Heat enough peanut or salad oil in a skillet to measure one-half inch and heat to 350 degrees F. Brown the chicken pieces on both sides and drain on paper toweling.

6. Peel just the yellow part of the lemon rind and cut it into small pieces. Squeeze out the lemon juice. Combine with the sugar, vinegar, broth, cornstarch mixed with the water and the monosodium glutamate in a small saucepan. Bring to a boil, stirring until the mixture thickens. Add the vegetables (except for the lettuce) and the canned pineapple to the sauce. Remove from the heat and stir in the lemon extract.

7. Spread the lettuce on a warm serving platter and cover with the chicken, cut in one-inch crosswise slices. Pour the sauce over the chicken and serve.

SERVES 4

The Pen & Pencil

While working in Paris in 1920, John C. Bruno frequented a specialty house, L'Oignon, which served only one item—the world's finest onion soup. In 1937, Bruno established in New York a restaurant which concentrated on one item—fine steak. The name of the establishment was chosen for the many authors, artists and newsmen who comprised the early clientele and who enjoyed the conducive clubby atmosphere, the ability to converse amid paneled walls while enjoying a hearty meal.

Pen & Pencil's steaks are large, juicy and of excellent quality because the owner has always prided himself on his care and knowledge of beef. The efforts of a staff of 65 are steered toward one goal: to produce the paragon of a beefsteak. Each piece of meat bought at the market each week has been selected and marked. The animals will be primarily Black Angus, 18 months old, weighing 1,300 pounds and classified as USDA Prime. The selection is consigned to a special four-week dry-aging process. Like fine wines and cheeses, beef also must undergo a natural enzymatic action to reach its peak of flavor. At this point, the beef is cooked—with no condiments, spices or chemicals added.

205 EAST 45TH STREET, NEW YORK CITY

Sliced Filet Mignon

4 4- to 5-ounce slices of
   prime aged tenderloin
¼ pound mushrooms
2 cups red wine
Butter
2 tablespoons flour
1 medium-size onion,
   chopped
1 carrot, finely diced
¼ teaspoon powdered
   thyme
2 bay leaves

1. Order the best beef possible.

2. Slice the mushrooms and wash them with warm water, drain well and soak in the red wine for 2 to 3 hours. Cook the mushrooms in the same wine until tender.

3. Heat 2 tablespoons of butter in a saucepan and add 2 tablespoons of flour. Stir until brown. Do not burn. Add 2 cups of the mushroom wine and simmer for 25 minutes.

4. At the same time sauté the chopped onion and carrot in 2 tablespoons of butter just until the onion is tender. Add the drained mushrooms, powdered thyme and bay leaves. Simmer for 5 minutes.

5. Transfer the mushroom slices to the thickened stock using a slotted spoon, discarding the onion, carrot and bay leaf.

6. Heat 4 tablespoons of butter in a skillet and sauté the meat slices, allowing 3 minutes to each side (rare). Transfer the slices to a heated platter and cover with the hot mushroom sauce.

SERVES 2

Le Périgord-Park

Somewhat like the French Department of Dordogne, the ancient province of Périgord, this restaurant is full of delightful surprises. The Dordogne region is noted for its splendid valleys graced with chestnut and walnut trees, with hidden truffles, and it is also remembered for its maze of caves. Some years back, two exploring youngsters literally slipped into the caves at Lascaux, there to discover the earliest known wall paintings of prehistoric man. At Le Périgord-Park, instead of intense darkness one finds the bright glow of sunlight playing on chandeliers and golden upholstery. But the wall paintings—of strollers in puckish attire—are just as jestful as the manner of the discovery at Lascaux. The cuisine is always surprising because it is unfailingly impeccable. France is noted for its pastries, and from the kitchens of this French restaurant come a marching procession of sweet things: beautifully bronzed apricot tarts, mouth-watering mousses and satisfying soufflés.

575 PARK AVENUE AT 63RD STREET, NEW YORK CITY

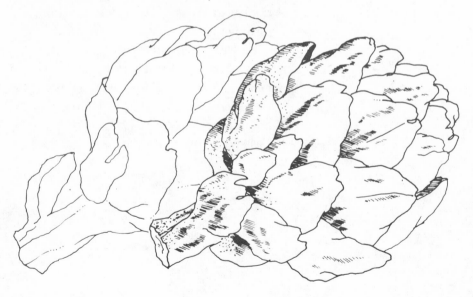

New York

Raspberry Mousse

⅔ cup sugar
⅓ cup water
8 egg yolks, well beaten
1 jar (10 ounce)
   raspberry jam
2½ pounds frozen
   raspberries, thawed
   and drained
4 tablespoons kirsch
½ teaspoon raspberry
   extract
1 quart heavy cream,
   whipped

Cook the sugar and water until it measures 240 degrees F on a candy thermometer or until it forms a medium-soft ball when a little is dropped in cold water. While beating the eggs, pour in the syrup in a thin stream. When all the syrup has been incorporated, beat in the raspberry jam and add the drained raspberries, the kirsch and the extract. Fold in the whipped cream and place in the refrigerator. Chill several hours before serving.

SERVES 6 TO 8

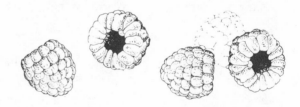

Sauce Vinaigrette

1 tablespoon wine
   vinegar
1 tablespoon French
   mustard
½ teaspoon salt
⅛ teaspoon white pepper
4 tablespoons olive oil

Mix together the vinegar, mustard, salt and pepper. Add the oil slowly, while stirring. If sauce is too thick, blend in a few drops of water. Serve on asparagus, artichokes, salads, etc.

Pierce's 1894 Restaurant

Elmira. Mark Twain lived there, and so did a straw-hat-maker named Crawford Henry Pierce. Perhaps the former riverboat pilot dandified his later years with the latter's products. Pierce bought two $200 lottery tickets for land parcels and struck it rich with prime lots in what was to become the downtown district of the new community of Elmira Heights. He built a spanking Victorian house on one lot and the Crawford Hotel on the other. Later called Pierce's 1894, this unique inn has been owned by the family for four generations. Many a weary traveler has enjoyed the warm turn-of-the-century atmosphere and the large comfortable chairs in the Village Room. Collectors especially will enjoy the display of bottles, one of the most comprehensive in the East. The restaurant offers an excellent menu and wine list. As a pioneering effort, a Chinese kitchen was added in 1955, and there is a fine bakery.

OAKWOOD AVENUE AND 14TH STREET, ELMIRA HEIGHTS, NEW YORK

Banana Daiquiri Torte

Cake:
- 1 cup sugar
- 1 cup dark brown sugar
- 2 cups cake flour, sifted
- ¾ cup butter
- 3 teaspoons salt
- 1½ teaspoons baking powder
- 1 teaspoon baking soda
- 3 large bananas, mashed fine
- 4 large eggs
- ¼ cup milk

1. Make the cake: Preheat the oven to 375 degrees F. Beat the sugars, flour, butter, salt, baking powder, baking soda and bananas with an electric beater for 5 minutes. Turn the beater down to low speed and add the eggs one by one, beating after each addition. Add the milk and continue beating for 10 minutes. Pour the mixture into a 10-inch springform pan and bake 35 to 45 minutes or until a toothpick inserted in the center comes out clean. Remove from the oven. Release the side of the pan but do not move cake from the pan until thoroughly cooled.

2. Make the custard filling: Soften the gelatin in the 1½ cups of milk and combine

Custard filling:

1 teaspoon gelatin
1½ cups milk
1 tablespoon butter
1 teaspoon vanilla
1⅓ cup sugar
½ cup milk
5 tablespoons cornstarch
2 eggs, slightly beaten

Butter-cream filling:

1 pound butter
2 cups confectioners' sugar
½ banana, mashed

Icing and garnish:

2½ pounds confectioners' sugar
¼ cup heavy corn syrup
½ cup water
1 teaspoon banana extract
1 drop yellow food coloring
2 tablespoons rum
2 tablespoons banana liqueur
2 large bananas

in the top of a double boiler with the butter, vanilla and sugar. Stir over direct heat until the mixture starts to boil. Set over hot water and add the milk combined with the cornstarch. Stir with a whisk until the mixture thickens. Add the eggs and continue cooking and stirring for 5 minutes. Cool and chill until firm.

3. Make the butter-cream filling: Cream the butter and sugar in an electric mixer until light and fluffy. Add the banana and the cold custard filling gradually, beating continuously.

4. Make the icing: Combine sugar, corn syrup, water, banana extract and food coloring in an electric mixer bowl and beat until the icing has the desired consistency. Add more water, if necessary.

5. Complete the cake: Cut the torte horizontally into 3 even layers. Sprinkle the bottom layer with rum. Sprinkle the second layer with banana liqueur. Spread both layers with butter-cream filling. Slice the 2 remaining bananas and cover the 2 layers with the slices. Assemble the 3 layers. Spread the top layer and sides with the remaining butter-cream filling and place in the refrigerator for 5 minutes. Cover top and sides with the icing and return to the refrigerator until time to serve. Slice in thin wedges.

SERVES 12

Quo Vadis

Whither goest thou? To the Quo Vadis—if you're Mrs. William Paley, Jackie Onassis, her sister Lee Radziwill, Truman Capote, Charles Collingwood, Mrs. Richard Rodgers, Mrs. Oscar Hammerstein, Kitty Carlisle, every Mayor of New York and every Governor of New York State since 1946, or if you are just you in search of a gourmet repast. Hosts Gino Robusti and Bruno Caravaggi, who arrived in the city in 1939 to man the famed Belgian Pavilion at the World's Fair, explain their secret of lasting success: "A restaurateur can't complete his job with just a quick smile at the desk, then stand around and admire himself in the mirror. He must be, at one time, a captain, a maître d'hôtel, a waiter, yes, even a bus boy, to assure a pleasant stay for the patron."

The cuisine also receives scrupulous attention as may be noted in the special treatment of fresh vegetables: delicious Aubergine Provençale sautéed to the brink of being burned and flavored with garlic; celery braised in a rich brown gravy; asparagus pared down to the soft white core and served with a thick Hollandaise sauce; spiced spinach; also crisp, sweet string beans. No less notable, the delectable strawberries that appear swimming in Grand Marnier and sweet cream.

26 EAST 63RD STREET, NEW YORK CITY

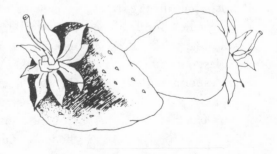

Strawberries Romanoff with Crème Chantilly

1 pint strawberries
4 tablespoons granulated sugar
Juice of 1 orange
½ teaspoon lemon juice
2 tablespoons Grand Marnier or Cointreau
1 tablespoon kirsch

Crème Chantilly
(Sweetened whipped cream)
1 cup heavy cream
2 tablespoons confectioners' sugar
1 teaspoon vanilla (or other flavoring)
1 egg white, beaten stiff (optional)

1. Choose fresh, firm, ripe strawberries. Wash and dry completely before removing the hulls.

2. Place the strawberries in a well-chilled glass dessert bowl. Add the sugar and toss until the berries are well coated.

3. Add the freshly squeezed orange juice, lemon juice and the liqueurs. Shake again.

4. Place the bowl, covered with Saran wrap, in the refrigerator for 2 hours.

5. To make the crème Chantilly: Pour the cream into a chilled electric mixing bowl and whip until it forms stiff peaks. Continue beating, adding the sugar 1 tablespoon at a time. Add the vanilla extract or kirsch or peach or apricot brandy. Fold in the egg white gently, if desired. (This is convenient if whipping the cream in advance.)

6. Serve the strawberries in individual dessert glasses topped with the crème Chantilly. These may be prepared in the kitchen or at the table.

SERVES 2

The Rainbow Room

To find where the rainbow ends, or begins, ascend the RCA Building in Rockefeller Center to the 65th floor and turn east. There, since 1934, has stood this "most talked about" restaurant, resplendent in its original art deco look, with glittering diamond crystal chandeliers, mirrored columns, plum-colored silk walls and golden draperies. On a clear day, through the two-story-high windows, you can see forever—or at least for 50 miles. This elegant dining room is redolent not only with present aromas of fine French and Italian fare but also with flitting memories of the past, of great personalities, great occasions which have constantly graced The Rainbow Room. The regular visits of Joan Crawford, Mrs. Woodrow Wilson, Elsa Maxwell, Gloria Swanson. The opening-night party for *Funny Girl* honoring Barbra Streisand. Zero Mostel doing a hora at the opening-night party for *Fiddler on the Roof.*

In the old days, there was an orchestra on a raised platform at the west end of the room, and in the center a revolving dance floor where patrons could dance cheek to cheek after the likes of Mary Martin, Beatrice Lillie, Carmen Cavallaro had performed. Then the dancing ceased after Pearl Harbor—to be renewed today under the baton of Sy Oliver and his orchestra.

30 ROCKEFELLER PLAZA, NEW YORK CITY

Roast Filet of Beef Wellington, Sauce Périgourdine

1 whole tenderloin of
  beef, well trimmed
  (4 to 4½ pounds)
8 tablespoons butter
4 large mushrooms

1. Make the pastry: Mix the salt with the flour. Using your fingertips or a pastry blender, work in the margarine until you have a fine mealy mixture. Moisten the mixture with just enough ice water to make a smooth ball. Wrap the ball in wax paper and chill thoroughly in the refrigerator.

2. Preheat the oven to 400 degrees F. Place the tenderloin in a roasting pan and rub

1 4-ounce can goose liver
3 eggs
Salt and pepper

Pastry:
2 cups all-purpose flour
½ teaspoon salt
1 cup margarine
Ice water

Périgourdine sauce:
2 tablespoons butter
1 shallot, minced
1 onion, thinly sliced
1 tablespoon chopped
   parsley
2 tablespoons finely sliced
   carrots
½ bay leaf
8 peppercorns
1 tablespoon flour
1 cup beef stock or
   bouillon
1 cup red burgundy
1 cup Madeira
1 small black truffle,
   minced
Salt and pepper

it with 6 tablespoons of butter. Roast 15 minutes, remove and cool.

3. Make the sauce: Heat the butter in a small saucepan; add the shallot, onion, parsley, carrots, bay leaf and peppercorns, and cook slowly until brown. Sprinkle with the flour and stir until the flour disappears. Add the liquids, blend well and simmer very slowly for 35 minutes. Strain and add the minced truffle. Season to taste.

4. Sauté the mushrooms in 2 tablespoons of butter until tender. Remove from the heat and mash the goose liver and mushrooms with a fork until blended. Add 2 eggs, slightly beaten, and season with salt and pepper. Spread this mixture all over the cold beef.

5. Roll out the pastry into a rectangle large enough to envelop the meat.

6. Place the beef in the center of the rectangle. Moisten the edges of the dough and wrap the dough around the beef, sealing the edges. Place in a baking pan.

7. Beat the remaining egg slightly with a tablespoon of water and paint the entire surface, giving an extra coating to the sealed edges. Bake for 25 minutes at 400 degrees F.

8. To serve: Let the Beef Wellington stand for 15 minutes before cutting it straight down in ¾-inch slices. Serve the sauce in a side dish.

SERVES 8

Sea Fare of the Aegean

The warm, limpid waters of the Aegean Sea are resorted to by vacationing bathers—and by teeming fish at the time of their procreating maturity. Inland lie the remains of ancient civilizations, especially the ruins of the striking Minoan palace of Knossos with its walls delicately painted with gorgeously dressed goddesses engaged in sacred ceremonies; a frieze of partridges, monkeys from Egypt, native wild goats and flowers that seem ready to be culled. The fish and the decor meet in the Sea Fare of the Aegean.

Fresh seaspray must just have splashed upon the Red Snapper Soup, flavored with lemon and a little celery. An Aegean salad is green with the vegetables of the countryside, and garnished with feta cheese, ripe olives, anchovies and a lemon dressing made with a very light oil. The ocean still sounds amid the fresh clams served in their shells.

There are some 60 main courses. In season, there may be as many as 20 kinds of fish that may be ordered broiled—broiled to perfection. The tastes, the decor bursting with freshly picked flowers are reminders of that carefree abundance so characteristic of Greece.

25 WEST 56TH STREET, NEW YORK CITY

Shrimp Santorini

Santorini Sauce:
- ¼ pound butter
- ½ cup minced onion
- 1 teaspoon minced garlic
- 1 tablespoon chopped fresh dill
- 1 tablespoon chopped fresh parsley

1. Begin by preparing sauce. Preheat oven to 350 degrees F. Melt butter in an ovenproof dish. Add the onions, garlic, herbs, sugar and tomatoes. Bake until golden brown.

2. Add the ketchup and chicken broth. Continue baking ½ hour.

3. Place the live lobster in a kettle, cover with the baked sauce. Add the water. Simmer for 1 hour or until half the liquid has

¼ teaspoon oregano
¼ teaspoon basil
2 bay leaves
1 teaspoon sugar
1 No. 2½ can stewed
  tomatoes (1 pint,
  10 ounces)
1 cup ketchup
1 quart chicken broth
1¼ pounds live lobster
1½ quarts water
½ cup sherry
1 teaspoon Maggi sauce

24 jumbo shrimp
2 tablespoons flour
¼ pound butter
2 whole fresh tomatoes
Oregano
Parmesan cheese
4 slices Greek Feta cheese

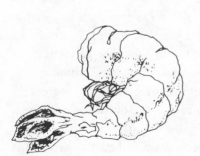

disappeared. Add the sherry, Maggi sauce, salt and pepper to taste. Simmer for 3 minutes.

4. Remove the lobster from the sauce and when cool, take out the lobster meat and return it to the sauce.

5. Press through a strainer or puree in a food processor. Set sauce aside.

6. Peel, devein and wash the shrimp. Dust lightly in flour. Sauté the shrimp in the butter until golden brown.

7. Cut the fresh tomatoes in half and place on a baking sheet. Sprinkle the cut halves with oregano and Parmesan cheese. Grill under a preheated broiler for 3 minutes.

8. Preheat the oven to 400 degrees F. Take 4 individual ovenproof casserole dishes and place 6 sautéed shrimp in each one.

9. Place the grilled tomato halves on top of the shrimp. Cover each half with a slice of Feta cheese. Pour over the Santorini sauce and bake for 5 minutes.

10. Serve with french fried potatoes and mixed green salad.

SERVES 4

Stone Ends Restaurant

Imagine offering to cook the hunter's prize, and after being confronted with the usual pheasant, rabbit and squirrel, suddenly finding at one's doorstep a 243-pound black bear, the successful hunter and 74 hungry friends. It happened at Stone Ends. The bear was hung up in the parking lot and prepared for the pot then and there. Such forbearance and such lengths to go to in order to satisfy one's customers!

The design of the building is Bauhaus inspired, with an exterior of contemporary angled roofs, gray stone and glass—a fitting tribute to the picturesque countryside of Albany County. An architectural firm was given a free hand to plan everything, right down to the coffee spoons. Owners Henry, Lou and Vincent Junco added their own touch of efficiency, cleanliness and exemplary cuisine.

Stone Ends is renowned for its rolling "International Trolley" laden with eighteen appetizers: Stuffed Vine Leaves, Fresh Beluga Caviar, Cherrystone Clam Cocktail. If you can muster ten companions good and true, Chef Emilio Muniz will prepare for your assembly a suckling pig—and for lesser occasions, there will be game in season and fresh vegetables from the Juncos' garden.

ROUTE 9W, GLENMONT, SOUTH OF ALBANY

Quail Broiled in Grape Leaves

4 quail, cleaned, singed and drawn
Salt and pepper
6 tablespoons butter
4 strips bacon
1 cup ginger ale

1. Preheat the oven to 450 degrees F. Rub each quail with salt, pepper and butter and wrap in a strip of bacon. Put 4 tablespoons of butter in a baking pan and place the quail in the pan. Roast for 5 minutes.

2. Reduce the heat to 300 degrees F. Take the pan out of the oven, add the ginger ale and cover each quail with grape leaves. Cover with aluminum foil and return to the

6 grape leaves, freshly
   washed
1 cup seedless grapes
2 small bunches seedless
   grapes
Fresh parsley

oven for 40 minutes. Remove the foil and transfer the quail to a heated platter.

3. Pour all the cooking juices into a small saucepan and add the cup of seedless grapes. Simmer until the grapes are heated through.

4. To serve: Place 2 quail on each of 2 heated plates, pour the sauce over the quail and garnish with small bunches of grapes and sprigs of parsley.

SERVES 2

Baked Acorn Squash

4 medium-size acorn squash
½ cup dark brown sugar
1 teaspoon cinnamon
½ teaspoon nutmeg
¼ teaspoon ground cloves
½ teaspoon salt
½ cup melted butter
½ cup maple syrup
8 ½-inch pieces of bacon
Boiling water

1. Preheat the oven to 350 degrees F. Cut each squash in half and with a spoon dig out the seeds and fibers.

2. In a small bowl combine brown sugar, cinnamon, nutmeg, cloves, salt and butter. Stir until well blended.

3. Arrange the squash in an ovenproof dish just large enough to hold them all. Spoon equal amounts of the spiced butter into the hollows. To each add a little maple syrup and 1 piece bacon.

4. Pour boiling water into the baking dish to a depth of about 1 inch. Place in the center of the oven and bake 30 minutes or until squash is soft.

SERVES 8

The "21" Club

You come of age at "21"—as a gourmet. And "21" came of age during Prohibition as a leading speakeasy. This called for a success dependent on ingenuity: a push-button trapdoor on the bar which funneled drinks into the sewer, secret doorways to the cellars. In 1932 Federal agents spent 19 hours ransacking the place for liquor, to no avail. Today the club—so called for its faithful patronage—is a furtive hideaway for the city's elite as they discuss a business deal or the latest newspaper scoop. Once past the iron-gated entrance, the atmosphere turns convivial. You are greeted by one of the principals, by name if you are a regular, and escorted past the lobby with its rich wood paneling, blazing logs in the fireplace and original Frederic Remington paintings. It's all very much like an exclusive English country hotel. Which makes sense of the unique iron figures on the portico, sporting the jockey colors of famous patrons. The "21" is alive with homey touches, the choice silver collection on display, the Remington bronzes scattered in casual munificence, the affectionately donated collection of miniature planes, trucks and buggies over the bar.

Even the well-laden cellars have that sporting, homey touch: cartoonist Charles Schulz's (Peanuts) Jack Daniels stored for his grandson's 21st birthday; bottles of Presidents, oil magnates, movie moguls awaiting a favored occasion. Obviously, this approach relates also to the food. As one executive noted: "We are old-fashioned enough to think that salmon and green peas belong on the 17th of June; the time for Scotch grouse is right after the 12th of August when the season opens in England; California figs should appear on the table only when God sees fit they are ready for human consumption."

21 WEST 52ND STREET, NEW YORK CITY

Mushrooms à la Daum

2 cups sliced mushrooms

Sauté the mushrooms, onions, ham strips and seasonings in butter, stirring gently with a wooden spoon. Just before serving, stir in

New York

1 cup minced onions
1 cup thin ham strips (julienne)
½ teaspoon salt
⅛ teaspoon freshly ground white pepper
2 tablespoons chopped parsley
8 tablespoons butter
1 cup brown sauce (see recipe below)
4 slices white bread

Brown Sauce

5 cups strong beef broth
4 tablespoons unsalted butter
4 tablespoons flour
1 clove garlic, peeled
1 bay leaf
½ teaspoon dried powdered thyme
1 small onion, chopped
¼ teaspoon Worcestershire sauce
Sherry wine to taste
Salt and freshly ground black pepper

the brown sauce. Serve on 4 pieces of freshly toasted white bread.

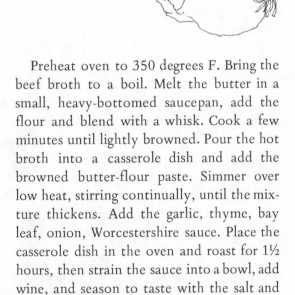

Preheat oven to 350 degrees F. Bring the beef broth to a boil. Melt the butter in a small, heavy-bottomed saucepan, add the flour and blend with a whisk. Cook a few minutes until lightly browned. Pour the hot broth into a casserole dish and add the browned butter-flour paste. Simmer over low heat, stirring continually, until the mixture thickens. Add the garlic, thyme, bay leaf, onion, Worcestershire sauce. Place the casserole dish in the oven and roast for 1½ hours, then strain the sauce into a bowl, add wine, and season to taste with the salt and pepper. Brown sauce may be prepared in advance and kept in the refrigerator until needed.

SERVES 2

71

La Bastille

It is a pleasant incarceration indeed to be confined in La Bastille—the fine French gourmet restaurant on the second floor of the Oliver Plaza in Pittsburgh. Your keeper, Belgian-born chef Alphonse J.G. Thomas, has prepared an extraordinarily ranging menu to make your stay memorable. A purist, Thomas insists on quality in his cuisine: "I myself will not tolerate changing French cuisine. The name that was given to a special dish must remain unchanged; too many changes arise between Paris and New York and when the dish is served, too many times the meaning of its origin is no longer known." Ingredients arrive from all over the world: caviar from Iran, wild boar and chanterelle from Germany, cheeses from France and Switzerland, goose liver and truffles from France, fish from the Pacific, Atlantic and Mediterranean. The bread served is French-style: La Flutte or Baquette.

Chef Thomas remembers well the great personalities he has served. The jovial smile of Maurice Chevalier, the charm and manners of Zsa Zsa Gabor. He thinks back to the late movie star, Van Heflin: "God rest his soul. He was such a sensitive and temperamental man. For an entree he would never order anything but bouillabaisse. Six out of ten times he would order tripe but he also loved escargots and wild boar." At a dinner given for former President Eisenhower, Thomas embedded the champagne bottles in the Pheasant Alsacienne au Champagne and when the waiters uncorked them, a lava of flavorful bubbly foam erupted over his choice creation.

ONE OLIVER PLAZA, PITTSBURGH

Pennsylvania

Polish Clodnick *(Borscht)*

1 quart buttermilk
1 cup sour cream
1 cup diced cucumbers
½ cup diced cooked beets
½ cup finely chopped green
  pepper
1 tablespoon grated new
  carrots
1 tablespoon finely
  chopped scallions
  (green onions)
1 tablespoon dill seed
1 tablespoon salt
½ teaspoon pepper
4 hard-cooked eggs (cut
  in fourths)
½ cup tiny bay shrimp
1 cup croutons

1. Blend the buttermilk and sour cream in a large bowl, using a wire whisk.

2. Prepare the cucumbers, beets, green pepper, carrots and scallions. Add them to the buttermilk mixture and stir.

3. Add the dill seed, salt and pepper. Mix well.

4. Pour the soup into a container with tight-fitting lid and place in the refrigerator for 24 hours or longer.

5. To make croutons, melt butter with 1 clove garlic in a heavy skillet. Remove garlic with a slotted spoon before adding cubes of stale white bread. Sauté the bread until light brown, stirring occasionally to brown all sides. Cool croutons on paper towels. Croutons may be prepared in advance and stored in a plastic bag until needed.

6. To serve: Fill bouillon cups or small bowls with the cold soup. Place a tablespoon of tiny shrimp in the center of each serving, and garnish with 4 egg wedges. Serve croutons in a side dish.

SERVES 4

Joe's Restaurant

This unusual restaurant specializes in original recipes that feature wild mushrooms. An examination of the menu reveals that mushrooms dominate or play an important part in 50 percent of the appetizers, soups, salads, entrees and sauces offered. Even the martinis are flavored by plump, pickled mushrooms. Joseph and Magdalene Czarnecki established Joe's as a tavern serving chicken platters back in 1916. Ownership passed to Joseph L. and wife Wanda in 1947, and it was then that a romance with exotic food and sophisticated service began. A third generation entered the picture when son Jack (now chef) and wife Heidi joined the business in 1974. Joe's is unpretentious, but it offers dishes served nowhere else in the country.

450 SOUTH SEVENTH STREET, READING

Piroshki Filled with Wild Mushrooms

Piroshki dough:
1¼ cups all-purpose flour
¼ pound very cold butter
3 tablespoons sour cream

Filling:
½ pound wild mushrooms
6 tablespoons butter
1 large onion, peeled and chopped
Pinch of savory
Salt and pepper

Both the piroshki dough and the filling must be made in advance and allowed to chill. For the uninitiated, store-bought mushrooms are safest, but wild mushrooms give a special and wonderful flavor. Dried wild mushrooms, soaked and chopped, are excellent for use in this recipe, which can be easily adapted to a food processor.

1. To make the dough: Sift the flour into a mixing bowl.

2. Slice the butter into the flour and cut it in with a pastry blender until the mixture resembles coarse crumbs.

3. Add the sour cream, tossing lightly with a fork just until the mixture holds together enough to form a ball.

4. Wrap the ball of dough in wax paper or plastic and chill thoroughly.

5. To make the filling: Clean the mushrooms and chop them fine.

6. Heat 3 tablespoons of butter in a skillet. Sauté the mushrooms until they are dry. Transfer to a small bowl.

7. Heat the remaining butter and sauté the onion until golden brown. Add to the mushrooms. Mix well and season with the savory, salt and pepper. Chill.

8. To assemble: Pinch off a scant tablespoonful of dough and roll out on a lightly floured surface to a circle 3 inches in diameter.

9. Trim the edges with a pastry wheel or cut with a 3-inch cookie cutter. Repeat until all the dough has been used.

10. Paint the edges of the circles with a little water.

11. Put a teaspoonful of filling in the center of each circle.

12. Fold over to make small turnovers, pressing the edges together with the tines of a fork. Pierce the tops once with the tines of a fork.

13. Place on a baking sheet and chill thoroughly.

14. Just before serving bake 15 to 20 minutes (or until golden brown) in a 400-degree oven.

MAKES APPROXIMATELY 24 PIROSHKI

Le Mont

Mountains are to be looked up to and so especially is a mountain on top of a mountain, as is the plush Le Mont restaurant atop Mount Washington, overlooking the sparkling new skyscrapers of Pittsburgh's Golden Triangle, at the confluence of the Allegheny and Monongahela Rivers as they form the mighty Ohio. Here, while dining superbly on French and Italian cuisine, you can gaze at this overpowering view through an expanse of windows 10 feet high and 106 feet long. Many have remarked on the mellow lavishness of the restaurant's total decor, which can only enhance the magnificence beyond. A soft mélange of beige and peach colors accents the Louis XV-style furniture. Design has been followed, and colors coordinated, down to the last detail. Tablecloths are of peach linen on deep brown liners, on which rest the dinner plates that pick up the soft blues in the dining room.

1114 GRANDVIEW AVENUE, PITTSBURGH

Chocolate Mousse

3 tablespoons water
1 cup plus 2 tablespoons sugar
4 egg whites
¾ cup (6 ounces) melted milk chocolate
2 cups heavy cream, whipped

1. Stir the sugar and water in a small saucepan with a wooden spoon over medium heat just until the sugar dissolves. Heat without stirring to 244 degrees F. or until a drop of syrup forms a medium soft ball when put in cold water.

2. Beat the egg whites until stiff in an electric mixing bowl and still beating, add the syrup in a slow stream.

3. Reduce the speed and add the melted chocolate.

4. Fold in whipped cream.

5. Serve very cold in individual sherbet glasses or custard cups.

SERVES 8

Pennsylvania

Marinara Sauce

⅔ cup olive oil
1 small onion, chopped
3 cloves garlic, minced
1 small can anchovy
   fillets, chopped fine
1 tablespoon oregano
¼ teaspoon thyme
1 teaspoon basil
¼ cup fresh parsley,
   chopped
¼ cup dry red wine
4 cups Italian pear-shaped
   tomatoes, crushed
Salt and pepper to taste

Heat the oil in a heavy-bottomed saucepan. Sauté the onion, garlic and anchovies for 3 minutes. Add the remaining ingredients, bring to a boil, then reduce heat, cover, and simmer for 30 minutes.

Serve with pasta, meat or fish.

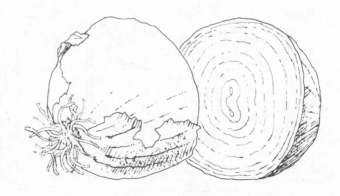

The South

It is impossible to separate food from religion in the South. Even the marriage contract here involves a deeper commitment than mere obedience, love or honor.

When the minister comes to call, honed on the households of his flock, aimed at salvation through his gastrointestinal tract, he dines at a table that does not groan, but purrs, recites creeds of aerial biscuits and hominy soufflés and Smithfield ham sliced Gillette thin. And even at funerals, Southerners go to their rewards cajoled by sweet-potato pie and okra soup, the final sacrament properly observed in the company of floating island or mourning doves roasted to a sort of heavenly perfection.

People sigh a good deal in the South. To the uninitiated it seems to be the heat. But to the chosen, it is the remembrance of things past: corn pudding served at a child's christening party from corn so sweet the very cobs would melt like butter in the skillet; a caramel cake with a pound of everything good in it on a table that stretches to kingdom come at a family reunion, Friendship Baptist Church, Vidalia, Georgia; a completely unpretentious wedding on a lawn in Mobile with a huge vat of shrimp creole and buckets of lemonade, salted and sweetened with the subtle hands of black masters; a great silver bowl of Savannah Artillery Punch so powerful that when the host sampled it he was unable to open the door for the guests. Sighs aplenty.

How comes this association of the sacred with the profane? The same combination that made jazz made Southern cooking: black and Bible; poverty and desire; field and hand. From Africa came the mothers of invention. Here, they found the land of the lotus, free and easy; but with it went the warning against indulgence, so there is always about Southern food a plainness, a *righteousness*. And then work, work in the fields planting an alien crop when the natural fruits of the earth are convulsed with laughter at your efforts. Don't give in.

It is of course a losing battle. Like sin and temptation. The easiest way to lick them is to give in.

Cantina d'Italia Ristorante

British diplomat James Bryce, the Alistair Cooke of American culture at the turn of the century, wrote of the nation's capital, "What you want is to have a city which everyone who comes from Maine, Texas, Florida, Arkansas and Oregon can admire as being finer and more beautiful than he had ever dreamed of." What resident and visitor admire about contemporary Washington is not only its obvious Americanism but also its cosmopolitan flavor. Italy is present in the passing Gucci purses and briefcases, and as well in Joseph Muran de Assereto's restaurant, which has been described by Robert Lawrence Balzer, *Holiday*'s Restaurant & Wine Editor, as providing "cuisine that is easily one of the finest repertoires of Italian food in America."

One enters an underground world of unicorns, lions and griffins, of tapestries featuring 16th-Century scenes from Italy's northern provinces. And from these same provinces come the recipes that have made the owner the Cabinet Minister of Cuisine: Antipasto con Bagna Cauda; Peperonata Lombarda; savory Gnocchi; duckling with pitted green and black olives, tomatoes and mushrooms, in golden Marsala wine, and piquant Coniglio al Limone.

1214-A 18TH STREET NW, WASHINGTON

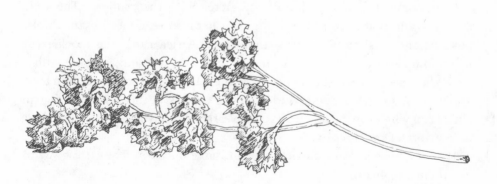

District of Columbia

Coniglio al Limone
*(Rabbit in Lemon
Raisin Sauce)*

24 pieces of rabbit
 1 quart lemon juice
½ cup olive oil
 8 ounces sweet butter
 1 cup grated lemon rind
 5 cloves garlic, minced
½ cup fresh chopped
   parsley
 1 cup dried sage leaves
½ cup crumbled
   bay leaves
Salt
 2 quarts heavy cream
 5 cups Chablis wine
 1 tablespoon wine
   vinegar
 1 cup potato flour
 3 cups Sultana raisins
Cracked black pepper

1. Marinate the rabbit pieces in enough cold water to cover, flavored with 3 cups of lemon juice, for 24 hours.

2. Drain and dry each piece of rabbit. In one or two large frying pans, put the olive oil and ½ cup of butter. Sprinkle with lemon rind and garlic. Heat the mixture. When it is hot, add the parsley and the rabbit. Add the bay leaves and sage and sprinkle with salt.

3. Reduce the heat and sauté the rabbit until golden brown on each side. Heat the cream and remaining butter in a large pan; add the browned rabbit pieces. Simmer for 15 minutes.

4. Remove the sage and bay leaves with a slotted spoon. Add the Chablis and vinegar to the drippings in the frying pan and simmer 5 minutes.

5. Return the rabbit to the frying pan with pincers. Add the potato flour to the cream. Stir briskly until blended. Pour the mixture over the rabbit and sprinkle with Sultana raisins and cracked black pepper. Stir well and place in a 300-degree oven for 30 minutes. Remove, transfer to heated platter and serve with fried potatoes.

SERVES 6

Le Provençal

If a bureaucrat in the nation's capital feels he is getting ironed flat by the system, he visits Le Provençal for a reinvigorating taste of individuality. The name is not just window dressing. Owner and executive chef Jacques Blanc hails from Aix-en-Provence and for the last decade has been serving the delectable specialties of this region of France: Moules Provençales, Sole Soufflée au Champagne, and dishes many times characterized by culinary gymnastics with tomatoes, garlic and other seasonings. On Fridays, everyone enjoys Blanc's noted Bouillabaisse Marseillaise.

In Provence, the countryside is given over to the solid occupations of sheep rearing and olive growing, while the azure coast fringes the Mediterranean with bikinis. And so, the bustle of Washington is juxtaposed to the charm of the country at Le Provençal; Mrs. Blanc greeting the lunchtime clientele and her husband appearing in the evening. The waiters have their own special forms of conviviality. The decor is also a blend of the countryside and the city: hand-painted murals, exposed beams—pink satin brocade panels and chandeliers. It's like crossing the Atlantic on a dinner plate.

1234 20TH STREET, N.W., WASHINGTON

Le Baby Pheasant des Gourmets

6 young pheasants, boned
¾ cup wild rice
6 ounces salt pork
1 onion, chopped fine
2 bay leaves
½ teaspoon powdered thyme
Salt and pepper
¼ pound chicken livers
2 tablespoons cognac

1. Ask your butcher to split the pheasants, remove all bones and save the bones and livers.

2. Cook the wild rice according to directions. Keep warm.

3. Cut the salt pork into small strips. Put in a pan of cold water. Bring to a boil. Simmer 5 minutes. Drain well.

4. Sauté the salt pork with the onion, bay leaves, thyme and a little salt and pepper.

5. Add chicken and pheasant livers and

District of Columbia

6 slices fat bacon
1 pound mushrooms
2 tablespoons butter
1 onion, sliced
1 carrot, sliced very thin
2 tomatoes, peeled,
  seeded and chopped
2 cups sherry
Chicken broth
1 tablespoon cornstarch
¼ pound cooked beef
  tongue
1 black truffle
6 4-inch rounds of white
  bread, ½ inch thick

cook gently 3 to 4 minutes, stirring frequently. Remove from the heat.

6. Grind the mixture or puree in a blender. Combine with the cooked rice. Season to taste and add cognac.

7. Stuff the pheasants with the mixture and wrap a strip of bacon around each bird. Secure with kitchen twine.

8. Preheat the oven to 375 degrees F. Place the pheasants in a roasting pan. Surround with the bones and roast for 30 minutes.

9. Cut the mushrooms in thin strips and sauté in butter just until tender. Set aside.

10. Cut the beef tongue and truffle into very thin strips.

11. Fry the rounds of bread in butter or oil until golden brown on both sides.

12. Remove the pheasants and bones from the pan, put in the onions, carrots and fresh tomatoes. Sauté until light brown. Add the wine and the cornstarch mixed with ¼ cup of chicken broth. Stir until blended.

13. Add the strips of tongue, truffle and mushrooms to the sauce and simmer for 2 to 3 minutes. Taste for seasoning. To serve: Remove the twine and bacon from the pheasants and place each on a heated plate, on top of a crouton. Cover with the sauce.

SERVES 6

Café Chauveron

The move from Manhattan to Florida did nothing to dim the gastronomic reputation of Roger Chauveron. The Parisian splendor of the Grand Véfour, or Taillevent, sends its rays over Miami Beach as this noted chef personally supervises dishes which have pleased Presidents and nobility: the Dover Sole Véronique, the Ris de Veau aux Marrons à la mode Périgourdine. The only word is *"superbe."* Or is it? As Chauveron jocularly explains, sometimes, and very rarely, one's lifetime experience is pitted against the inadequacies of the patron. Once he had served the dessert Mousse au Chocolat avec Saboyon to a party of four. One of them called him over and remonstrated, "This is cake instead of the real mousse!" The chef had to suggest that the mousse was authentic, had been served in the same way for 18 years, that it was a mousse encased on four sides by a quarter-inch layer of pound cake which is coated with the same Swiss chocolate that constitutes the mousse, the entire mousse serving 15 people, a portion being one slice. Chauveron sighs, "Obviously these people had been inculcated with different types of chocolate pudding masquerading as mousse." But he counters, "The dining public as a whole has shown striking changes in the knowledge it brings to ordering, especially wines."

9561 EAST BAY HARBOR DRIVE, BAY HARBOR ISLAND

Dover Sole
or Pompano Véronique

4 fish fillets
Salt and pepper
4 tablespoons butter
4 shallots, chopped

1. Place the fish seasoned with salt and pepper in a pan that has been rubbed with 2 tablespoons of the butter and sprinkled with the shallots. Add the wine. Bring to a boil and simmer very gently for 30 minutes. Remove the fish with a wide slotted spatula to a heatproof serving dish and keep warm.

3 cups dry white wine
½ cup Béchamel sauce
(page 416)
4 tablespoons cream,
whipped
1 cup seedless muscat
grapes, skinned

2. Cook the liquid in the pan down to a third of its original quantity.

3. Mix the Béchamel sauce with the rest of the butter and whip until blended. Add to the fish liquid. Season to taste and fold in the whipped cream.

4. Surround the fish with the grapes and pour the sauce over all.

5. Brown quickly under a preheated broiler. Serve at once.

Note: Any firm white fish fillets can be substituted for the Dover sole or pompano.

SERVES 4

Café Chauveron Fond Brun *(Brown Stock)*

2 pounds beef skin
2 pounds veal knuckle
¼ pound lean raw ham
with the bone
2 carrots
2 onions
5 quarts water
1 bouquet garni (celery,
parsley, thyme and
bay leaf tied in a
bit of cheesecloth)
2 teaspoons salt

1. Cut the meat in fairly small pieces and spread on a flat pan. Sprinkle with a little cooking oil and brown well in a moderate oven (350 degrees F.) or on top of the stove, stirring occasionally.

2. Slice the carrots and onions and place them with the meat to brown for a few minutes.

3. Transfer all to a 2-gallon kettle and add the water, the bouquet and salt. Bring the water to a boil, remove any scum from the surface and simmer for about 3 hours.

4. Cool and remove fat that congeals on top. Strain through a fine sieve or cheesecloth and store in the refrigerator or freezer.

MAKES ABOUT 3 QUARTS

Café L'Europe

"**H**ow did you come so far, so quickly?" is a question that might be asked of the youthful owners of Café L'Europe, Titus Letschert and Norbert Goldner. The restaurant is beginning its fourth year of operation and these men are still in their mid-30s. Still, their success rests on a solid foundation, because both served apprenticeships of several years, and when they opened L'Europe they knew what it was all about.

Their expertise is reflected in the high level of the service, the sophistication of the menu and the pleasing setting they have created, a kind of indoor garden where luxuriantly green and tropical plants contrast with salmon-pink brick walls and harmonizing salmon-pink tablecloths.

The menu is essentially French, though there are pastas, steaks and curried lamb chops to add international accents. Brandied Duckling is popular. For dessert there are tempting and luxurious homemade pastries and soufflés. For luncheon, lighter fare—salads, omelettes, crêpes and open-faced sandwiches.

431 HARDING CIRCLE, SARASOTA

Curried Lamb Chops

8 thick lamb chops
4 tablespoons flour
1 tablespoon Madras curry powder
2 tablespoons butter
4 tablespoons chopped mangoes, fresh or canned
1 tablespoon chopped preserved kumquat
4 tablespoons coconut

1. Ask the butcher to French-cut the chops. This means to cut out the eye of the chops and trim off all fat. Shape them into nice round medallions with your hands.

2. Combine the flour and curry powder and coat each piece of meat on all sides.

3. Before cooking the chops prepare the sauce: Sauté the onion, ham and bacon in the butter in a small pan until the onion is golden.

4. Add the curry and cook for 1 minute, stirring constantly.

5. Stir in the flour, apple, preserved fruit

Curry Sauce:
- 1 small onion, finely chopped
- 4 tablespoons finely diced cooked ham
- 1 slice bacon, diced
- 1 tablespoon butter
- 2 tablespoons Madras curry powder
- 1½ teaspoons flour
- 1 small apple, cored, peeled and coarsely chopped
- 2 tablespoons preserved mango or kumquat
- 1½ teaspoons tomato paste
- ½ teaspoon salt
- Juice of ½ lemon
- 1½ teaspoons honey
- 1 cup chicken stock

(coarsely chopped), tomato paste, salt, lemon juice and honey. Cook for 1 minute more and add the chicken stock. Simmer 25 minutes. Remove from the heat and cool. Taste for seasoning.

6. Spin the sauce in a blender until smooth.

7. Heat 2 tablespoons of butter in a large skillet and sauté the chops 2 minutes on each side. Add the mango, kumquat, curry sauce and lemon juice. Simmer 3 minutes.

8. Serve the chops and sauce in a preheated serving dish and sprinkle with coconut which has been lightly toasted in the oven.

SERVES 4

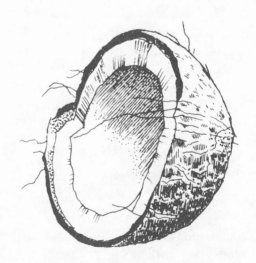

Chalet Suzanne

Alice can still find her Wonderland, if she looks through central Florida. At Lake Wales, just east of Tampa, Chalet Suzanne Inn and Restaurant has nonsense to rival the Mad Hatter's. It is a crazy collection of 30 brightly colored guest rooms and 5 interconnected dining rooms, all knotted together with winding walks, heavy iron gates, and cobblestone courtyards—an odd but delightful maze with a surprise at every corner.

It all began in 1931 as the home of Bertha Hinshaw, who collected many of the colorful doo-dads displayed and used throughout the unusual rooms—objects gathered through 18 trips around the world. Bertha's son, Carl, who now runs the inn, has never hired a trained chef, preferring to man the kitchens himself and employ people who just happen to enjoy preparing good food.

The unusual touch is everywhere. There is a yellow building named "Pink Cottage," a guest room called "Banana," and one room that is squeezed among two others called "In-between." Each table is set with different china—Royal, Windsor, Wedgwood, Spode. Here and there are inexpensive Hong Kong reproductions, accorded equal billing among the good china, simply because they are attractive and in good taste. One favorite dinner opener, a Chalet original, is cinnamon broiled grapefruit with grilled chicken livers roosting in the center. Gourmet critics, alarmed at first, soon marvel at the taste. Guests can enjoy it all while dining, perhaps, in the Round Room which, not surprisingly, just happens to be hexagonal.

FOUR MILES NORTH OF LAKE WALES, BETWEEN U.S. 27 AND 27A

Seafood-Mushroom Soup with Sherry

6 tablespoons butter
9 tablespoons flour

1. Melt the butter in the top part of a double boiler. Add the flour and stir with a whisk until well blended. Add the milk and cream and stir until the mixture starts to simmer. Place over hot water and add the

3 cups light cream
2 cups milk
1½ cups chopped cooked
   seafood (cod, haddock,
   shrimp, lobster or a
   combination)
½ cup mushrooms,
   sautéed in 1
   tablespoon butter
1 hard-cooked egg,
   finely chopped
½ teaspoon grated
   lemon rind
1 tablespoon salt
¼ teaspoon white pepper
½ teaspoon sugar
4 tablespoons Harvey's
   Bristol Cream Sherry
3 hard-cooked egg yolks
2 tablespoons chopped
   chives

remaining ingredients except for the sherry. Cook 25 minutes.

2. Add the sherry 5 minutes before serving.

3. To serve: Pour the soup into hot soup bowls and garnish with sieved egg yolk and chopped chives.

SERVES 6

Baked Grapefruit

Grapefruit
Butter
Sugar
Cinnamon
Chicken livers
Flour, salt, pepper

Cut fresh grapefruit in half. Cut out the center and cut around the sections, being careful not to pierce the skin. Fill center cavity with melted butter. Sprinkle a mixture of sugar and cinnamon over the top. Place under the broiler until slightly browned, or in the oven about 10 minutes at 375 degrees F. Garnish each half with a grilled chicken liver and serve as a first course.

Chez Guido

Chez Guido has recently passed through a conversion—from dim English tavern to bright tropical rattan—and installed a new chef in the kitchen. The new decor is lighter and so is the food. Chef Pierre Jaun is a disciple of the "new cuisine Française" that strives to cut back calories and carbohydrates without sacrificing flavor. It calls for more fresh meats and vegetables, and less thickening in the sauces. Nothing is overcooked.

"Diners must be educated to eat duck rare rather than overcrisp, for better flavor," chef Pierre rules. "Whether vegetables or meat, overcooking kills the natural flavor of food. Sauces should be delicate, to complement a dish rather than smother it."

Will all of Chez Guido's patrons become slim and willowy under this regime? It's hard to believe, when they have placed before them such entrees as Brook Trout Stuffed with Shrimp Mousse, Turtle Soup, Quail in Truffle Sauce, Steak Diane and Steak Poivre.

The knowledgeable and gregarious host, Guido Gerosa, is Swiss and Italian; the chef is French. So what can the style be but cosmopolitan? The elegant entrees are served up on lacy rattan tables against a background of cool lime-green and white and lush foliage, a second feast for the diner's eye.

PLAZA CENTER, ROYAL PALM WAY, PALM BEACH

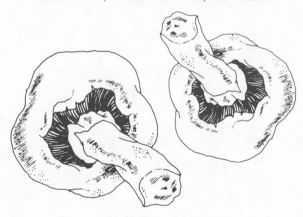

Florida

Steak Diane Chez Guido

2 6-ounce sirloin steaks
4 tablespoons butter
2 tablespoons brandy
2 shallots, minced
¾ cup sliced mushrooms
2 teaspoons Dijon
  mustard
1½ teaspoons Worcestershire
  sauce
4 tablespoons red wine
1 cup Madeira sauce
¼ cup heavy cream
Salt and freshly ground
  pepper

Madeira Sauce:
1½ tablespoons butter
1½ tablespoons minced
  shallots
1 cup brown sauce
  (page 418)
3 tablespoons Madeira
2 teaspoons lemon juice

1. Make the Madeira sauce: Heat the 1½ tablespoons butter in a small saucepan and simmer the 1½ tablespoons shallots until soft but not brown. Add the brown sauce, Madeira and lemon juice. Cover and simmer for 10 minutes.

2. Heat the 4 tablespoons of butter in a metal skillet and pan-broil the steaks 3 to 4 minutes on each side according to taste. Add the brandy and ignite with a lighted match, spooning the sauce over the steaks until the flames are extinguished. Remove the steaks and discard the butter.

3. Using the same very hot pan, add the shallots, mushrooms, mustard, Worcestershire sauce and wine. Cook rapidly over high heat for a few minutes and then add the Madeira sauce. Stir well and cook 4 minutes.

4. Lower the heat, add the heavy cream and season with salt and several twists of a pepper mill. Replace the steaks in the sauce and reheat.

5. Serve on two heated plates along with white rice and a green vegetable.

SERVES 2

Le Cordon Bleu

Never heard of Dania? You may have driven right through it and not noticed. It's bounded on the north by Fort Lauderdale, on the south by Hollywood and on the east by two miles of glorious golden sand, blue sea and green palms.

What does one do in Dania, besides laze on the beach? One watches jai alai in plush surroundings, or takes the children to the Pirates World amusement park, and has dinner at Le Cordon Bleu. Many a native Floridian and sophisticated tourist drives out of his way to locate what appears at first glance to be a modest white cottage but turns out to be one of the country's finest French restaurants, complete with fresh flowers, candlelight and the gleam of well-polished silver on white napery.

The remarkably varied menu is the result of Anne and Harold Kane's long love affair with fine cuisine (she has carried on alone since his death). The featured preparations are treasures the Kanes discovered on their European travels. Waterzooi, for example, comes from Belgium where many consider it the national dish. There are also such delights as Sole Albert, prepared by chef André Pernod on request; Mousseline de Grenouilles; and a delectable combination of spinach, mushrooms and artichoke hearts in sauce they call Le Gratin Normand.

Remember Dania then. It gets its name from the Danish settlers who founded it, and it was once famed as a tomato-growing center. Today, the name is enshrined in the memory of happy diners who, in pleasant surroundings, consumed memorable repasts.

1201 NORTH FEDERAL HIGHWAY, DANIA

Belgian Waterzooi

1 capon (6-7 pounds)
2 tablespoons soft butter
8 stalks celery
4 leeks

1. Truss the capon as though for roasting. Rub with the butter and brown it on both sides under a preheated broiler, turning it with large pincers so as not to prick the skin.

2. Transfer the capon to a deep casserole, large kettle or Dutch oven.

1 carrot
1 small onion
4 sprigs parsley
4 cloves
½ bay leaf
⅛ teaspoon powdered
   thyme
⅛ teaspoon ground
   nutmeg
Chicken broth
4 egg yolks
¼ cup heavy cream
Juice of 1 lemon
1 tablespoon chopped
   parsley

3. Cut well-washed celery into 4-inch lengths. Trim the leeks so that they measure 4 inches and wash very thoroughly to remove any sand. Scrape the carrot and dice coarsely. Peel the onion and chop coarsely. Add all to the chicken.

4. Add the cloves, bay leaf, thyme and nutmeg.

5. Add enough chicken broth or diluted chicken base to cover the capon. Bring to a boil. Reduce the heat, cover and simmer for 1 hour or until the chicken is tender.

6. Remove the capon from the stock and let it cool slightly. Remove and discard the skin and cut the meat into large serving pieces. Keep the pieces warm.

7. Strain the chicken stock into a large saucepan and reheat almost to the boiling point.

8. Beat the egg yolks and cream adding a little of the hot stock. Gradually add the mixture to the rest of the hot stock, stirring vigorously with a whisk until the mixture thickens. Do not let it boil. Season to taste with salt, pepper and lemon juice.

9. Place the chicken pieces in a small tureen or deep serving dish. Cover with the sauce and sprinkle with the chopped parsley. Serve the Waterzooi with thinly sliced, buttered whole wheat bread.

SERVES 4

The Down Under

Fort Lauderdale is the Venice of America and, for years, Florida's yachting capital. Within an area of 35 miles of what was once a swamp, some 300 miles of navigable canals and waterways have been carved, so that wherever you are in the city, you are never more than a few steps from water. As Stephen Birmingham pointed out, "Where else but in Fort Lauderdale would you find a yacht with not one but *two* wood-burning fireplaces?"

In such a setting, along the Intracoastal Waterway, Leonce Picot and Al Kocab created their happy two-story wooden-beamed tavern, hidden in a profusion of plants and flowers, alive with Belle Epoque antiques and art nouveau objets d'art.

The young and talented chef, Christian Planchon, serves a menu that is basically French, with Russian, Italian and New Orleans influences. Try the Chicken Madagascar, piquant with green peppercorns and wine vinegar.

3000 EAST OAKLAND PARK BEACH BOULEVARD, FORT LAUDERDALE

Crippen Salad

2 bunches watercress
3 hearts of palm (canned)
¼ pound sliced raw
   mushrooms
Vinaigrette sauce (page 428)
½ cup toasted sliced almonds
Salt and pepper to taste

Wash watercress well, discard stems and cut into 1-inch lengths. Cut hearts of palm into ¼-inch pieces. Combine with the mushrooms in large bowl and toss with vinaigrette sauce (French dressing), salt and pepper. Divide into 4 salad bowls and sprinkle each with the almonds.

SERVES 4

Chicken Madagascar

2 2½-pound chickens,
   cut up
½ pound butter
2 tablespoons green
   peppercorns, crushed
2 tablespoons wine vinegar
2 tablespoons brandy
1 cup dry white wine
Chicken stock or broth
1 pint cream
½ cups sifted all-purpose
   flour
Salt
White pepper

1. Sauté the chicken pieces in ¼ pound of butter until brown on all sides. Remove with pincers and set aside.

2. In the same pan put the peppercorns, vinegar, brandy and wine. Boil for 2 minutes.

3. Add the chicken and enough chicken stock or broth to cover. Sprinkle with salt and pepper. Cover and let simmer 25 minutes.

4. Heat the rest of the butter in a saucepan and stir in the flour, blending completely. Cook very slowly for 10 minutes.

5. Strain the chicken liquid into a large saucepan and boil it down for 5 minutes. Slowly add the flour-butter mixture, stirring constantly with a whisk. When the ingredients are well blended, add the cream and boil for 1 minute. Place the chicken in the sauce and let set for 1 hour. Reheat before serving.

6. Serve with white rice (p.426), wild rice (p.428), spätzle or noodles.

SERVES 8

The Forge

It was a treasured moment when, with sudden inspiration, *Holiday* editors hit upon a worthy title—"Alvin's Magic Anvil"—for Robert Lawrence Balzer's account of The Forge restaurant, which appeared in the April/May, 1975, issue of the magazine. Alvin Malnik is the inspired entrepreneur who has turned this former blacksmith's shop into a flamboyant masterpiece of dining pleasure. As Mr. Balzer pointed out, "It takes the rebellion of youth against starchy formality to find a new beauty and individuality." Even an experienced Restaurant and Wine editor could stand amazed at the succession of lavishly decorated rooms in this gastronomic Bluebeard's Castle.

Particularly stunning was the Dome Room—"This small area, seating only 16 people, cost more than a million dollars. The walls are arched panels of stained glass; soft colors reflect from 10th-Century Venetian mirrors, glancing off the prisms of the central chandelier; table-high wainscoting of carved rosewood circles the room in peacock design. In niches high above, abstract contemporary goddess-of-the-grape figures in carved wood lean out in gestures of grace. The decor is its own idiom."

Even the wine cellar is breathtaking. One walks by walls lined with locked storage cases and notes a bottle of red Bordeaux Château Lafite Rothschild 1822 vintage, with an eye-popping $10,000 price tag. Nearby is a similar bottle—but 1858 vintage—for a mere $7,500! Need we hammer the point of The Forge's uniqueness further?

432 ARTHUR GODFREY ROAD, MIAMI BEACH

Artichoke Hearts
Monte Carlo

1 cup lump crab meat
2 cups watercress leaves

1. Shred the crab meat with a fork in a small bowl.

2. Combine all the remaining ingredients, except for the artichoke hearts and lettuce, in a blender until smooth and creamy.

¼ cup chopped chives
2 tablespoons chopped parsley
1 clove garlic, minced
3 anchovy fillets, chopped
1 cup mayonnaise
3 tablespoons lemon juice
½ teaspoon salt
¼ teaspoon freshly ground black pepper
½ cup sour cream
3 tablespoons chopped dill
12 canned artichoke hearts, drained
Bibb lettuce

3. Add half of the sauce to the crab meat and toss well.

4. Trim the bottom of the artichoke hearts so that they will sit evenly on the plate. Take out some of the center leaves to form a cup. Fill each heart with crab meat.

5. Place 2 filled hearts on beds of lettuce on individual plates and cover with the remaining sauce.

6. Optional garnish: Decorate the artichokes with small pimiento cut-outs or tiny strips. Surround with a few asparagus spears and cross 2 strips of pimiento over each spear.

7. Refrigerate 30 minutes before serving. Serve with thin buttered slices of pumpernickel bread.

SERVES 6

Joe's Stone Crab Restaurant

Florida developer Henry M. Flagler died in 1913, the same year the Stone Crab Restaurant was born: the end of one era, the beginning of another. After honeymooning at St. Augustine in 1883, Flagler had become infatuated with the Sunshine State. There he created opulence, starting with the fashionable Spanish Renaissance-style Ponce de Leon Hotel in St. Augustine, moving to the Ormond Hotel at Ormond Beach, the Royal Poinciana at Palm Beach and the Royal Palm at Miami. He pushed his railroad southward, moving the citrus industry with it, and reached Key West despite all odds. His private coach traversed that series of impossible bridges to the tip of the nation a year before he died. Then came the boom-and-bust years of the '20s and '30s. Through all these vicissitudes, the Stone Crab continued with its simple formula, down-to-earth food served to perfection. The buildings came and went but the family and the service remained the same, so that, to this day, gourmets by the hundreds cram this eating place for stone crab, crisp salads, famous cole slaw, clam chowder, Key Lime Pie, Shrimp Creole and other delectable dishes from the diversified menu.

227 BISCAYNE STREET, MIAMI BEACH

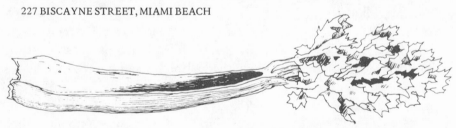

Mustard Sauce

½ cup English mustard
1 quart mayonnaise
¼ cup A-1 Sauce
¼ cup Lea & Perrins
1 pint light cream

Combine all ingredients in a large bowl and beat well, using whisk or electric beater, until thoroughly blended. Continue beating while adding the cream, a little at a time, till the mixture has the desired creamy consistency.

Shrimp Creole

½ cup chopped celery
½ cup chopped onions
4 tablespoons diced
   salt pork
1 No. 2½ can (1 pint
   10 ounces) tomatoes
¾ cup chili sauce
½ teaspoon thyme
1 teaspoon Maggi
2 cloves garlic, minced
Salt and pepper
2 pounds cooked shrimp
White rice (p.426)

1. Simmer the celery and onion with the salt pork until the vegetables are tender and the pork has rendered its fat. Add all the remaining ingredients except the shrimp and simmer 30 minutes.

2. Add the cooked shrimp and spoon the mixture over cooked white rice.

3. Serve on individual heated plates. Garnish with chopped parsley.

SERVES 4 TO 6

Petite Marmite

Imagine the scene: a boatload of tipsy Spanish sailors scrambling up a white sandy beach as their ship, the *Providencia*, lay foundering, its hold still laden with 20,000 coconuts. The crazy fellows had broken into the cargo of 100 barrels of wine with disastrous results. In such inglorious fashion was founded Palm Beach, as glorious, svelte and glamorous a resort as any in the world. Once sobered up, the sailors did their bit by retrieving the bobbing coconuts and planting them. Succeeding generations planted mansions under the swaying palms. Good cheer prevailed in the hands of capable restaurateurs, and the tradition nobly prevails at Costanzo Pucillo's Petite Marmite.

Pucillo had come from another fairyland surrounded by a sea of blue, the island of Capri, where once the Emperor Nero built 12 villas for his weekends off. After training under the great chefs of Europe, the owner brought the serenity of Italy, the gourmet excellence of the Continent, to fashionable Worth Avenue. One dines imperially under chandeliers from Venice, by lanterns under which gondoliers once sang and vivid paintings undertaken by an artist from—Capri.

315 WORTH AVENUE, PALM BEACH

Florida

Veal Chops
Petite Marmite

6 thick veal chops
6 large slices of
   prosciutto (Italian ham)
3 large truffles
Flour
3 eggs, well beaten
2 cups fresh white fine
   bread crumbs
½ cup freshly grated
   Parmesan cheese
½ pound butter
Salt and pepper
Parsley

1. Ask the butcher to butterfly the chops. He will split each chop horizontally leaving the meat attached to the bone. Fill each chop with a slice of prosciutto and 3 slices of truffles and press the flaps closely together.

2. Pat a little flour on both sides of each chop. Dip into the beaten egg and finally coat with a mixture of the bread crumbs and cheese.

3. Heat the butter in a large skillet and sauté the chops slowly for 10 to 12 minutes on each side, depending on the thickness of the chop. Season with salt and freshly ground pepper.

4. Serve on a heated platter garnished with fresh parsley.

SERVES 6

Note: Montrachet, a fine white Burgundy wine, is particularly good with Veal Chops Petite Marmite.

Raft and Reef

He came for the potato pancakes. A German, from a land of potatoes, and no less a personage than Chancellor Willy Brandt. As Mayor of West Berlin, Willy Brandt had first visited the Far Horizons Resort and its Raft and Reef Restaurant in 1965, but he returned for an unprecedented three weeks' stay in 1971, lured by memories of those pancakes, the fine cuisine, and the beachfront setting. In Germany, he asserted, this kind of food is made from pre-mixes or taken from cans, whereas at Far Horizons the pancakes are made from "scratch" in the old time-consuming way by the German chef. The Chancellor equally enjoyed the wide range of veal dishes including Schnitzel à la Holstein and Plume de Veau, Lemonata Doré. Great men are allowed their eccentricities, so no eyebrows were raised when Brandt and his family ordered fresh strawberries for dessert each day during their entire stay. It seems that strawberries are a rarity in Germany and nonexistent during those wintry weeks while he was basking in Florida.

Manager Jack Chris Kahn is aware that many of his guests stay for several weeks. Accordingly, a new menu is prepared on a daily basis. Kahn notes the growing awareness of his visitors: "Our guests are becoming much more sophisticated in their dining proclivities. We have had to create a far more elaborate menu than we used to offer. The sophistication of our guests is also apparent in their wine selections for they no longer rely on famous first growth names or on the price list for selections. They realize that great glasses of wine do not necessarily come from high-priced bottles."

At Far Horizons Jack Kahn is assisted by his brother Bill. Both innkeepers are in constant attendance to see to their guests' comfort and enjoyment while at their resort. In fact, they take special pleasure giving tours of their showplace kitchen where you may see Chef Harold Wuelfrath preparing some of his specialties, perhaps even those famous potato pancakes?

FAR HORIZONS RESORT, 2401 GULF OF MEXICO DRIVE, SARASOTA

Mixed Seafood en Coquilles

¼ cup chopped shallots
3 tablespoons butter
1 tablespoon chives
½ cup dry white wine
12 shucked oysters
12 freshly shelled and
   deveined shrimp
½ pint Bay scallops
10 white mushrooms,
   quartered
1 cup light cream,
   heated
Salt and pepper
½ pound lump crab meat
3 tablespoons flour
½ cup whipped cream

1. Sauté the shallots in 1 tablespoon of butter until they are transparent. Add the chives and wine and simmer until reduced by half.

2. Add the oysters, shrimps, scallops and mushrooms and simmer 4 minutes.

3. Add the hot cream and season to taste with salt and pepper.

4. Add the crab meat and remove from the heat.

5. Knead the remaining butter with the flour and drop in small portions into the seafood mixture while stirring very carefully with a wooden spoon. Return to the heat and simmer 2 more minutes.

6. Spoon the mixture into 6 heatproof shells or ramekins. Top with a spoonful of unsweetened whipped cream and brown under a preheated broiler. Serve very hot.

SERVES 6

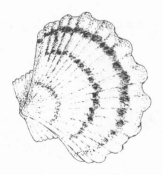
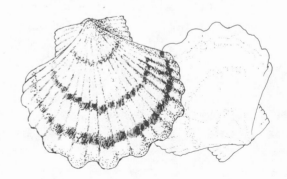

Raimondo's

"O Sole Mio," sing Floridians in tribute to the sun that sparkles on their blue waterways as brightly as on the Bay of Napoli, and in celebration of a happy wedding of their unmatched fresh vegetables and seafoods to Italian cuisine. It all happens at Raimondo's, a small place with a large reputation. The restaurant seats just 65 persons but almost everybody who is anybody in show business, politics or the arts ends up there sooner or later, sampling the Zuppa di Pesce, Veal Piemontese, Stuffed Beef Bones Jule and the tangy Onion Soup di Mare.

The dining room is finished in tones of brown and beige to serve as a quiet background for the colorful foods that are artistically presented to the diners and then prepared at tableside: emerald green spinach, sun yellow cheeses, scarlet tomatoes. They provide all the bright accents an interior decorator could desire.

Host Raimondo Laudisio was born in Brooklyn but grew up in the Miami area where he learned the rudiments of the restaurant business. Later, he served an apprenticeship at the Hotel Excelsior in Rome and toured Europe, tasting and testing the best foods offered by the old countries before returning to Miami, in 1972, to open his own place.

201 NORTH WEST 79TH STREET, MIAMI

Fettuccine Verdi "Organic John"

1 pound green fettuccine
  (homemade or
  store-bought)
4 mushrooms, sliced thin

1. Put a large kettle of water and ½ teaspoon of oil on high heat and bring to a boil.

2. Assemble all the remaining ingredients except the butter and mix together as if for a salad dressing.

3. Cook the noodles for 6 minutes or just until tender (al dente). Drain well and rinse for 1 second in cold water. Put back in the

2 large tomatoes (peeled,
  seeded and diced)
2 cloves garlic, minced
½ cup pine nuts
½ cup chopped parsley
2 tablespoons chopped
  fresh sweet basil
½ cup freshly grated
  Parmesan cheese
1 teaspoon grated lemon
  peel
¼ cup olive oil
Salt (preferably sea salt)
Freshly ground black pepper
4 tablespoons sweet butter

hot kettle and toss with butter over heat until the noodles are all coated with butter.

4. Add sauce, mix well and serve very hot.

SERVES 2 OR 3

Homemade Green Noodles

3½ cups flour
  (approximately)
3 eggs
½ pound spinach, cooked
1 tablespoon oil
½ teaspoon salt

Drain the spinach well and put it through a blender or food mill. Mix with the eggs, oil and salt, in a large bowl. Add the flour, a little at a time, stirring at first and then kneading with the hands, to make a smooth, solid dough. Cover and let rest 30 minutes.

Turn onto a floured board and roll into very thin sheets. They should be dry but not brittle. Fold the sheets and slice into noodles ¼ inch in width. Or, divide in thirds and put through a noodle maker according to directions that come with the machine.

The Abbey

It's the only church in Atlanta that is as busy weekdays as on Sundays. A clergyman's dream, the spot is packed for service each day. Of course, since 1969, this former place of worship has been William Swearingen's highly successful restaurant.

The church dates back to 1915, when the First Unitarian Church of Atlanta finished 32 years of wandering like the chosen people in the desert and dedicated the edifice. In 1951, the Unitarians merged with the Universalists and celebrated their holy union by moving again. After serving a variety of purposes, both lay and religious, the building was purchased by the present owner in 1968. The altar and pews were removed but the glowing stained-glass windows remained. Tables and chairs were imported from Mexico and medieval-style tapestries from the Middle East; period paintings were hung on the walls. To provide an aura of prayerful attention, waiters donned monastic habits.

But any sermons of praise should not stop at the unusual setting. The Abbey has become known for its French cuisine, its offerings of Crabe Dante, Venaison St. Hubertus, Couronne d'Agneau.

669 WEST PEACHTREE STREET, N.E., ATLANTA

Georgia

Roast Duckling with
Stewed Cinnamon
Apples, Raisins and
Orange Sauce

2 4-4 ½ pound Long Island
  Ducklings
2 tablespoons marinated
  green peppercorns
2 apples, peeled, cored
  and diced
2 celery stalks, diced
1 carrot, diced
2 medium onions, chopped
1 can (20 ounces)
  stewed apples
2 tablespoons light
  brown sugar
1 cup raisins
½ teaspoon cinnamon
½ cup dry white wine
1 teaspoon lemon juice
2 teaspoons arrowroot
  or cornstarch
3 tablespoons white sugar
1 quart fresh orange
  juice
1 tablespoon each Triple
  Sec, Kirschwasser and
  Curaçao
Salt and pepper

1. Remove the giblets from the ducklings and rub the insides with salt and white pepper.

2. Preheat the oven to 350 degrees F.

3. Crush the green peppercorns and mix with the diced apples. Stuff the ducklings with this mixture and place them in a roasting pan. Surround them with a mixture of the diced celery, carrot and onions and add 1 cup of water to the pan.

4. Roast 1 to 1¼ hours.

5. Put the stewed apples in a saucepan. Add the brown sugar, raisins, cinnamon, white wine and lemon juice. Bring to a boil and simmer very gently for 5 minutes. Do not stir very much because the apples will break up.

6. In another saucepan combine the orange juice, white sugar and a cup of water. Bring to a boil and add the arrowroot or cornstarch softened in a little water. Add the liqueur.

7. When the ducklings are done, split in half and remove the inside bones. To serve: Place a serving of stewed apples on a heated plate. Top with half a duckling and spoon over the orange sauce. Serve very hot.

SERVES 4

The French Restaurant

The SS *Queen Mary* is docked at Long Beach, California. The SS *France*, in Atlanta, Georgia. Well, not the entire French superliner—but at least its famed dining room is berthed in Atlanta. Pierre Caillet, manager of the restaurant that graces the elegant new Omni International Hotel (470 rooms, skating rink, six movie theaters, boutiques), tells us that he and his staff feel they are still aboard the ocean liner, on a long sunshine cruise that will never end. After all, the chef, the waiters, Pierre himself, were on the *France* together for many years.

Those were the days when they enjoyed serving Chicken Calvados, superb omelettes—to the likes of the late President Eisenhower, James Stewart, Brigitte Bardot, Mel Ferrer, Audrey Hepburn. By a lucky turn of fate, the culinary team can still offer the same great dishes, on a luxury land cruiser forever at anchor, and to a new stellar clientele that includes Pauline Trigere, Eugenia Sheppard, Barbara Rush, the Cornelius Vanderbilt Whitneys. Favorites on shipboard have become the specialties of the present menu: Roast Duckling Bigarade, Filet of Beef Périgourdine, Tournedos Henri IV, Stuffed Sea Bass Herbed With Fennel, Trout Meunière and, for the final sweet moments, Pear Poached in Bordeaux Wine, Orange Flavored Chocolate Mousse. A new wave of excellence has crested in Atlanta.

OMNI INTERNATIONAL HOTEL, ONE OMNI INTERNATIONAL, ATLANTA

Chicken Calvados

- 1 2½-3 pound chicken
- 2 large onions
- 4 tablespoons butter
- 1 apple, peeled, cored and quartered

1. Order the chicken cut in 4 pieces with the backbone and wing tips removed.
2. Cut the onions in ½-inch dice.
3. Heat 2 tablespoons of the butter in a deep pan and sauté the chicken and onions until the chicken is browned on all sides.
4. Remove the chicken from the pan

2 stalks celery, sliced
1 carrot, sliced
2½ cups water
2 cups chicken stock
  or bouillon
2 tablespoons flour
White rice (page 426)
2 cups whipping cream,
  heated
6 tablespoons Calvados
  or Apple Brandy

and add the apple, celery and carrot. Sauté for 2 minutes, stirring frequently.

5. Add the water. Season with salt and pepper and put back the chicken. Cover and simmer 30 minutes.

6. Drain and set the chicken aside to cool.

7. Combine the strained broth with the chicken stock or bouillon and boil it down to half its original volume.

8. Mix the remaining butter with the flour until well blended and drop in small portions into the hot stock, whisking constantly until the mixture thickens. Add the hot cream and simmer 10 minutes.

9. Meanwhile cook the rice according to directions.

10. Remove the skin and bones from the still warm chicken and discard. Cut the meat into serving pieces.

11. Add 4 tablespoons of Calvados to the sauce. Mix well.

12. Place the chicken in the sauce and remove from the heat.

13. Make a ring of rice around a shallow heated serving platter and fill the center with the chicken. Sprinkle the remaining Calvados over the chicken.

SERVES 2

The Midnight Sun

The mind of space-oriented architect John Portman creates buildings that belong as much to the next century as to our own. Best known of his innovations to date is the Peachtree Center in Atlanta, where you shop with "moonbags" and sleep in ultramodern hotels that wink back at the stars. An architectural gem in this huge complex is the Midnight Sun Restaurant, named after Denmark, the "land of the midnight sun." Accordingly, the menu is replete with Danish specialties, prepared by Danish chefs and served in the Danish manner. Notable is the Kabaret, a private smorgasbord. Also served is Reindeer (Lapia Style), Saddle of Venison Châtelaine and Lobster Soufflé.

As befits the latest in modern luxury, the Midnight Sun has the distinction of being the first operation of its kind in the country to have all its food and beverage accounts and cash receipts handled by computer. But the technology does not detract from the warm glow of the woods that uniquely spring like trees from the floor and fan out over the ceiling, or from the comfortable design of the Scandinavian furniture. The pièce de résistance is a central atrium with a marble-tiered fountain. Of an evening, lights play under the marble, which becomes translucent, and the waters channel down among the tables. It is like living in the Land of the Lotus, or on some balmy planet visited by the crew of Star Trek.

235 PEACHTREE STREET, N.E., ATLANTA

Gravad Lax

6-7 pound salmon
2 tablespoons salt
2 tablespoons crushed
  pepper
2 cups sugar
2 cups fresh dill

1. Fillet the salmon and remove all bones or ask your fish dealer to do it. Place in a deep dish just large enough to hold the fish.

2. Sprinkle the fish with the salt, pepper, sugar, dill and fennel seeds, pricking the flesh to let the spices seep through.

3. Cover with the oil and refrigerate for 3 days.

1 cup fennel seeds
2 cups salad oil

Mustard-dill sauce:
  1 cup Dijon mustard
  ½ cup sugar
  ½ cup white wine vinegar
  2 cups salad oil
  2 cups fresh chopped dill

4. To make the sauce: Combine the mustard with the sugar mashed or blended together with the dill. Stir in the vinegar and oil and mix well.

5. To serve: Cut the fish into paper-thin slices slightly on the diagonal. Each side of the salmon will make 50 to 60 slices. Serve with the mustard-dill sauce and thin slices of pumpernickel bread. Estimate 3 slices per person when serving the dish as an appetizer. In northern Sweden, Gravad Lax is also served as a main dish accompanied by either creamed spinach or creamed potatoes.

SERVES 20 TO 40 AS AN APPETIZER

The Pirates' House

And there was Billy Bones, the faithful first mate alongside Cap'n Flint as the old leader muttered his last words, "Darby, bring aft the rum!" Legend has it that this scene from Robert Louis Stevenson's *Treasure Island* took place in what is now the Pirates' House restaurant. Many will swear that the ghost of Cap'n Flint still haunts the place on moonless nights. If this all sounds piratically jolly, then that's just what owner Herb Traub wants. He's taken Frances McGrath's old tea room of twenty years ago and created one of the most unusual and intriguing dining places in the nation. Frances's recipes are still the gourmet staples of the very reasonably priced menu, but more traditionally, Herb Traub has been able to blend fine cuisine with the Jolly Roger exuberance of his 23 dining areas as he daily brings new life to his trust, one of Savannah's historic landmarks.

When General Oglethorpe and his fellow colonists landed here in 1733, they established an experimental garden on this site only one month after their arrival. The following year, they built the "Herb House"—today the oldest building in Georgia—and as seafaring increased, an inn (now the Pirates' House) was constructed nearby, a scant block from the Savannah River. To this rendezvous repaired sailors and pirates in search of some fiery grog. Many a man was shanghaied, to have his stupor broken by salt spray blowing across a strange ship. This lusty past is relived in the patch-eye decor of the restaurant. Anywhere else, such would be only a gimmick. At the Pirates' House it's a genuine wink at history.

20 EAST BROAD STREET, SAVANNAH

Georgia

Onions Au Gratin

5 cups boiled onions,
   drained and chopped
5 cups grated Cheddar
   cheese
½ cup self-rising flour
¼ teaspoon black pepper
½ teaspoon salt
6 tablespoons butter,
   melted

Preheat the oven to 350 degrees F.

Combine the onions and 4 cups of the cheese with the flour, pepper, salt and butter. Pour into a 2-quart buttered casserole. Sprinkle with the remaining cup of grated cheese. Bake 30 minutes.

SERVES 10 TO 12

Ham Buffet Ring

1 can condensed tomato
   soup
¾ cup water
2 tablespoons gelatin
½ cup cold water
3 ounces cream cheese
2 tablespoons lemon juice
1 tablespoon grated onion
½ cup mayonnaise
2 teaspoons prepared
   mustard
2 cups ground cooked ham

Soften the gelatin in the ½ cup cold water. Combine the soup and ¾ cup water and bring to a boil. Remove from heat and add the softened gelatin and the cream cheese. Beat smooth with a rotary beater. Cool.

Add lemon juice, onion, mayonnaise, mustard and ham to the cooled but not stiff soup-gelatin mixture. Rinse a ring mold (8½-inch size) in cold water and pour in mixture. Chill 3 to 4 hours.

To serve: Unmold on salad greens. Garnish with hard-cooked eggs and stuffed olives.

SERVES 8 TO 10

Stanley Demos' Coach House

That acerbic reporter, Henry L. Mencken, became honey-tongued after his visit to the Lexington region. He had once been invited unexpectedly to a Bluegrass farmhouse for breakfast, and years later he wrote of the encounter: "Never in all my wanderings have I seen a more idyllic spot . . . or had the pleasure of being entertained by more pleasant people. . . . The place was truly Arcadian." In 1969, Stanley Demos opened his Coach House to extend Kentuckian hospitality to the discerning traveler and the horse-loving folk of the locality. He operates his establishment in the spirit of Woodrow Wilson's dictum that the ancient traditions of a people are their ballast, as has proved true in the calm solidity of Lexington.

The dining room is entirely French in decor, a pavilion-type setting. Gold and white flocked wallpaper is used throughout, accented with deep red draperies and carpet and off-white woodwork. The light fixtures and the paintings of fashion models are originals from La Belle France. But more original are the dishes, all special creations of Stanley Demos—whether it's the Gazpacho or Fresh Florida Snapper Coach House. With well-justified flamboyance, the Dover Sole is billed "My Way."

855 SOUTH BROADWAY, LEXINGTON

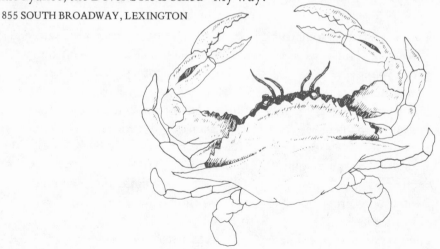

Kentucky

Crab Demos

2 cups mayonnaise
4 tablespoons curry powder
4 tablespoons Dijon mustard
2 tablespoons lemon juice
2 cups cooked wild rice
  (page 428)
1 pound lump crab meat
6 tablespoons freshly
  grated Romano or
  Parmesan cheese
Paprika

Preheat the broiler.

1. Mix the mayonnaise, curry, mustard and lemon juice and set aside.

2. Divide the cooked rice between 6 sea-shells or ramekins.

3. Cover the rice with the crab meat.

4. Spoon the mayonnaise mixture over the crab and sprinkle with the cheese and a dash of paprika.

5. Heat under the broiler until hot and bubbly.

6. Serve on individual plates, garnished with lemon wedges and fresh parsley.

SERVES 6

Gazpacho

½ cup peeled, diced
  cucumber
½ cup peeled, chopped
  fresh tomato
¼ cup chopped green pepper
¼ cup chopped onion
¼ cup chopped celery
3 tablespoons olive oil
2 tablespoons wine
  vinegar
1 teaspoon salt
½ teaspoon pepper
Tomato juice

Combine the finely chopped vegetables in a quart jar. Add the oil, vinegar, salt, pepper and about 1 cup of tomato juice. Put lid on the jar and shake well to blend seasonings. Add more tomato juice, filling jar to the top. Stir, cover and refrigerate overnight. Taste and correct seasoning as desired, before serving.

Serve very cold, in chilled bouillon cups, as a first course.

SERVES 6

Bon Ton Restaurant

The Cajuns were once despised. Descendants of French Canadians who had been driven by the British from the captured French colony of Nova Scotia, they had trekked to the fertile bayou lands of southern Louisiana, there to form their own compact and self-contained communities. To this day they speak their own patois, perform their own spinning, weaving, and other home crafts. But they keep to themselves, and outsiders once returned their aloofness with prejudice for the supposed Black and Indian Cajun ancestry.

From this background comes the independent spirit of Alvin Pierce, a French-speaking native of Bayou Lafourche. Still clutching many of his old Cajun family recipes, he opened his establishment in New Orleans and popularized his people's indigenous cooking with a fine chef's hand. He uses only the freshest foods and seasonings that the locale has to offer. When something is out of season, it disappears from the menu. Try his Fried Catfish, the Crawfish Jambalaya or the bread pudding with a whiskey sauce. The decor follows the easy-going, warm feel of the 1800s, the tablecloths are checkered red and white—and that is all that is checkered in the progress of this notable small restaurant.

401 MAGAZINE STREET, NEW ORLEANS

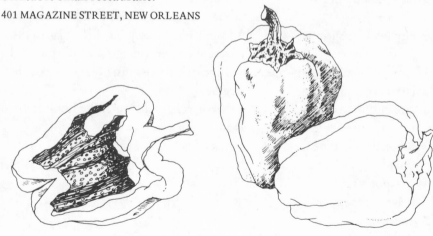

Shellfish in Eggplant

6 medium-size eggplants
Olive oil
4 green peppers, seeded
  and diced
4 medium onions, chopped
½ cup chopped celery
3 cloves garlic, minced
1 pound small shrimp
1 pound white lump crab
  meat
½ cup chopped parsley
Bread crumbs
Salt and pepper
Paprika

1. Boil the eggplants in a large kettle of salted water just until soft. Remove, cool and cut in half. Carefully scoop out the flesh, leaving a shell ½ inch thick.

2. Heat 3 tablespoons of olive oil and cook the peppers, onions, celery and garlic just until soft. Do not brown. Add the scooped-out eggplant and cook until almost dry.

3. Add the shrimp and cook 20 minutes, stirring frequently over moderate heat.

4. Place the mixture in a bowl and fold in the crab meat and parsley. Season to taste with salt and pepper.

5. Add enough bread crumbs to give the mixture the texture of stuffing.

6. Stuff the eggplant shells and place them on an oiled baking sheet.

7. Preheat (now or later) the oven to 350 degrees F.

8. Sprinkle the eggplant with bread crumbs and paprika and dribble with a little olive oil. Bake until browned.

SERVES 12

Brennan's Restaurant

Call it the luck of the Irish, or better, the flair of the Irish. In 1946, Owen E. Brennan, Sr., opened his first New Orleans restaurant in the French Quarter, on the corner of Bourbon and Bienville Streets. A colorful and flamboyant man, Brennan was urged into the restaurant business by the legendary Count Arnaud, who told him, "You Irishman! You open a dining spot in the French Quarter, you open a *French* restaurant." Brennan had actually been contemplating a steakhouse. The restaurant flourished and in a few short years friends like novelist Robert Ruark had helped give Brennan's an international reputation. But the owner was not satisfied. Despite the culinary brillance of the city's dining rooms, he found them lacking in elegance. So he conceived something on the grand scale—the lovely and opulent establishment he created on Royale Street, where gorgeous women could dine of an evening by candlelight. Owen Brennan died a few weeks before his dream came to fruition.

The torch passed to his wife Maude, who continued her late husband's quest for the definitive New Orleans restaurant. Fortunately their three sons became imbued with the same passion, and to this day one or more of the family will be there to supervise the premises. As the family slogan recalls: "Some famous restaurants are merely famous . . . but there's one famous restaurant that's also great."

417 ROYALE STREET, NEW ORLEANS

Louisiana

Trout Nancy, Lemon Butter Sauce

  8 fillets of speckled trout
Melted butter for basting
  2 tablespoons butter
1½ pounds lump crab meat
 ⅓ cup capers

Lemon butter sauce:
 ½ cup brown sauce
     (page 418)
  2 tablespoons lemon
     juice
1½ pounds butter, melted

1. Preheat the broiler.
2. Brush a rack in an open roasting pan with melted butter.
3. Place the fillets on the rack and sprinkle with salt and white pepper. Brush with melted butter. Set aside.
4. Heat the 2 tablespoons butter in a heavy skillet over medium heat and add the crab meat and capers. Reduce the heat a little and sauté for 5 minutes, tossing the pan occasionally so that the crab meat will not break up. Keep warm in a 175-degree oven.
5. To make the sauce: Combine all the ingredients and cook, stirring over low heat until blended.
6. Broil the fish 3½ to 4 inches from the broiling unit for 6 or 7 minutes, until the fillets flake when pierced with a fork.
7. Place the broiled fillets on preheated dinner plates. Top each one with several heaping tablespoons of the sautéed crab meat and capers and spoon a generous amount of lemon butter sauce over each fillet. Serve immediately.

SERVES 8

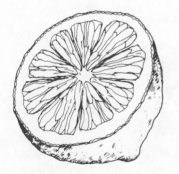

The Caribbean Room

Bankers and lawyers are fine friends when you are running a successful gourmet restaurant, but they are the devil's own advocates when you want to start one. So found E. Lysle Aschaffenburg when, in 1948, he conceived the idea of the Caribbean Room in his Pontchartrain Hotel. These friends thought the man was out of his mind that he would dare to compete against such culinary giants of New Orleans as Antoine's and Galatoire's, with their 100-year-old histories. The pundits were proved wrong and the restaurant has reached the pinnacle of acclaim in this gourmet's city.

Although the Caribbean Room is noted for its Crab Meat Remick, Trout Véronique and famous Mile High Ice Cream Pie, President Albert Aschaffenburg speaks of the behind-the-scenes philosophy that builds a general reputation: "We have deliberately attempted to avoid being representative of what I call a 'pseudo haute cuisine.' In the first place, we feel that New Orleans people don't want such a menu and the tourist who comes to New Orleans seeks something different from what can be found in New York or Chicago. So we bear in mind the fascinating truth about our regional cuisine, that it is a happy combination of Cajun, Creole and French cooking. I would never want to operate a local restaurant with chefs who could not prepare Red Beans and Rice, Jambalaya, Gumbo and Red Fish Courtbouillon."

PONTCHARTRAIN HOTEL, 2031 ST. CHARLES AVENUE, NEW ORLEANS

Louisiana

Oyster Broth

2 quarts shucked oysters
1 small onion, chopped
2 stalks celery, chopped
½ pound butter
2 tablespoons flour
Salt and white pepper
Parsley, chopped

1. Look over the oysters to be sure there are no shells. Save the juice carefully.
2. Sauté the onion and celery in the butter. Do not let them brown.
3. Add the flour and blend well. Add the oysters and the oyster juice and simmer gently 20 to 25 minutes. Strain. Taste for seasoning.
4. Serve in bouillon cups, garnished with chopped parsley.

SERVES 8

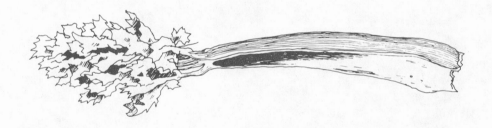

Lemon Icebox Pie

1 can sweetened condensed
   milk
½ cup lemon juice
Grated rind of 1 lemon
2 eggs, separated
1 8-inch baked pie shell
2 tablespoons sugar

Blend condensed milk, lemon juice, grated lemon rind and egg yolks. Pour into cooled pie shell.

Beat egg whites until foamy. Add sugar gradually, beating until stiff but not dry. Cover lemon filling with meringue and bake at 350 degrees F. for 10 minutes or until slightly browned. Chill and serve cold.

SERVES 6 TO 8

Christian's

Founded in 1973 by Christian Ansel, a member of the well-known Galatoire family of culinary experts, this immaculate, small and unpretentious French restaurant has already a tremendous following in this food-conscious region. You have only to take a mouthful of the red fish *froid* appetizer in its tantalizing sour cream and pecan masking to know you are in the presence of a great tradition. Emphasis is placed on French and Creole preparation of fish from local waters. Chef Roland Huet is especially proud of his Oysters Roland, Bouillabaisse, Filet stuffed with oysters. Also try his Quenelles and Baby Veal Christian. The wine list includes domestic and imported labels at reasonable prices.

1519 VETERANS MEMORIAL BOULEVARD, METAIRIE

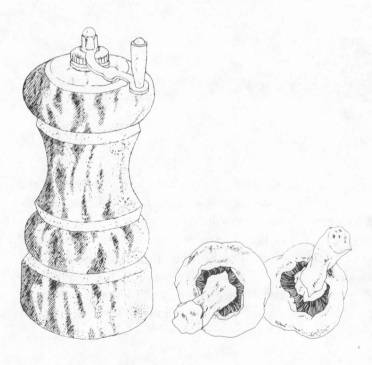

Louisiana

Lobster Tails Madeleine

2 tablespoons dry English
  mustard
4 tablespoons butter
3 pounds cooked lobster
  meat
⅓ cup brandy
2 cups heavy cream
Salt and pepper

Mix the mustard with a little water to make a light paste.

Melt the butter over high heat and sauté the lobster until all water evaporates from it. Then pour over brandy and ignite.

When the flames subside, add the cream and cook, stirring, till a smooth sauce is obtained. Add the mustard paste and season to taste with the salt and pepper.

Serve in individual casserole dishes or on a platter, garnished with parsley.

SERVES 6

Oysters Roland

1 bunch parsley
2 cloves garlic, pressed
1 12-ounce can mushrooms
  (stems and pieces)
1 pound butter, softened
1 teaspoon salt
1 teaspoon black pepper
¼ teaspoon nutmeg
1 cup soft bread crumbs
5 dozen shucked oysters

1. Process in a blender or food processor: first the parsley, then the garlic and mushrooms, drained of their liquid (reserve the liquid). Add the butter and spices and blend well, then the mushroom juice and bread crumbs. Blend well.

2. Poach the oysters in their own juices just until the edges curl.

3. Place 6 oysters in each of 10 4½-inch *au gratin* dishes. Spread the butter mixture over them with a small spatula. Cook under a preheated broiler until brown and bubbly.

4. Serve very hot.

SERVES 10 AS AN APPETIZER

Commander's Palace

For most of us, "magnificent moments" are few and far between, but for the Brennan family of Commander's Palace such a moment occurs every workday. As Ella Brennan, who along with sister Adelaide and brothers John and Dick presides over this charming place, describes it, "I cannot think of any business I would rather be in, if only for the exciting and satisfying time when I walk through the kitchens each morning and make my way among the festoons of copper pots and pans to hear the chefs call out excitedly, 'Miss Ella, Miss Ella, come taste this Shrimp Bisque' or 'The crawfish are in, and here's the beginning of today's Crawfish Etouffée.' I feel for the people who don't have the good fortune to work with these marvelous people we have, to serve our fine clientele and enjoy putting out great dishes in a city where they are so much appreciated."

But the Brennans are as much a legend for hospitality as for fine food. (One once confessed, "The worst thing about·running a restaurant is giving people the check.") So they mingle with the patrons, Charles Bronson and his actress wife Jill Ireland, playwright Tennessee Williams, Robert Mitchum, or the likes of you and me, and oversee the 60 waiters (each one serves no more than two tables).

Commander's Palace is one of the great houses of the Garden Quarter and the Brennans keep this premier rendezvous throbbing with the pulse of New Orleans.

WASHINGTON AVENUE AT COLISEUM STREET, NEW ORLEANS

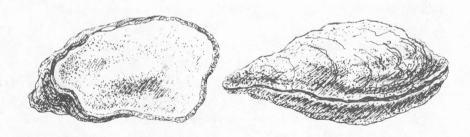

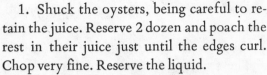

Oysters Commander's

4 dozen raw oysters in
  the shell
¾ cup clarified butter
  (page 420)
1 cup flour
½ bunch green onions,
  chopped
½ cup artichoke bottoms,
  chopped
Pinch of cayenne pepper
½ teaspoon white pepper
Salt
3 dashes of Lea & Perrins
  sauce
½ cup Parmesan cheese

1. Shuck the oysters, being careful to retain the juice. Reserve 2 dozen and poach the rest in their juice just until the edges curl. Chop very fine. Reserve the liquid.

2. Preheat the oven to 450 degrees F.

3. Heat ½ cup of butter and blend in the flour. Stir and cook for 1 minute. Set aside.

4. Heat the remaining butter in a small pan and sauté the green onions with the seasoning just until soft. Add the butter-flour mixture and cook 2 or 3 minutes. Remove from the heat and whisk in the oyster liquid until thick and well blended. Add a little water if necessary. Cook 5 minutes.

5. Stir in the chopped cooked oysters and artichoke bottoms.

6. Lay the raw oysters in the half shells or in ramekins.

7. Spoon the mixture over the oysters and sprinkle with Parmesan cheese.

8. Bake 10 to 12 minutes. Serve very hot in individual ramekins.

SERVES 6

Note: If oysters in the shell are not obtainable, allow 4 raw oysters to a serving.

LeRuth's

Owner-chef Warren LeRuth is proud of his front door, and equally proud of his back door. In fact, his recipe book for patrons is called *Front Door, Back Door Cook Book*.

The front door stands for his fine haute cuisine establishment, which looks over the French Quarter of New Orleans, four and a half miles away. With Gallic bravado he mentions that "the distance between the left bank of Paris and the west bank of the Mississippi is not too far—especially if you go by way of LeRuth's." The building is a 90-year-old Victorian-style house, its walls hung with an art collection that includes an original Picasso. The menu features choice delicacies: Crab Meat St. Francis, Crawfish Cardinal, Veal Désir du Chef. The artichoke and oyster soup is so much LeRuth's own that he will not part with the recipe.

The back door represents the kitchens, where his staff dines on sumptuous regional fare, such as Fried Catfish Bellies, Pannée Pork Chops and Lyonnaise Potatoes and the popular Red Beans and Rice. The lively spirit of the chef makes all the food preparation an adventure—as the mushroom salad with Bibb lettuce and vermouth dressing. Why vermouth? The simple answer: "Vinegar is an archenemy of good wine. Eat a salad containing vinegar and any wine that follows will hardly taste at all. But vermouth, which is made of wine, won't kill the taste buds."

636 FRANKLIN STREET, GRETNA

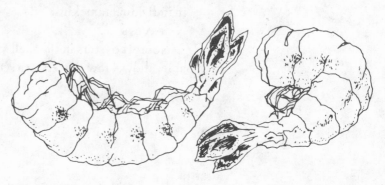

Louisiana

Trout à la LeRuth

4 6-ounce trout fillets
4 very large shrimp
4 tablespoons butter
¾ cup dry white wine
Salt and pepper

Sauce:

2 green onions
   (scallions), chopped
4 tablespoons butter
12 large fresh oysters
1 cup all-purpose cream
3-4 tablespoons flour
Salt and red pepper

1. Preheat oven to 400 degrees F.

2. Wrap a trout fillet around the edge of each shrimp. Place in a buttered pan. Dot with butter. Add the wine and sprinkle with salt and pepper. Cover with foil and bake 15 to 20 minutes.

3. At the same time sauté the chopped onions in butter until soft.

4. Add the oysters and poach just until the edges of the oysters curl. Do not over-cook. Set aside and keep warm.

5. Bring the cream to a boil. Pour off ¾ cup of liquid from the trout pan. Whisk the fish liquid with the flour until smooth and add to the cream.

6. Add the onions and oysters. Season with salt and pepper.

7. Place a portion of fish on a heated plate and cover with sauce.

Note: If a thicker sauce is desired add a beaten egg yolk.

SERVES 4

Masson's

Masson's is a restaurant having the better of two worlds. Located far from the French Quarter and the Garden District, at West End—near Lake Pontchartrain—it combines the quaintness of New Orleans outside and the charm of Paris within. Once inside, a glance at the menu reveals the name of the restaurant's original owner, Albert Dubos, in the title for one delightful dish, Poisson Du Bayou Dubos. Dubos built, in 1915, what is now Masson's, proudly serving the epicures of New Orleans with fabulous seafood recipes. Later, Dubos's daughter married Ernest Masson, and a new family became a joint proprietor of the restaurant.

Today, Ernest Masson, Jr., and Albert Masson, Sr., have taken charge of what their family built from scratch. Ernest, who studied at the Cordon Bleu, and Albert, who trained in Bordeaux, have combined their knowledge of French cooking and fine French wine in a manner that has brought them international honors. Spécialités de la Maison include Baked Oysters Albert, Crayfish Etouffé, and, of course, Quiche Lorraine. Here in the delightful atmosphere of Masson's, savoring the French culture and unique cuisine, a fine meal of stuffed flounder, broiled in butter sauce, or marinated rack of lamb, must be followed by the tempting Sabayon, a soft French custard, light to the tongue, yet rich in sherry and cream and topped with grated chocolate. Afterward, a short stroll around the changing West End, in this rapidly expanding city, brings many new sights for visitors. The new causeway across Lake Pontchartrain, the ultramodern expressway from downtown New Orleans to the lake—all spell progress. Masson's holds the distinction of being *the* French restaurant chosen by visitors and locals alike—a reputation that can only grow in a city that attracts tourists from all over the world.

7200 PONTCHARTRAIN BOULEVARD, NEW ORLEANS

Tournedos Sauce Provence

1 cup olive oil
2 large onions, coarsely chopped
1 carrot, cut in large dice
2 cloves garlic, sliced
½ bunch parsley, coarsely chopped
½ cup flour
2 tablespoons tomato paste
1 cup dry red wine
4 cups light beef stock or 2 cups bouillon plus 2 cups water
2 cloves garlic, chopped
2 tablespoons parsley, chopped
8 3-ounce tenderloin slices

1. Heat ¾ cup of oil and sauté the onions, carrots, garlic and parsley until golden brown.

2. Add the flour and stir until blended. Cook 5 to 8 minutes.

3. Add the tomato paste and cook 3 to 4 minutes.

4. Add the wine and beef stock and simmer until the mixture is reduced by half. Strain through a fine strainer or puree in a blender or food processor.

5. Sauté the chopped garlic in a tablespoon of oil but do not brown. Add to the strained sauce and add the parsley. Season the sauce to taste.

6. Season the tenderloin slices with salt and pepper and sauté in oil to desired doneness, rare, medium-rare, etc.

7. To serve: Place the 8 slices on 4 heated plates and cover with the sauce.

SERVES 4

Chesapeake Restaurant

For more than 70 years, the Friedman family has owned and operated this Baltimore institution that serves seafood from a region that is up to its gills in watery wonders. The excellence that comes from tradition and individualism is found in the preparation of oysters, lobster, soft-shell crab, crab lumps Chesapeake. For this is a rugged individualist's corner of America. Think of the rivers themselves, with such names as the Sassafras, the Pocomoke, the Chicamacomico, the Mispillion, the Nanticoke, the Big and Little Annemessex. And the place names, such as Modest Town, Little Heaven, Ending of Controversy; even Tedious Creek and Ornery Point.

Families here go back generations and are unperturbed by newfangled nuclear silos and Washington overspill. The great tides of immigration of the 19th and 20th Centuries, flowing into and through the big cities, bypassed the small coastal towns. On the Shore "everybody is everybody else's tenth cousin." Against such a background, a father and son opened a small eating place on a main thoroughfare in Baltimore at the turn of the century, and the family has maintained high standards of cuisine to this day through three generations, not only with seafood but also with choice cuts of U.S. Prime Western Beef, and exotic dishes like Steaks Teriyaki and South African Lobster Tails.

1701 NORTH CHARLES STREET, BALTIMORE

Teriyaki Sauce

2 ounces fresh ginger, finely chopped
6 cloves garlic, minced
4 cups granulated sugar
1 teaspoon Accent
2 cups peach nectar
2 cups soy sauce

Combine all ingredients in an earthenware crock or stainless steel container—do *not* use aluminum. Let the mixture stand 8 to 10 hours, stirring occasionally. Strain sauce into glass jars, cover tightly and store in the refrigerator. The sauce will keep for 2 to 3 weeks. To serve 6, marinate 2 pounds of beef sirloin in the sauce for about 2 hours, then broil over charcoal.

Maryland

Crab Imperial Chesapeake

1 green pepper, finely diced
2 pimientos, finely diced
1 tablespoon English
    mustard
1 tablespoon salt
1 teaspoon white pepper
4 hard-cooked eggs
1 cup mayonnaise
3 pounds lump crab meat
Mayonnaise for topping

Mix diced pepper and pimiento. Add mustard, salt, pepper, eggs and mayonnaise; mix well. Add crab meat and mix in with fingers so lumps are not broken. Divide the mixture into 8 crab shells or individual casseroles, heaping it in lightly. Top with a light coating of mayonnaise and sprinkle with paprika. Bake at 350 degrees F. for 15 minutes. Serve hot or cold.

SERVES 8

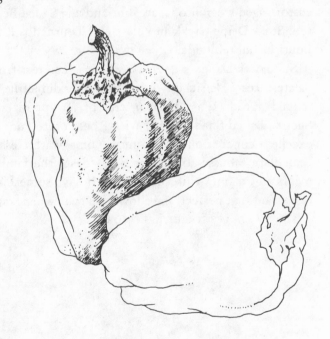

131

Danny's

Nineteen sixty-one—the year that fast food chains began to stack up to the ceiling of America; the year Danny Dickman decided to open a gourmet restaurant in the heart of Baltimore, that "beer and crab town." The burghers of Baltimore scoffed at the new Escoffier—yet he made it, by distinguished menus and fine service. After all, there were the choice catches from nearby Chesapeake Bay, and there's more to be drunk than beer. Oysters can be ordered Bernard style: stuffed with mushrooms, shrimp, anchovies, shallots, in Mornay sauce; Striped Bass is served in a mousse of lobster sauce; Crab Mornay in a puff pastry shell with Gruyère cheese.

If you want to make a go of it, throw your line even farther—and purchase the best beef year round from the Timonium, Denver and Chicago shows. You make sure your veal is pure milk-fed, *Plume de Veau*—the whitest of white veal. And then the kitchen wizardry of turning prime Black Angus custom-aged steer into Chateaubriand à la Sauce Béarnaise or Beef Wellington. Steak Diane, Steak au Poivre and Tournedos Rossini are prepared with flourishes, at tableside.

Sunday is Danny's day off, when he can rest from pandering to others' palates. Rest? He sits down to the family dinner he has prepared, still in his striped apron. It's a little matter of an appetizer, Baked Grapefruit au Sherry; Baked Shad Stuffed With Roe, Potato Pancakes, Beatrice Salad—an excellent concoction of raw mushrooms, watercress and endive—and a rich Chocolate Mousse for dessert. He toasts the family and the dinner with Meursault, a fine white Burgundy. It says something for the man and his restaurant that perfection follows him even when his feet are up.

1201 N. CHARLES STREET, BALTIMORE

Maryland

Beatrice Salad

½ pound raw mushrooms,
    sliced
1 bunch watercress
½ pound Belgian endive
1 cup olive oil
¼ cup red wine vinegar
4 teaspoons Dijon mustard
1 teaspoon salt
Freshly ground black pepper

1. Wash the mushrooms. Dry them completely and slice them quite thin by hand or by a food processor.

2. Cut off the root ends of the watercress and wash the leaves and tender stems thoroughly. Chill in the refrigerator.

3. Cut off the root tip of the Belgian endive and separate the leaves. Wash well. Dry and chill in the refrigerator.

4. Place the oil, vinegar, mustard, salt and pepper in a small bottle with a cap or stopper. Shake well.

5. To serve: Arrange the vegetables in a cold salad bowl. Shake the dressing well and add it just before serving or at the table. Toss well with a wooden salad fork and spoon.

SERVES 4

Note: If Belgian endive is not available, substitute other salad greens.

Justine's

Memphis was once the city of cotton bales piled high along Front Street, of proud riverboat captains and elegant old-time hotels, of wailing jazz from Beale Street. Alas, much has passed away—and much has taken its place: the festivities of Memphis in May, the parades of the Secret Societies, the blocks-long hospital complex, St. Jude's Children's Hospital and, surviving the decades, the elaborate system of wonderful city parks. Memphis is still a fine city and one of its finest landmarks is Justine's restaurant. The locale and cuisine are so superior that the owners never have to advertise; word-of-mouth is sufficient.

In 1958 Dayton and Justine Smith took over the Coward place, a mansion built in 1843, and made it into one of the most elegant dining places in America. Restoration lasted 14 months. The warm pink exterior was uncovered after peeling away eleven layers of paint, and the building now glows in its former glory. The chandelier in the East Room once belonged to one of Napoleon's generals; the banister of the Colonial stairway is made from the balustrade in the city's old Gayoso Hotel; the wrought-iron gate leading to the courtyard reached Memphis from Louisiana in 1881. A veritable museum restaurant, the rooms are complemented by antique Georgian silver and precious Baccarat crystal. As one critic pointed out after dining at Justine's: "It was like finding the perfect frame for a fine old painting." Just the setting for the midnight-to-dawn champagne parties the Smiths host for Metropolitan Opera openings.

919 COWARD PLACE, MEMPHIS

Tennessee

Crème d'Epinards
(Creamed Spinach)

2 cups cooked chopped
   spinach
2 generous tablespoons
   cream sauce
Dash of Lea & Perrins
   sauce
Dash of Tabasco
Salt and pepper to taste
4 tablespoons Hollandaise
   sauce (page 424)

1. Drain the spinach well and mix it with the cream sauce and seasonings in a saucepan. Heat.

2. Divide the hot spinach mixture into 4 individual casserole dishes. Top each with 1 tablespoon Hollandaise and place in a hot oven (450 degrees F.) until lightly browned.

SERVES 4

Lotus Ice Cream

4 quarts coffee cream
6½ cups sugar
Grated rind of 10 lemons
2 cups lemon juice
2 cups chopped toasted
   almonds (cool)
2 teaspoons vanilla
1 teaspoon almond
   extract

1. Mix all the ingredients together.

2. Pour the mixture into an ice cream freezer container and freeze according to the directions of the freezer.

3. When the mixture is very firm, remove the dasher from the freezer. Cover the top with 2 sheets of wax paper and aluminum foil. Store in ice or in a cabinet freezer.

4. Serve in individual dessert glasses garnished with toasted almonds.

SERVES 24

Arthur's Restaurant

Totally American in concept, this unique restaurant takes great pride in presenting "the best of America" in its selection of foods and wines. Arthur's recipes are designed to complement the finest of American beef, chicken, crab meat and the fresh 3-pound Maine lobsters that are brought to the table for the customer's selection. The menu runs the gamut from Steak Diane to a delicious Country Fried Fillet. The chef is American, and he recommends his crisp Cottage Fried Potatoes rather than *pommes soufflés* as the perfect companion for his entrees.

Breads are baked daily for the fancy sandwiches served during lunch, as well as for the individual loaves that appear with your dinner. The vegetables and produce featured are fresh, and regional varieties are added as available. By prior arrangement Arthur's customers can bring their own wild game bags to the chef for preparation.

Also unique is Arthur's "all-American" wine list, and the only female sommelier in town.

Arthur's bar is a world unto itself. It is a sleek and sophisticated lounge noted for fine entertainment. One can order Arthur's Cadillac, Arthur's Velvet Hammer or, more conventionally, a martini reputed to be the best in town.

8350 CAMPBELL CENTRE, DALLAS

Arthur's Special Stuffed Filet Mignon

4   8-ounce filets mignons
8   tablespoons butter
3   shallots, sliced
½   pound fresh lump crab meat
1   tablespoon chopped chives
8   medium-sized mushrooms, sliced
2   cups beef stock or bouillon
1   cup Madeira wine

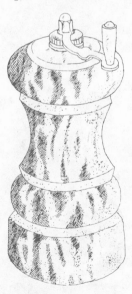

1. Ask the butcher to butterfly the steaks. If that is not possible, cut each steak in half horizontally, leaving the left side uncut to make a kind of hinge.

2. In 2 tablespoons of butter sauté the shallots just until soft. Add the crab meat and chives and cook until the crab is well coated with the butter. Spoon the mixture between the halves of the steaks, closing the flaps to cover.

3. Sauté the mushrooms in 2 tablespoons of butter just until tender. Set aside.

4. Heat the remaining butter in the skillet and when very hot quickly brown the steaks on both sides and transfer to a 350-degree oven to cook to desired doneness, rare or medium rare.

5. Add the beef stock to the skillet. Scrape the juices from the bottom of the pan with a fork. Add the mushrooms and Madeira and boil down quickly to half its original volume. Season with salt and pepper. This sauce may be thickened with *beurre manié* (page 417) if desired.

6. Place the filets mignons on individual heated dinner plates. Top with the sauce and garnish with parsley. Serve with wild rice (page 428).

SERVES 4

Brennan's French Restaurant

By now it's almost a saying of the land, "Where there's a Brennan, there's a restaurant." And a fine one at that. The branch of the family that runs the Commander's Palace in New Orleans operates the Houston Brennan's with the same high traditions. The building was constructed in 1929 and served as the home of the Junior League until 1966. At that time, the Irish moved in and redecorated in New Orleans style. The red brick, two-story structure has several charming dining rooms. The main area is French Provincial with shades of terra-cotta, royal blue and brown fabric-covered walls. The L-Room, as it is called, overlooks the patio and is decorated in stripes of bright orange, blue-green and yellow. The chairs are wrought-iron with striped cushions. Cocktails are served on the patio from nine in the morning until midnight. Upstairs, there are three private dining rooms. The recently renovated Garden Room is known for its fabulous trellis work which overlooks seating for 150 people. There is also a Wine Room where guests dine surrounded by walls lined with bins of Bacchus' pleasure.

3300 SMITH STREET, HOUSTON

Turtle Soup au Sherry

4 pounds turtle meat
4 quarts water
2 bay leaves
2 teaspoons cayenne
2 tablespoons salt
1 cup butter
3 cups chopped onion
1 cup flour
¼ cup tomato puree
1 cup sherry
½ cup Lea & Perrins sauce
3 hard-cooked eggs, chopped
1 cup finely chopped parsley
1 lemon, thinly sliced

1. Cook the turtle meat in water seasoned with the bay leaves, cayenne and salt. Add water if needed to keep liquid at about 3 quarts. When meat is very tender, chop it into small cubes. Strain stock and reserve.

2. In a large kettle over medium heat melt butter, add onions and sauté until transparent. Stir in flour and cook until browned. Add tomato puree and cook 5 minutes. Add stock, sherry and Lea & Perrins and simmer 15 minutes more. Add turtle meat and egg and cook 10 to 15 minutes longer. Stir in parsley and lemon slices and serve at once.

TWELVE 1-CUP SERVINGS

Bananas Foster

2½ cups light brown sugar
½ pound sweet butter
½ cup Banana Liqueur
8 ripe bananas, peeled and sliced lengthwise
½ cup white rum
8 large scoops vanilla ice cream

Heat the brown sugar and butter in a skillet until smoothly blended. Add the liqueur and the sliced bananas. Simmer slowly, basting the bananas with the sauce and slowly adding the rum. Touch with a lighted match and continue basting until the flames subside.

Serve immediately over ice cream.

SERVES 8

The Fig Tree Restaurant

If The Fig Tree had been around in 1836, instead of being founded on St. Patrick's Day in 1973, and had Davy Crockett and his companions been able to regale themselves at the restaurant while defending the Alamo, then perhaps a page of history would have ended gloriously as well as courageously. The house is endearingly tiny, the last of the private dwellings in the historic La Villita section of town. The Phelpses had bought the old Henshaw residence in 1970, but their house guests had "oohed" and "aahed" so much over its charm that Frank had to open it as a restaurant to let others enjoy its homey elegance—right down to the period furnishings, German crystal goblets, and International silverplate flatware.

The menu is equally elegant and served in the classic style from the days of plenty: Black Caviar, Terrines Strasbourg, Chateaubriand, Brown Quails. It is a re-creation of how Great-Grandfather enjoyed his Sunday repast.

515 PASEO DE LA VILLITA, SAN ANTONIO

Heavenly Hash Dessert

12 miniature marshmallows
1 tablespoon crushed
   pineapple
2 teaspoons coarsely
   chopped nuts
1 cup cooked rice
Whipped cream

The whipped cream should be sweetened and flavored with vanilla. All the ingredients should be thoroughly chilled.

Just before serving, combine ingredients in a chilled mixing bowl and fold gently, using just enough whipped cream to moisten the ingredients and hold them together. Serve in chilled champagne glasses and garnish with more whipped cream and fruit if desired.

SERVES 2

Texas

Stuffed Mushrooms

8 large mushroom caps
Monterey Jack cheese

Stuffing
4 tablespoons cooked
   shrimp
4 tablespoons king crab
   meat
2 tablespoons chopped
   celery
2 tablespoons chopped
   green pepper
⅛ teaspoon garlic powder
½ teaspoon salt
½ teaspoon white pepper
¼ cup Tokay wine

1. Chop all ingredients for the stuffing very fine, mix well, and bake in a buttered baking dish 15 minutes at 350 degrees F. Taste, correct seasoning if needed, cool and then refrigerate.

2. Later, clean the mushroom caps and place them stem side up on a buttered baking pan. Top each with a spoonful of the chilled stuffing and a slice of the cheese about 1 inch square and ¼ inch thick. (If Monterey Jack is not available, substitute any sharp Cheddar.) Refrigerate until serving time.

3. To serve: Heat under the broiler just until the cheese begins to brown. Serve on small plates with cocktail forks. Garnish with lemon wedges.

SERVES 2 AS AN APPETIZER

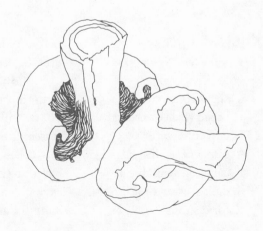

La Louisiane

In 1935, the nearest restaurant to San Antonio that served authentic French cuisine was some 500 miles distant in New Orleans. Max Manus, born of Greek parentage in Istanbul, took up the challenge in Texas that year, beginning with a cook and two waiters in a small stucco building with a shed-roof kitchen. With the help of his wife, Antoinette, he began training a small staff in the preparation of French food, emphasizing seafood and chicken dishes. His brother-in-law, George Dareos, came under his training, and today, from those humble beginnings, George continues a greatly refined tradition in Louis XV elegance. The two-story building has grown graciously, and the wine cellar would have pleased a French monarch. The restaurant has won the *Holiday* Dining Award continuously from the inception of the program.

Texas has changed a lot since 1935; the cities have become far more cosmopolitan, the diners more sophisticated. There are today in the Lone Star State at least a dozen restaurants where authentic French dishes are prepared and served with an authentic Parisian flourish. La Louisiane led the way, and the rest of Texas has been happy to follow.

2632 BROADWAY, SAN ANTONIO

Taramosalata (Carp Roe Spread)

6 slices coarse white bread (free of crusts)
1 cup cold water
4 ounces tarama (salted carp roe available at delicatessen or gourmet food shops)

1. Soak the bread in the water for 5 minutes. Squeeze it dry with your hands.

2. Combine with the tarama in a blender or food processor and blend until smooth.

3. While the blender is still spinning, add the lemon juice and onion and then pour in the olive oil in a very slow stream as for mayonnaise. Add only as much oil as is necessary to make it hold its shape.

4. Taste for seasoning and refrigerate.

142

¼ cup fresh lemon juice
¼ cup finely grated onions
¾ to 1 cup olive oil

5. Serve as part of an hors d'oeuvre platter with crackers, melba toast or thin slices of French bread.

Oysters Kilpatrick

Sauce Kilpatrick:
7 strips bacon
1½ cups chili sauce
1½ cups ketchup
1 stalk celery, chopped fine
3 teaspoons Worcestershire sauce
6 drops Tabasco (or to taste)
2 cloves garlic, minced
2 teaspoons lemon juice

2 dozen oysters on the halfshell

Fry the bacon crisp and chop or crumble it into small bits. Combine with the other ingredients and mix well. Store in the refrigerator. (This sauce is also delicious with clams, snails or king crab.)

Arrange oysters on the half-shell on a bed of rock salt in a large roasting pan. Place under the broiler or in a hot oven (450 degrees F.) until just warmed through. Add a spoonful of the sauce to each oyster and continue cooking until the sauce bubbles (4 to 5 minutes in the oven).

SERVES 4

Mario's

The familiar blackamoor figure that has been a trademark at Mario's for years holds a place of honor in the restaurant's plush new premises in Turtle Creek Village, one of the most beautiful areas of Dallas. Mrs. Christine Vaccaro, Mario's widow, exhibits her fine collections of Chinese porcelain and Venetian glass in the Peacock and Plate rooms. The 9-foot doors, made of rosewood and bronze, were brought all the way from an 18th-Century house in London. In the vestibule, walls are covered in a flame-color Belgian linen, and brightened by chandelier lights reflected in oval mirrors with gold lacquer frames. Another set of doors, New Orleans style, with the original cranberry glass leaded panes, opens upon a foyer, where opulence blossoms in the huge arrangement of flowers on the marble-topped console, flanked by tall Renaissance Italian chairs. In the dining areas, the walls are covered in brilliant paisley and Florentine patterns, in velvets and cotton damasks. The bar is an original late 19th-Century soda fountain, with the mirror behind it reflecting the sparkling crystal and glassware. At Mario's, you can step into another world, savor the finest specialties of Northern Italy and enjoy the proud traditions of this fine Italian family's heritage.

135 TURTLE CREEK VILLAGE, DALLAS

Veal Scallopini with Artichoke Hearts and Mushrooms

12 thinly sliced scallopini
Flour
½ pound butter
8 medium mushrooms, sliced

1. Dip the scallopini into flour and shake off any excess.

2. Heat half the butter in a skillet and brown half the scallopini on both sides. Lift from pan and reserve. Melt the rest of the butter, brown the rest of the scallopini and lift from the pan.

3. In the same pan sauté the mushrooms until tender. Add the artichoke hearts, white

12 artichoke hearts
½ cup white wine
Juice of 2 lemons
 1 cup chicken stock or
   bouillon

wine, lemon juice and chicken stock. Simmer until the liquid is reduced by a third of its volume.

4. Return the veal to the skillet to reheat. Simmer in the sauce 2 to 3 minutes, then serve at once.

SERVES 4

Special Salad Maison

½ pound spinach leaves
 1 head Boston lettuce
½ pound cherry tomatoes
 2 Belgian endive
½ cup pine nuts

Dressing:
 2 fillets of anchovy,
   crushed
 1 small clove garlic,
   crushed
⅛ teaspoon dry mustard
½ cup light olive oil
 2 tablespoons wine vinegar
Juice of ½ lemon
Pinch of tarragon leaves,
   crushed
½ teaspoon Worcestershire
   sauce
Salt and pepper

Combine ingredients for the dressing and mix well.

Remove stems of the spinach leaves. Wash thoroughly all the greens and cut up as desired. Toss all ingredients with the dressing, just before serving.

SERVES 4

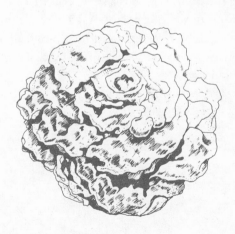

Old Swiss House

Fourteen years ago, when Nancy and Walter Kauffmann opened this restaurant, Fort Worth was a city where dining out meant steak.

"I had a hard time selling people on veal," chef Walter Kauffmann recalls. "And salmon. Sometimes I would go out into the dining room carrying a fresh salmon; I'd show it to the customer and beg him to let me prepare it for him. He'd look doubtful and order steak.

"Now it's all changed. Fort Worth is a city of knowledgeable diners who order veal, salmon—even escargots and frog legs. A part of the same picture is a change in drinking habits. My sales of hard liquor are way down—sales of wine, way up. Young people, in particular, order wine as a matter of course."

The Old Swiss House is doubtless one of the factors—along with the television shows of Julia Child and Graham Kerr and countless articles in women's magazines—that changed Texans' dining habits. It's a comfortable, not overpowering place, and Nancy Kauffmann, who acts as hostess and supervises the dining rooms, is a native of Fort Worth who can help bridge the gap between Texans and her Swiss-born husband's haute cuisine.

Yes, there are Swiss wines and several Swiss specialties—Escalope de St. Moritz, a veal preparation, is one. Other preparations are classic French, because Switzerland is a small country and Swiss chefs borrow the traditions of their next-door neighbors. There are fabulous appetizers—one combining lobster and artichokes, another crab meat and avocado.

Also, to please unreconstructed Texans, there are excellent charcoal-broiled steaks!

5412 CANT BOWIE, FORT WORTH

Hot Avocado
and Crab Meat "Boyo"

3 tablespoons butter
1 teaspoon chopped
   shallots
2 cups crab meat
1 cup sliced mushrooms
4 teaspoons chopped chives
Juice from ½ lemon
2 tablespoons brandy
1 cup whipping cream
2 tablespoons sherry
1 teaspoon cornstarch
2 avocados
2 teaspoons lemon juice
Hollandaise sauce (page 424)
Salt, pepper and cayenne

1. Heat the butter in a skillet and add the shallots. When the shallots are well coated with butter, add the crab meat, mushrooms, chives and lemon juice.

2. When the mixture is well heated, add the brandy and touch with a lighted match. Stir gently until the flames subside.

3. Add the cream and stir until the mixture boils.

4. Combine the sherry and cornstarch and stir into the mixture. Continue stirring until the mixture thickens slightly. Season to taste with salt, pepper and cayenne. Set aside.

5. Preheat the oven to 400 degrees F.

6. Peel, seed and halve the avocados. Place them side by side, cavity side up, in a glass heatproof oven dish. Sprinkle with the lemon juice and bake 3 minutes.

7. Remove from the oven and turn on the broiler.

8. Fill the cavities with the crab mixture. Top with the Hollandaise and brown under the broiler. Serve on individual plates, garnished with lemon wedges and watercress.

SERVES 6

Old Warsaw (La Vieille Varsovie)

An evening at the Old Warsaw takes you back to a time when life was lived with taste and style. Classical music, freshly cut flowers, photographs of the famous who have dined here set the stage for the meal to come. Even the menu has a distinct touch of Europe, with the purple ink script of the Table d'Hôte. Complementing your selections, and in the finest traditions of "le service Français," a full band of waiters will bring your meal to the table in gleaming silver dishes.

The actual fare is thoroughly and classically French. From the *hors d'oeuvres* to *les viandes*, the dishes are a triumphal march down the Champs Elysées of dining. Soufflé Grand Marnier for dessert with Café Espresso completes a truly sumptuous meal; or, if you wish, choose the perfect cigar from the beautiful Honduras mahogany humidor created especially for the Old Warsaw by Alfred Dunhill of London. There is even a special cigar for the ladies! Add a snifter of brandy and you have created a truly memorable evening.

2610 MAPLE AVENUE, DALLAS

Crevettes Provençal
(Hot Shrimp Appetizer)

24 shrimp, peeled and
    deveined
Flour
¼ pound butter
2 shallots
Juice of 2 lemons
2 cloves of garlic, minced
3 tablespoons Pernod
    liquor
Salt and pepper to taste

1. Dust shrimp lightly with flour. Melt butter in a heavy skillet and sauté shrimp, a few at a time, until almost done. Use slotted spoon to lift shrimp to another container.

2. Add garlic and shallots to the skillet and cook, stirring, until the shallots are transparent but not browned. (Do not overcook.)

3. Return shrimp to the skillet. Add the lemon juice and Pernod. Simmer for 3 minutes. Add salt and pepper to taste and serve at once in a chafing dish or candle warmer.

SERVES 4 AS AN APPETIZER

Tournedos de Chevreuil Grand Veneur
(Venison Steaks)

8 3-ounce slices of
   sirloin of venison

Marinating sauce:
2 cups salad oil
2 cups dry red wine
1 onion, quartered
2 cloves garlic
2 carrots, diced
2 stalks celery, diced
1 tablespoon cracked
   pepper
6 bay leaves
½ teaspoon thyme
½ cup red wine vinegar

¼ pound butter
4 tablespoons cognac
½ cup heavy cream
2 tablespoons cranberry
   sauce

1. Combine all the ingredients for the marinating sauce and soak the steaks for 1 week in the refrigerator, turning from time to time.

2. Wipe the venison slices dry and sauté in butter to desired doneness on both sides.

3. Add the cognac and touch with a lighted match.

4. Remove the meat and keep warm.

5. Add to the pan 2 cups of the marinating sauce and stir with a fork until the mixture boils. Simmer until it is reduced by one third of its volume.

6. Add the cream and cranberry sauce and stir until the mixture simmers. Simmer 1 minute and taste for seasoning.

7. Place 2 pieces of venison on each of 4 heated plates. Top with the sauce and serve with a chestnut puree, wild rice and currant jelly.

SERVES 4

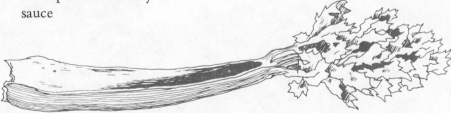

The Pyramid Room

This restaurant offers the unexpected.

The pyramid for which it is named extends not up but down; it is a chandelier of gold metal and amber glass that nearly fills the ceiling and tapers to an apex near the floor.

The wine cellar, a glass-enclosed, temperature-controlled rack as tall as a house, extending not down but up, is accessible only to a young and agile sommelier. He is Silvano Zanetti, and his specialty is clambering Tarzan-like up the wine rack's ladder, then striking a triangle for pitch (or to attract the attention of his audience) and announcing the diner's selection with a snatch of operatic aria.

It follows, somehow, that the wandering violinist whose name is Jose Singer is really an accomplished pianist, and each waiter an actor who stars in a dramatic performance at tableside. After all this, it is almost a surprise to find the food superlative.

Diners enthroned in comfortable high-backed chairs enjoy some very special fillips and garnishments: between appetizer and entree, a wine-flavored sherbet to refresh the taste; between entree and dessert, huge strawberries in a glaze coating that makes them crunchy. Who would expect a crunchy strawberry?

THE FAIRMONT HOTEL, ROSS AT AKARD, DALLAS

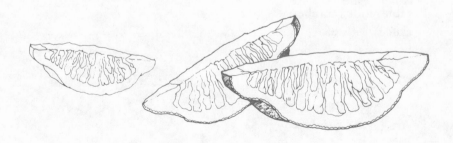

Lemon Soufflé

2 tablespoons butter
1½ tablespoons flour
½ cup milk
5 egg yolks
3 tablespoons sugar
1 lemon
6 egg whites
1 tablespoon sugar

1. Melt the butter and add the flour. Stir over medium heat until it starts to brown.

2. Add the milk and stir until thick and smooth. Reduce the heat and continue to cook for 5 minutes. Stir constantly.

3. Beat the egg yolks and sugar until lemon-colored and add to the sauce.

4. Add the grated rind of the whole lemon and the juice of half a lemon. Remove from the heat. Preheat the oven to 375 to 400 degrees F.

5. Prepare two large (1 pint) individual soufflé dishes or four 1-cup dishes by buttering them lightly and sprinkling them with sugar.

6. Beat the egg whites until stiff but not dry. Add the 1 tablespoon of sugar.

7. Fold the egg whites into the egg yolk mixture, lifting the batter high as you fold to incorporate more air.

8. Fill the soufflé dishes three quarters full and place on a baking sheet. Bake 20 to 35 minutes or until well puffed and golden brown. Sprinkle with powdered sugar and serve immediately. This can be served with a variety of sweet sauces—vanilla, apricot, chartreuse or clear lemon sauce.

SERVES 2 TO 4

Tony's

Tony Vallone deserves an Oscar—or is it a Tony?—for the exquisite way in which he has brought the splendor of continental cuisine to the Lone Star State. The French like to use the word impeccable, and it would be fitting here. This is one of the most beautiful dining rooms in America. The dark, wine-hued walls come alive with the owner's collection of Chinese porcelains and French, German and American impressionist paintings, precisely lighted. The stark white menu bears a simple subtitle: "The Poetry of French Food"—and that's just what it is. Never before such red snapper. The version captioned André arrives with mushrooms, artichokes glistening with *beurre blanc*. The Veal Acapulco is masterfully garnished with tomato and avocado, a touch of demiglaze and Mornay. Dessert time is celebrated with Italian macaroons and strawberries, or soufflés of the berries in season.

The wine cellar at Tony's is one of the most notable in the country. The move from the former location on Sage Road was held up owing to the complexities of excavating this new cellar. A breathtaking underground retreat, this room houses a collection of more than 20,000 bottles from which to choose and the inventory is kept at a constant $250,000 value. The rare wines date back to 1889. Some of the truly magnificent dinner parties in Texas' recent history have taken place in these bibulous surroundings.

1801 SOUTHPOST OAK, HOUSTON

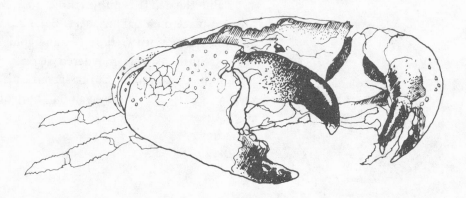

Red Snapper Noisette

2 fillets red snapper, sole
  or other firm fish
¼ cup flour
⅛ cup cornstarch
Milk
1½ sticks (12 tablespoons)
  butter
1 cup lump crab meat,
  cut in bite-size pieces
3 tablespoons raw
  almonds
1 lemon
4 slices large mushroom
  (cap and stem)
Salt and pepper

1. Dip the fillets in a combination of the flour and cornstarch, then in milk and again in the flour mixture.

2. Heat 4 tablespoons of butter in a skillet and sauté the fish until nicely browned on both sides. Transfer to a heated platter and place in a 300-degree oven to keep warm.

3. Put 8 pieces of lump crab meat on each fillet and let warm while preparing the sauce.

4. Put the remaining butter in a very hot clean skillet. When it is very hot add the almonds, sizzle a moment and then reduce the heat. Simmer 3 to 4 minutes. Add the juice of 1 lemon.

5. Remove the almonds with a slotted spoon and discard.

6. Add the mushrooms and simmer 1 minute.

7. Place 2 mushroom slices on each fish and pour the dark brown butter over the fish. Serve very hot.

SERVES 2

The Midwest

The plains were settled by those who carried their cooking pots across the Alleghenies and the Appalachians and laid them down firmly on the prairie land. The people were not beholden, they subsisted, grew tall and strong on butter soup, baked squash, apple salad; on salted cherries that disappeared as fast as small hands could snatch them. The tradition lives, exemplified in the recipes passed down through the generations, in those wonderful Thanksgiving dinners where the four corners of the earth convene for a meal in a Kansas farmhouse. The Midwesterner grew to be practical, open, a welcomer of nationalities, until his cities came to be a transplanted northern tier of Europe. And so he learned to relish the Continental dish along with the fare of grandmother's kitchen; he became a heartlander who was not embarrassed to be a sophisticate.

The Midwest is a swathe of white farmhouses, but also of surprising cities: fountained Kansas City, arched St. Louis, brewered Milwaukee, turbine-engined Indianapolis, production-lined Detroit. But then there is that host of smaller communities, twinkling their lights every few miles at the passing airliners. Unusual, and yet not so unusual, that many fine gourmet restaurants are located in small Midwest towns.

The soaring shapes of the Chicago skyline seem planted at the center of America, of the whole complex we call the modern world. Isn't O'Hare International the busiest airport on earth? Like Chicago, the Midwest is outward-looking—but with roots lying deep in the home. There is something special about Middle America's rooting for the local high school basketball team, for the Buckeyes or Wolverines. A Detroit executive will feel as much at home throwing baseballs for Kewpie dolls at his daughter's 4-H fair as he does throwing out an idea that will shape the U.S. economy. For never far away is the consciousness of the dented ear of corn, the rounded rib of steer and pig, the tang of rhubarb pie. A hot dog never tasted so good as when present at a touchdown; a gourmet meal never tasted so good as after a day in a Midwest state park under a brisk October sky.

The Bakery

"Here at The Bakery we place the accent on food," says chef/owner Louis Szathmáry. "We buy the highest quality available, prepare it ingeniously, serve it expertly and hope that our guests enjoy it thoroughly." They do! For the privilege of dining on Szathmáry's unique eastern European, French and American creations, diners book reservations weeks in advance.

"Chef Szathmáry amazes guests with some of the most eclectic and innovative preparations in the country," writes Jim Villas in *Town and Country*. "One of the greatest chefs and most colorful proprieters in the country," writes another restaurant critic.

There is no regular menu, since the offerings change constantly. This is partly because chef Szathmáry feels that the major part of any meal should feature fresh ingredients that are in season, and partly because he is continually experimenting with new preparations. There are no ethnic barriers here. Szathmáry, though Budapest-born, is an authority on American cookery (his personal library includes some 6,000 books on American food)—and he serves Baked Pork Chops, Bear Sausage and Beef Stew along with Beef Wellington, Roast Duckling with Cherry Glaze, Ragoût of Venison and Spring Lamb in Tarragon Cream Sauce. The desserts, wonderfully varied and all homemade, are memorable.

2218 NORTH LINCOLN AVENUE, CHICAGO

Illinois

Hungarian Christmas Balls

1 cup sugar
2 tablespoons grated orange rind
2 tablespoons orange juice
2 tablespoons lemon juice
1 cup finely ground walnuts
½ cup finely chopped candied fruits
½ cup cocoa

1. In a saucepan over low heat melt the sugar with grated orange rind, orange juice and lemon juice. Cool.

2. Add the walnuts and fruits and mix with your hands.

3. Rub a little oil or butter on the palm of your hands. Pinch off small pieces of the fruit mixture and roll into ¾ inch balls. Roll in cocoa until well coated.

4. Freeze balls for an hour. Place each ball in a small candy paper or wrap in foil. Store covered in a cold place.

MAKES 20 SMALL PIECES

Sauce Louis

2 eggs
3 tablespoons prepared mustard
3 tablespoons sugar
½ teaspoon salt
⅛ teaspoon ground white pepper
Juice of 1 lemon
1 teaspoon vinegar
1 pint sour cream

1. In a medium-sized bowl, using a wire whip or electric beater, blend together the eggs, mustard, sugar, salt, pepper, lemon juice and vinegar.

2. Slowly fold in the sour cream. Keep refrigerated, in a covered jar. Serve with fish or meat.

MAKES 2½ CUPS

Café de Paris

A touch of Paris on the shore of Lake Michigan? For this, *merci*!

For 35 years this excellent French restaurant has been an institution on Chicago's North Side. Others have come and gone, Café de Paris remains to serve faithful patrons who come to feast on authentically Parisian fare.

Café de Paris is the place to come for a bird and a bottle; the bird being Duckling à la Belasco, long the reigning favorite among the restaurant's entrees. Oranges, lemons, sherry and caramelized sugar go into the sweet-tart sauce in which it swims.

One may also order Le Crabe Suprême au Chablis, lump crab meat sautéed in butter and wine, or tender Tournedos Rossini in classical preparation. These, too, go well with a bottle from the restaurant's wine cellar.

Intimate rather than overpowering, the Café de Paris flourishes under the supervision of long-time restaurateur Henri Eschman. On hand to see that things go smoothly in the dining room is maître d' Alex Abraham; the kitchen is undisputed realm of chef Agripino Sanchez. Together, they maintain the high standards of cuisine and impeccable service that have made this restaurant so successful.

1260 LINCOLN PARKWAY, CHICAGO

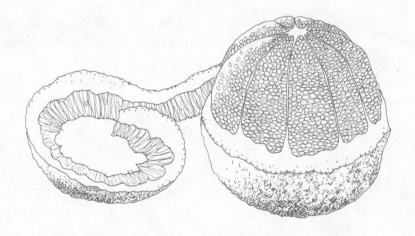

Duckling à la Belasco

1 5-pound duckling
2 medium-size oranges
1 lemon
½ cup sugar
1 teaspoon currant jelly
1 quart brown sauce
   (page 422)
1 teaspoon cornstarch
½ cup dry sherry

1. Preheat oven to 350 degrees F.

2. Roast the duck for 2 hours.

3. Peel the outer skin from the oranges and lemons and cut it into fine strips.

4. Heat the sugar in a heavy saucepan until it turns into dark brown caramel. Add the currant jelly and the juice from the oranges and lemon.

5. Remove the duck from the roasting pan. Keep warm.

6. Pour off all the fat. Add a little hot water to the pan and scrape off all the duck juices from the bottom of the pan. Add to the brown sauce. Combine with the caramel and add the orange and lemon strips.

7. Dilute the cornstarch in the sherry and add to the sauce. Simmer 20 minutes.

8. Halve the duck, remove the breast bones and reheat for a moment in the oven.

9. Pour the sauce over the duck. Garnish each serving with sliced oranges and watercress.

SERVES 2

Cape Cod Room

Was it the wind or the big-city league dream that blew in those small-town Midwesterners, Theodore Dreiser, Sherwood Anderson, Upton Sinclair to find fame and fortune in Chicago? Like so many others, they were surely lured by the sophistication of the big city on the lake, by the equivalent of today's unusual skyscrapers and elegant dining places. For many years, a jewel in fashionable Lake Shore Drive has been the luxurious Drake Hotel, and since 1933, the year of the World's Fair, that minute but shining example of seafood dining at its best: the Cape Cod Room of the hotel.

The late Ben Marshall, architect, builder and part owner of the Drake, had wanted a room specializing in the fish dishes garnered from the four corners of the globe, and he appropriated some unused space in one corner of the arcade for that purpose. Peter Hunt, an artist from Provincetown, Massachusetts, and an authority on Cape Cod lore, was employed to help bring a touch of the eastern seaboard to the Midwest. Hunt arrived with copper pots, chowder kettles and lobster traps to ornament the room. Some old bottles, relics of Prohibition days, were added. A few tables with checkered tablecloths, some ships' captains' chairs, a few fish nets and an old pot-bellied stove retrieved from a second-hand store finished off the unpretentious decor.

But the food was to be far from humble. The menu became a gastronomic delight, a bountiful catch of seafood sallies: Maine lobster served seven different ways, crab meat five ways, scallops six, and seven variations for shrimp. After nearly half a century of exemplary service, the menu has grown to include another twenty-three dishes besides the above skipper's treats.

THE DRAKE HOTEL, LAKE SHORE DRIVE AND UPPER MICHIGAN AVENUE, CHICAGO

Bookbinder
Red Snapper Soup

4 tablespoons diced
   onions
½ cup diced celery
1 cup diced green pepper
2 tablespoons butter
2 pints fish stock
   (page 423)
1 teaspoon Worcestershire
   sauce
½ teaspoon salt
1½ cups sherry
1 cup diced, raw red
   snapper
1 pint canned tomato
   sauce
1 quart brown sauce
   (page 418)

1. Make fish stock, if there isn't a supply on hand. (To make fish stock, place about 1 pound of fish trimmings—heads, tails, bones—in a large kettle with 1½ quarts cold water. Add a bay leaf, an onion stuck with 1 clove, a carrot and a stalk of celery, 1 teaspoon salt and 4 white peppercorns. Bring slowly to a boil, removing any scum that rises to the surface. Cover and simmer 45 minutes, then strain through a fine sieve or cheesecloth. Fish stock may be prepared in advance and stored in the refrigerator or freezer till needed.)

2. To prepare soup: Sauté onions, celery and green pepper in butter until soft but not brown. Add the fish stock, Worcestershire sauce and ½ cup of the sherry. Simmer 25 minutes.

3. Add red snapper and cook 10 minutes. Add tomato sauce and brown sauce, simmer for 5 minutes more and then taste for seasoning.

4. Serve very hot, dipping the soup into large bowls and then adding ¼ cup sherry to each of the 4 servings.

SERVES 4

La Cheminée Restaurant

You tread the wine press on Near Northside Chicago. Or nearly so. The wine cellar of La Cheminée stretches under the sidewalk on North Dearborn, so your feet tap softly to the reclining Burgundies and Bordeaux.

In this cosmopolitan city, it was only natural for Katja and Burton Kallick, two ardent Francophiles, to provide some Gallic countryside feeling for the feet of those giant new skyscrapers with their authentically bucolic restaurant, breezy (if not windy) with checkered tablecloths and fresh-cut flowers. The building combines two converted brownstones, an advantage when striving for an informal, warm atmosphere.

The presiding chef is Chef-of-the-Year Willy Maes, and Chicago has no finer maître d'hôtel than Pierre Vimont. If the place is "split-level tiny," the menu itself is expansive. Do not pass up Le Poulet Sauté aux Concombres. The Salade Cheminée of avocado and hearts of palm is outstanding. You will never taste a caramel custard so superbly rich, smooth and peaking in caramel flavor. The latter is a simple dish but, in this case, a little masterpiece.

Chef Maes was granted his title as chef of the year for 1976 by Chicago's International Food and Wine Society, so it is an accolade from the experts and a crown worthy to fit over his chef's cap.

1161 NORTH DEARBORN STREET, CHICAGO

Les Escalopes de Veau au Marsala *(Veal in Marsala Sauce)*

18 thin veal slices,
   3 ounces each
1 cup flour
8 tablespoons sweet
   butter
2 teaspoons finely
   chopped shallots
3 cups thinly sliced fresh
   mushrooms
1½ cups dry Marsala wine
Salt and pepper
Lemon

1. Pound the veal lightly between sheets of wax paper. Dip in flour. Season with salt and pepper. Shake off any excess flour.

2. Heat the butter in a large skillet and sauté the veal over moderate heat for 3 to 4 minutes or until brown on both sides. Place veal on a heated platter and keep warm.

3. Cook the shallots and mushrooms in the same pan for 3 minutes. Add the wine and simmer until reduced to half its quantity.

4. Pour sauce over the veal and garnish with thin slices of lemon.

SERVES 6

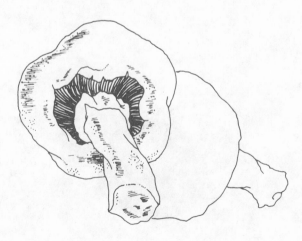

L'Epuisette

Chicago is generously endowed with seafood restaurants and tucked neatly away at the corner of North Dearborn and Goethe Streets is one of the finest of these—L'Epuisette—a cozy little spot fitted into the side of a high-rise apartment building. L'Epuisette is a classic French seafood restaurant in all respects but one. The menu is in English, making those of us who feel less than confident about our *français* a little more comfortable. The name? It's the French word for a small net used to catch fish.

Specialties of the house include Lake Superior whitefish with lemon butter—tender to the touch, brimming with the rich flavor of the sea. Crêpes L'Epuisette, stuffed with crab meat and served in white sauce, is another favorite. Dover sole Marguery, fresh shrimp Newburg, Rocky Mountain trout are all highly recommended. Patrons may choose from a long list of French, German and American wines.

During dinner, a capable staff of waiters see to it that every customer is satisfied. That extra bit of attentiveness, the owners reason, can make a meal infinitely more enjoyable. Gleaming silver, china and soft candlelight are parts of an atmosphere that every employee works hard to achieve.

21 WEST GOETHE STREET, CHICAGO

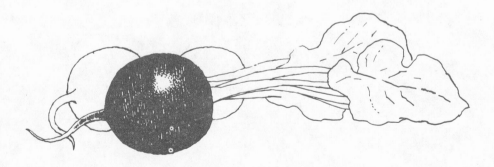

Stuffed Boneless Brook Trout

- 2 10-ounce Rainbow trout
- ½ pound butter
- ½ pound crab meat
- ½ cup chopped mushrooms
- ½ teaspoon chopped shallots
- ½ teaspoon chopped chives
- 2 cups Béchamel sauce (page 416)
- 1 cup dry white wine
- 2 lemons
- Salt and pepper to taste
- Radish flowers
- 2 tablespoons chopped parsley

1. Sauté the trout in 8 tablespoons of heated butter until brown on both sides. Open the trout on the belly side and deftly remove the backbone which will remove the rest of the bones. Keep warm.

2. In 4 tablespoons of butter sauté the mushrooms and crab meat. Add the shallots and chives, stir gently and cook 5 minutes. Add the white sauce and dry wine. Mix well and season to taste.

3. Place the trout on a hot serving platter, fill each with the crab mixture, sprinkle the tops with lemon juice and with the remaining butter, heated until bubbling.

4. Garnish with flowered radishes and chopped parsley.

SERVES 2

Farmer's Daughter Restaurant

Kandy Henely's establishment has been operating 12 years and has gained 35 International awards (that's about three a year!). It's only a freeway jaunt from Chicago and worth the day's outing. Rustic, but quietly elegant, the restaurant has two dining rooms: one in authentic Spanish decor of blacks and reds, with pewter service plates; the other in contemporary brick, accented with copper artifacts, beige and orange cloths.

Pastries, muffins and over 20 desserts are made in the kitchens, and the coffee beans are ground there before brewing—a much-appreciated finer touch. Customers enjoy most the Filet au Poivre, Tournedos Dijon, Shrimp de Jonghe and the newest addition, Veal Katsu, a Japanese delicacy.

14455 LAGRANGE ROAD, ORLAND PARK

Cream of Lettuce Soup

4 tablespoons butter
½ cup dark green lettuce leaves, chopped
⅓ cup flour
3 cups hot chicken broth
1 cup all-purpose cream
½ cup shredded lettuce (½-inch pieces)
1 teaspoon salt
¼ teaspoon white pepper

1. Melt the butter in a small casserole. Add the dark green lettuce leaves. Stir until the leaves are well coated. Cover and cook over gentle heat for 10 to 15 minutes.

2. Strain the mixture into a saucepan and stir in the flour. Cook until blended. Add the chicken broth combined with the cream and stir until the mixture thickens.

3. Add the shredded lettuce and seasoning. Heat 5 minutes but do not let the mixture boil. Serve immediately. (If this soup is made in advance you may have to thin it a little with milk when reheating.)

SERVES 6 TO 8

Irish Whiskey Pie

1½ teaspoons unflavored
   gelatin
½ cup cold water
2 squares of unsweetened
   chocolate
½ cup hot water
¼ teaspoon salt
½ cup sugar
¼ cup egg yolks
¼ cup milk
2 tablespoons Irish
   whiskey
¼ cup egg whites,
   beaten stiff
1 cup of heavy cream,
   whipped
¼ cup sliced almonds
1 9-inch baked pastry
   shell, chilled
Garnish: whipped cream and
   sliced almonds

1. Dissolve gelatin in cold water and melt over simmering water until clear.

2. Combine chocolate, water, salt and sugar in a saucepan. Bring to a boil and cook until smooth. Remove from the heat.

3. Mix egg yolks and milk and stir into the chocolate mixture.

4. Add the gelatin and whiskey to the chocolate mixture.

5. Pour into a mixing bowl and place it inside a larger mixing bowl filled with crushed ice. Stir the mixture until it cools and becomes syrupy.

6. Fold in the egg whites.

7. Fold in the whipped cream and almonds. Pour the mixture into the pastry shell. Chill 4 hours. Before serving, garnish with additional whipped cream and sliced almonds.

SERVES 6 TO 8

Le Français

If you are going to be a born chef, where better to enter the world than in the town of Roanne in French Burgundy. Jean Banchet had this distinction—the stork let him down only yards from the celebrated Troisgros restaurant. The chef's hat beckoned when he was 15, and there was no job available in the Troisgros kitchen—so Banchet apprenticed at the lesser Terminus. Eventually, he landed a position with the legendary Fernand Point at the Pyramide restaurant in Vienna.

Borne on the crest of the New Wave in French cuisine, Banchet splashed down, with his excellent training, in the Midwest. When he planned to open his own restaurant a few years back, he listened to his wife, Doris, who was convinced that people who dine in top French restaurants live in the suburbs. The result of such wisdom was a striking bonus for the village of Wheeling, 40 miles north of Chicago.

This disciple of the Troisgros brothers, and another friend, Paul Bocuse, delivers his testaments to fine dining from a French country cottage by a busy roadside. Here the serious eaters gather, to savor the Troisgros salmon with sorrel sauce, or the Bocuse-style cold salmon in pastry. Banchet will serve his own special creation: lobster tail, smeared with lobster mousse, baked in puffed pastry, served with tarragon and Pernod sauce. Given six days' notice, this chef will supply any dish requested by a patron.

269 SOUTH MILWAUKEE STREET, WHEELING

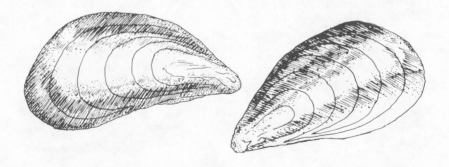

Soupe de Moules au Basilic *(Mussel Soup with Basil)*

    3 quarts fresh mussels
   10 shallots, chopped
    ½ bunch parsley
    2 stalks celery, chopped
    1 pint of dry white wine
Salt and pepper
    1 quart fish stock
       (page 423)
    2 tablespoons chopped
       basil leaves
    1 quart heavy cream
    2 egg yolks, slightly
       beaten
    ½ pound butter

1. Wash and scrape the mussels well. Place in a kettle with ½ cup of water the shallots, parsley, celery, wine and a little salt and pepper. Bring to a boil and simmer, covered, for about 6 minutes or until the shells open.

2. Remove the mussels with a slotted spoon and reserve. Strain the liquid through a fine sieve or cheesecloth, to remove the herbs and any sand, and return to the kettle. Boil down until it measures 1 quart. Chop the mussels coarsely.

3. Add the fish stock, 1 tablespoon of basil leaves and 3 cups of cream. Boil and stir 2 to 3 minutes. Season to taste.

4. Just before serving, add the rest of the cream mixed with the egg yolks and fresh butter. Heat but do not boil.

5. Serve the soup in soup bowls or bouillon cups. Garnish with the mussels and sprinkle with basil. Serve very hot.

SERVES 8 TO 12

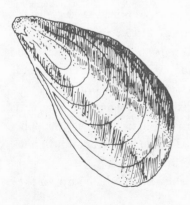

Maxim's de Paris

"The night they invented champagne," the night they opened Maxim's—in Chicago—eight Paris-trained chefs prepared a repast from a gargantuan menu once used for a King Edward VII Dinner. It was once more the days of La Belle Epoque from which a Liane de Pougy or a Lily Langtry emerged, dripping in diamonds. Instead, Chicago's most discriminating gourmets were there ready to indulge in French fanfare. The Maxim's of the Windy City was on its way!

And just a few years later, expert chef Bernard Cretier arrived from Vichy to add even more epicurean delights to the menu. His Crêpes Veuve Joyeuse and Poulet Sauté au Vinaigre de Vin are Maxim's originals.

"Ghosts are invisible assets," said Monsieur Vaudable, owner of the Paris Maxim's. But the ghosts of a wild, untroubled generation inhabit Chicago's Maxim's as well. Surrounded by polished brass, mirrored walls and plush red decor, you can easily imagine yourself in the company of the royalty and genteel folk of Europe. And why not? Some of the wilder spirits may have remained in Paris, but this Maxim's perpetuates the imperial tradition.

1300 NORTH ASTOR STREET, CHICAGO

Sole Albert *(Fillet of Sole in Vermouth)*

3 1-pound sole or 6 fillets
1 pound butter
3 shallots, chopped
1 teaspoon each chopped parsley, tarragon
¾ cup fresh bread crumbs
Dry vermouth
½ lemon
Salt and pepper

1. Preheat oven to 425 degrees F.
2. Skin the sole by ripping the skin from head to tail with a pair of pliers.
3. Melt ¾ cup of butter in an ovenware dish large enough to hold the 3 sole or 6 fillets side by side. Mix the chopped shallots and herbs and spread over the bottom of the dish. Place the dish over low heat.
4. Melt ½ cup of butter in a shallow pan. Dip one side of the sole in butter and then in the fresh bread crumbs.
5. Place the sole, breaded side up, in the

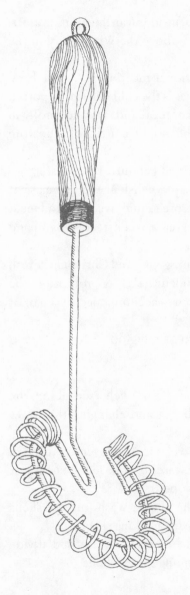

hot ovenware dish. Season with salt and pepper.

6. Carefully pour in enough dry vermouth to half submerge the fish without wetting the bread crumbs. Pour another ¾ cup of melted butter over the fish.

7. Bake in oven for 30 minutes or until golden brown.

8. Remove from the oven. Transfer the fish with a wide spatula to a heated platter.

9. Quickly boil down the pan juices to about 2 tablespoonfuls. Remove from the heat and stir in the remaining butter, whisking vigorously until you have a light frothy sauce. Add the lemon juice and taste for seasoning. Pour some of the sauce around the sole and serve the rest separately.

SERVES 3

Note: If sole is not available, substitute fillets of flounder.

The Ninety-Fifth

You dine in space, part of a frozen film clip, inside an airliner poised aloft. Such is the feeling at The Ninety-Fifth, high above the Windy City in the John Hancock Center.

From its inception in 1970, this International meeting place has been noted for its cuisine. Among the hors d'oeuvres is the cold Rillete, or potted meats, a smooth pâté laced with solid chunks of meat and rich and smoky in taste. Among the hot hors d'oeuvres is the popular artichoke bottom covered with beef marrow and truffle sauce.

For the seafood dishes, the preparations are all genuine. Live lobsters are cooked, for instance, to flavor the Lobster Bisque, a dish in which the use of short cuts has become, unfortunately, a widespread practice. Fish and meat dishes range from the familiar to the culinary greats, to Entrecôte Marchand de Vin and Filet Mignon Grille Béarnaise.

Special holiday menus are featured at Thanksgiving and Christmas. Fresh venison was served one Christmas. For a St. Valentine's Day promotion, the Harry Love Trio played during the serving hours—accompanied by a pair of live love birds.

JOHN HANCOCK CENTER, 172 EAST CHESTNUT STREET, CHICAGO

Baked Clams

1 dozen fresh little neck clams (steamers)
12 tablespoons butter, melted
1 medium tomato, peeled, seeded and chopped
3 large cloves of garlic, chopped

1. Wash the clams well, scrubbing the shells with a brush and changing the water several times.

2. Cook the clams in a covered saucepan with ¼ cup of water over moderate heat just until the shells open.

3. Shuck the clams. Wash out the shells and place them on a baking sheet.

4. Chop the clams coarsely and divide them evenly among the 24 shells.

2 tablespoons chopped
   shallots
4 tablespoons chopped
   parsley
2 tablespoons dry white
   wine
Salt and pepper
¾ cup of bread crumbs

5. Preheat the oven to 350 degrees F.

6. Mix the 8 tablespoons of butter with tomato, half the bread crumbs, the garlic, shallots, parsley and white wine. Season to taste with salt and white pepper. Divide the mixture evenly among the 24 shells.

7. Sprinkle with remaining bread crumbs and dribble with the remaining butter.

8. Bake for 10 minutes and serve piping hot.

SERVES 4 AS AN APPETIZER

The Presidents

The name and the theme are American—the menu and letterhead bear a motif of stars and stripes—and in the kitchen the chef's aim is to create a "finely defined regional and classical American cuisine." This has engendered the construction of imaginative entrees and accompaniments from varied traditions: oysters baked New Orleans style in a peppery sauce, chilled mulligatawny with just the right touch of curry, a feather-light avocado soufflé, a watercress salad with almond dressing, a special Presidents cheesecake. Here the themes of the American experience are served up on elegant silver service for the edification of lunchers and diners.

The setting is spectacular, as The Presidents is part of the First National Plaza, and diners have, from their tables, an unparalleled view of the Plaza fountain. The entrance is next to the Marc Chagall mosaic. Food for the eye, sustenance for the spirit!

DEARBORN AND MONROE STREETS, CHICAGO

Snails and Mushrooms

- 4 tablespoons butter
- 2 tablespoons garlic
- 2 tablespoons shallots, chopped fine
- ½ tablespoon ground black pepper
- ½ tablespoon salt
- 24 snails (canned)
- ¾ cup red wine
- 24 large mushrooms
- 2 tablespoons chopped parsley

1. Sauté the garlic and shallots in 2 tablespoons of butter for 2 minutes. Add salt and pepper and cook 3 minutes.

2. Add the snails and cook just 2 minutes.

3. Add red wine and cook 3 minutes.

4. Stem the mushrooms and clean the caps. Sauté the caps in 2 tablespoons of butter for 5 minutes.

5. To serve: Place 4 mushroom caps stem side up in each of 6 small round dishes. Place a snail on each mushroom cap, and pour the sauce over each snail. Sprinkle with parsley and serve hot.

SERVES 6 AS AN APPETIZER

Avocado Soufflé

5 tablespoons butter
6 tablespoons flour
2 cups milk
1 teaspoon salt
Freshly ground black pepper
Grated nutmeg
2 medium-size avocados
5 egg yolks
6 egg whites

1. Preheat the oven to 375 degrees F. Melt the butter in a saucepan, add the flour and stir with a wooden spoon until blended. Scald the milk, then add it all at once to the butter-flour mixture and beat with a wire whisk until smooth. Season with salt, pepper and a little nutmeg.

2. Peel and seed the avocados. Press the pulp through a sieve or spin it in a blender. Beat in the egg yolks, then combine this mixture with the sauce. Cook over low heat, removing pan from the heat before contents reach the boiling point.

3. Beat the egg whites until stiff, then fold them into the hot avocado mixture. Pour into a buttered and floured 2-quart soufflé dish. Bake about 35 minutes (or about 1 hour with soufflé dish placed in a pan of boiling water). Serve immediately.

SERVES 6

Tower Garden and Restaurant

Since 1968, Reinhard Barthel has been the Pied Piper of Skokie, with Chicago suburbanites being perennially charmed by the notes of his symphony of menu and setting. Although the Tower Garden was founded in 1934, only recently have vast changes been introduced by Barthel, managing partner and a graduate of a hotel management school in Lausanne, Switzerland. New buildings were added and the wine cellar upgraded to make it one of the best stocked and best equipped in the country.

Featured dishes include Rack of Lamb Bouquetière, Filet of Walleyed Pike Doria, and Truite au Bleu (the trout freshly netted from a tank of live fish). During the week many of the items are prepared at the table, including the Medallions of Venison Hunter-Style when in season. During the summer, guests can dine outdoors in a delightful garden.

9925 GROSS POINT ROAD, SKOKIE

Walleyed Pike Doria

2 10- to 12-ounce fresh
   pike fillets
Salt
Lemon juice
Worcestershire sauce
Flour
4 tablespoons butter
1 small cucumber, diced
2 tablespoons capers
½ cup Chablis
Chopped parsley

1. Marinate pike fillets in lemon juice with salt and a dash of Worcestershire sauce. Peel the cucumber, remove seedy portion and dice.

2. Dredge fillets in flour and sauté in melted butter, in a heavy skillet. When fillets are golden brown on both sides, remove to a heated platter and keep warm.

3. Add capers and diced cucumber to the skillet and sauté, stirring frequently.

4. Just before serving, pour a little Chablis into the skillet, remove from heat and stir. Pour sauce over the fish and sprinkle with chopped parsley.

SERVES 2

176

Chicken à la Tarragoneza

1 cup wild rice
Boiling water
Salt
Butter
6 boned chicken breasts
1 cup flour
1 teaspoon salt
¼ teaspoon pepper
8 tablespoons butter
Hollandaise sauce (page 424)
½ teaspoon tarragon leaves, crushed

1. Prepare the wild rice: Wash well and place in saucepan. Pour over the rice enough boiling water to cover, put a tight-fitting lid on the pan and let stand until cool. Drain well. Repeat this process 3 times.

2. Dip the boned chicken breasts in flour seasoned with salt and pepper. Shake to remove excess flour.

3. Heat the butter in a large skillet and sauté the chicken breasts until golden brown on both sides. This should take about 25 minutes.

4. While chicken is cooking, make the Hollandaise sauce and finish preparing the wild rice by seasoning it with about 1 tablespoon each of salt and butter and rewarming it in the oven or in the top of a double boiler.

5. To serve: Place the chicken breasts on beds of wild rice. Top each with Hollandaise, sprinkle with the crushed tarragon leaves and brown under a preheated broiler.

Café Johnell

"**A**nything the Kennedys do, I can do better." Such was the philosophy of big 6-foot-5-inch, 280-pound John Spillson, as he read of the lavish entrees served at Presidential dinners. Accordingly, he reincarnated his pizza parlor as an elegant French restaurant and ran it with such panache that kings, stars of screen and field, everyone within a 200-mile radius who wanted a truly decent meal, flocked to his Café Johnell. Today, in a city noted for auto pistons, life insurance and high school basketball, it's Spillson's restaurant that attracts new top executives.

The kitchen is small, so small it has only one 16-burner stove and, for lack of space, a huge pressure cooker and a pastry oven hang from the ceiling. Yet the menu offers 82 dishes—and 16 different coffees. As Spillson points out, "It's not the space that's important—it's the quality of the food." To back up his remark, he daily sets out for a local supplier and pays 10 percent over wholesale to get first pick of the produce. Meanwhile, fresh fish is flown in from the East Coast and Scotland, beef trucked in from Chicago. Everything must be perfect. Once, he used up a whole case of eggs while experimenting with a Béarnaise sauce. The wine inventory is exemplary, including one of Napoleon Bonaparte's personal bottles of brandy.

The staff now includes daughter Nike, food director, and son Jon, the maître d'.

2529 SOUTH CALHOUN STREET, FORT WAYNE

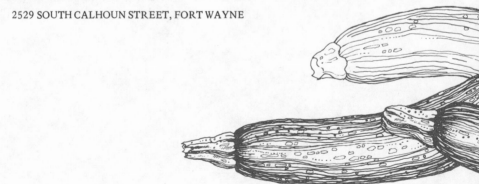

Ratatouille *(Provençal Vegetable Casserole)*

4 tablespoons olive oil
2 garlic cloves, crushed
2 large onions
2 carrots
2 stalks of celery
3 green peppers
6 tomatoes
1 medium eggplant
1 pound zucchini
Salt and pepper
¼ cup chopped parsley
1 large pinch each thyme, basil and chervil
1 tablespoon Worcestershire sauce

1. Prepare all vegetables before starting to cook. Peel and slice the onions. Cut the carrots and celery into narrow strips about 2 inches long. Seed the green peppers and cut them into narrow strips. Peel the tomatoes, cut them in quarters and squeeze gently to remove the seeds. Peel the eggplant and cut the flesh into large cubes. Wash the zucchini and cut it into thin slices.

2. Heat the olive oil and sauté the crushed garlic for 2 minutes. Remove the garlic with a slotted spoon.

3. Add the onions, carrots, celery and pepper. Stir until slightly softened.

4. Add the tomatoes, zucchini and the eggplant. Season with salt and freshly ground black pepper. Add the herbs and Worcestershire sauce.

5. Cook over low heat, stirring occasionally, until vegetables are tender or for about 35 minutes. Do not cover.

SERVES 6 TO 8

Note: Ratatouille may be served hot or cold as an appetizer. It may also be served hot as a vegetable, or cold as a salad.

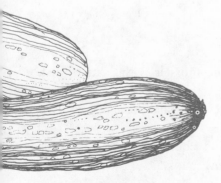

King Cole

The King Coles are among a surprising number of great American restaurants that opened their doors in the years just before the Great Depression and managed—through the lean years that came before they were well established—to keep their doors open. Max Comisar's two were, in those days, modestly priced family restaurants of Spanish persuasion called Seville's. Midwesterners who are graying at the temples still remember them fondly.

Changes came. In the postwar era Comisar redecorated both restaurants and reopened with new names, French cuisine, and menus planned to attract a new and more affluent clientele. Shadowing Max as he tirelessly commuted between Indianapolis and Dayton was son Bruce, who also tagged along on fact-finding visits to other fine restaurants all over the country. What he learned has stood him in good stead since Max's death in 1974.

"I'm optimistic about the future of the fine restaurant," Bruce Comisar says today. "We're now seeing a change in America's lifestyle. The pendulum is swinging back, at last, from the overly casual to increasing formality. Not snobbery, but a sincere appreciation of nice things. People are buying formal clothes again, and when they get dressed up they want someplace to go."

He looks forward to the day when the blue-jean generation, wearing neckties and nylons at last, arrives to dine on his Châteaubriand Sauce Béarnaise, and Cherries Jubilee.

7 NORTH MERIDIAN, INDIANAPOLIS

Moules Marinière
(Mussels in White Wine)

2½ quarts mussels
1½ cups dry white wine

1. Scrub the mussels with a stiff brush until clean.

2. Place the wine, shallots and mussels in a saucepan.

3. Cover and cook just until the shells open. Do not overcook.

5 shallots, finely
  chopped
4 tablespoons butter
1½ teaspoons flour
1 tablespoon finely
  chopped parsley

4. Remove the mussels from the pot and keep warm.

5. Boil down the liquid in the pan to half its original quantity.

6. Mix the butter and the flour and add to the liquid.

7. Add the parsley.

8. Put the mussels in soup plates and pour the sauce over them. Fingers and a soup spoon are the utensils for this dish.

SERVES 4 TO 6

Cherries Jubilee

2 dozen fresh Bing cherries
1 cup water
3 tablespoons sugar
1 tablespoon red currant
  jelly
1 teaspoon cornstarch
3 tablespoons Cherry
  Herring
3 tablespoons brandy
4 scoops vanilla ice cream

Wash the cherries and remove the pits.

Mix together the water and sugar. Bring to a boil and add the cherries. After about 4 minutes remove the cherries with a slotted spoon. Add the currant jelly and continue to cook the liquid until it is reduced to about ¾ cup.

Dissolve the cornstarch in a little cold water and stir it into the hot cherry liquid. Cook until it begins to thicken, then put the cherries in and cook just until they are heated through.

To serve: Add the Cherry Herring and brandy. Bring to a boil and quickly ignite with a match. While still burning, pour the cherries and sauce over ice cream.

SERVES 4

Shambarger's

The first course is a Bloody Redkey, a Bloody Mary made with Budweiser instead of vodka and mixed to the accompaniment of "Bloody Mary" blasting away on the stereo. John Shambarger's way-out restaurant in the tiny community of Redkey is pure Hoosier hysteria. He likes it that way since his unique mix of a gargantuan repast and performing histrionics have served the place well for the last 45 years. The 7-course meal, served only on weekends (to 75 people at a sitting, who have reserved months in advance) begins in a decor of "American Attic," as John Shambarger moves to an antique oak table equipped with a chopping block (under a picture of Christ and a collection of wild-looking clocks and memorabilia) to prepare his legendary dishes. The 5-hour extravaganza begins. Between courses, John will entertain with song and dance. Meanwhile, the privileged diners are eating like epicureans.

The second course, Guacamole Dip, made with fresh avocados, chopped red onions and green peppers, will be accompanied by the sound of the Tijuana Brass, if John is too busy. The fantastic courses creep toward the pièce de résistance, seven huge beeves of prime rib, flambéed with 151-proof rum. Between the fifth and sixth courses there is an intermission—a tour of Redkey. There should be another lull before the dessert, but it rolls in relentlessly: Strawberry Skyscrapers, giant 18-inch-high pie creations, mounded with plump fruit.

On the way home, guests have their bag of popcorn, given by John to lighten the nocturnal return. They will be carrying another gift, a flower—a token of the "power" of Shambarger's.

WEST HIGH STREET, REDKEY

Shambarger's Antique Salad Dressing

3 quarts cottonseed oil

Combine all ingredients and mix well. Store in covered jars in the refrigerator.

MAKES 12 PINTS

2¼ quarts wine vinegar
4 tablespoons chopped red onions
2½ cups sugar
6 ounces concentrated lemon juice
4 tablespoons ground pepper
4 tablespoons salt
¾ cup catsup
½ cup apple butter

Guacamole
(Avocado salad)

3 ripe avocados, peeled and seeded
2 large ripe tomatoes, peeled, seeded and chopped
5 tablespoons chopped onions
1 teaspoon chili powder
1 crushed garlic clove
½ teaspoon Tabasco
Salt and pepper
½ cup crushed crackers
1 teaspoon lemon juice
1 teaspoon rum

1. Prepare all the ingredients and chop them together, adding the rum last. Taste for seasoning, and add more lemon juice, if necessary.

2. Serve on beds of lettuce with crisp crackers or melba toast.

La Tour

Patrons enjoy a panoramic view of Indianapolis along with lunch or dinner at this restaurant perched atop a downtown bank building.

Currently in charge of masterminding the classic dishes is executive chef Christian Frappier, a 29-year-old who is one of the nation's youngest culinary experts. His apprenticeship started in France at age 14. As Christian explains, "The first year I peeled a lot of potatoes, the second year I was allowed to help the head chef, and the third year I actually did some cooking." Frappier is a dedicated artist, spending up to 14 hours daily in the kitchen. He lives to carve in ice. A basket will take him a mere couple of hours, while a swan, made from a massive 300-pound block, may take up to three days.

The chef is sensitive to the qualities that separate the mediocre from the great in his profession. "A good chef can make 25 recipes from the same ingredients," he notes. He refuses to smoke since this could affect his taste buds. A particular feature of his offerings is the Pheasant Souwaroff, which is cooked classically in an earthenware oval cocotte. The diner opens the earthenware at the table by breaking the sealed lid with a small mallet. It took a lot of searching to find a maker of these pots. The sleuthing ended in the small town of Vallauris, France, where a particular potter's family had been fashioning this earthenware for six centuries.

ONE INDIANA SQUARE, INDIANAPOLIS

Mousse de Saumon Guillaume Tirel, Sauce Mousseline (Salmon Mousse with Mousseline Sauce)

1. Make the salmon mousse: Using finest blade of meat grinder or food processor, grind salmon fillets twice. Place in mixing bowl. Add the egg whites gradually, beat vigorously until blended. Add 1 teaspoon salt and ⅛ teaspoon pepper. Place bowl with the mixture over another bowl filled with ice

1¼ pounds skinless,
  boneless salmon fillets
 2 egg whites
 2 teaspoons salt
 ¼ teaspoon white pepper
 2 cups heavy or
  all-purpose cream
 2 whole eggs, slightly
  beaten
 2 tablespoons chopped
  fresh tarragon
 4 tablespoons chopped
  fresh parsley
 1 tablespoon chopped
  fresh chives
Butter
 10 asparagus tips
1½ pounds skinless,
  boneless sole fillets,
  cut into strips
Mousseline sauce (page 426)

Garnish:
 ½ pound cooked peeled
  shrimp
 10 mushrooms, sauteed
  in butter
 2 truffles, sliced

and gradually beat in 1½ cups cream. Place in refrigerator.

2. Make bread stuffing: Put bread crumbs into a mixing bowl and blend with eggs, remaining cream, 1 teaspoon salt, ⅛ teaspoon pepper and the chopped herbs.

3. Preheat oven to 350 degrees F. Brush the sides and bottom of a 2-quart soufflé or ring mold with melted butter. Spread half the salmon mousse evenly in the mold and on it lay half the strips of sole and asparagus tips alternately, side by side. Spread over them half the bread stuffing. Lay the remaining strips of sole and asparagus on the stuffing. Cover with the remaining mousse and spread with the remaining stuffing, smoothing the top.

4. Set the mold in a baking dish containing boiling water and bake for 1½ hours. If the stuffing gets too brown, cover with foil. When it is cooked, remove from the oven and let the mold stand in the hot water, to keep the mousse hot.

5. Prepare the mousseline sauce and the garnish.

6. To serve: Unmold the mousse onto a warm serving platter. Decorate with the garnish and cover with about a third of the sauce. Serve the remaining sauce in a side dish.

SERVES 8 TO 10

Pzazz! Starlight Room

Pzazz it is! A conglomeration of restaurants, cocktail lounges, auditoriums, and bars (nine of them) all housed under one roof. There's a newly created 300-seat discothèque called "Flapper Fanny's," with entertainment appealing to all ages; a 500-seat auditorium that features rock bands; a 250-seat room housing a contemporary dance band and an 1890's-style lounge complete with a ragtime piano player.

For a taste of the Old West, a peanut bar, known as "Red Rat Saloon," serves highballs and beer. Sports buffs will enjoy the raucous atmosphere of the "Lusty Lady," which exhibits a 6-foot TV screen for athletic events of all kinds. A 24-hour cafe and a steak house offer luncheons daily. Future plans envision a 3-story motel unit directly tied in with the rest of the complex.

Here also one finds the quietly beautiful Starlight Room with Georgian marble, walnut paneling, velvet booths and stunning gold place settings. The menu is set in a bold typeface large enough to be read from 100 paces. Nevertheless, subtlety arrives with every course, from the fresh Tomato Bisque to the Pheasant Under Glass, fresh spinach with dill and lemon butter, Cornish Hen Kiev, and Fresh Fruit Compote (crystal from Gumps of San Francisco).

Inventor John Winegard put the complex together, and it now is directed by his son.

3003 WINEGARD DRIVE, BURLINGTON

Orange Rice Stuffed Trout

6 12-ounce boned rainbow
   trout
1 cup diced onion

1. Wash the trout and dry them well inside and out. Lay them out on a working surface.

2. Sauté the onions, pepper and garlic in 2 tablespoons of butter until the onions are tender.

½ cup diced green pepper
2 cloves garlic, peeled
   and finely chopped
Butter
1 thin-skinned orange
3 cups boiled rice
½ teaspoon powdered thyme
Salt and pepper
3 tablespoons chopped
   parsley
2 lemons

3. Grate the orange and squeeze out the juice.

4. Combine the boiled rice, which must be tender but not overcooked, with the vegetables, orange rind and juice and the thyme. Mix well and season to taste with salt and pepper.

5. Preheat the oven to 350 degrees F.

6. Stuff the fish with the mixture and sew up the cavities with needle and thread.

7. Place the fish in a single layer in a well-buttered baking-serving dish. Bake the fish 20 minutes, basting almost constantly with melted butter.

8. Garnish the fish with chopped parsley and twists made from thin slices of lemon.

SERVES 6

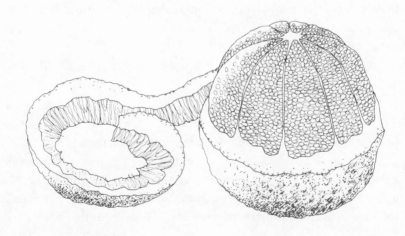

Joe Muer's Restaurant

The moment could not have been more inauspicious. Joe Muer the First opened his seafood restaurant the day before the 1929 stock market crash. The founder owned a cigar factory in the German section of Detroit but the demand for cigars was down drastically, largely due to Prohibition, and he decided to open the city's first public oyster bar. It was a time to try men's souls but somehow Joe survived, and his establishment grew from the original five tables to a seating capacity of 420. Nowadays the much expanded restaurant grosses $5 million annually. Why the success? Somebody once asked son Bill what would have happened if his father had started things back in the boom years of the '20s. He replied, "I guess it wouldn't have made much difference to Pa, because he was doing his level best to please people with what he had to provide. That's what we have been doing ever since."

Today the business is operated by second-generation Bill Muer along with third-generation Tom and Joe, and there's a fourth-generation Joe waiting in the wings.

Over a thousand meals are served daily, with hearty seafood: Maine lobster, Pacific salmon, Boston scrod, Lake Superior trout, Cape Cod bluefish—and for the meat lovers, prime steak and great American wines. It is without a doubt one of the most down-to-earth, solid, value-conscious restaurant operations you could find anywhere.

All this, and there are still freshly printed menus daily!

2000 GRATOIT AVENUE, DETROIT

Crab Canapés

2 egg whites
1 cup mayonnaise
3 tablespoons grated onion

Beat egg whites until stiff. Fold in mayonnaise. Add grated onion and Worcestershire sauce and mix gently. Fold in crab meat. Season to taste with salt and pepper. Spoon mixture onto bread rounds 1 inch in diame-

1 tablespoon
  Worcestershire sauce
¾ pound crab meat
Salt and pepper to taste

ter. Place on baking sheet and broil, 8 inches from broiler element, until browned.

Deviled Crab Cakes

1¼ pounds 3-day-old bread
  5 hard-cooked eggs,
      chopped
  1 heaping tablespoon salt
  1 heaping tablespoon
      dry mustard
  1 large onion, chopped
  2 tablespoons butter
  7 teaspoons cider vinegar
  7 teaspoons
      Worcestershire sauce
  3 tablespoons mayonnaise
  2 pounds fresh crab meat

1. Cut the crust from the bread and crumble the bread into small bits and place in a large mixing bowl. Add the eggs, salt and mustard.

2. Sauté the onions in 2 tablespoons butter just until tender and add to the bread crumbs along with the vinegar and Worcestershire sauce and mayonnaise. Mix well.

3. Add the crab meat, tossing it lightly with 2 forks. Preheat oven to 350 degrees F. Form the mixture as you would a small snowball to make your crab cakes and place on a buttered baking sheet. Bake for 15 minutes.

SERVES 6 TO 8

London Chop House

Detroit was asking, "Ever tried an eight-cylinder car?" and offering a Chrysler Brougham, tax paid, for under $1,000. The year was 1938 and the London Chop House opened in the city's financial district to help celebrate the Ford Motor Company's 26-millionth auto. But the assembly line of patrons stretched beyond the business world as many show business celebrities dropped in. Part of the restaurant's unique decor consists of dozens of caricatures of personalities who have made the Chop House their headquarters over the years.

The basement location of the 154-seat dining area imitates the charm of a British eating place, with oak-beamed ceiling, leather banquettes and plaid table coverings. Owners Lester and Sam Gruber offer Continental cuisine, gleaned from their extensive travels abroad, and the staff is noted for its cordiality. For those patrons who reserve in advance, the London Chop House is pleased to add the amenities of name-imprinted table cards and matches.

155 WEST CONGRESS, DETROIT

Celery Root Puree

5 celery roots (celeriac or knob celery) 4 to 4½ inches in diameter
1 medium or large potato
1 tablespoon Kosher salt
3 tablespoons soft butter
1 tablespoon lemon juice
1 tablespoon sugar
Salt and white pepper to taste.

1. Choose celery roots that are not too large—large ones tend to be fibrous. Wash and peel the celery roots and potato. Cut in quarters and place in a large saucepan.

2. Add water to cover and the Kosher salt. Bring to a boil, cover and simmer 15 to 20 minutes or until pieces are tender.

3. Drain and put through a food mill, ricer or food processor. Whip in the butter, lemon juice, sugar and a little salt and pepper. Taste and add more salt and pepper if needed. Serve as a vegetable.

SERVES 6

Michigan

Pea Pod Soup

7 tablespoons clarified
  butter (page 420)
¾ cup coarsely chopped
  onion
¾ cup sliced leeks (white
  portion only)
3 tablespoons flour
1 tablespoon sugar
1 bay leaf
½ teaspoon white pepper
¼ teaspoon freshly ground
  nutmeg
Salt
4 cups of rich, clear
  chicken broth, heated
1 package (12 ounces)
  frozen peas
1 cup fresh Chinese pea
  pods, trimmed and cut
  in ¼ inch pieces
2 egg yolks
1 cup heavy cream

1. In a heavy skillet or 3-quart enamel saucepan sauté the onion and leek in 6 tablespoons of butter until transparent.

2. Add flour, stir 1 minute and add the sugar, bay leaf, pepper, nutmeg and season to taste with salt.

3. Add chicken broth and stir until blended. Bring to boil and simmer 15 minutes.

4. Add the frozen peas, bring to a boil and cook 2 to 3 minutes.

5. Puree in blender or food processor and strain through a fine sieve. Reheat.

6. Sauté the Chinese pea pods in a tablespoon of butter until they start to color. Do not overcook. Add to the soup.

7. Using a fork, beat the egg yolks with the cream, and add gradually to the soup before serving. Taste for seasoning.

SERVES 6

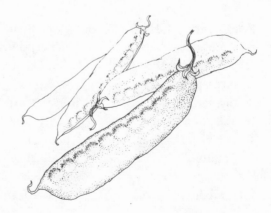

191

Pontchartrain Wine Cellars

"The Cellars," as it is affectionately known to patrons from the Motor City, is a small French bistro, a quiet, friendly place which serves surprisingly good food. Founded in 1935 by Harold Borgman, the Cellars originally served only soups, sandwiches, cheese and wine. The initial growth of the menu came from the efforts of Mr. Borgman's daughter, who worked several summers in France tracking down new dishes. While the menu has increased in scope, the Wine Cellars has maintained its loyalty to wine by serving neither liquor nor water. One is reminded of those delightfully informal wine restaurants in Australia that draw on a sophisticated clientele.

This noted Detroit eating place has received national recognition as the home of Cold Duck, a drink consisting of champagne and still Burgundy, which derives from an old German wine-festival custom of pouring together the last wines—one red and one white—for one final drink. Joan Redhead, a former proprietress of the Wine Cellars, had the distinction of introducing the beverage in the United States. But as you imbibe, do not forget to order—especially the Gigot d'Agneau with Ratatouille de Provence.

234 WEST LARNED, DETROIT

Pork Chops Charcutière

1 large onion, sliced thin
5 tablespoons lard or
    margarine
1 teaspoon flour
1 cup beef stock or
    bouillon
½ cup white wine
Salt and pepper

1. Sauté the onions in a saucepan with 2 tablespoons of lard or margarine until tender. Do not brown.

2. Stir in the flour and when the flour has disappeared, add the beef stock and wine. Stir until thick. Season to taste with salt and pepper.

3. Bring the sauce to a boil and skim if necessary. Let simmer 30 minutes.

4. Meanwhile, brown the pork chops in

6 large pork chops
2 tablespoons gherkins,
  coarsely chopped
1 teaspoon Dijon mustard
2 tablespoons chopped
  parsley

Cold Boeuf en Salade
(Cold Beef Salad)

2½ pounds cooked and
    trimmed cold beef
2 onions, sliced
¼ cup wine vinegar
½ cup olive oil
4 tablespoons capers
2 tablespoons chopped
   parsley
2 teaspoons chopped
   tarragon
2 teaspoons chopped
   chives
1 tablespoon chopped
   pimiento
1 hard-cooked egg,
   chopped
¼ teaspoon dry mustard
Tabasco
Freshly ground pepper

the remaining fat. Reduce the heat. Cover
and cook until tender.

5. Skim the sauce again if need be and
add pickles and mustard.

6. Pour the sauce over the cooked chops
and sprinkle with chopped parsley.

SERVES 6

Cut the beef into thin slices across the
grain and place on a non-metal platter.

Separate onion slices into rings and spread
over beef. Combine the vinegar, oil, capers,
herbs, pimiento, egg, mustard, Tabasco and
pepper and pour over the meat. Let stand at
room temperature for 3 hours.

Serve on leaf lettuce, garnished with
watercress.

SERVES 6

The Vineyards

Culinary expert James Beard places Detroit among the four leading U.S. cities for gourmet dining. Helping attain this distinction is The Vineyards, 45 miles northwest of the city in the suburb of Southfield. Located on a 10-acre vineyard, in a rambling Normandy-style building, Frederick Gracyk's eating place is host to thousands. The patrons' problem may be getting a table—Gracyk's only problem occurred years ago, when he moved in. The raccoons had arrived first. Everything was tried in an effort to remove them: pesticides, traps—but to no avail. Finally, the owner took up a nocturnal vigil on the roof (that is where the raccoons were) and waited for them to go foraging. Once they departed, steel plates were put over their entrance and the creatures never returned.

For his patrons, Gracyk is the ideal host, as he serves enviable dishes in graceful surroundings of red-brick alcoves and vaulted ceilings. Sweet and Sour Pork Roast is the specialty of the house, and is slow-cooked for two hours. Other delights are ethnic-type casseroles.

Gracyk attributes his success to the "fun" he has in running the restaurant. This includes making sure his staff has three weeks paid vacation each year, and when he hosts a women's club, he sees that its members receive a bonus, such as a lesson on roast-cutting or ice-carving.

29230 FRANKLIN ROAD, SOUTHFIELD

Pork Roast with Sweet and Sour Sauce

4 1-pound center cut rib pork roasts
2 cups sugar
1 cup distilled vinegar

1. Preheat oven to 450 degrees F.

2. Place pork roasts in roasting pan, bone side down, and roast for 30 minutes. Meanwhile, prepare the sauce by mixing sugar, vinegar, green pepper and salt with 1 cup of water. Simmer 5 minutes.

3. Combine cornstarch with 2 table-

2 tablespoons chopped
  green pepper
1 teaspoon salt
1 cup water
4 teaspoons cornstarch
2 tablespoons water
2 teaspoons paprika
2 tablespoons finely
  chopped parsley
4 small baked apples

spoons water. Add to the sauce and stir over heat until sauce thickens. Strain and add the paprika and parsley.

4. Remove the pork from the oven and transfer to a deeper baking dish with bone side up.

5. Pour the sauce over the pork and bake for 2½ hours at 300 degrees F., basting occasionally.

6. To serve: Place on platter with sauce ladled over the pork. Garnish with baked apples.

SERVES 4 VERY GENEROUSLY

Pauline's Bourbon Pie

1 8-inch graham cracker
  piecrust
1 egg, separated
4 tablespoons sugar
Pinch of salt
3 tablespoons bourbon
  whiskey
¾ cup chopped pecans
½ pint whipping cream
Nutmeg

Beat the egg yolk and add the sugar, salt, bourbon and chopped pecans. Mix well.

Whip the cream and fold it into the mixture. Beat the egg white and fold it in.

Pour mixture into the pie crust. Sprinkle with nutmeg and place in freezer. Serve frozen.

SERVES 8 GENEROUSLY

Win Schuler's

Today, outside of a return to the pages of Dickensia, where can one spend an entire evening in the company of such rogues as Fagin and the Artful Dodger, such clowns as Mr. Pickwick and Sam Weller, such innocents as Esther Summerson, David Copperfield, Oliver Twist and Pip? If you guessed the Charles Dickens Society of London, England, you're close—but wrong. For in order to "resurrect" the master's more famous characters that way, you must wait until the Society convenes—a delay which, no matter how slight, is frustrating.

At Win Schuler's in Marshall, Michigan, on the other hand, such frustrations are unknown. Indeed, whenever you wish (although a reservation is helpful), you can enter this classic restaurant, select the table closest to your favorite hero or villain and order a meal fit for kings and Cartons alike. Or, if not a Dickens buff, you are invited to choose the Centennial Dining Room, or, for banquets, the Heritage Room. Regardless of personal preference, the cuisine of each hall remains dedicated to the Schuler ideals of tradition and excellence, ideals that become increasingly apparent as you move from Bar-Scheeze and Schipps, to Swiss Onion Soup and salad, to a superb main course and delectable dessert. Clearly, no hard times can be found here: at Win Schuler's, great expectations still do come true.

115 SOUTH EAGLE STREET, MARSHALL

Fresh Blueberry Glacé Pie

1 quart blueberries,
  washed and drained
¾ cup water
3 tablespoons cornstarch
1 cup sugar

1. Simmer 1 cup of berries in the water for 3 or 4 minutes. Combine the sugar and cornstarch and add to the cooking fruit, stirring constantly until the syrup is thick and ruby-clear.

2. Add lemon juice to taste.

3. Spread the softened cream cheese on the bottom of the pastry shell and cover with

1 teaspoon-1 tablespoon
   lemon juice
1 small package (4 ounces)
   cream cheese, softened
9-inch baked pastry shell
Whipped cream or ice cream

the remaining berries. Pour the cooked fruit mixture over and mix in very gently with a fork.

4. Chill thoroughly before serving with whipped cream or ice cream.

SERVES 6 TO 8

Swiss Onion Soup

½ cup butter
2 pounds onions, thinly
   sliced
1½ teaspoons paprika
6 cups beef stock
   (page 416)
½ cup vegetable oil
¾ cup flour
¾ teaspoon celery salt
Salt and pepper to taste
8 ounces dark beer
12 slices bread
½ cup Parmesan cheese
Paprika

1. Cook onions in butter until soft. Stir in paprika, then add beef stock and bring to a boil.

2. Make a roux by browning the oil and stirring in the flour. Stir into the soup the roux, celery salt, and salt and pepper. Simmer at least 2 hours.

3. Shortly before serving, sprinkle the slices of bread liberally with Parmesan cheese and paprika and toast them in the oven. Add the beer to the soup and allow it to return to serving temperature, then remove from heat.

4. Pour soup into bowls, add a slice of toast to each and sprinkle with additional Parmesan cheese.

SERVES 12

The Blue Horse

The day they tore up the streets of St. Paul to eliminate the streetcar tracks, architect Roland Terry was there to pick up the pieces—pieces of paving stone, that is. Some of the stones ended up as walls of The Blue Horse, where they create a French wine cellar atmosphere and a fitting background for the beaten-copper bas relief that gives the restaurant its name—a stallion gone mellow greenish-blue with patina.

Cliff Warling brought a tang of salt-scented Seattle with him when he returned to his native Twin Cities in 1964, and he serves Dungeness crab and Puget salmon. Warling also takes credit for introducing the "authentic" West Coast Caesar salad to Minneapolis and it remains the most popular item on his bill of fare. As a concession to Minnesota freshwater chauvinists, he also offers flaky walleyed pike harvested from Minnesota lakes. Diners who are not enthusiastic about seafood or freshwater fish may dine on excellent Steak Tartare or Italian specialties expertly prepared by chef George Wandzel.

Reason enough for the blue horse to join the select zoological company of the purple cow and the pink elephant!

1355 UNIVERSITY AVENUE, ST. PAUL

Steak Tartare

1 pound freshly and finely ground tenderloin or sirloin steak
2 egg yolks
1 teaspoon Dijon mustard
1 teaspoon salt
½ teaspoon fresh ground black pepper

1. Ask the butcher to grind fat-free beef twice.

2. In a shallow bowl, mix the egg yolks, mustard, pepper and salt. Whisking constantly, add the vinegar and, very gradually, the oil until the sauce thickens.

3. Add all the remaining ingredients except for the garnish. Blend thoroughly.

4. Add the ground meat and stir gently with a fork until thoroughly mixed.

1 teaspoon red wine vinegar
2 tablespoons olive oil
1 tablespoon chopped
   onion
1 tablespoon capers
1 teaspoon salt
1 tablespoon chopped
   parsley
1 tablespoon Worcestershire
   sauce
1 tablespoon chopped
   dill pickles

Garnish:
1 medium fresh tomato,
   quartered
4 fillets of anchovies
Pumpernickel bread

5. To serve: Serve immediately on individual plates. With a small spatula, form the meat mixture into rectangular or oval shapes. Garnish with tomato wedges covered with pieces of anchovy fillets. Serve with pumpernickel bread. (The meat mixture may be spread on small pieces of pumpernickel bread and served as a canapé.)

SERVES 2 TO 3

Camelot

Banners and pennants flutter over a 15th-Century-style castle; inside, platefuls of regal nourishment are hoisted high—"that's how conditions are" at Camelot, Hans Skalle's legendary restaurant in Twin Citied Minnesota. At suburban Bloomington, behind the protection of a moat and turreted walls, the royal days of King Arthur—complete with round tables, hand-carved in Mexico, and high-backed, hand-carved chestnut chairs—are reborn. Authentic medieval weapons and armor are placed tastefully around the six cozy hexagonal rooms. The giant chandelier in the Great Hall required ten men and two hydraulic lifts to install.

This royal style is nothing new to Skalle, who spent years in culinary service to King Haakon and the royal Norwegian family. He sees that you and your fellow knights partake of a tasty selection from the Continental menu, which includes specialties such as scampi, fresh river trout, prime rib, pheasant, and young partridge. Camelot's talented chefs are periodically joined in the kitchen by Skalle, who enjoys rolling up his sleeves and skillfully filleting a Dover sole. Camelot is noted for its seafood, but prime rib is the most popular entree.

JUNCTION OF HIGHWAYS 494 AND 100, BLOOMINGTON

Soft Shell Crab Sautéed Grenobloise

24 soft shell crabs, cleaned
Salt and pepper
Flour
 1 cup butter
 ¼ cup oil
Juice of 1 lemon
 2 tablespoons butter

1. Wash and dry the crab.
2. Sprinkle with salt and pepper and dredge with flour.
3. Heat 1 cup of butter and the oil in a large skillet.
4. Sauté the crab back side down for 5 minutes. Turn the crab and sauté 3 more minutes.
5. Transfer the crab to a heated platter and sprinkle with lemon juice.

4 lemons, peeled and
  diced
1 cup capers
2 tablespoons chopped
  parsley
2 tablespoons
  Worcestershire sauce

6. Heat the remaining 2 tablespoons of butter in the same skillet. Add the diced lemon and capers, 1 tablespoon of chopped parsley and the Worcestershire sauce. Stir until hot and pour over the crab. Sprinkle with the remaining parsley.

7. Serve with parsleyed new potatoes and garnish with sprigs of parsley.

SERVES 6 TO 8

Scampi Amoureuse

3 pounds shelled scampi
  or jumbo shrimp
½ pound butter
2 10-ounce cans prepared
  lobster sauce or
  lobster bisque
1 cup heavy cream
2 tablespoons Pernod

1. Wash scampi and blot dry with paper toweling. Melt butter in a large skillet. Add the scampi and sauté for about 5 minutes, shaking the pan constantly so that all scampi are well covered with butter and none stick to the pan.

2. Drain scampi and discard butter. Return skillet to the heat, adding lobster sauce, cream and liqueur. Stir while heating; do not allow mixture to come to a boil.

3. Add scampi and simmer 2 minutes. Taste; correct seasoning if needed. Serve in a chafing dish, with white rice or patty shells on the side.

SERVES 6 TO 8

Charlie's Café Exceptionale

The New York City Establishment was appalled in 1929 when "Scherzo," a joyous, bronze nude nymph, was first unveiled. No one flinches anymore. Instead, the modern Establishment is welcomed by Scherzo at the entrance of Charlie's Café Exceptionale. In 1948 she was moved to Charlie's in Minneapolis and now surveys the rambling Tudor structure which houses four dining rooms, each with its own distinctive personality. Dark oak-paneled walls, 16th-Century watercolor murals, and massive stone hearths grace the formal dining area. For informal occasions Charlie's Pub Room is a cozy niche featuring a 22-foot oil mural that depicts the classic tale of the young knight and the dragon. Small chandeliers fashioned from wine bottles enlighten the proceedings.

No matter what your preference, Charlie's cuisine is exceptional, indeed. Feast on Shrimp Sebastian served with a delightful Chablis sauce, or try the Roast Peppered Rib Eye of Beef. Charlie's is famous for festive desserts. Flaming Crêpes are the perfect finale to any meal.

701 FOURTH AVENUE SOUTH, MINNEAPOLIS

Roast Peppered Rib Eye of Beef with Savory Wild Rice

5 pounds boneless rib eye beef roast, trimmed of excess fat
½ cup coarsely cracked pepper

1. (Start this recipe 1 day in advance.) The day before serving, rub the entire roast with a combination of pepper and cardamom seed, pressing the spice in with the heel of the hand. Place in a shallow baking dish.

2. Combine the tomato paste, garlic powder, paprika, soy sauce and vinegar. Mix well with a whisk and pour over the beef. Let stand at least 12 hours in the refrigerator, spooning the marinade over the meat several

½ teaspoon ground
  cardamom seed
1 tablespoon tomato
  paste
½ teaspoon garlic powder
1 teaspoon paprika
1 cup soy sauce
¾ cup red wine vinegar

Savory wild rice:
1½ cups wild rice
4 cups water
1 teaspoon salt
1 small onion
4 strips bacon, diced
4 green onions, chopped
  fine
6 fresh mushrooms,
  sliced thin
Fresh ground pepper to taste
1 teaspoon poultry
  seasoning

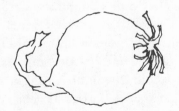

times. Soak the wild rice in water overnight.

3. Next day, remove the meat from the marinade 3½ hours before serving. Let stand at room temperature 1 hour. Then wrap the meat in foil and roast in a shallow pan for 2 hours at 300 degrees F.

4. Open the foil and spoon out all the drippings into a saucepan. Return the meat to the oven, unwrapped, and turn temperature to 350 degrees F., so the meat will brown while the gravy is being made. Strain the meat drippings and skim off excess fat. To 1 cup of meat juices, add 1 cup of water. Bring to a boil, taste and add a little of the marinade if desired. If the gravy seems too thin, add 1½ tablespoons of cornstarch mixed with ¼ cup cold water.

5. Meanwhile, begin to prepare the wild rice at least 1 hour before serving time. Rinse the rice and combine with the 4 cups water, salt and the whole onion. Simmer, covered, 40 to 45 minutes, then remove onion and drain rice in a colander. Fry the bacon until crisp, add the green onions and mushrooms and cook just until tender. Add the drained rice, stir, and season to taste with salt, pepper and poultry seasoning. Keep hot. Serve with the meat and gravy.

SERVES 8

International Rosewood Room

The immigrants arrived, the newly arrived, *les nouvelles arrivées*. If they were Scandinavian, they tended to settle in Minnesota. As a reminder of this pattern in American history, Scandinavian Savories are served at luncheon Monday through Friday in the comfortably paneled Rosewood Room restaurant on the seventh floor of the Northstar Inn in downtown Minneapolis. But an even more international touch to the menu is the "Nouvelles Arrivées" featured weekly. Typically, on one such day, patrons were treated to "Specialties from 1001 Nights," Middle Eastern dishes that included the following:

Couscous Marocaine—A traditional dish in the Middle East. Lamb and various vegetables steamed with semolina. Served with Harissa sauce.

Joojhe Kebab—Special marinated spring chicken roasted on a large skewer. Served with saffron rice and a creamy curry-flavored sauce.

Veal "Maharadshah"—Slices of veal sautéed with mango, apple, raisins and almonds; tossed with a hot curry sauce. Served with Patna rice.

Very cosmopolitan dining in Minneapolis!

NORTHSTAR INN, 618 SECOND AVENUE SOUTH, MINNEAPOLIS

Scampi Costa Brava

12-20 large Spanish shrimp

Saffron rice:
  ¼ cup butter
  1 small onion, chopped
  1 cup long-grain
      white rice
  2 cups hot water

1. Prepare the saffron rice: Melt the butter in a heavy saucepan and sauté the onion until softened but not brown. Add the raw rice and cook slowly 3 to 4 minutes or until the rice is opaque. Stir in the hot water, cover tightly and cook over low heat until all the liquid is absorbed and the rice appears dry and fluffy—about 20 minutes. Add saffron and salt and pepper to taste. Mix gently. Keep warm until shrimp is ready to serve.

⅛ teaspoon powdered
   saffron

Tarragon Butter:
   ½ pound softened
      butter
Juice of ½ lemon
   1 tablespoon chopped
      parsley
   1 tablespoon dry
      white wine
   1 tablespoon chopped
      fresh tarragon
Salt and pepper

   ½ cup dry Spanish
      sherry

2. Preheat oven to 425 degrees F. Remove all the legs from the shrimp but do not remove the shells. Place the shrimp in a baking dish.

3. Mix all ingredients of the tarragon butter until blended. Put a little of the tarragon butter on each shrimp and sprinkle the sherry over all. Bake 12 to 15 minutes.

4. To serve: Arrange 4 to 6 shrimp on a bed of saffron rice on each of 4 plates. Garnish with a lemon slice and a sprig of parsley. Each diner should have a small sauceboat of the tarragon butter, and a finger bowl.

SERVES 4

Lowell Inn

Nellie Palmer had her hair in braids and wore a smart brown flowered dress as she greeted fellow Stillwater residents on that bright Christmas Day in 1930 for the opening dinner at the Lowell Inn. She and her husband were carrying on a tradition of hospitality, which began in 1848 when the stately Sawyer House was built on the site. It had provided 75 years of good cheer to the lumber barons and their wives before demolition by the wrecker's ball in 1923.

Arthur, Sr., and Nellie, he a pianist and she an actress, had spent much of their early lives on the road, living from suitcases; and when they had a chance to settle down and start an inn, they were determined that it would be just like a home, with excellent food served from a home kitchen. So today, guests arrive as much for the notable pear bread and pecan pie as for a look at the exquisitely furnished dining rooms serving an elaborate menu.

The rooms of the Lowell Inn are unique. The Matterhorn Room is eye-catching with its collection of antique wood carvings. A Swiss wood-carver, Herr Blatter, spent two and one-half years at the inn fashioning some of the pieces. Woven into the backs of the chairs are sections of climbing rope used in ascents of the Matterhorn and Mt. Everest. The dinner itself is Swiss with wines from the same country: a dry sherry, a white Johannisberg, a white Fendant, and finally the Merlot Rosé.

Among other dining areas are the George Washington Room, reflecting the owners' regard for Williamsburg Colonial antiques; the Garden Room, with polished agate tables and an indoor trout pool, and a cocktail lounge where guests are served "doubles" in sparkling glassware.

102 NORTH SECOND STREET, STILLWATER

Lowell Inn Sweet and Sour Red Cabbage

1 medium-size red
   cabbage

1. Wash and remove outer leaves of cabbage. Cut out core and slice very thin.
2. Peel and slice the onion.
3. Peel, core and quarter the apples.
4. Place all the ingredients except the

1 medium-size onion
2 large apples
1 large tablespoon
   melted bacon fat
1 teaspoon salt
½ cup sugar
1 cup cider vinegar
1½ cups water
1 bay leaf
2 whole allspice
2 cloves (heads removed)
6 peppercorns
2 teaspoons cornstarch

cornstarch in a large bowl and toss together.

5. Put in a non-metal lined pan. Cover and simmer 1½ hours.

6. Before serving, thicken the juices with 2 teaspoons of cornstarch, dissolved in a little water.

SERVES 8 TO 10

Pecan Pie

5 eggs
Pinch of salt
1¼ cups sugar
¼ pound butter, melted
½ cup plus 2 tablespoons
   Karo syrup
½ cup plus 2 tablespoons
   Alaga syrup
Nut meats from 8 large
   pecans
Unbaked pastry shell

Preheat oven to 300 degrees F.

Beat eggs well. Add salt and sugar. Stir in melted butter, then syrups. Pour in pastry shell and bake about 50 minutes. Arrange nuts on top of pie, then bake 10 minutes longer.

American Restaurant

"**E**verything's up to date in Kansas City." Over the last few years, literally billions of dollars in private money have been spent to make the metropolis even more spectacular. ("Cow town" is a crass misnomer.) Splashing in among the myriad fountains have been new stadiums, a fun park, riverfront developments—and Joyce C. Hall's $350-million Crown Center complex, a small city in itself. Anyone who has admired the artistry of a Hallmark card will appreciate the care that went into this development by the founder of the company. The same may be said for the stunning American Restaurant that is part of the Crown Center Hotel.

Wanting a sophisticated eating place offering the best of strictly American cuisine, Hall fashioned the interior to look like a huge lace valentine. The effect was achieved with a fan-shaped network of glass and oak bentwood canopies that created intimate areas while retaining a feeling of airiness. A panoply of clear filament lamps and sprays of light from the windows make their own shimmering reflections, and theatrical projectors throw showers of dappled light for a walking-in-the-woods-on-a-sunny-day illusion. The Plymouth Clam Pie, Montana Elk and Long Island Duckling dishes provide their own refulgence.

ATOP HALL'S, CROWN CENTER, KANSAS CITY

Plymouth Clam Pie

Pie pastry for 2 9-inch pies
- 2 tablespoons butter
- 3 tablespoons chopped shallots
- ½ cup diced mushrooms
- 2 tablespoons diced salt pork

1. Mix the pastry and let it rest.
2. Heat the butter in a saucepan and saute the shallots, mushrooms, salt pork and garlic for 3 minutes.
3. Stir in the flour and cook for 1 minute.
4. Add the clam juice; bring to a boil and cook 1 minute.
5. Add the cream and boil for 10 minutes.

½ teaspoon chopped garlic
2 tablespoons flour
1¼ cups clam juice
4 tablespoons heavy
  cream
1 pint chowder clams
1 teaspoon chopped
  parsley
¼ teaspoon grated lemon
  rind
½ teaspoon chopped
  tarragon
⅛ teaspoon thyme
1 egg yolk, slightly
  beaten

6. Add the chopped clams, parsley, lemon rind, tarragon and thyme.

7. Remove from the heat and gradually beat in the egg yolk. Let the mixture cool.

8. Preheat the oven to 375 degrees F. Roll out the pie pastry ⅛ inch thick and cut into 16 4-inch circles with a large cookie cutter or small saucepan cover. Line 8 individual pie tins or foil pans. Trim the edges and moisten slightly. Fill each one with the clam mixture and cover with one of the remaining circles. Crimp and seal the edges and slash the top in several places to allow the steam to escape.

9. Bake for 15 minutes. Serve very hot.

SERVES 8

Chocolate Velvet

1 pint heavy cream
3 egg yolks
2 tablespoons shaved
  semi-sweet chocolate
¼ cup kirsch
½ cup hazelnuts

1. Heat the cream just to the boiling point. Immediately reduce heat and whip in the egg yolks. (Do not let the mixture return to a boil or it will separate).

2. Add the chocolate and stir gently over moderate heat until the mixture begins to thicken slightly. Stir in the kirsch and the hazelnuts and remove from heat.

3. Pour into mold or into individual paper pastry cups and refrigerate for 2 hours or longer before serving.

SERVES 6 TO 8

Anthony's

First there was Tony's, then Anthony's.

As the names suggest, the two restaurants are part and parcel of the same operation, owned by brothers Vincent and Anthony Bommarito. The former is usually to be found at Tony's, which specializes in Italian dishes, and the latter at Anthony's, where the cuisine is French. The two restaurants are eight blocks apart.

The "new" restaurant—it opened in 1972—is contemporary, all browns and smoked glass, a little dim but with hanging lamps that center each table in an intimate island of light.

"We visited fine restaurants everyplace before opening Anthony's," says Anthony. "We planned every detail carefully, and we feel we've created the finest restaurant setting in the country. We're particularly pleased with the acoustics."

Diners admire the decor and enjoy the acoustics, but it's primarily chef Peter Ferronato's culinary skill that makes it necessary to phone for a reservation before dropping in at Anthony's for lunch or dinner.

10 SOUTH BROADWAY, ST. LOUIS

Tomato and Eggplant Glacé

1 medium eggplant, peeled
2 large ripe tomatoes
Salt, pepper and sugar
2 tablespoons butter
2 tablespoons flour
1 cup rich chicken broth
½ cup Hollandaise sauce
½ cup cream, whipped
½ cup Parmesan cheese

1. Preheat oven to 350 degrees F. Cut the peeled eggplant into ½-inch slices. Peel the tomatoes, cut in half and gently squeeze out the seeds. Cut in ½-inch slices.

2. Alternate the eggplant and tomato slices in a shallow, ovenproof serving dish. Sprinkle with salt, pepper and sugar.

3. Bake 15 to 20 minutes or until tomato and eggplant are tender.

4. Meanwhile, heat the butter in a small saucepan and blend in the flour. Whisk in the chicken broth until smooth and bring to a boil. Simmer 10 minutes.

210

5. Remove the vegetables from the oven and drain the juice into the chicken sauce. Blend in the Hollandaise and whipped cream.

6. Cover the eggplant and tomato with the sauce. Sprinkle with Parmesan cheese and brown under a preheated broiler. Serve very hot.

SERVES 4

Breast of Capon à L'Antoine

4 bay leaves
Pinch of rosemary
1 teaspoon peppercorns
½ cup chopped celery
½ cup chopped onion
1 3-pound capon
½ cup Chablis
½ cup chicken stock
  (page 419)
2 slices white bread
2 slices cooked ham
2 large cooked mushroom
  caps
½ cup Hollandaise sauce
  (page 424)
¾ cup cream, whipped
½ cup Parmesan cheese

1. Tie bay leaves, rosemary and peppercorns in a bit of cheesecloth and place in a large saucepan. Add the celery and onion. Remove legs and wings from the capon and place all parts in the saucepan. Add the wine and chicken stock, cover and cook at a gentle boil for 20 minutes.

2. Cut the slices of bread heart-shaped and fry in a little butter. Place on a heatproof Pyrex or deep silver platter. Top each with a slice of ham and half the breast of capon, skinned and boned. Place a mushroom on each.

3. Fold together the Hollandaise and whipped cream and spoon half over each serving. Sprinkle with the Parmesan cheese and put under the broiler until browned. Serve at once.

SERVES 2

Dominic's

Whom do you thank for a fine meal at Dominic's? Do you thank owner and chef Giovanni Galati? Or his wife, Jackie, the hostess? But there is the owner's father-in-law at the door. And Joe, the brother-in-law, is the manager. Perhaps one should thank the mother-in-law, who helps with the cooking? No matter. Just remember how much of an effort the whole family has made to make your dining pleasurable.

Everything is Sunday-best at Dominic's. The decor is intimate, with candlelight settling on fresh roses blushing over white tablecloths. The walls are colored brightly Italian in wine accents—for days of wine and roses. The male waiters attend in tuxedos.

Each entree is made to order and served only with fresh vegetables. Specialties include: Veal Fiorentina, Sicilian Veal Kabobs, Chicken Cardinale, Lobster alla Gusta. Wife Jackie supervises the delectable desserts. The community of St. Louis has drawn close to this family affair.

5101 WILSON AVENUE, ST. LOUIS

Spiedini Siciliani
(Sicilian Veal Kabobs)

18 pieces of veal ¼-inch thick (2 ounces)
18 thin small slices of prosciutto or salami
1½ cups of shredded Mozzarella cheese
Salt and pepper
4 cups chopped parsley
1 onion, quartered and broken into sections

1. Put the veal pieces between sheets of wax paper. Flatten each one with a mallet.

2. Preheat oven to 450 degrees F. Put a small slice of prosciutto on each piece of veal and cover with the shredded cheese. Roll each slice up.

3. Place the veal rolls on skewers, alternating them with pieces of bay leaf and onion. Allow 3 veal rolls to a skewer.

4. Combine the bread crumbs with Parmesan cheese, garlic, parsley and a little salt and pepper. Mix well.

5. Pour the oil in a shallow dish and

18 small pieces of bay leaf
3 cups dry bread crumbs
1 cup grated Parmesan
   cheese
1 teaspoon garlic powder
Parsley
1½ cups olive oil

spread the bread crumbs on a plate. Dip the skewered meat in oil and then in bread crumbs. Place on a broiling rack in a roasting pan. Cook 10 to 15 minutes, turning the skewers occasionally and basting frequently with olive oil.

6. Serve the skewers on a heated platter, garnished with lemon juice and parsley.

SERVES 6

Bianco Mangiare

Pound cake
½ cup sugar
½ cup cornstarch
1 quart milk
1 teaspoon vanilla
   extract
1 teaspoon cinnamon
1 cup chocolate
   sprinkles
1 cup chopped pecans
½ cup maraschino cherries,
   chopped

Chocolate Sauce (optional)

1. Cut the cake into ½-inch slices and place one layer in the bottom of a 9-inch cake pan. Set aside.

2. Combine the sugar and cornstarch in a saucepan. Set over medium heat, add the milk gradually and cook, stirring, until the mixture comes to a boil and thickens. Remove from heat and stir in the vanilla and cinnamon.

3. Pour half the pudding over the sliced cake. Scatter over the pudding half the chocolate and half the pecans. Add another layer of cake, the rest of the pudding and the remaining chocolate and pecans. Top with the cherries and refrigerate.

4. Serve cold on chilled plates, with chocolate sauce if desired.

SERVES 10 TO 12

Jasper's Italian Restaurant

The waiter who recites the list of desserts at Jasper's is likely to add: "The chocolate cake's very good—my mother made it." He's Jasper Mirabile, Jr., 14, youngest of four Mirabile sons who don dress suits and help out at a restaurant that is truly a family affair. Mother Josephine Mirabile prepares some of the specialties with her own hands; others are from recipes she personally collects and tests. Father Jasper is father, founder and namesake.

Featured mostly on the menu are the great dishes of northern Italy and southern France. One, Fettuccine Pope John XXIII, is made from a recipe given to Jasper *père* by the late Pontiff's personal chef (it combines fettuccine, prosciutto, grated Parmigiano cheese, egg yolks, white wine, freshly whipped cream and butter; the final blending is done at tableside). Desserts include a delectable Brandy Alexander Mousse.

The foyer and dining areas at Jasper's are formally Italian; the new bar is informally American Modern under a rakishly tilted skylight. *Bere, mangiare bene*—that translates "Good eating and drinking."

405 WEST 75TH STREET, KANSAS CITY

Missouri

Brandy Alexander Mousse

½ pound semi-sweet
   chocolate bits
2 tablespoons cold water
1 tablespoon instant
   coffee
5 egg yolks
2 tablespoons brandy
2 tablespoons Crème de
   Cacao
5 egg whites

Topping:
½ cup heavy cream, whipped
2 teaspoons sugar
2 teaspoons ground
   almonds
2 teaspoons Kahlua
   (coffee liqueur)

1. In the top of a double boiler, heat and stir the chocolate bits, and the coffee mixed with the water until the mixture forms a smooth paste.

2. Beat the egg yolks until they are a pale lemon color. Add to the chocolate mixture and stir until well blended.

3. Add the brandy and Crème de Cacao and stir until the mixture begins to thicken. Pour into a bowl and let the mixture cool.

4. Beat the egg whites until stiff and fold carefully but completely into the cooled chocolate mixture.

5. Put the mixture into a pastry bag fitted with a medium-size fluted tip. Pipe the mixture into stemmed dessert glasses or into a pretty cocktail glass. Chill thoroughly in the refrigerator.

6. Whip the cream until thick. Add the sugar, almonds and the Kahlua liqueur. Continue whipping the cream until stiff enough to hold its shape. Spoon the cream over the mousse just before serving.

SERVES 6

Tony's

Like the Arch, Tony's restaurant is part of the modern spirit of St. Louis. With justifiable civic pride, Joe Pollack of the *St. Louis Post-Dispatch* proclaimed, "Tony's stands alone and far above anything in the area and will rank with the dozen or so finest eating places anywhere."

Tony's started in 1949 as a spaghetti house. Each year, owner Vincent Bommarito made improvements to the building and to the menu so that by the mid-50's, when he was joined by his brother Anthony, the "Spaghetti House" had evolved into a white-tablecloth, beautifully appointed restaurant serving notable Italian cuisine.

All service is conducted at tableside with exquisite silver dishes. As Vincent points out, everything must be geared to a "pleasant dining experience." Neither the menu nor the waiter must be intimidating. The staff is trained to put the dining party at ease, to ask "May I help you with the menu?" Friendly service makes the pasta appetizers, the large assortment of baby veal offerings and the seafood entrees even more enjoyable.

Today Vincent is almost always on hand to greet arriving patrons and make sure things go smoothly; the kitchen is under the capable supervision of Rico Lonati, his chef for 25 years. St. Louis wouldn't be St. Louis without them.

826 NORTH BROADWAY, ST. LOUIS

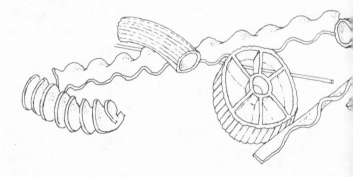

Tagliatelle con Pesce
(Noodles with Shellfish)

1 pound butter
1 cup fresh sliced
   mushrooms
1 large tomato, peeled,
   seeded and chopped
8 cups combination cooked
   crab meat, lobster
   and shrimp
½ cup chopped parsley
2 pounds Tagliatelle
   (fine noodles)
Salt and pepper

1. Bring a large kettle of salted water to boil for the pasta.

2. Meanwhile, prepare all the ingredients for the sauce.

3. Heat 8 tablespoons of butter.

4. Put the noodles in the boiling water, bring to a boil and cook 5 to 6 minutes or just until tender (al dente).

5. Simmer the mushrooms, tomato and seafood in the melted butter.

6. Strain the cooked pasta thoroughly and return to the kettle. Add the remaining butter and the seafood mixture. Stir and simmer 5 minutes. Season well and add the chopped parsley.

7. Serve on preheated plates.

SERVES 8

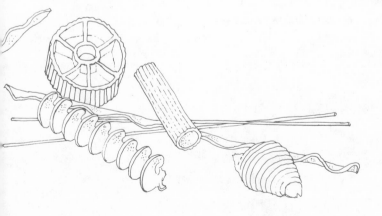

Au Père Jacques

Host Jack Schindler is a poacher. The dishes at his well-regarded restaurant have been "lifted" from all over the world. But why worry when the menu lists 34 different preparations of Dover Sole alone . . . and the recipes are handed down from the Mount Olympus of haute cuisine—from the great restaurant kitchens of Europe.

The Escargots Au Père Jacques were "stolen" from the famed Taillevent restaurant in Paris, a Dover Sole preparation from Wheeler's of London, Ecrevisse à la Crème from the Hôtel de la Poste in Beaune, that quaint town in Burgundy country. The Scampi Méditerranée came from the chef aboard the *Leonardo da Vinci*, the Veal in Cream with Dill from a Cologne kitchen, the Lobster Père Jacques from chef George Bise at Talloires on the shores of Lake Annecy. It says something for Schindler's enthusiasm and charm that he has been able to use these notable chefs as tutors and to strike up lasting friendships with all of them.

Perhaps his good humor can be traced in part to the computer he uses for the restaurant finances. It costs him over $10,000 per year to operate, but every night, before he has had time to lay a spoon to his soup, he has a masterly tally of all the day's transactions. Even if the figures, some nights, would make an ordinary man choke, they would not faze big Jack Schindler. After all, he's just paid $60,000 to reduce his seating from 120 to 80!

34105 CHAGRIN BOULEVARD, CHAGRIN FALLS

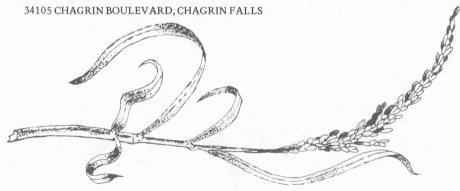

Poulet Portugaise
(Portuguese Chicken)

2 3-pound chickens, each
   cut into 6 pieces
Flour
1 cup chicken stock
1 clove garlic, minced
½ cup dry white wine
1 large Bermuda onion,
   chopped
1 red pepper, chopped
1 green pepper, chopped
3 tablespoons olive oil
3 tablespoons butter
1 tablespoon chopped
   parsley
½ teaspoon chopped fresh
   tarragon
½ teaspoon chopped basil
Pinch of thyme
Salt and pepper
4 ripe tomatoes, peeled,
   seeded and chopped
½ cup pitted ripe olives
½ cup stuffed green olives
2 cups sliced mushrooms
2 cups heavy cream
Rice pilaf (page 427)

1. Wash and dry the chicken pieces and dip each piece in seasoned flour.

2. Using a pressure cooker, make the cup of stock from the backbones, breast bones, wings and trimmings.

3. In an electric skillet or large iron skillet heat the butter and olive oil. The bottom of the pan should be covered by ⅛ inch. Brown the dark meat for a few minutes before adding the breasts. When all pieces are browned on all sides, add the crushed garlic clove and cover with the wine and chicken stock.

4. Add the onions, peppers and herbs. Cover and simmer for 10 to 15 minutes.

5. Add the tomatoes, olives and mushrooms and simmer slowly uncovered just until the vegetables are cooked.

6. At this point, the sauce should be fairly thick. If not, pour off all liquid except 1 cup.

7. Add the heavy cream, bring sauce to a boil and cook until very thick.

8. Serve on a bed of rice pilaf.
SERVES 4 TO 6

Gourmet Restaurant

Like Rome, Cincinnati spills over seven hills, and from the penthouse-like Gourmet Restaurant perched atop the Terrace Hilton you can view all seven and a slice of the mighty Ohio River for good measure. The riverfront is worth an extra look if the Cincinnati Reds are playing a home game, or if one of the stern-wheeler passenger boats—the *Delta Queen* or the *Mississippi Queen*—is docked to load passengers.

Inside, the view is only slightly less spectacular. Managing somehow to look at home in 20th-Century mid-America is a six-foot-in-diameter chandelier that Queen Victoria once presented to London's Army-Navy Club, and a pair of 12-candle terra-cotta sconces made for the palace at Versailles.

The food? Authentically French haute cuisine which has rated applause from restaurant critics ever since the doors opened for business. Jean-Paul Metaiguer is executive chef.

The restaurant is open for dinner only and can serve just 54 happy diners at a time with such delicacies as Potage Billi Bi, Lougoustine Fine Champagne, Le Carré d'Agneau aux Fines Herbes and Soufflés Tous Parfums.

15 WEST SIXTH STREET, CINCINNATI

Potage Billi Bi

4 pounds fresh mussels
1 medium-size onion,
  chopped fine
3 sprigs parsley
1 stalk celery, chopped
1 cup sliced carrots
⅛ teaspoon freshly
  ground black pepper
½ teaspoon thyme
1 cup dry white wine
2 cups water
1 cup fish velouté
½ cup whipping cream
Salt
Chopped parsley or chives

1. Rinse the mussels very well in a colander.

2. Put the mussels in a large kettle and add the vegetables, pepper and herbs, white wine and water.

3. Cover the kettle tightly and cook over high heat for 10 to 12 minutes, or until the shells open. Shake the kettle occasionally so that all the mussels will cook.

4. With a slotted spoon, transfer the mussels to another pan and keep warm.

5. Strain the broth through a very fine sieve or through 2 thicknesses of cheesecloth.

6. Shell the mussels.

7. Reduce the broth to almost half its original quantity. Add the velouté and bring to a boil. Remove from heat and add the cream. Season to taste with salt and pepper.

8. Serve in individual soup bowls, adding 2 to 3 hot mussels to each. Sprinkle with chopped parsley or chives.

SERVES 6

King Cole

W ith or without his fiddlers three, Old King Cole would have been a far merrier soul could he have stopped by Dayton's King Cole Restaurant to enjoy a flavorful steak or chop; there to dine in Old World and regal fashion, admiring the Gainsboroughs and Remingtons that adorn the walls while taking in the custom-scrolled French benches, quartered oak tables and chairs, pure Irish linen and elegant Wedgwood coin gold service plates.

But elegant though they may be, the appointments of the King Cole fade away when the meal arrives. From soup to nuts, from aperitif to after-dinner drinks, the food and beverage selections tempt and please the discriminating epicure. The choicest meats, distinctive seafoods, rare and unusual desserts, a wine list selected by experts and representing the most superb vintage wines of Europe—such are but a few of the many continental delights that await the diner. And, finally, when the last dish has been removed, you can sit back and call for your coffee—or, like King Cole, for your pipe and your bowl.

WINTERS' TOWER LOBBY, DAYTON

Chopped Chicken Livers

¾ pound hen livers
1½ teaspoons salt
½ cup rendered chicken
   fat
1 hard-cooked egg,
   finely chopped
1 teaspoon dry mustard
2 tablespoons minced
   onion

Place livers in a saucepan and add water to cover. Bring to a boil, reduce heat and simmer 15 minutes. Drain on paper towels, then mince finely in a food mill or blender. Add other ingredients, mix well, cool and refrigerate.

Serve on lettuce, garnished with tomato wedges and olives, and accompanied by dark rye bread or melba toast.

SERVES 6 TO 8 AS AN APPETIZER

Oyster Bisque

1 quart fresh oysters
2 cups chicken stock
    or broth
¼ small onion
1 cup finely sliced celery
4 whole cloves
Salt and white pepper
2 tablespoons sherry
4 cups scalded milk
2 tablespoons butter
Nutmeg

1. Shell the oysters, saving the juices.

2. Place the chicken stock in a saucepan with the oyster juice, onion, celery and cloves. Simmer for 25 minutes.

3. Strain the mixture through a fine sieve.

4. Add oysters and heat well. Add salt and pepper and sherry.

5. Just before serving, stir in the scalded milk and butter.

6. Serve in bouillon cups with a dash of nutmeg. Soda crackers should accompany the bisque.

SERVES 4 TO 6

Maisonette

The year is 1949—native Cincinnatian Robert A. Taft is still recovering from his defeat by Tom Dewey; sportsman-sheriff Dan Tehan has just begun a city-wide crackdown on gambling; and Nathan L. Comisar founds La Normandie-Maisonette, named after the old Maisonette Room in New York's St. Regis Hotel. Comisar began his business in a tiny basement hideaway. The Maisonette was a reflection of the more worldly appetites of Cincinnatians returning from the war.

By 1966, the owner's sons Lee and Michael had taken over the management, and Cincinnati Urban Renewal dictated a change in location. So in May of '66, the Maisonette opened at its present address, but the original hideaway charm remained. There one encounters little surprises of endless variety such as Quail with Fresh Pineapple and Curaçao—a gastronomic inspiration!

114 EAST SIXTH STREET, CINCINNATI

Salmis de Cailles aux Ananas *(Quails with Fresh Pineapple and Curaçao)*

1 large ripe pineapple
8 quail
4 tablespoons butter
4 tablespoons diced carrots
4 tablespoons diced celery
4 tablespoons diced onion
½ pound mushrooms, quartered

1. Cut off both ends of the pineapple. Cut the remaining pineapple in 4 equal slices. Peel the outer rind and, with a melon ball cutter, hollow out each piece of pineapple into pineapple balls, forming a shell. Do not pierce through the bottom. Reserve the pineapple balls and the juice.

2. Split the quails and remove the backbones. (Reserve backbones, necks, giblets and liver.)

3. Sprinkle the quails with salt and pepper. Sauté them in butter in an ovenproof skillet until golden brown. Remove the

Ohio

Sprig of thyme
1 bay leaf
¾ cup dry white wine
6 tablespoons Madeira
6 tablespoons Curaçao
1 cup veal stock
Salt and pepper
3 tablespoons sweet butter

quails with pincers and set aside. Preheat oven to 375 degrees F.

4. Add the vegetables, thyme, bay leaf and giblets and cook for 5 minutes. Pour off any excess butter.

5. Pour in the wine, Madeira, and half of the Curaçao, and cook over medium heat, scraping the bottom of the pan with a fork until the mixture boils. Place the quails back in the skillet, add the pineapple juice and the veal stock, and bring to a boil again. Cover the skillet and place in the oven for 15 minutes or until done.

6. Remove quail and place them in the pineapple shells. Add the pineapple balls. Keep warm in oven.

7. Quickly boil down the sauce to half its quantity. Season to taste and strain through a fine strainer. Add 3 tablespoons of sweet butter and the rest of the Curaçao. Stir until the butter melts. Do not boil. Pour the sauce over the quail.

SERVES 4

Le Bistro

Milwaukeans, it has been noted, habitually think in terms of convenience, so stocked is the downtown area with good food *and* good lodging. Visitors to the nation's beer capital quickly find that the best hotels and restaurants are within a short walk of each other. A prime example is the newly renovated Marc Plaza—a popular complex that includes 550 lavish guest rooms, three floors of convention facilities, a health club and Le Bistro—one of the city's finest and most preferred restaurants. Shops, theaters, galleries and the city's new MECCA Convention Center are within minutes. A short walk brings you to the world-renowned County Zoo, the Mitchell Park Conservatory, and the Milwaukee Performing Arts Center.

Le Bistro—which is, incidentally, an outstanding example of Art Deco—offers an extensive menu of Continental cuisine that has, since the restaurant opened a few years ago, pleased the particular palates of Milwaukee. Filet de Boeuf Tartare Garni (Steak Tartar), Le Dome d'Argent (Roast Prime Rib of Beef) and Le Carré d'Agneau à la Provençale (Rack of Spring Lamb) are all specialties of the house. The dining room features stained-glass windows, the best in concert piano, and complimentary hors d'oeuvres. The waiters, many of whom are college students, were each trained for six weeks before the room opened, taught the basics of fine service by Henry Schielein, the vice-president of hotel operations for the Marc Plaza and the also popular Hotel Pfister. Salads are prepared at tableside, prime rib carved from a rolling rib cart, cognac glasses brought to the proper serving temperature, as patrons look on.

509 WEST WISCONSIN AVENUE, MILWAUKEE

Stewed Chicken Hunter Style

1 3½-pound chicken, cut in 6 pieces

1. Wash and dry the chicken.
2. Heat the oil in a large skillet and sauté the onion, carrot and celery lightly. Add the chicken and brown over high heat, turning the chicken until golden brown on all sides.

Wisconsin

½ cup olive oil
1 onion, chopped
1 carrot, chopped
1 stalk of celery, chopped
2 tablespoons butter
¼ cup flour
¾ pound fresh mushrooms
Salt and pepper
2 cups dry white wine
2 medium-size tomatoes,
  peeled and sliced

3. Mix the butter and flour together with a fork until smooth. Stir into the sauce and, when blended, add the mushrooms, salt and pepper.

4. Add the wine and boil 3 minutes. Add the tomatoes. Bring to a boil, cover and reduce the heat. Simmer for at least 1 hour or until chicken is tender.

5. Transfer the chicken pieces to a heated platter. Taste the sauce for seasoning and pour over the chicken. Serve very hot.

SERVES 2

Veal Port au Prince

2 3-ounce portions of
  sliced veal
Flour
Salt and pepper
2 tablespoons butter
1 teaspoon finely chopped
  shallots
1 tablespoon sliced
  mushrooms
½ teaspoon chopped
  tarragon
¼ cup sherry
¼ cup chicken stock

1. Flatten the veal slices by pounding them gently between pieces of waxed paper. Dredge with flour and season with salt and pepper.

2. Melt the butter in a heavy skillet. Brown the slices of veal on both sides, then remove to a platter and keep warm.

3. Saute the shallots and mushrooms in the skillet, then add the tarragon, sherry and stock and cook, stirring with a fork, until the quantity is reduced by half.

4. Pour the sauce over the veal slices, garnish with lemon wedges and parsley. Serve at once.

SERVES 2

The English Room and Pub

Bringing out the most creative instincts of its chefs by naming the evening's main entree after the chef who prepared it is The English Room and Pub's unique way of bringing out the best in its culinary personnel. This is one of the gambits that has made the restaurant in the Pfister Hotel one of Milwaukee's favorite places to dine.

Dinner in the English Room takes on a theatrical aura, with an instrumental trio playing on weekends and a harpist strumming delicate melodies on weekday evenings. The setting is intimate but impressive; the walls are ornately papered and hung with rare 19th-Century oil paintings.

To supplement the more than 100 carefully chosen items on the wine list there is a "treasure barrel" for those seeking a taste discovery at prices meant to stimulate the most budget-minded of wine lovers.

Complimentary personalized matchbooks are a small dividend for those who make reservations in advance.

The numerous English Room specialties are listed on the regular menu and on a special gourmet one; especially recommended are the fresh Lake Michigan Whitefish, the Broiled Shropshire Lamb Chops and the Lobster and Pork Curry Bombay.

THE PFISTER HOTEL, 424 EAST WISCONSIN, MILWAUKEE

Lobster and Pork Curry Bombay

Pilaf Rice, seasoned
    with saffron (page 427)
4 shallots, diced
2 cups sliced, fresh
    mushrooms

1. Prepare the rice.
2. Sauté the shallots, mushrooms and pork in 4 tablespoons of butter until the pork is brown. Add the lobster meat, curry powder and white wine. Cook for 1 minute.
3. Add the fish velouté, cover and simmer 20 to 24 minutes. Halve and quarter the bananas and fry in the remaining butter.

Wisconsin

1 pound 2 ounces finely
  diced pork tenderloin
6 tablespoons butter
1 pound 2 ounces diced
  cooked lobster meat
4 tablespoons curry
  powder
4 tablespoons white wine
1¼ cups fish velouté
  (page 423)

Accompaniments:
3 bananas
Chutney sauce
Toasted coconut

4. To serve: Serve the curry accompanied
with the chutney sauce, fried bananas, toasted coconut and saffron rice.

SERVES 6

Strawberry Beignet

Beer batter:
12 ounces beer
 3 eggs
Pinch of salt
⅓ cup sugar
 1 cup flour

36 fresh strawberries
Flour
Confectioners' sugar

1. Prepare the batter: Separate the eggs
and whip the egg whites. In a mixing bowl,
beat the egg yolks until light. Add the beer,
salt, sugar and flour. Fold in the egg whites.

2. Dip 1 strawberry at a time in flour,
then in the beer batter. Fry in deep fat until
golden brown.

3. Dredge strawberries with confectioners' sugar and serve at once.

SERVES 6

Karl Ratzsch's

Milwaukee was once called the "Munich of America." So thoroughly had German culture been transplanted to the Wisconsin city, it remained only for men like Karl Ratzsch to cultivate the garden. Ratzsch's Old World Restaurant, which began operations more than 50 years ago, flowered with the atmosphere of the New World Germany—with sounds from lively beer gardens and homesick Germans singing lusty stein songs till the early hours of the morning.

Although the German character of the city has somewhat changed, Karl Ratzsch's little bit of Munich continues to thrive, giving many a German immigrant and other hungry patrons a nostalgic tour of the precious homeland complete with an unequaled collection of rustic Germanic dishes. The menu is divided into two parts: "New World Favorites" which include filet mignon, broiled African lobster tails, pork chops; and "Old World Suggestions" like Kassler Rippchen, Wiener Schnitzel, Hungarian Goulash and Schnitzel à la Holstein. Everywhere there are delightful antiques—heavy pewter platters, English copper mugs with elk-horn handles, wooden carvings, a meerschaum pipe as big as an alto saxophone. The bar displays an enormous collection of rare glassware—clear liqueur glasses, hearty two-fisted beer glasses. Above the taps are rows of beer steins, in all shapes and sizes—one in the form of a castle, another modeled after a Prussian soldier's head.

320 EAST MAIN STREET, MILWAUKEE

Karl Ratzsch's Hungarian Goulash with Potato Dumplings

2 pounds lean beef (bottom sirloin, butt or round)

1. Cut the meat into 1½-inch squares.
2. Sauté the onions in butter until transparent, not brown.
3. Add the meat, stir and cook together 5 minutes.
4. Sprinkle flour over the meat and stir until the flour disappears.

4 cups sliced onions
4 tablespoons butter
4 tablespoons flour
3 teaspoons salt
½ teaspoon pepper
3 cups beef stock
or bouillon
1½-2 tablespoons Hungarian
paprika

Potato dumplings:
1 large raw potato,
ground
½ small onion, ground
4 strips of bacon, diced
and fried
½ cup small croutons
2 eggs, slightly beaten
1 teaspoon chopped
parsley
1 cup flour
½ teaspoon salt
⅛ teaspoon pepper
⅛ teaspoon nutmeg
Melted butter

5. Add beef stock and just enough water to cover the meat. Add the salt and pepper and cover and bring to a boil.

6. Lower heat, stir in the paprika and simmer for 1½ hours or until tender.

7. Mix all the ingredients for potato dumplings.

8. Form into small balls about the size of an egg and simmer in boiling salted water for 30 minutes. Remove dumplings from water with slotted spoon.

9. Serve immediately topped with melted butter as an accompaniment to the goulash.

SERVES 6

Mader's German Restaurant

Mader's restaurant in Milwaukee began in the era of the "bucket boy"—when youths, toting boards carrying half a dozen buckets of frothy beer, offered daily refreshment to office workers, the beer capital's version of the coffee break. Then, the restaurant was called "The Comfort," an unpretentious little place with wooden chairs and oaken tables, owned by Charles Mader.

Prohibition struck in 1919, and Mader gave full attention to the varied collection of hearty, Germanic dishes served by his capable chefs. Sauerbraten, Wiener Schnitzel, German Potato Salad and pork shank quickly gained a wide reputation. When the tap was turned on once again, and beer flowed freely through the restaurants of Milwaukee, Mader's was credited with serving the first legal stein of beer in the city.

Today's $100,000 collection of medieval weaponry, displayed attractively about the "Armour Room," reflects the success that the restaurant has enjoyed over nearly 75 years of service. Magnificent hand-carved wooden murals grace the dining room walls. Here can be found all the beautiful charm of a castlelike Old Bavarian Inn.

1037 NORTH THIRD STREET, MILWAUKEE

Kartoffelsalat
(Potato salad)

 4 cups sliced freshly cooked potatoes
1¼ pounds bacon, diced
 ½ cup chopped onion
 ¼ cup sugar
 1 teaspoon salt
 2 tablespoons flour

1. Cook the potatoes without peeling. Drain, peel and slice while still warm.
2. Fry the bacon until crisp. Remove to paper toweling with a slotted spoon.
3. Pour off all but 2 tablespoons of bacon fat. Add the chopped onion and stir until the onion is transparent. Do not brown.
4. Add the sugar, salt and flour. Mix until blended. Add vinegar and water and cook until thickened.

½ cup cider vinegar
½ cup water
Chopped parsley
½ cup thinly sliced
     radishes (optional)

5. Add potato slices and bacon bits, folding very gently to avoid breaking the potato slices. Allow to stand in a 140-degree oven with the door open for 30 minutes, so potatoes will absorb flavor of the dressing.

6. Transfer to a warm serving dish and garnish with parsley and radishes.

Kummelroggenbrot
(Caraway Rye Bread)

2 cakes compressed
    yeast
2 cups lukewarm
    water
3 tablespoons dark
    molasses
3 tablespoons melted
    butter
3-3¼ cups sifted flour
2½ cups whole rye flour
3 teaspoons salt
2 tablespoons
    caraway seeds

Crumble yeast in a large mixing bowl and pour on water; add the molasses and melted butter. Mix flour and whole rye flour and add the salt and caraway seeds; add approximately half to the yeast mixture. Beat until smooth. Add the remaining flour mixture and knead until smooth and elastic to the touch, about 10 minutes. Place in a buttered bowl, cover and let rise in a warm place until double in bulk—about 1 hour. Turn out on a lightly floured board; divide into 2 equal parts and cover. Allow to rest for 10 minutes. Mold into round loaves; place on buttered pan. Allow to rise until double in bulk, about 1 hour. Bake in a preheated oven for 35 minutes at 400 degrees F.

The West

When Hollywood gave up one of its brightest luminaries to reign as Princess Grace over the principality of Monaco, a group of public-minded citizens of Beverly Hills got together to discuss the possibility of declaring the town a principality. The plan bogged down in an argument as to who should be the Crown Prince. Most favored the late Howard Hughes, but a vociferous faction opted for Mike Romanoff, the self-styled Russian prince from Illinois who had brought so much panache to cuisine in the West. After all, had not "His Highness" dubbed himself "one of the few authentic geniuses of the day"? Romanoff, like the West itself, was larger than life. The mountains, the deserts, the coastlines are so grand that they seem only ethereally connected to the globe. Romanoff, the supreme restaurateur, could be an actor among actors, like the Rockies chuckling at the competition. The West is so fantastic, it has to breed fantasy. And so Mike Romanoff, Prince of Beverly Hills, could cast a frozen stare at a reigning movie queen who had arrived at his restaurant on Rodeo Drive in slacks, and could peremptorily order her, "Go home and change your clothes at once. You are a disgrace to your profession, your town, and *my* restaurant."

That which seems apocryphal is, in the West, true. For high individualism and perfect talent can flourish side by side. The jesting on Rodeo Drive was lovable; the Chicken Romanoff and Omelette Sylvia (named after Romanoff's wife) were divine. In California and the surrounding states, elite restaurants surprise not only by the quality of their cuisine but by their uniqueness, whether it is a special decor or an engaging, informal atmosphere.

But in the final analysis, the West defies any generalization. The vastness does not numb; rather it breeds a vast progeny of delightfully fractious children, each wanting to be very much himself. Otherwise, how could San Francisco be so triumphantly a gastronome's city, how could Cannery Row live a second charmed life? The seas and the farmlands provide the bounty— to keep the "children" healthy.

Alexis Restaurant

"**C**ome with me to the Casbah" is an invitation not to be disregarded if the Casbah referred to is the picturesque red-and-gold cocktail lounge of the Alexis. Order a Cobra, made with Balkan plum brandy and served in an ornate brass cup, and sip it to the romantic music of a gypsy trio.

The Casbah is just one part of a restaurant complex that may be America's most beautiful; it is certainly one of the most lavishly decorated establishments in the country. The prevailing mode is Byzantine, but a banquet room that doubles as a discothèque on weekends is in the medieval style, as is the brick-arched wine cellar where parties as large as 18 may be seated in splendid tooled-leather armchairs around a refectory table.

If it all seems a bit like a stage set, that may be because the Alexis whose dream is realized here (Alexis Merab) was once an actor. He appeared in movies in his native Georgia—the Georgia that is part of the Russians' southland—before coming to the U.S. in 1947.

To design and decorate his showplace, Alexis imported from France one Serge Sussouni, an École des Beaux Arts graduate, who was responsible for several unusually beautiful eating places in Europe. Alexis' trust in him was not misplaced, and the oh's and ah's of guests arriving for the first time make it all worthwhile.

The menu is primarily French, but there are also specialties from Georgia and central Europe: Blinis, Stroganoffs, and so on.

1001 CALIFORNIA STREET, SAN FRANCISCO

Blinis à la Russe
(Russian Blinis)

1 cake compressed yeast
 or 1 envelope powdered
 yeast
2 cups lukewarm milk
3 egg yolks, beaten
½ cup buckwheat flour
½ cup white flour
½ teaspoon salt
1 pound Beluga Malasol
 caviar
½ cup sweet butter,
 melted
1 cup sour cream

1. Dissolve yeast in warm milk. Add beaten egg yolks, flour and salt. Mix well. Let rise in a warm place until doubled in volume.

2. Heat a lightly greased skillet and drop batter by the tablespoonful onto the skillet. Cook to golden brown on each side. Allow 2 thin pancakes about 4 inches in diameter per person. Stack on a pie plate in a warm oven until all the pancakes are cooked.

3. To serve: Place a pancake on a small serving dish, spread with melted butter and a thin layer of sour cream. Cover with another pancake, spread with melted butter and sour cream. Then top with 2 ounces of caviar, spreading evenly over sour cream. Repeat the process for each serving. Serve at once, while pancakes are still warm.

SERVES 8

Anthony's Star of the Sea

There are two ways to arrive at this restaurant—by land and by sea. There is a parking lot for cars, and a dock for the convenience of guests who arrive in their own boats. And what could make a pleasanter break in a day or weekend of cruising than stepping ashore to feast on Abalone Gourmet, Sole à l'Admiral, Deviled Crabs, or the succulent Charcoal Broiled Broadbill Swordfish?

Memo to meat lovers: Go elsewhere if you must have steaks or chops. Here is a seafood restaurant that serves seafood, period. It belongs to the Ghio family, fishermen for generations, who maintain their own fishing fleet to supply the finest "fruits of the sea" to their several restaurants. This one, facing San Diego's beautiful and busy bay, is their pride and joy. The view is a pageant of constant change and motion as planes and clouds trace patterns on the sky and ships and sails crisscross the blue-green sea.

The menu's accents are predominantly Italian (put on a bib and try Catherine Ghio's own cioppino), with the offerings richly varied. Where else can you order Squid Cutlets?

HARBOR DRIVE AND ASH STREET, SAN DIEGO

Charcoal Broiled Broadbill Swordfish

4-8 swordfish steaks
(8- to 12-ounce)

Marinating sauce:
1¼ cups garlic oil
(page 424)
1 pint catsup
2 tablespoons

1. Trim the skin from the swordfish steaks. Place steaks in a deep bowl.

2. Combine all the ingredients for the marinating sauce. Pour over the fish and marinate for several hours, turning the fish occasionally.

3. Cook the swordfish on a medium charcoal fire for about 20 minutes, turning the fish gently and basting each time with the marinade, using sprigs of parsley as a brush. Transfer to a heated platter. Serve garnished

Worcestershire sauce
3 tablespoons Dijon
  mustard
1 tablespoon Tabasco
¾ cup sherry
1 teaspoon monosodium
  glutamate
Juice of ½ lemon
2 drops of liquid smoke
Pinch of thyme
Salt and pepper

Poached Fish de Pesca

2 potatoes
4 10-ounce portions of
  whitefish, halibut,
  snapper or salmon
1 quart water
2 bay leaves
1 teaspoon pickling spice
¼ teaspoon salt
¼ teaspoon monosodium
  glutamate
4 tablespoons olive oil
1 teaspoon chopped
  parsley
1 lemon
Freshly ground pepper
Butter

with parsley. Rice pilaf (page 427) is an excellent complement to this dish.

SERVES 4 TO 8

1. Peel and quarter the potatoes. Cover with the water and bring to a boil. Add the bay leaves, spice, salt and monosodium glutamate. Add the fish. Cover and reduce heat. Simmer for 10 minutes.

2. Remove fish and potatoes to individual dishes or a large shallow casserole. Dribble the olive oil over the fish and potatoes and sprinkle with parsley, lemon juice and pepper. Serve with melted butter and lemon wedges.

SERVES 4

Au Relais

Sonoma is the home of Harold Marsden's Au Relais. Having outgrown his original building, he moved the restaurant just three years ago to an old farmhouse in Sonoma, saw to each step of the remodeling, and is today the proud owner of one of northern California's most spectacular French dining spots.

Resawn redwood and Art Deco, circular windows and a relaxing airy patio—the design comes close to Marsden's long-cherished dream of erecting a French country inn in California. There is stained glass, and beautiful iron work, but the greatest triumph is the food.

Marsden prepares the menu from the dishes of his repertoire, a collection of fine offerings accumulated over his many years as a chef in France, Switzerland and Alsace. The Seafood Bisque is extraordinary, as is the Moussaka, Cassoulet, and Tart Tatin, examples of what the Au Relais has picked up from chefs that Marsden visits overseas.

As for wines, a restaurant couldn't be situated in a better spot; the vineyards of Sonoma are responsible for producing some of the finest labels. And not too far down the coast are several other noted wine centers—Buena Vista and Simi.

691 BROADWAY, SONOMA

Clams or Mussels Poulet

2 dozen clams or mussels, thoroughly scrubbed
2 tablespoons chopped shallots
2 tablespoons chopped parsley
¼ teaspoon fresh marjoram

1. Place the clean shellfish in a saucepan. Add all the other ingredients except ½ of the heavy cream and egg yolks. Cook over high heat, allowing 20 minutes for clams and 5 minutes for mussels.

2. Remove the shellfish with a slotted spoon and place them on a platter. Remove the top shells. Strain the liquid through cheesecloth and boil it down by half.

2 tablespoons butter
1 cup dry white wine
1 cup heavy cream
2 egg yolks
½ teaspoon curry powder
  (optional)

3. Beat the yolks with the remaining cream and add very gradually to the cooking liquid. Whisk until thick but do not boil. Add the curry powder if desired.

4. Coat the shellfish with the sauce and brown quickly under a preheated broiler. Serve immediately.

SERVES 2

Compound Butter Café de Paris

4 shallots
Red wine
1 pound butter, softened
1 teaspoon brandy
1 teaspoon Dijon mustard
1 teaspoon horseradish
4 anchovy fillets, crushed
1 teaspoon parsley, chopped
Juice of 1 lemon
Few drops of Tabasco
Few drops of Lea & Perrins
1 teaspoon each: oregano,
   thyme and sage
Salt and pepper

Chop the shallots fine and place them in a small saucepan with red wine to cover. Cook, stirring, until the wine evaporates. Combine with the butter and all other ingredients and mix until evenly blended.

Shape into a roll, wrap in waxed paper and store in the refrigerator. Cut off bits or slices to use as needed.

Compound butter gives a delicious and distinctive flavor to steaks or chops—just cut off a thin slice and place it on the meat to melt and season it.

Aux Délices

"**A** place of deliciousness" is an appropriate name for this restaurant, which is widely known for the elegant pastries and desserts created in its kitchens. On Thursdays or weekends one can order Paris Brest, a memorable confection that unites almonds and hazelnuts in a sugary praline that is, in turn, combined with a creamy custard and feather-light pastry circles. On another evening try the strawberry tart. At all times Aux Delices offers fresh seafoods and fresh vegetables impeccably prepared.

Aux Délices is one of the best of many good restaurants that have appeared in Los Angeles suburbs in the last two decades. It was one of the first to locate on a stretch of Ventura Boulevard that subsequently became known as Restaurant Row. The competition does not worry host Roger Martine or chef Marcel Frantz as their fairly small and not-at-all-pretentious restaurant has earned a reputation that brings eager diners from all parts of Los Angeles and its sprawling suburbs to their door.

15466 VENTURA BOULEVARD, SHERMAN OAKS

Paris Brest (Cream Puff Cake Praliné)

Praline:
½ cup peeled almonds
½ cup hazelnuts
½ cup sugar
 cup water

Cream Puff Pastry:
½ cup water
3 tablespoons butter
½ cup flour
2 eggs
1 egg, slightly beaten

1. Prepare the praline: Preheat the oven to 375 degrees F. Place the nuts on a baking sheet and bake until light brown. Combine the sugar and water in a saucepan and cook until light brown. Add the nuts and continue to cook until dark brown. Pour into a pie tin and allow to harden. Break into pieces and pulverize in a blender.

2. Prepare cream puff dough: Bring the water and butter to a boil. Add the vanilla and remove from the heat. Add the flour all at one time and stir until well blended. Put the pan back on the heat and cook for 3 minutes or until the dough is almost dry and no longer sticks to the pan. Transfer to a

½ cup sliced almonds
Granulated sugar

Filling:
⅓ cup sugar
2 whole eggs
2 egg yolks
1 teaspoon vanilla extract
½ cup flour
1 teaspoon gelatin
1 cup milk
1 tablespoon butter
4 egg whites, beaten stiff

½ pint whipping cream
½ teaspoon vanilla
Confectioners' sugar

mixing bowl and add the 2 eggs one at a time, beating hard after each addition.

3. Place the dough in a pastry bag fitted with a plain ½-inch tip. Lightly flour a baking sheet and outline a circle by placing an 8-inch saucepan cover in the center. Trace the circle with the dough, joining the ends. Put an inner circle of dough just inside the first, and a third ring on top, where the two join. Brush the entire surface with the beaten egg. Sprinkle with sliced almonds and granulated sugar. Bake 1 hour at 375 degrees F.

4. Prepare the filling: Combine sugar, eggs, egg yolks and vanilla in a mixing bowl. Beat vigorously and then beat in flour. Stir the gelatin into the cold milk and bring to a boil. Pour into the egg mixture, beating constantly. Cook over moderate heat, stirring constantly, until mixture thickens. Add the butter. Pour into a bowl, mix in half the praline and fold in the egg whites. Allow to cool.

5. To assemble: Cut the pastry ring in two, horizontally. Fill bottom half with the filling. Whip the cream, sweeten it to taste and fold in the vanilla and the remaining praline. Spread over the filling. Put the other pastry ring on top and sprinkle with confectioners' sugar. Refrigerate until time to serve.

SERVES 8

La Bella Fontana

The Beverly Wilshire is one of the world's great hotels. Which means a room there is like a room in a house where the host has nothing to do but make you comfortable. The new wing of the hotel is a joyous Mexican festival; the older part, like one of those marvelous silent film stars you see driving around Beverly Hills in a narrow, high Rolls-Royce, the back seat full of memories and well-maintained glamour.

La Bella Fontana is the jewel of the hotel's restaurants. The fountain from which the restaurant takes its name is in the center of the room and perfectly appropriate with a cherub perched atop. Hand-carved and gilded lighting fixtures give a rich glow to the velvet-covered walls.

Bouillabaisse on Friday is a never-failing delight. Godiveau Périgourdine (forcemeat served with Périgord sauce), redolent with truffles, is a great classic, an education in the possibilities of French cooking. Salmon braised in Riesling is another specialty to make you remember the proximity of California to the cold rivers of the north.

9500 WILSHIRE BOULEVARD, BEVERLY HILLS

Godiveau *(Forcemeat with Périgord Sauce)*

1½ pounds veal
¾ pound lean pork
¾ pound boned chicken
  breasts, skinned
2 ounces truffles,
  chopped
Salt and pepper
⅓ cup heavy cream
2 tablespoons cognac
2 egg whites, beaten
  stiff
Fresh white bread crumbs
6 tablespoons clarified
  butter (page 420)

Périgourdine Sauce:
2 cups brown sauce
  (page 418)
4 tablespoons Madeira
  sauce
2 truffles, sliced
1 tablespoon butter

1. Put the meats through the finest blade of a meat grinder twice or puree in a food processor.

2. Place the mixture in a bowl, add the truffles, cream, cognac and egg whites. Mix well and taste for seasoning.

3. Divide the mixture into 6 parts and mold each one into the shape of a veal chop.

4. Coat each one with bread crumbs.

5. Preheat oven to 425 degrees F. Heat the clarified butter in an ovenproof skillet.

6. Sauté the "chops" until golden brown on the underside. Turn the meat over and place the pan in the oven. Bake 15 minutes.

7. Meanwhile, make Périgourdine sauce: Boil down the brown sauce until very thick, add the Madeira, truffles and butter. Heat but do not boil. Taste for seasoning.

8. To serve: Place the meat on a heated platter and pour a little of the sauce over it. Accompany with the rest of the sauce in a sauceboat, wild rice and the vegetable of your choice.

SERVES 6

Blue Boar Inn

San Francisco's Lombard Street is named for a famous thoroughfare in London's financial district, so it's an appropriate address for a restaurant conceived in the spirit of an English pub. On the ground floor are 19th-Century leaded-glass windows representing the coats-of-arms of British cities: Liverpool, Glasgow, Sheffield and Birmingham. Old sporting prints of hunting and racing scenes hang beneath a Tudor ceiling that copies one in a 16th-Century English manor house. Upstairs, high-ceilinged, oak-paneled rooms offer settings of baronial splendor for private parties.

All this is the creation of Brian Weatherhill, who styles himself "Governor," and Bernhard Jansen, "Host and Master of Decor." Jansen is from Holland, and his special contribution is the bar, hung with blue Dutch tiles and Delft plates and lighted by a Dutch chandelier.

From Executive Chef Henri Bot's kitchen comes a balanced fare of English and Continental specialties. There are Beef Wellington and London Mixed Grill, Rack of Lamb and Orange Duckling. And steaks and succulent seafoods, served with or without the appropriate French sauces.

The wine cellar contains some 6,000 bottles, among them such collectors' items as a jeroboam of Château Lafîte 1961.

Anglophiles find at the Blue Boar Inn a home-away-from-home on the shores of the blue Pacific. Hail Britannia!

1713 LOMBARD STREET, SAN FRANCISCO

Potted Shrimp

10 tablespoons finely chopped shallots
½ cup dried tarragon leaves
Pinch of cayenne

1. Sauté the shallots, tarragon and cayenne in 5 tablespoons of butter without browning. Remove from the heat and cool to lukewarm.

2. Whip in the remaining butter and, when the mixture is creamy, add the shrimp which should be at room temperature.

10 tablespoons butter
 1 pound cooked shrimp
Salt

3. Mix well so that the shrimp is well coated with butter. Place in a jar, cover and refrigerate for several hours.

4. Arrange on a bed of dressed shredded lettuce, garnished with lemon wedges, and serve with toast.

SERVES 4 AS AN APPETIZER

Coquille Pacifique (Seafood Curry)

Sauce:
 4 tablespoons butter
 1 large onion, diced
 1 apple, diced
 4 tablespoons shredded coconut
 4 tablespoons strong Indian curry powder
 ½ cup flour
 2 quarts fish stock (page 423)

2½ pounds cooked king crab legs
 2 pounds cooked scallops
1½ pounds cooked shrimp
Cayenne, ginger, salt

1. Prepare the sauce: Sauté onions in melted butter until soft but not brown. Add apple and coconut. Remove from heat and blend in flour and curry. Cook on low heat for a few minutes stirring occasionally. Add the fish stock, bring to a boil and simmer 20 to 25 minutes.

2. Place the seafood in large saucepan. Strain the sauce over it, then bring to a boil. Season to taste with cayenne, ginger and salt.

3. Serve over rice pilaf (page 427) with condiments and Major Grey's Chutney on the side.

SERVES 8 GENEROUSLY

Blue Fox Restaurant

It's almost a rule of thumb that the finest restaurants in the Bay area are found in dim alleys or off main thoroughfares. So it was with some concern that the management at The Blue Fox saw the city morgue and city-county jail move away from the other side of dark and dingy Merchant Street. The more eerie the scene without, the better is set off the warmth and splendor within. There's a feel for "the good old days," when the Pony Express terminated only a block away; or, in this century, when a great boxer like James J. Jeffries and a great criminal lawyer like John J. Taafe used the restaurant as their headquarters.

Out of the darkness and the fog, you step into the elegance, the brilliance of the Palatina Room with its Roman Ionic columns, Directoire chairs—and an English silver serving cart, cosing $3,000. Then there's the Lafayette Room with its early American scenes—and the Hunt Room. More spectacular are the private dining rooms: the wine cellar where one dines before Venetian lace and silver candelabra, surrounded by 300 varieties of wines, many of them collector's items. In the champagne room, the chairs change from Napoleonic Era high-backs to 18th-Century Florentine. And here, for a touch of local history, the beams date back to the 1906 earthquake and fire.

The Blue Fox serves quality Continental cuisine, the quality extending even to the dinner plates of elegant china, with royal blue trim and a fox's head in the center.

659 MERCHANT STREET, SAN FRANCISCO

California

Tomato Timbale with Broccoli à la Blue Fox

6-8 medium-size, very cold tomatoes

Broccoli Filling:
- 4 tablespoons butter
- 1 teaspoon chopped shallots
- ¼ cup flour
- ½ teaspoon chopped sweet basil
- ¼ teaspoon nutmeg
- ½ cup sherry
- ½ cup chicken broth
- 12 ounces chopped, cooked broccoli

Salt and pepper

1. Dip the cold tomatoes in boiling water and peel. Slice ¼ inch from the bottom. Scoop out the center, removing as much excess moisture as possible. Place each tomato in a 5-ounce fluted jelly or brioche mold. Lacking these, use large custard cups. Press down with the palm of the hand. Sprinkle each tomato with salt and pepper.

2. Make the broccoli filling: Heat butter in a small skillet. Sauté the shallots or onions until tender but do not brown. Remove from the heat, stir in ½ cup of flour, add basil and nutmeg and mix together into a paste. Put back on the heat, add the sherry and chicken broth. Cook for 1 minute, stirring well till mixture thickens. Add chopped, cooked broccoli (fresh or frozen) and mix well. Let cool 2 or 3 minutes. Taste for seasoning.

3. Spoon stuffing into tomatoes. Place the molds in a pan of water and bake for 25 minutes at 350 degrees F.

4. To serve: Arrange the molds on a serving platter and garnish with sprigs of parsley. This may also be used as a garnish for beef or lamb.

SERVES 6 TO 8

La Bourgogne

"**T**he restaurant which sets the standard for the whole city of San Francisco," says one professional gourmand. "Sophisticated travelers usually put it in any listing of the top ten restaurants in the world," says another.

These tributes to La Bourgogne reward owner Jean Lapuyade's unswerving devotion to classic French cuisine, meticulously presented in a setting that is quietly elegant rather than ostentatious. The carpet is royal blue, the walls champagne and gold. Antiqued mirrors reflect the sparkle of crystal chandeliers and wall sconces. There are fresh roses on the tables.

From the kitchens of chef Louis Marticorena flow delectable entrees of veal, lamb, Dover sole—and authentic Parisian desserts like the Soufflé Grand Marnier.

Great food makes a restaurant great, and cuisine of a remarkably high standard has been responsible for the success of this one since its opening in 1961.

320 MASON STREET, SAN FRANCISCO

Marinated Roast Rack of Lamb with Chestnut Puree

1 rack of lamb (6 chops)
1 carrot, sliced
1 medium onion, sliced
2 shallots, chopped
6 peppercorns
4 sprigs of parsley
¼ teaspoon powdered thyme

1. Place the rack of lamb, trimmed free of all fat and tendons, into a deep earthenware dish which has a layer of half the vegetables on the bottom. Sprinkle with salt, the remaining vegetables, the crushed peppercorns, parsley, thyme and bay leaf. Pour in the red wine and finally pour the oil over the meat to prevent the top from becoming dark. Keep in the refrigerator for 24 hours, turning the meat occasionally.

2. Shortly before cooking the lamb, make the chestnut puree: Combine the

1 bay leaf
½ teaspoon salt
2½ cups dry red wine
6 tablespoons oil
2 tablespoons butter

Chestnut puree:
2 cups peeled chestnuts
½ stalk celery
2 sprigs parsley
½ bay leaf
¾ cup beef bouillon
Water
2 tablespoons butter
Salt and pepper

Bordelaise sauce (page 418)

chestnuts, celery, parsley, seasoning, bouillon and enough water to cover the chestnuts. Simmer for about 45 minutes or just until tender. Drain, remove the celery and herbs and spin in a food processor or force through a food mill. Season with salt and pepper and keep warm in a double boiler.

3. Make the Bordelaise sauce.

4. Remove the meat from the marinade and wipe it dry. Brown lightly in a skillet using 2 tablespoons of butter and 2 tablespoons of oil. Transfer the meat to a 425-degree oven; roast 15 minutes. Reduce heat to 375 degrees and cook 10 to 15 minutes longer.

5. Take 6 tablespoons of the marinade and boil it down to 2 tablespoons. Add 1 cup of Bordelaise sauce and simmer for 2 minutes.

6. To serve: Place the meat on a serving platter and carve at the table. Cover each serving with Bordelaise sauce and serve with the chestnut puree.

SERVES 2

The Carnelian Room

"**E**ast is East, and West is San Francisco, according to Californians," wrote O. Henry, and one of the dramatic spots in which to experience the city is the Carnelian Room atop (52nd floor) the Bank of America Center at 555 California Street.

Unlike Sandburg's catlike fog of Chicago, San Francisco's four o'clock phenomenon churns its way inland with rolling turbulence and natives, as well as visiting guests, come to see the show. By day the Carnelian Room serves as a private Bankers' Club wherein city money handlers look down on their domain while lunching in exclusivity; after business hours candles in the Room are lit, the lights of the city begin to glitter, and the public arrives for a 360-degree view of the Bay area and some of the finest Continental dining in the country.

The cuisine is properly haute under the direction of Chef Wolfgang Schweinberger. The menu, French in concept, changes three times a year, and includes California classics—shrimp, Olympia oysters from Washington, Pacific salmon when in season—all prepared with the superb professionalism of "Davre's" restaurants. Strawberries Carnelian (prepared with Port, Madeira, and Armagnac) is a house favorite.

Floor to ceiling glass walls at that height add a spacy exhilaration to French antiques and furnishings. Carnelian-red tables are divided by glass cases of fine china and objets d'art. An enormous glassed-in wine cellar keeps rare vintages under the watchful eye of Master Sommelier Lawrence de Vries.

O. Henry and Sandburg would be pleased with the setting.

BANK OF AMERICA CENTER, 555 CALIFORNIA STREET, SAN FRANCISCO

Noisettes D'Agneau Henri *(Médaillons of Lamb)*

1. Ask your butcher to cut 12 4-ounce steaks (médaillons) from lamb racks. Ask him to give you 2 pounds of the bones.

Lamb sauce:

- 2 pounds lamb bones
- 4 tablespoons cooking oil
- 1 cup chopped onion
- 1 cup chopped carrots
- 1 cup chopped celery
- 2 whole tomatoes, quartered
- 1 tablespoon tomato paste
- 1 quart beef stock or bouillon
- 12 artichokes (canned artichoke bottoms can be substituted)

- 3 pounds boneless lamb fillet
- ¼ pound butter
- 2 teaspoons chopped shallots
- ½ cup dry white wine
- ½ cup chopped fresh tarragon
- 3 tablespoons goose liver pate, diced
- 5 tablespoons diced fresh tomatoes

Cooked asparagus

Small boiled potatoes

2. Lamb sauce: Brown lamb bones in oil in a large skillet. Add the vegetables and tomato paste. Stir well and cook for 2 minutes. Add the beef stock and boil for 10 minutes. Strain and skim off any excess fat.

3. Artichoke bottoms: Remove the stems and hard leaves and cut off the top third of each artichoke; boil them in salted water 25 minutes. Remove the remaining leaves and scoop out the prickly choke with a spoon. Keep the artichoke bottoms warm.

4. Médaillons: Heat 2 tablespoons of butter in a skillet and sauté 6 lamb steaks, browning both sides until medium rare. Transfer the steaks to a heated platter and keep warm. Repeat the process with the remaining steaks and transfer to the same platter.

5. Add the shallots and white wine, lamb sauce and tarragon to the pan, stir well and simmer for 30 minutes. Add remaining butter and diced pâté to the sauce. Remove from the heat.

6. To serve: Place hot artichoke bottoms on a large silver platter. Fill each one with diced tomatoes and top with médaillons of lamb. Spoon a tablespoon of the sauce over each one. Garnish with hot asparagus and small boiled potatoes and serve with side dishes of lamb sauce and Hollandaise.

SERVES 6

Chasen's

There's no mystery about the reputation of Chasen's. The answer is simply fine cuisine, fine service. That's why the Wizard of Whodunits, Alfred Hitchcock, has been coming to this restaurant for the past 30 years, one Thursday after another. Seated before his evening repast, Hitch, as he is known to his familiars, indulges in his customary exuberant pose, a coverup for a very sly wit. He holds a glass of translucent Pouilly-Fuissé Latour (1974 vintage) to the light and confesses to his old friend Maude Chasen, widow of the restaurant's founder and present proprietor: "This isn't wine at all! I've just killed seventeen people and the police are on their way to get me. But they won't." He raises the glass to his lips, and remarks, after a suitable cliff-hanging pause: "I'm drinking cyanide . . . ."

Hitchcock relaxes before his evening meal. Maître d' Ronald Quint, who has been waiting on the Hitchcocks for 21 of their 30 years' patronage, has prepared for the maestro strained barley soup, followed by breaded veal cutlet, hash browns and a dessert of vanilla ice cream topped with a strawberry sauce. The superb fare plus the attention is enough to make Chasen's Hitch's prime solace when he is in Hollywood. (And here is a diner who has 1,200 bottles of wine in his own cellar.)

As the meal draws to a close, the famous client muses over those scenes in *Frenzy* with Vivien Merchant cooking one gourmet recipe after another for an unappreciative husband. Then comes the afterthought: "I want to know, I really want to know, why do they always serve stew in Westerns?" Chasen's serves, instead, Chili, Hobo Steak and a very special Peperonata.

9039 BEVERLY BOULEVARD, LOS ANGELES

Spinach Salad

2-3 cups raw spinach
4 slices bacon

Wash the spinach well and remove stems. Fry the bacon crisp and chop or crumble into small bits. Reserve 2 tablespoons hot bacon fat.

Vinaigrette Sauce
(page 428)
Lea & Perrins sauce
Freshly ground black pepper

Toss the spinach with a little French dressing, the bacon and bacon fat, a dash of Lea & Perrins sauce, and pepper to taste.

SERVES 2

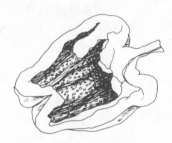
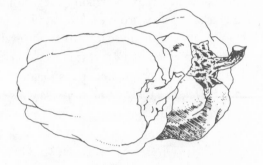

Chasen's Peperonata
(Pepper Steak)

2 pounds sirloin steak
1 medium onion, sliced thin
4 tablespoons sweet butter
1 green pepper, seeded and sliced thin
4 large mushrooms, sliced thin
1 medium-size can red pimientos (4½ ounces)
2 tablespoons cooking oil
2 tablespoons sherry
2 tablespoons chives

1. Cut steak into small, thin squares, approximately 1 inch in diameter.

2. Sauté the onions in 2 tablespoons of butter for 2 minutes. Add the peppers, mushrooms, pimientos and continue cooking for 2 to 3 minutes. Remove from the heat.

3. Sauté the beef in the oil and remaining butter, using a high heat. When it is browned, add the vegetables, sherry and the chives. Season to taste with salt and pepper. Serve immediately.

SERVES 4 TO 6

La Chaumière

La Chaumière—"the cottage"—a fitting name for this cozily appointed rustic French restaurant, almost an anachronism among the luxuries and glitter that spell Beverly Hills.

Yet a visit here is like taking a tour of the French countryside. Photographs of the actual Normandy region have been enlarged and hand-painted to create the view from each window; linens, specially ordered and imported from France, enhance each table, preserving that all-important air of authenticity; and when a guest tastes chef Georges E. Peyre's splendid entrees, he will wonder if, perchance, he is magically being transported to the land of *la tour Eiffel*, to a real *"chaumière française."*

207 SOUTH BEVERLY DRIVE, BEVERLY HILLS

Sole Soufflée

- 6 ounces fresh sea bass or other ocean whitefish
- 1 egg white
- 1¾ cups fresh cream
- 4 Dover sole, 14 ounces each, skinned and boned
- 2 tablespoons sweet butter
- 1 tablespoon finely chopped shallots
- 1¾ cups Champagne Brut

1. Prepare the stuffing: Force the sea bass free of skin and bones twice through the food grinder, using the finest blade, or puree in a food processor. Force the fish through a fine strainer and place in a small mixing bowl. Place the mixing bowl in a larger bowl containing crushed ice. Beat in the egg white and a little salt and pepper. Still beating rapidly, add 1 cup of fresh cream and continue to beat until the mixture becomes light and fluffy. Chill in the refrigerator.

2. Ask the butcher to remove the backbone of the fish, leaving the fish intact and forming a pocket for the stuffing. Prepare the Hollandaise and keep it warm.

½ cup Hollandaise sauce
(page 424)
1 truffle

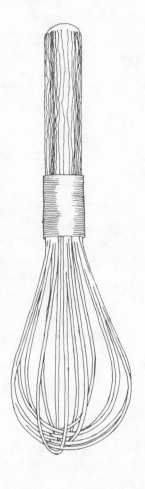

3. Spread the butter and the shallots on the bottom of a flat pan, large enough to hold the 4 fish. Place the fish in the pan and season with salt and pepper.

4. Put the stuffing in a pastry bag fitted with a small fluted tip. Pipe the stuffing into the fish.

5. Pour the champagne on top of the fish, cover and cook over medium heat for 6 minutes. Remove from heat and leave covered for 6 more minutes.

6. Remove the fish from the pan with a wide spatula to a clean towel and blot dry. Place the pan over high heat and let the liquid cook until reduced by one third. Add the remaining cream and whisk until thick. Remove from the heat and add the Hollandaise sauce. Season to taste.

7. Place the fish on serving plates. Strain the sauce directly onto the fish and place 4 thin slices of truffle on the center of each.

SERVES 4

Chez Cary

This long-established restaurant, close to the ocean and an easy 75-minute drive from Los Angeles and San Diego, is under the expert guidance of Mary Louise Frazier and chef Fred Hossli. The decor is brightly inviting: red velvet high-back chairs, flocked wallpaper, white linens, chimney-style napkins and high-class crystal. The accent is on service, as a captain and two waiters attend each table, seeing to the final perfection of the flambéed entrees and desserts. (Such pampering even extends to footstools for the ladies.)

The French traditional menu is characterized by succulent surprises, such as Abalone Sauté Doria, tender abalone garnished with glazed cucumber; or Suprême de Poulard Sauté Cyntia, breast of capon, sautéed with grape, orange and avocado slices.

571 SOUTH MAIN STREET, ORANGE

Poitrine de Poularde Bombay (Breast of Capon in Curry)

¼ pound butter
½ onion, chopped
1 cup chopped celery
2 apples, peeled and
  chopped
3 bananas, sliced
Curry powder
1 quart chicken stock
  (page 419)
2 tablespoons soft butter
2 tablespoons flour

1. Melt 4 tablespoons of butter in a skillet. Sauté the onions, celery, apples and bananas until the onions are tender. Add 2 teaspoons of curry powder and the chicken stock to the skillet.

2. Bring to a boil and simmer. Blend the flour and butter. Drop them in small portions into the sauce, whisking until the sauce starts to thicken. Season to taste and simmer for 1 hour.

3. Dust the capon breasts in flour. Sprinkle with salt, pepper and a little curry powder.

4. Sauté the breasts in the remaining butter until golden but not brown on both sides.

8 large capon breasts
Flour
½ cup white wine (Chablis)
½ cup pineapple juice
4 pineapple slices
 (canned)
½ cup whipping cream
Toasted coconut
Rice pilaf (page 427)
Chutney

5. Add the white wine, curry sauce, sliced bananas and pineapple. Simmer 15 minutes.

6. Place the capon breasts in a deep platter or shallow baking dish and garnish with pineapple slices and bananas taken from the sauce with a slotted spatula.

7. Blend the cream gently into the sauce and pour over the capon. Brown quickly under the broiler. Sprinkle with toasted coconut and serve with rice pilaf and chutney.

SERVES 8

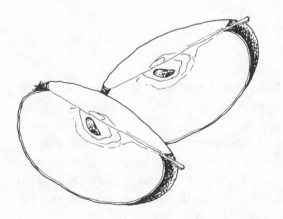
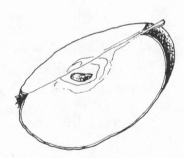

Doros

The rugged gray stone structure that houses this restaurant was part of the famed Barbary Coast in the gay, bad old days of San Francisco's youth. Solidly built, it survived the earthquake to house a winery up until Prohibition. Then, in more sober days, it contained a printing plant. After World War II, more changes. The neighborhood, rejuvenated as a center of shops and interior designers, prospered. Doros opened its doors, and again there are laughter, wine, and well-dressed people enjoying an evening out—albeit in more conservative fashion than those who drank, danced and dined here before the turn of the century.

"We call our menu 'Continental Cuisine,' but in truth it is world cuisine," says owner Don Dianda. "Food knows no boundaries." Chef Paul Bermani, like Dianda, is a native of Italy, but he prepares dishes from all over the world, and the menus change frequently. As a matter of fact, if a guest comes in and asks for a dish not on the bill of fare at the moment, chef Bermani will make it for him.

"We seek to provide the kind of food our customers enjoy," says Bermani. So there is Russian Breast of Chicken à la Kiev, French Medallion of Beef Tenderloin Pompadour, Italian Saltinbocca à la Romana with Risotto, and that uniquely American combination, Steak and Lobster. All delicious!

714 MONTGOMERY STREET, SAN FRANCISCO

Breast of Chicken à la Kiev

2 large chicken breasts,
  boned and halved
Salt and pepper
¼ pound butter
Flour

1. Trim the skin and flatten each chicken breast gently between sheets of wax paper, using a small mallet. Season with salt and pepper.

2. Divide the butter in half and shape it into rolls three inches long and approximately one inch in diameter. Lay the roll of butter on the flattened breast and roll the

2 eggs, slightly beaten
1 quart vegetable oil
½ cup fine white bread
   crumbs
2 cups heavy cream
½ cup sour cream
2 cups cooked rice
   (page 426)

meat tight around the butter. Dip the rolled breast in flour, then in the beaten eggs and in the bread crumbs.

3. Preheat the vegetable oil to ‹370 degrees F. Fry the chicken breasts for approximately 9 minutes or until golden brown.

4. Make the sauce: Boil the cream and remove from the heat. Add the sour cream and whisk until well blended. Season with salt and pepper.

5. To serve: Pour the sauce into a heated deep platter. Set the chicken on the sauce. Garnish with rice and serve immediately.

SERVES 2

Risotto with Mushrooms à la Doros

4 tablespoons butter
1 large onion, chopped
2 cups sliced mushrooms
1 cup rice
2½ cups chicken broth
Dash of saffron
Salt and pepper
¼ cup minced prosciutto
   (Italian ham)
6 tablespoons grated
   Parmesan cheese

1. Sauté the onion in butter until soft and lightly browned. Add mushrooms and cook for 5 minutes.

2. Add the rice and stir until it is impregnated with butter. Add the chicken broth, dash of saffron, salt and pepper to taste. Bring to a boil, cover, reduce heat and simmer gently 20 to 25 minutes or until rice is nearly done.

3. Add minced prosciutto, stir and cover.

4. Just before serving, mix in the Parmesan cheese.

SERVES 2

Empress of China

Housed in splendid surroundings atop the China Trade Center, this luxurious eating place occupies two whole floors, from whose eminence guests may cast an imperious eye over the city and Bay. The classic beauty of the architecture reflects the Han era of 206 B.C., set off by silk-brocade walls, antique palace chandeliers, gilt and teak carvings and imperial peacock feathers. The upstairs entrance is an actual garden court housed in a wide pavilion modeled after one in the royal park in Peking. The bar has that carry-me-back-to-China feel, with its windows lined with traditional goldfish aquariums.

Featuring the distinctive cuisine of all China (not just Cantonese) the Empress harks back to the age of the Five Emperors some 4,500 years ago. Delectable appetizers from the Dowager's court are being served for the first time, and even an American dish, Chicken Li Hung Chang, has royal connections. Lord Li Hung Chang, China's first ambassador to the United States, was able to sample the delicacy in America, and later spirited the recipe into the royal household back home.

But not all the dishes are regal; there's room for the simple home-style offerings. Country broth is available alongside the more exotic brews of the good women of Szechwan, sizzling rice soup from Shanghai, Peking's bird's nest soup and Canton's shark's fin soup. The menu is as populous as the nation from which it comes.

838 GRANT AVENUE, CHINATOWN, SAN FRANCISCO

Empress Sai See Gai (Chicken Salad)

1 3-pound whole chicken
4 tablespoons best-grade Chinese soy sauce
4 tablespoons oyster sauce

1. Wash the chicken and hang it up until very dry. Fry in hot deep fat (370 degrees) until brown and cooked through.

2. Mix the soy sauce, oyster sauce, sugar, oil and honey in a bowl. Do not refrigerate. Cut the onions into 2-inch-long shreds. Cut lettuce into shreds.

1 tablespoon sugar
1 tablespoon sesame oil
1 tablespoon honey
4 green onions (scallions)
1 small heart of crisp
  lettuce
1 bunch Chinese parsley
¼ pound chopped almonds,
  toasted
¼ pound fried Chinese fun
  see (Chinese vermicelli)

3. Chop the parsley and toast the almonds.

4. Deep fry the fun see for 1 minute. Cut the meat off the bones and cut flesh into thin strips with a sharp knife.

5. Mix the shredded chicken first with the sauce and then add the onions, parsley, chopped almonds, fried fun see and the lettuce. Toss well and serve with white rice.

SERVES 4

Empress Beef

½ pound sirloin steak
Vegetable oil
3 stalks celery
1 large white onion
1 small can button
  mushrooms
½ small can water chestnuts
¼ pound snow peas (or
  French-cut green beans)
1 tablespoon cornstarch
5 tablespoons best-grade
  Chinese soy sauce
½ tablespoon sugar
½ cup water
Cooked rice (page 426)

1. Cut the beef into shoestring strips. Chop the celery and water chestnuts coarsely and cut the onion and mushrooms into thin slices. Cut snow peas once diagonally.

2. Heat the oil in a heavy skillet. Brown the beef, seasoning it with the salt. Add the vegetables and cook for a few minutes over high heat, stirring slowly.

3. Cover the pan, reduce heat and simmer 3 minutes. Just before serving, stir in a thickening sauce made by heating together the cornstarch, sugar, soy sauce and water. Serve with rice.

SERVES 2

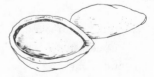

L'Ermitage

Weight watchers, beware. That is, if you think you are the type that is likely to be easily tempted. With profusion, and no apologies, this restaurant offers fourteen desserts at each seating—and then you must add the homemade sherbets. To make matters worse, the laden pastry cart is placed close to the entrance. But the lavishness only starts with the Chocolate Charlotte. Over half a million dollars have been spent refurbishing this former antique shop on La Cienega. Candles flicker, silver gleams and fresh flowers bloom in a French château milieu. Napoleon wanted to capture Russia, including Catherine the Great's Hermitage in Leningrad; you will want to capture the pâtisserie called Napoleon at L'Ermitage in L.A.

Marching backward from the desserts, one finds entrees such as the choice Aiguillette de Canard au Medoc. This is not your Long Island duckling but a special thin-skinned, California-raised bird that is a cross between the Peking and Muscovy strains. The bird is called a mallard and because it lacks the usual heavy layer of fat, it requires less cooking, with more moisture remaining in the meat. Other worthy dishes include Côte Veau Prince Orloff, Veal Chop with Puree of Mushrooms Soubise Sauce and Suprême de Pigeon Ermitage. Fish fanciers will enjoy the Whitefish à la Julienne de Légumes. The Salade is correctly called "Gourmande" as it includes lobster, chicory and string beans. Another introductory course is Fish Dumpling with Truffles Sauce. All makes for wonderful dining—as you watch, not your weight, but the Rolls-Royces and Jaguars purring by the antique shops outside.

730 NORTH LA CIENEGA BOULEVARD, LOS ANGELES

Chocolate Charlotte

¾ pound semi-sweet
    chocolate
1 cup sugar

1. Melt the chocolate in a double boiler over simmering water.

2. Bring sugar and water to a boil with the vanilla bean. Boil 1 minute. Cool to room temperature. Remove from heat and cool.

1⅓ cups water
1 vanilla bean or 1
⅛ teaspoon vanilla
extract
1½ quarts whipping cream
12 egg yolks
2 dozen ladyfingers

Remove vanilla bean or stir in the vanilla extract.

3. Whip the cream and place in the refrigerator. Place egg yolks in the top of the double boiler. Start beating the eggs with a large whisk or with a rotary beater. Add the syrup slowly to the yolks, beating constantly.

4. Place top of the double boiler over boiling water and continue beating until the mixture has a creamy consistency. This will take approximately 5 minutes.

5. Put the mixture in a blender and spin until cool. Stir in the chocolate and fold the mixture into the whipped cream.

6. Cover the bottom of a 3-quart soufflé dish or 12 individual soufflé dishes with a round of wax paper. Lightly butter the paper and sides of the dish or dishes. Line the bottom and sides with ladyfinger halves. Fill with the chocolate mixture and place in the refrigerator for several hours.

7. To serve: Unmold the Chocolate Charlotte on 1 dessert platter or 12 dessert plates. This may be served plain or piped with sweetened whipped cream.

SERVES 12

Ernie's Restaurant

If you saw Alfred Hitchcock's *Vertigo* you have seen the interior of Ernie's. Strange, in a way, since Ernie's is the epitome of solid footing, of the down-to-earth cozy splendor of the Victorian era. The walls are lush crimson silk with mahogany wainscoting. Brass candelabras came from the mansions of Pacific Heights, chandeliers from the estates of William Sharon, the Comstock King, and Claus Spreckels, the Sugar Baron. Massive sideboards, elaborate gold-leafed floor-to-ceiling mirrors, cut-glass hurricane lamps, Charles Dana Gibson sketches of Victorians at dinner make this an empire of memories of San Francisco's Golden Age.

Ernie's is history, one of the city's great dining places, founded on the site of the lusty Frisco Dance Hall that perished in the quake and fire of 1906. The new building was called the European Hotel, then Il Trovatore Hotel, and finally, in the early '30s, it became Ernie's, named after a beloved North Beach character, Ernie Carlesso, who took over the management.

The restaurant almost expired with the death of aged chef Hugo Carismo, but Victor and Roland Gotti decided on some empire building, bought the luxury of the past and remodeled with their stunning Ambrosia and Elysian rooms and the Bacchus Cellar.

The menu at Ernie's is à la carte. This is the place to try Cracked Crab in season, to have melon with prosciutto, Olympian oysters, Bay shrimp, pâté with truffles. You can have sweetbreads with morels, soothing vichyssoise and those delicious quenelles, expertly made of sea bass and baked in Nantua sauce. Should you come with a partner, order the marvelous double New York cut sirloin and dine like a Disraeli and a Metternich.

847 MONTGOMERY STREET, SAN FRANCISCO

California

Sweetbreads aux Morilles

2 pairs of sweetbreads
½ teaspoon salt
3-4 white peppercorns
2 teaspoons vinegar
2 small bay leaves
1 clove
½ cup flour
6 tablespoons butter
2 teaspoons chopped
   shallots
1 4-ounce can morilles
   (morels)
1 tablespoon brandy
2 tablespoons dry white
   wine
¾ cup heavy cream
Salt and pepper
1 teaspoon parsley

1. Poach the sweetbreads for 5 minutes in enough water to cover plus the peppercorns, vinegar, bay leaves and clove. Bring to a boil and simmer 5 minutes. Drain and plunge into ice water, then remove all tendons and tissues.

2. Cut the cooled sweetbreads in ¾-inch slices. Season with salt and pepper and dip in flour.

3. Heat the butter in a skillet and when it is very hot, sauté the sweetbreads until golden brown on both sides, turning them very gently. Add the shallots and morels and continue cooking until the shallots are soft.

4. Add the brandy and touch with a lighted match.

5. Add the wine and bring to a boil.

6. Add the cream and simmer 5 minutes.

7. Remove the sweetbreads and mushrooms to a warm serving dish. Quickly boil down the sauce until the quantity is reduced by half. Mix the cornstarch with a little of the juice from the canned morels. Stir into the sauce until thickened. Pour the sauce on the sweetbreads and sprinkle with chopped parsley.

SERVES 4

L'Escargot

There are a number of good reasons for visiting Carmel. One can see artists at their easels or shop in chic boutiques or walk the beach or play the Pebble Beach course familiar to television watchers. Still another good reason is L'Escargot, a charming restaurant that is far more like *bistrots* in France than most that call themselves French restaurants. L'Escargot is family-owned, family-operated. The kitchen closes at 9 p.m.; there's an excellent wine cellar but no bar.

The decor is Norman Country Kitchen. The ceiling is beamed, the walls hung with copper and pewter utensils, old menus and maps. Chairs and banquettes are covered with a toile print, producing an effect charmingly relaxed and informal.

Privileged patrons receive the benefits of owner-chef Yvan Nopert's experience as chef of the Belgian Embassy in Washington, from 1950 to 1953. If the thought of eating escargots—snails—is not appealing, one may order Fonds d'Artichauts aux Oeufs as an accompaniment to Poulet Crème aux Truffles, Bourride or Moules Marinières (in season), or Vin de Veau Archiduc or quenelles.

MISSION NEAR FOURTH, CARMEL

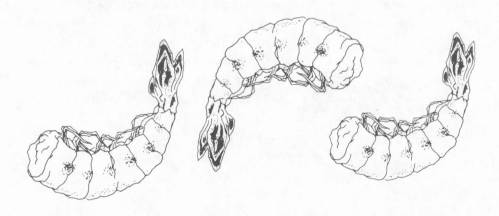

California

Bourride Yuan Nopert

16 thin slices of French
    bread
5   pounds large shrimp,
    shelled and cleaned or
    5 pounds boned white
    ocean fish (cod, sea
    bass, halibut), cut
    in pieces
15 egg yolks
10 garlic cloves
4   quarts of clam broth
    or fish stock

Aioli:
3   large cloves garlic,
    pressed
3   egg yolks
1½ cups olive oil
Salt and black pepper

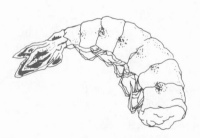

This dish should be prepared at the last minute. Prepare the aioli (garlic mayonnaise) in advance, and toast the French bread rubbed with garlic, but cook the fish just before serving.

1. Prepare the aioli: Put the garlic and egg yolks in a blender or food processor. Spin the egg yolks and gradually add the oil till the mixture has the consistency of mayonnaise. Season with salt and pepper.

2. Prepare the toast: Rub the cut surface of a garlic clove over the slices of bread. Toast them lightly and keep them warm.

3. Prepare the bourride: Bring the clam broth or fish stock to a simmer and add the shrimp or fish. Cook 3 to 4 minutes.

4. Mix the egg yolks with the pressed garlic cloves.

5. Use a slotted spoon to lift the poached fish or shrimp from the clam juice to a deep serving dish.

6. Combine the egg mixture and the hot clam juice. Heat, stirring continuously, but do not allow the mixture to come to a boil. Pour over the shrimp or fish.

7. Serve in soup plates with the French bread and the aioli.

SERVES 8

L'Escoffier

It was the great L'Escoffier himself who told of a woman of much charm who averred that she knew true gourmands by the way they pronounce the word *good* in their conversations. "Here is something *good*," or "Here is something very *good*." She assured the master of cuisine that real connoisseurs put into this short word an accent of conviction, of pleasure and of enthusiasm, which people of dull palate can never hope to attain. And so, at L'Escoffier, the gourmands chant *good*, not only because the view is wonderful, as the eye wanders over the sumptuous appointments of the restaurant atop the Beverly Hilton Hotel and the captivating scene of Century City, but because the service is so personal and the food is so divine.

You can order à la carte or choose one of the two complete dinners offered at reasonable prices. Diners are recommended to try the à la carte menu for the number of interesting dishes. Live lobster tanks have been installed—a useful point to remember when ordering.

BEVERLY HILTON HOTEL, 9876 WILSHIRE BOULEVARD, BEVERLY HILLS

Filet of Veal Gentilhomme

4 6- to 8-ounce veal cutlets
Flour
2 eggs, slightly beaten
4 tablespoons butter
4 fresh tomatoes
2 ripe avocados

Mornay sauce:
2 tablespoons butter
2 tablespoons flour

1. Cut each cutlet in half. Place between sheets of waxed paper and pound gently until quite thin. Dip each slice in flour and egg and let stand.

2. Peel and seed the tomatoes. Chop rather fine and cook in a small saucepan until thick.

3. Make the Mornay sauce: Melt the butter in a saucepan and blend in the flour. Add the hot milk and cook until sauce thickens. Remove from heat. Add mustard and cheese and stir until cheese melts.

4. Make the Madeira sauce: Melt the but-

1 cup hot milk
Salt and pepper to taste
2 teaspoons Dijon mustard
¾ cup grated Cheddar
cheese

Madeira sauce:
1½ tablespoons butter
1½ tablespoons minced
scallions
1 cup brown sauce
(page 418)
3 tablespoons Madeira
2 teaspoons lemon juice

ter in a saucepan and simmer the minced scallions until softened but not brown. Add the brown sauce, Madeira and lemon juice. Simmer 10 minutes.

5. Peel and slice the avocados, sprinkling lightly with lemon juice to prevent discoloration.

6. Heat the 4 tablespoons butter in a skillet and sauté the veal over high heat until golden brown on both sides.

7. Place the veal on a heatproof serving platter. Place a little of the tomato on the center of each piece and top with slice of avocado.

8. Cover with the Mornay sauce and brown under a preheated broiler. Surround the meat with the Madeira sauce. Serve immediately.

SERVES 4

L'Etoile

L'Etoile has the classic air of splendor that must have existed in France just before the Revolution. The purity of Louis XVI neo-classicism, the invisibility of the service, the never-failing genius of the dishes make L'Etoile a brilliant rendezvous.

Henri Barberis worked with the great Henri Soulé when Soulé's Le Pavillon was the greatest restaurant in America; partner Claude Rouas received his training at Maxim's. L'Etoile's chef, Claude Bougard, cooked at La Réserve in Beaulieu, France, before coming to this country to work his magic.

An ecstasy of flaming apricot sauce, caramelized sugar, almonds and ice cream known as La Marquise Alice Pralinée might cause you to renounce your citizenship. La Poularde aux Morilles (chicken with mushrooms sparked with brandy) or Dover Sole Soufflée Ile de France are monuments to the delicacy and tact with which a great chef avoids blandness. The Salon de Cocktails, where brandy fumes and piano music mingle, is open until 1:30 a.m.

1075 CALIFORNIA STREET, SAN FRANCISCO

La Poularde aux Morilles (Chicken with Morels)

1 2½- to 3-pound chicken
Salt
White pepper
1 bay leaf
Vegetable oil
1 cup sauterne
4 ounces canned morels

Preheat the oven to 400 degrees F.

1. Season chicken inside and out with salt and white pepper. Brush with oil and bake 35 minutes. Lift chicken onto serving platter and keep warm.

2. Add sauterne to pan and place over moderate heat. Cook, stirring with a fork to loosen pan juices, until the quantity is reduced by half. Strain and set aside.

3. In a large saucepan simmer the sherry

½ cup sherry
2 cups heavy cream
¾ cup brandy

and morels until the liquid is almost all absorbed. Add the cream and simmer until thickened. Blend in the strained pan drippings and the brandy. Taste for seasoning and add salt and pepper as needed.

4. Pour the sauce over the roast chicken and serve at once.

SERVES 2

La Marquise Alice Pralinee

½ cup sugar
½ cup whole almonds
½ pint vanilla ice cream
1 pint whipping cream
2 tablespoons kirsch
1 jar (8 ounces) apricot
   jam
2 tablespoons Grand
   Marnier or Cointreau
2 tablespoons cognac

1. Heat the sugar in a small heavy pan until melted. Place the almonds in a small dish and pour the sugar over them. When they are hardened, chop very fine or pulverize in the blender.

2. Mix the vanilla ice cream with the whipped cream and the pulverized almonds. Stir in the kirsch and pour into individual serving glasses. Place in the refrigerator.

3. Blend the orange liqueur and brandy with the apricot jam. Whisk until smooth.

4. To serve: Top the dessert with apricot sauce just before serving.

SERVES 4

Five Crowns

A bit Norman, a bit Scandinavian, somewhat Teutonic and very much Anglo-Saxon: such is the patchwork composition of Ye Olde English Inn. But despite this goulash of nationalities, the inn has remained . . . well, typically English—shy and unpretentious, yet warm and incredibly hospitable. Nor has time succeeded in changing this gentlemanly reserve; the characteristics remain. Deep bay or trellised windows; heavy, blackened timbers; narrow, winding stairs; small gardens; horse brasses; brass bugles; men drinking Watney's or Guinness from tankards and ladies sipping shandies. Find these traditional landmarks in Great Britain, and you will have found the English inn. Go looking for them in Los Angeles, and you will doubtless discover the Five Crowns, a faithful and convincing reproduction of one of England's oldest coaching inns.

A consistent winner of the *Holiday* Magazine Award as well as the recipient of much local tribute, Five Crowns offers warm respite to the traveler and superb food for the most discriminating palate. For to accompany its excellent stouts and ales, the restaurant serves equally outstanding specialties—Roast Rack of Lamb, Roast Prime Ribs of Beef and Bristol Sherry Chicken. As you can see, the same courses served during the Brueghelian festivals of four centuries ago can still tempt travelers today.

For dessert, try Trifle.

3801 EAST COAST HIGHWAY, CORONA DEL MAR

Creamed Spinach à la Lawry's

1 package (10 ounce) frozen chopped spinach
3 slices lean bacon, very finely chopped
½ cup finely chopped onion
1 clove garlic, minced

1. Cook spinach according to package directions and drain well.

2. Sauté the bacon, onions and garlic together for 10 minutes or until the onions are tender. Remove from the heat. Add flour and seasonings. Mix well. Return to the heat, add the milk gradually and stir until thick. Add spinach and mix well.

SERVES 4

2 tablespoons flour
1 teaspoon Lawry's
  Seasoned Salt
¼ teaspoon Lawry's
  Seasoned Pepper
1 cup milk

English Trifle

1 package (3¼ ounces)
  vanilla pudding
2 cups light cream
2 tablespoons dark
  Puerto Rican rum
2¼ cups heavy cream
3 tablespoons sugar
2 tablespoons red
  raspberry preserves
Sponge cake (round, 10
  inches diameter)
¼ cup brandy
¼ cup dry sherry
30 whole strawberries

1. Combine pudding mix and light cream in a saucepan. Cook, stirring constantly, until mixture comes to a boil and thickens. Add rum and chill.

2. Whip 1¼ cups heavy cream with 1 tablespoon sugar until stiff. Fold into the chilled pudding.

3. Coat the inside of a deep 10-inch bowl with raspberry preserves to within 1 inch of the top. Slice the cake horizontally into 4 even slices. Place top slice, crust side down, in the bottom of the bowl, curving edges upward. Combine the brandy and sherry and sprinkle about 2 tablespoons over the cake slice. Spread a third of the chilled pudding over the cake. Repeat procedure twice.

4. Whip the remaining 1 cup of heavy cream, sweeten with the remaining 2 tablespoons of sugar and spread over the pudding. Garnish with the strawberries. Chill at least 6 hours.

5. To serve: Spoon onto chilled dessert plates.

SERVES 12

Fleur De Lys

Surely, no gypsy encampment was ever as warm, as charming and as captivating as the restaurant Fleur De Lys of San Francisco. More festive, perhaps; more rustic, certainly—but never more enchanting. Here is found a special kind of magic, a spell that mixes the rural with the regal, surrounding diners with tentlike enclosures of exquisite, hand-painted, billowing fabric while crowning all with the royal iris. A novel combination, to be sure, but one that continues to draw customers—merely curious at first, confirmed patrons thereafter.

True to the traditional American success story, the original Fleur De Lys was comfortable in the small and unpretentious village of San Anselmo. But success soon leads to greater things, and as the word went out and hungry diners crowded in, it was decided to move the whole operation to larger and more opulent quarters in San Francisco. Thankfully, expansion has not eclipsed the high standards and personal attention management devotes to every detail. Thus, while captains and waiters stand respectfully at the ready, owner Maurice Rouas himself composes the menu which, predominantly à la carte, features such specialties as Smoked Salmon, Escargots en Coquilles, Broiled Brochette of Fillet of Beef and various other delights—all calculated to satisfy an entire caravan.

777 SUTTER STREET, SAN FRANCISCO

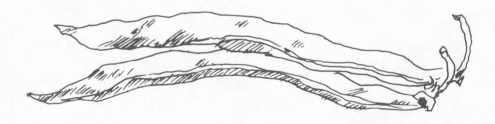

California

Veal Champagne

18 veal scallopini
    (2 pounds)
1   cup flour
1   teaspoon salt
¼   teaspoon white pepper
4   tablespoons butter
5   shallots, chopped
1   pound mushrooms,
    sliced
2½ cups dry white wine
1   quart whipping cream

1. Put the veal between sheets of wax paper and pound lightly with a mallet.

2. Mix the flour with salt and pepper and dip each piece in the mixture.

3. Heat the butter in a large skillet and brown the scallopini on both sides. Remove to a platter and keep warm.

4. Simmer the shallots in the same skillet and when they are soft add the mushrooms. Simmer and stir until tender. Add the white wine and boil down for 2 to 3 minutes.

5. Add the cream, stir until well blended. Simmer until the sauce is slightly thickened.

6. Put the veal back into the sauce and reheat.

7. Serve with rissolées potatoes and string beans.

SERVES 6

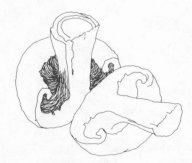

Fournou's Ovens

On the corner of California and Powell streets atop Nob Hill the new-old Stanford Court Hotel provides the perfect setting for the experience known as Fournou's Ovens. The building's façade, with a lofty leaded-glass dome over the porte cochere entrance, is a San Francisco landmark dating back to 1912, but within all is up-to-the-minute and luxurious to the tune of $17 million spent recently on reconstruction and furnishings. Item: Every guest room is equipped with *two* telephones and *two* television sets.

In the restaurant, chef Marcel Dragon presides expertly over the massive tile-faced open-hearth ovens (that suggested the name). Fired with seasoned live oak, these units produce roasts of every description, which are served with accompaniments of Continental cuisine and offerings from a distinguished wine cellar. The multi-level dining room is richly decorated with antiques and artifacts from five continents, and there's a separate wine-tasting room.

The menu includes Steak au Poivre, Bay Shrimp in Sour Cream, veal, duck and, of course, lamb racks basted with an aromatic sauce which contains bay, fresh mint, rosemary and thyme. Fabulous!

CALIFORNIA AND POWELL STREETS, SAN FRANCISCO

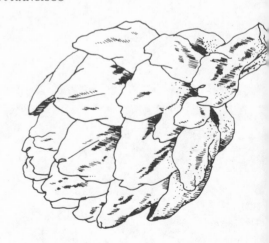

California

Cream of Artichoke Soup with Crushed Hazelnuts

4-6 artichoke bottoms, depending upon size
⅓ cup hazelnuts
4 cups rich fat-free chicken stock
3 tablespoons rice flour
6 tablespoons cold water
½ cup heavy cream
1 tablespoon dry sherry (optional)

1. Remove the top inch and the stem from the artichokes and snip off the prickly tip of the leaves. Cook in boiling water with a teaspoon of lemon juice for about 40 minutes until a leaf pulls off easily. Remove with tongs and drain upside down on paper towels.

2. Blanch the hazelnuts in salted water for 10 minutes. Rinse in cold water. Spread on a baking sheet for 10 minutes in 250-degree oven.

3. Remove the leaves and scoop out the choke from the artichoke. You will only need the bottoms.

4. Place the bottoms in a pan containing the chicken stock.

5. Crush the hazelnuts in a blender or food processor or put them in a food grinder. Add to the stock and simmer for ½ hour.

6. Spin the soup in a blender or food processor and return to the pan.

7. Mix the rice flour with the cold water. Stir into the soup, gradually bringing it to a boil. Reduce the heat and simmer 15 minutes.

8. Season to taste with salt and pepper and stir in the cream and the sherry, if desired. Serve in bouillon cups.

SERVES 4

François' Restaurant

Beneath the Bank of America Tower in the Atlantic Richfield Plaza, François' exudes corporate splendor and well-being. The diners are likely to be patrons on their way to the Music Center, as François has a special pre-theater dinner menu for them. Or, a la carte, they order appetizers (mushroom caps stuffed with crab meat, fresh salmon mousse, duckling pâté) or bits and pieces of elegant desserts (frozen raspberry soufflé, a wonderful wine-poached pear).

If you can make a night of it—and you really ought to—be prepared for *les entrées en force*. Feuilleté de Ris de Veau à la Reine is sweetbreads in a heavenly light pastry. Canard à la mode de Tillières is duckling flamed with Calvados and served with fried apples and bananas. Mountain Trout Stuffed with Salmon Mousse—you can close your eyes for a moment and imagine yourself above the timberline where the night and the stars run together. Pheasant for two cooked in a sealed earthenware vessel—almost sinful in an oozing succulence of foie gras and truffles. Primarily French, François' menu offers the highest of haute cuisine underground.

555 SOUTH FLOWER STREET, LOS ANGELES

Canard à la Mode de Tillières—(*Roast Duckling Flambé Calvados*)

2 4-pound ducklings
1 small onion, quartered
1 teaspoon salt
1 pinch pepper
4 bay leaves
1 pinch thyme
½ cup sugar
½ cup red wine vinegar

1. Preheat the oven to 375 degrees F. Remove all the giblets from the ducklings, wash the birds and wipe dry inside and out.

2. Inside each duckling place ½ the onion, salt, pepper, thyme and bay leaves.

3. Place the ducklings in an ovenproof skillet that has been lightly oiled. Wipe oil over the ducklings and roast 1½ hours, basting ducklings twice during this time.

4. When ducklings have cooked for 1 hour, place the giblets in the pan and continue cooking.

5. Remove the ducks and cut in half,

1 whole orange
3 cups chicken stock or bouillon
1 teaspoon tomato paste
2 tablespoons red currant jelly
2 tablespoons cornstarch
4 teaspoons white wine
4 teaspoons Calvados
½ apple
1 banana
1 egg, slightly beaten
½ cup coconut, shredded

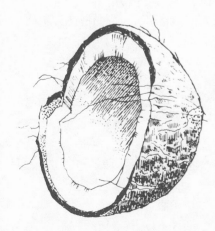

leaving the leg and breast section together. Remove all the bones, saving them for the sauce. Set aside.

6. To make the sauce, pour off the oil from the duck pan. Add sugar, duck bones and red wine vinegar and bring to a boil, stirring constantly with a fork. Slowly reduce the temperature and when the sugar is brown, squeeze juice from the orange into the sauce and then add the entire orange.

7. Add chicken stock, tomato paste, currant jelly and simmer for 15 minutes.

8. Strain the sauce into a small saucepan. Mix the cornstarch with the wine and add to the sauce. Boil 2 to 3 minutes. Add 2 teaspoons of Calvados. Keep warm.

9. Heat 2 inches of oil in a deep skillet and heat to 370 degrees F. Peel the apple, core it and cut into rings. Peel the banana and cut into 4 pieces. Dip the fruit in egg and roll in the coconut. Deep fry until golden brown.

10. To serve: The ducklings may be reheated by covering with foil and placing in the oven until hot. Place on a heatproof platter and surround with the fruit. Pour 2 teaspoons of Calvados over the ducklings and touch with a lighted match. Bring to the table flaming and serve with a side dish of sauce.

SERVES 4

Gulliver's

"**M**ay you live every day of your life," said Jonathon Swift, whose *Gulliver's Travels* inspired this restaurant's name.

An 18th-Century English pub, with leaded glass, antiques, old prints, pewter, brass, clay pipes, memorabilia and, overlooking all, a proud portrait of Swift above the study mantel. It's a warm masculine environment, strong on conviviality as well as food.

Neo-hedonists, professionals and a lot of others weary of mad paces and faceless people enjoy the single entree dinner—roast beef, lean and juicy. The only decision is the cut (a Gulliver? Prime Minister? or a Big Endian?). Pottage, Sallet Greens, Yorkshire Pudding au Jus, and wines chosen by Bacchus (but moderately priced) are superb. True old English pubgoers drink the imported Whitbread Beer on tap, and join the dart players after lunch. No Lilliputian drinks. It's Brobdingnagian all the way.

The baked creamed corn served as a side dish at Gulliver's is such a favorite that the recipe has been neatly printed on a card for handing out to guests, and it is the recipe that appears here—by special request. The cayenne pepper and Parmesan cheese are very important additions to a dish that too often is bland and characterless.

Al Levie's dining concept has expanded from the original location at Irvine to a second at Marina Del Rey and a third in Burlingame. Each maintains the successful combination: picturesque atmosphere, superb roast beef.

18482 MACARTHUR BLVD., IRVINE

California

Gulliver's Creamed Corn

2 packages frozen kernel
  corn
1 cup whipping cream
1 cup homogenized milk
1 teaspoon salt
¼ teaspoon Accent
6 teaspoons sugar
Pinch of white or cayenne
  pepper
2 tablespoons melted
  butter
2 tablespoons flour
Parmesan cheese

1. Combine all the ingredients except the butter, flour and cheese. Bring to a boil in a saucepan and simmer 5 minutes.

2. Combine the butter with flour and drop into the corn. Stir until blended and remove from heat.

3. To serve: This can be served immediately or it can be placed in a heatproof casserole, sprinkled with Parmesan cheese and browned under a broiler.

SERVES 8

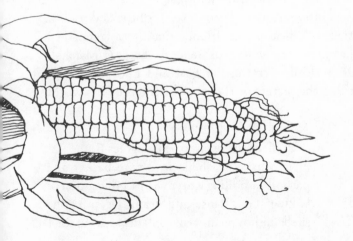

Imperial Dynasty

Wings have taken flight over Hanford, a small community at the southern end of California's San Joaquin Valley. It would seem an unlikely place, especially since the wings are the Chinese Wing family and their restaurant in the city revered for its haute cuisine. The matter is cleared up when it is noted that Chow Gong Wing, grandfather of the present owner, Richard, left China aboard a Flying Cloud sailing ship bound for California as a railroad labor camp chef. In 1883, he opened his restaurant in Hanford, which still has enthralling relics of a former busy Chinatown. What was once a basement network of opium dens has been transformed over the years into comfortable dining rooms with intricate ivory carvings, jade Buddhas and porcelain teapots. Beauty has been created from chaos.

Proprietor Richard Wing explains his unique approach to the culinary arts: "In the West, French cuisine remains the basic foundation for most Occidental food concepts. In the East, Chinese cuisine is still the basic foundation for Oriental cooking. Basically, my food concept, 'Continental-Chinoise,' is an exciting culinary combination of the two great cuisines, namely, French cuisine with a bit of Chinese culinary accent."

Wing speaks with authority on the International dimensions of fine dining. After having studied international relations, law, politics and trade at the University of Southern California, he found himself assigned, as a member of the State Department, to the staff of General George C. Marshall. He traveled with the General all over the Far East and Europe, even to Russia, all the time learning the secrets of the great kitchens of the world.

CHINA ALLEY, HANFORD

Escargots à la Imperial Dynasty

48 empty imported snail
    shells

Preheat the oven to 450 degrees F.

1. Wash the shells in a wire basket and parboil in boiling water with 1 tablespoon of baking soda. Rinse and drain. Deep fry the shells in hot peanut oil (350 degrees F.) for 1

48 imported French snails
   (canned)
Peanut oil

Sauce:
1½ cups butter
 4 cloves garlic, mashed
 2 tablespoons chopped
   shallot
 4 slices ginger root,
   mashed
½ teaspoon pepper
Pinch of nutmeg
 1 tablespoon cashew
   spread (or peanut
   butter)
 2 tablespoons puree of
   cornish hen or
   strained baby food
   chicken
 1 cup white wine
 1 tablespoon chopped
   parsley
½ teaspoon salt
Juice of 1 fresh lime

 2 tablespoons fine
   bread crumbs
 1 medium-sized onion,
   thinly sliced

minute. Drain and sprinkle the inside of each shell with garlic salt. Place shells on a baking sheet and bake 3 minutes. Now the shells are ready to give a good flavor to the snails.

2. Remove the snails from the can and place in a wire basket. Lower into boiling water for 10 seconds and drain. Plunge into the hot oil for 5 seconds. Drain.

3. Heat the butter in a wok or skillet and stir-fry the garlic, shallots and ginger root but do not brown. Add all the other ingredients and stir until the mixture bubbles.

4. Add the snails but do not let the mixture reach the boiling point.

5. With a pair of bamboo chopsticks or a small cocktail fork, stuff each snail into a shell by placing the soft part in first. Then fill each shell with the butter sauce and put in small snail plates.

6. Sprinkle with the bread crumbs and drape with rings of onion.

7. When ready to serve, bake at 450 degrees F. for 8 to 10 minutes or until the sauce bubbles. Serve very hot with plenty of French bread for dunking.

Note: The snails may be prepared in advance and kept in the refrigerator until ready to serve. The fresh ginger root deodorizes the garlic.

SERVES 6 TO 8 AS AN APPETIZER

Imperial Palace

The Dowager Empress of China would have bowed sedately in approval of this restaurant's original drink, "Imperial Jade," served in oversized goblets. Ever since its opening in 1960, the Imperial Palace has enjoyed success, bringing to its clients the centuries-old recipes of Imperial China in a selection of choice dishes from the Canton and northern China provinces.

Suitably situated in the heart of San Francisco's Chinatown, the establishment is authentically decorated with display cases of beautiful Chinese covered teacups and even larger displays of porcelain vessels from the Ch'ing Dynasty. A cozier touch in the foyer are the masses of photographs signed by visiting celebrities. There is also a cozy-looking bar with stained-glass dividers sporting Chinese motifs. The entrance to the dining room is flanked by massive tables laden with large bowls of freshly cut flowers, which also abound on long side tables in the main room, as well as on individual candlelit tables.

You are escorted to your table by a hostess dressed in a long Chinese-style evening gown, and served by waiters in tailor-made tuxedos. An appetizer of Minced Squab Imperial is suggested, to be followed by Lobster Imperial and Flaming Black Leaf Lichee for dessert. The restaurant is proud of its large selection of California wines. As Confucius would say, "When in Chinatown, do as the Chinese do."

919 GRANT AVENUE, CHINATOWN, SAN FRANCISCO

Chicken Walnut

1 pound boned breast of chicken, cut in thin strips
2 tablespoons peanut oil
1 teaspoon salt

1. Preheat a wok or frying pan and add the oil. Swirl the oil over the bottom of the pan. Add the chicken strips and salt and stir-fry for 2 to 3 minutes.

2. Add the snow peas, mushrooms, bamboo shoots and chicken broth. Stir quickly and cook for 2 minutes. Add the soy sauce,

¾ cup snow peas
¼ pound small mushrooms
2 ounces bamboo shoots
2 cups chicken broth
1½ cups roasted walnuts, coarsely chopped
1 tablespoon soy sauce
½ teaspoon sugar
1½ teaspoons cornstarch
1 teaspoon water

sugar and walnuts. Stir well and add the cornstarch mixed with water. Cook just until slightly thickened.

3. Serve with white rice.

SERVES 6

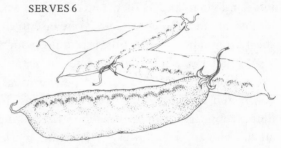

Dried Shredded Scallop Soup

½ cup dried shredded scallops
2 quarts chicken stock (page 419)
¼ cup shredded black mushrooms
¼ cup shredded bamboo sprouts
2 teaspoons cornstarch
2 egg yolks
¾ teaspoon salt
1 teaspoon soy sauce
2 slices ginger root
2 tablespoons minced Virginia ham

1. Buy shredded dried scallops, black mushrooms and ginger root at an Oriental food shop. Soak the scallops overnight, then drain them. Soak the black mushrooms and clean them carefully.

2. Combine scallops with the chicken stock in a large saucepan. Bring to a boil, then cover, reduce heat and simmer 30 minutes.

3. Add the mushrooms and bamboo sprouts and cook 2 minutes.

4. Mix together the egg yolks and cornstarch. Add to the soup along with the salt, soy sauce and ginger root. Cook, stirring constantly, until soup is thickened.

5. Just before serving remove the ginger root and garnish with the ham.

SERVES 6

India House

Pimm's Cup was invented in 1841 by the owner of James Pimm's Oyster Bar in London. It was so popular that it was later bottled and shipped around the world, arriving first in the American West at the India House restaurant in San Francisco. Even today, the India House sells more of this drink—fruit juice and gin mixed, cooled, and garnished with borage and cucumber rind, a bright summer cooler—than anyone else in the country. The drink is part of the heritage absorbed by this restaurant from the British era in India.

A small bar at the entrance to the establishment reminds visitors of a typical British pub, the frosted pewter mugs hanging from the wall. When contrasted with the heads, skins and tapestries of Bengal tigers that fill the dining room area, one feels the mood of pre-independence India. The waiters are all scholars from India and Pakistan, working toward degrees at Bay area universities; Hindus and Moslems working side by side.

The menu naturally emphasizes curry—lamb, chicken, beef, shrimp, all blended well with this interesting mixture of exotic Eastern spices. Whatever you decide upon, try chapatties—unleavened whole wheat bread baked full and puffy to the customer's order, best when eaten hot, dripping with melted butter. The recommended drink with curry is a large bottle of Liebfraumilch or several bottles of Guinness Stout.

350 JACKSON STREET, SAN FRANCISCO

Khorma *(Lamb Curry)*

4 pounds fat-free shoulder of lamb

1. Cut the lamb into 1-inch cubes and roll in the turmeric.
2. Heat the oil and add the onions and garlic and brown over moderate heat.

1½ tablespoons turmeric
2 cups salad oil
6 medium onions, chopped
3 cloves of garlic, minced
6 whole cardamom seeds
6 bay leaves
6 cloves
1 stick of cinnamon
1 cup water
2 tablespoons ground cumin
¼ teaspoon mace
¼ teaspoon ginger
1 teaspoon ground coriander
⅛ teaspoon cayenne
¼ teaspoon nutmeg
1½ teaspoons dill
Salt

Condiments:
Grated coconut
Ground peanuts
Mustard Pickle
Limes, quartered
Onions, chopped
Raisins
Chutney

3. At the same time, boil the cardamom seeds, bay leaves, cloves and cinnamon stick in the 1 cup water for 10 minutes.

4. Combine the other spices and dill.

5. When the onions are brown, add the mixed spices and cook for 10 minutes.

6. Stir in the meat and sprinkle with salt.

7. Strain the boiled spices and add the liquid to the meat. Cook 30 minutes or until the meat is tender.

8. While the meat cooks, prepare a set of condiments to be served with the curry. These condiments may include, but should not be limited to, those listed.

9. Serve the meat in the cooking liquid, very hot, along with boiled rice and the desired condiments in separate small dishes.

SERVES 8 TO 10

Jack's Restaurant

To think that venerable Jack's Restaurant, in operation since 1864, could have been called Brer's or even Cottontail's. Although the present owner, Jack Redinger, comes from a family that has lavished its expertise on the establishment since the turn of the century (his father, Paul, worked here tirelessly for 70 years), the name has nothing to do with the Redingers; it merely refers to the rabbit dishes that first made it a popular eating place. Jack Rabbit is as good a derivative as any, after all.

Jack's is disarmingly simple: bentwood chairs, white linens, hat racks, a five-foot bar—one of the smallest in the country. (True, the deep frieze of gilded garlands gives an air of turn-of-the-century grandeur.) The bill of fare is simple and old-fashioned, the waiters are as venerable as the establishment. But then, financier Louis Lurie lunched at his round table for 55 years, a movie producer used Jack's for his dining scenes because it looked more like a restaurant than any place he knew, a group of businessmen lingering over a fine lunch found it was already time for dinner. And a U.S. senator requested a menu to decorate his dining room in the capital. Jack's rose from the ashes of the 1906 earthquake and performed a similar Phoenix act after a devastating fire in 1958. Only superb service and cuisine could maintain its foremost role throughout the years.

Like everything else in this respected institution, the menu has stayed much the same over the years. English mutton chops with broiled kidneys has been a favorite for generations. Lucius Beebe, the doyen of gourmet reporters, called Jack's chops "superb." There are popular French preparations—chicken with mushrooms and artichokes, frog's legs sautéed with mushrooms and served in brown sauce or in a classic white-wine cream sauce. Some places would give up on trying to sell customers on tripe, but at Jack's the chef orders some 50 pounds a week to meet the demand for first-rate honeycomb Tripes à la Mode de Caen.

615 SACRAMENTO STREET, SAN FRANCISCO

California

Fried Cream with Rum

1 quart milk
1¼ cups flour
1¼ cups sugar
3 whole eggs
6 egg yolks
¼ teaspoon salt
¼ pound butter
2 tablespoons vanilla

Coating:
2 eggs, slightly beaten
   with 2 tablespoons
   of water
1 cup fine bread crumbs
½ cup rum, heated
Cooking oil

1. Bring milk to a boil.
2. Combine eggs and egg yolks and beat slightly. Add the flour, sugar and salt and mix to a paste.
3. Add the paste to the milk, stirring continuously and gradually adding the butter. This mixture must be stirred continuously while cooking as it burns easily.
4. Remove from the heat and stir in the vanilla. (Other flavors may be substituted.)
5. Pour the mixture into a buttered cake pan. Spread the top with a little butter and cool. Chill in the refrigerator until very firm.
6. Preheat hot oil in deep frying pan. Cut the cream into squares and dip first in egg and then in bread crumbs. Fry until golden brown. Place on a heatproof serving dish and keep warm until all the squares have been fried. Sprinkle with sugar. Add the heated rum and touch with a lighted match. Serve immediately.

SERVES 6

Kan's Restaurant

Had Johnny Kan established his now famous restaurant 713 years earlier and had he elected to locate somewhere in northern China rather than in San Francisco, California, Genghis Khan might not have been so eager to leave Mongolia for the Asian steppes and parts west. After all, quality won ton was hard to find in 1240, as were good bamboo shoots, water chestnuts and crab curry. No wonder Genghis and his followers had to travel so far and were so upset when they got there.

But, as historians will attest, Kan's was not even a glimmer at the time of the Mongol scourge, and, at least, for present-day San Franciscans, it's just as well. Now they can enjoy authentic and superb Chinese cuisine which offers everything from seaweed, bird's nest or shark's fin soup, to snow peas and bean sprouts, to Curried Tomato Chicken and Pineapple Pork Sweet and Sour. While feasting, diners can feast their eyes upon the luxuries of the main hall: T'ang Dynasty teak and rosewood latticework and gold-paneled walls accented with rich Mandarin red. Upstairs, in the smaller salon used for parties, hang 12 giant watercolors. Painted on commission by famous artist Jake Lee, they depict the history of the Chinese in the United States, progressing from the first immigrants of 1849 to the champion Chinese fire-hose team of Deadwood, South Dakota, 1888.

Genghis never had it so good.

708 GRANT AVENUE, SAN FRANCISCO

Curried Tomato Chicken

3-4 pounds chicken, boned
4 cups vegetable oil

1. Remove the skin from the chicken and cut the flesh into 1-inch slices.

2. Make the batter by whisking the salt, water, egg yolk, cornstarch and a dash of white pepper in a small bowl until thoroughly blended.

California

Batter:
½ teaspoon salt
1 tablespoon water
1 egg yolk
3 tablespoons cornstarch
White pepper

Sauce:
3 tablespoons vegetable
  oil
1 clove garlic, crushed
1 teaspoon salt
2 tablespoons curry
  powder
1 cup finely diced
  green pepper
1 cup sliced onions
3 tomatoes
1 cup chicken broth
5 tablespoons tomato
  catsup
4 tablespoons sugar
1 teaspoon Accent
1 teaspoon sesame oil

Thickening:
2 tablespoons cornstarch
2 tablespoons water

3. Dip the chicken slices in the batter so that each piece is well coated.

4. Preheat the oil to 375 degrees F. Drop the chicken pieces in, one by one, and stir slowly to prevent the pieces from sticking together. Fry for 2 minutes or until the chicken begins to brown. Remove from the fat and drain on several layers of paper toweling. Keep warm.

5. Prepare the sauce: Place the oil, garlic and salt in a wok or a skillet and cook over high heat until the garlic turns brown. Add the curry powder, green pepper and onion. Toss rapidly for 1 minute.

6. Cut the tomatoes into 4 parts each. Add the tomatoes and the chicken broth to the curry mixture.

7. Combine the catsup, sugar, Accent and sesame seed oil. Add to the mixture in the wok. Stir rapidly. Cover and cook 4 to 5 minutes.

8. Meanwhile make a paste of the cornstarch and water. Uncover the wok or skillet and stir in the paste. Stir until the mixture is very hot and the sauce thickens.

9. Serve the sauce and the chicken with boiled rice (page 426).

SERVES 3 TO 4

Kee Joon's Cuisine of China

The era 960-1279, as we know it, witnessed the signing of the Magna Carta, and Louis VIII of France departing on his final Crusade; but in China they were enjoying the splendors of the Sung Dynasty, one of the golden ages of Chinese history. At Kee Joon's, the recently opened penthouse restaurant that overlooks the bay three miles south of San Francisco's airport, over a million dollars was spent to recreate the opulence of the Sung Dynasty. So wide has been the acclaim that the establishment already does over a million dollars in business a year.

The decor here is classical, not gaudy, with emphasis on good taste. The dynamic, professional Kee Joon was lucky in being able to have the hand-carved panels and marble fountain specially made and imported from China. This is a quiet spot, far removed from the snarls of every day. As the proprietor notes, Kee Joon's was built for a leisurely, pleasurable dining experience. But as he so politely mentions, "If for any reason you wish for service with greater expediency, a word with your captain or your waiter and he will be more than happy to meet your needs."

The endeavor has been to provide a menu selection that is representative of the best in Chinese cuisine, including the choicest dishes from Peking *(Ging)* in North China, Yanchow *(Yang)* in Central China, Szechuan *(Chuan)* in Western China and Canton *(Yuet)* in South China. If a favorite dish is missing, let your wishes be known; the chef will be informed—and the kitchen will go to work for you. The regular fare is well worth a detour to this view by the Bay. Try the sizzling Rice Soup, fresh Lemon Chicken, Smoked Tea Duck or the Szechuan spicy-hot classics.

433 AIRPORT BOULEVARD, BURLINGAME-BY-THE-BAY

Fresh Papaya Soup

1 pound lean boneless
    beef
1½ quarts water

1. Bring the water to a boil and add the lean beef, cut into 1½-inch cubes. Simmer 2 hours.

2. Wash the papaya thoroughly and peel. Cut in half and spoon out the seeds. Cut into

1 large firm papaya
(must be firm)
1 teaspoon salt

Chicken Egg Roll

¼ cup vegetable oil
1 pound boneless breast of
chicken
¼ cup water
½ cup chopped water
chestnuts
½ cup chopped bamboo
sprouts
½ cup Chinese black
mushrooms
2 green onions
¼ teaspoon salt
½ teaspoon sugar
2 tablespoons light soy
sauce
1 teaspoon cornstarch
Egg roll skins (store-bought)
Beaten egg
Vegetable oil for frying

1-inch cubes and add to the broth. Simmer for 30 minutes.

3. This soup can be served strained as a broth or unstrained.

SERVES 2 TO 4

1. If using dried black mushrooms from an Oriental food shop, soak the mushrooms 1 hour in warm water or simmer 30 minutes in boiling water. Drain. Chop the chicken coarsely and mince the green onions.

2. Heat the vegetable oil in a wok or skillet. Add the chicken and cook it for about 5 minutes or until browned, stirring constantly.

3. Add the water and all other ingredients except cornstarch and egg roll skins. Cook, stirring constantly, about 5 minutes. Dissolve the cornstarch in a little water and add. Continue cooking, stirring constantly, just until the mixture is thickened. Transfer to another pan or dish and cool.

4. Spoon mixture onto egg roll skins and fold as desired—square, rectangle or triangle. Seal edges by brushing with a little beaten egg and then pressing firmly with the fingers.

5. Fry the completed egg rolls in 1 inch of vegetable oil heated to 300 to 350 degrees F., turning once to brown the second side. Serve at once.

SERVES 4 TO 6 AS AN APPETIZER

Lubach's

San Diego harbor is the home of 137 naval vessels, a fleet of tuna-fishing superseiners and a lot of industry, and yet it is one of the cleanest bodies of water in the nation. It is also home for some fine restaurants, including Lubach's, which has dispensed dining excellence since its founding in 1956. Mr. R.C.A. Lubach began his gourmet career in Amsterdam at the age of 14, and he has passed along his training to his son Bob, who now helps him run the renowned establishment on the Embarcadero, the centerpiece of San Diego's long waterfront.

Lubach's is divided into three dining rooms. In one, parties *à deux* enjoy picturesque views. The other rooms offer a comfortable and hospitable atmosphere of warm wood paneling, illuminated ship models and crackling fireplaces. Single bud vases grace the snowy tablecloths, and a bottle of clear spring water waits to clear the diner's palate.

The food is simply delicious, watched over by a staff that has been with the restaurant for many years. A buffet hung with copper pans displays salads at noon and a handsome array of raw seafood and steaks at night. Luncheon consists primarily of seafood salads and open-faced sandwiches, though diners can choose from Lubach's full menu anytime.

The specialty is seafood. Rare totuava from the warm waters of Baja California is served in season. Entrees include Broiled Baby Pacific Coast Lobster; fresh Columbia Salmon, poached and served with a Hollandaise sauce; Dover Sole, Shad Roe and Swordfish. Shrimp Cabrillo, another specialty, will pique the appetite—giant shrimp broiled on a skewer with bell peppers and mushrooms. Lubach's also excels in perfectly prepared steaks.

When the main course is completed, a specially designed pastry cart is wheeled to the table, laden with magnificent confections from the restaurant's own bakery. Try the Parisian-style Baba au Rhum—it's sinfully mouthwatering.

2101 NORTH HARBOR DRIVE, SAN DIEGO

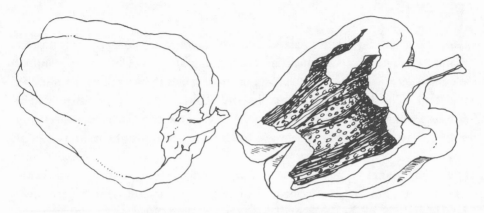

Broiled Jumbo Shrimp Cabrillo

Cabrillo sauce:
½ pound butter
2 teaspoons English mustard
2 bottles catsup, 10 ounces each
Juice of 2 lemons
10 dashes Worcestershire sauce
4 dashes Tabasco sauce

Shrimp Skwers:
48 jumbo shrimp
4 green peppers
1 pound bacon
16 large mushroom caps

1. Make the sauce: Melt butter in a skillet, add the dry mustard and stir a few minutes over a very slow fire. Add the remaining ingredients and stir while bringing to a boil. Reduce the heat and simmer 20 minutes.

2. Peel, clean and devein the shrimp. Cut the peppers into 1-inch squares, removing the seeds and membranes.

3. Cut bacon into 1-inch pieces.

4. Alternate shrimp with bacon and peppers on 16 skewers. There should be 3 of each on every skewer. Add the mushroom caps to the end of the skewers. Brush lightly with oil and cook for 8 to 10 minutes on each side over charcoal or under a broiler.

5. To serve: Allow 2 skewers to a person and serve with white rice and Cabrillo sauce.

SERVES 8

The Mandarin

In Ghirardelli Square, in part of a former factory, is a corner that is forever China. Designed by a Chinese architect and crafted by Chinese carpenters, electricians and plumbers, the restaurant manages to be both handsome and efficient. The kitchen was installed by Robert Yick of the firm whose Chinese woks and grills serve distinguished Chinese cooks worldwide (Danny Kaye, Oriental chef better known for other accomplishments, has one of Yick's woks in his kitchen).

Here Madame Cecilia Chiang, a North China aristocrat turned San Franciscan, cares for the real gourmets of California, patrons who have known her since the days she ran a small restaurant on Polk Street.

At lunch Madame Chiang offers a Chinese-style buffet so the diner can see before he tastes. Slices of abalone are quickly cooked with Oriental mushrooms; baby shrimp are lightly sautéed and served with fresh green peas. At dinner there's a Mongolian chafing pot of bubbling chicken broth in which diners dip thin slices of chicken, oysters, bean curd or crisp vegetables until they are cooked. Afterward they consume the broth. Beautiful set worthy of Mr. Moto. Interesting artifacts, and inscrutable, lively drinks.

GHIRARDELLI SQUARE, 900 NORTH POINT, SAN FRANCISCO

Sweet and Sour Fish

1 3-pound fish (rock cod, haddock, carp or red snapper)
2 tablespoons soy sauce
2 tablespoons sherry
1 egg, slightly beaten
4 tablespoons cornstarch
Vegetable oil

1. Order the fish cleaned, leaving the head, tail and fins intact. Make 5 to 6 deep parallel slashes on both sides so that the seasoned paste will soak into the meat.

2. Combine the soy sauce, sherry, egg and cornstarch and rub the mixture on both sides of the fish. Let stand for 20 minutes.

3. Heat 2 inches of salad oil in a pan large enough to hold the fish.

4. Deep-fry the fish until a deep golden brown on both sides. Remove the fish with 2

Sauce:
8 tablespoons catsup
4 tablespoons wine vinegar
8 tablespoons sugar
6 tablespoons soy sauce
4 tablespoons cornstarch
2 cups water
1 sweet pepper, shredded (optional)
1 carrot, shredded (optional)

spatulas to a long fish platter. (The fish may be fried in advance and refried again just before serving to make it crisper.)

5. Prepare the sauce: Combine the catsup, vinegar, sugar and soy sauce in a small saucepan. Mix and boil for a few minutes. Gradually add the cornstarch mixed with the water and stir until the sauce is thick.

6. Pour the sauce over the hot fish just before serving. Garnish, if desired, with the pepper and carrot shreds.

SERVES 4

Asparagus à la Shangtung

½ pound asparagus
Salt
Sugar
Soy sauce
Sesame oil

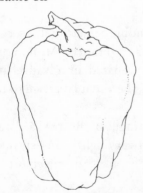

1. Snap off the tender tips of the asparagus and discard the rest—the stems will naturally break where the tender part begins. Cut the tips diagonally into pieces 2½ inches long.

2. Bring water to boil in a large saucepan, over high heat.

3. Drop asparagus into the water and cook 2 to 3 minutes. Drain, rinse in cold water and drain again.

4. Sprinkle over the asparagus a little salt (about ¼ teaspoon), a smaller amount of sugar, a few drops of soy sauce and a few drops of sesame oil. Stir to blend seasonings and refrigerate in a covered container. When chilled, taste and adjust seasoning if necessary. Serve cold.

SERVES 2

Maurice et Charles' Bistrot

Californians and visitors alike make pilgrimages to this gourmet's shrine in San Rafael, a bistrot in the finest sense of the word, to participate in the artistry of Messrs. Robert Charles, Maurice Amzallag, and chef Claude Collomb. In part, for the quenelles—the stuff dreams are made of. When asked for his quenelle recipe, M. Charles replies, "Always when asked I give the dictionary definition of a kiss. To kiss means to touch with the lips as a token of love or affection; but how it is accomplished is open to wide interpretation."

In the spirit of its name, the Bistrot setting is a long room with wooden bar, oversized wine glasses, and white, graffiti-covered walls (visitors are invited to express themselves) hung with oils and a gouache by Marilyn Rabinovich, whose *Anemones* graces the menu. Many regulars stay with the lamb, a traditional Charles specialty from his "Fleur de Lys" French landmark of the '60s where virtually no meat but lamb was served—succulent, medium-rare, exquisite. Others are enraptured over Marcassin Grande Chasse (young wild boar), served with a masterful sauce, chestnut puree and cranberries, or the authentic Parisian Vacherin.

A 15-minute drive north from the Golden Gate Bridge takes you to one of the finest French dining experiences available. Ah, those quenelles.

901 LINCOLN AVE. AT THIRD, SAN RAFAEL

Vacherin Glacé Imperial

Meringue:
8 egg whites
2¼ cups fine granulated sugar
Few drops lemon juice

A vacherin is a noble dessert that is served on great occasions in France. All its component parts are prepared in advance and then assembled just before it is carried to the table.

1. Prepare meringues: Butter a large, heavy baking sheet very lightly and sprinkle with flour. Using a saucepan cover 6 to 7

Confectioners' sugar

Filling:
1 cup diced candied
    fruit
2 tablespoons kirsch
1 pint chocolate ice
    cream
½ pint vanilla ice cream

Topping:
Crème Chantilly (p. 420)
1 tablespoon cocoa or
    2 tablespoons shaved
    semi-sweet chocolate
1 tablespoon toasted
    almonds

inches in diameter, outline 4 circles on the flour, leaving a little space between.

Whip the egg whites until fairly stiff. Gradually add the sugar and continue beating until very stiff, smooth and glossy. Do not underbeat. Beat in lemon juice.

Fill in the circles with the meringue (use pastry bag with ½-inch tip or spoon and spatula). Sprinkle with confectioners' sugar. Bake the meringues in a 200-degree oven until very dry but not browned (1½ to 2 hours).

2. Stir the kirsch into the candied fruit. Allow the ice creams to soften but not melt. Prepare the Crème Chantilly.

3. To assemble dessert: Place 1 meringue on a round platter and cover with a layer of chocolate ice cream. Cover with another meringue and gently spread with vanilla ice cream. Sprinkle with half the candied fruits. Add another meringue and cover with chocolate ice cream and top with the fourth meringue. "Frost" with Crème Chantilly. Sprinkle the sides with cocoa or shaved chocolate and the top with the remaining candied fruit and the almonds.

4. Present the confection to the guests, then cut into wedges and transfer to dessert plates at the table.

SERVES 6

Mister A's Restaurant

Unlike the gloomy *Scarlet Letter* of literary fame, the red "*A*" on Mister A's Restaurant is a happy symbol marking the scene of good eating and drinking.

Perched atop the 12-story Fifth Avenue Financial Centre—a skyscraper by downtown San Diego standards—the restaurant offers diners a choice of views: the blue bay with harboring ships, the majestic trees in Balboa Park, planes headed for Lindbergh Field, so low in their flight paths that they appear life-size as they glide silently by (the silence due to careful planning by the building's architects and engineers).

In the evening one watches the sunset drown itself passionately in the restless Pacific; at night there is communion of city lights and heavenly stars.

The name is the result of a contest held before the restaurant opened, the Mr. A referred to being John Alessio. For him the building and its crowning glory, the restaurant, represent a dream come true and a fitting ornament for the city he loves.

Dining is suitably cosmopolitan. Order Oysters Rockefeller (complemented by emerald-green spinach), Fettuccine Alfredo (compounded at tableside for the patrons' edification), Scampi Français (featuring a superb herbed butter sauce) or Risotto alla Milanese.

2550 FIFTH AVENUE, SAN DIEGO

Risotto alla Milanese
(Milanese Chicken Rice)

7 cups chicken stock or
  bouillon
8 tablespoons butter
½ cup finely chopped onions

1. Bring chicken stock to a simmer in a saucepan and keep over low heat.

2. Melt 4 tablespoons of butter in a heavy 3-quart heatproof casserole over moderate heat. Cook the onions in the butter for 7 to 8 minutes, stirring frequently. Do not let them brown.

2 cups white raw rice
(preferably imported
Italian)
½ cup dry white wine
⅛ teaspoon powdered
saffron
½ cup freshly grated
Parmesan cheese

3. Add the rice, preferably imported Italian, and cook, stirring, for 1 to 2 minutes or until all the grains are coated with butter and are somewhat opaque.

4. Pour in the wine and boil until it is almost all absorbed.

5. Add 2 cups of simmering stock to rice and cook uncovered, stirring occasionally until all the liquid is absorbed.

6. Add 2 more cups of stock and cook, stirring occasionally.

7. Put the saffron in 2 cups of stock and let steep for a few minutes.

8. When the rice is almost dry, add the saffron stock and cook until the rice is dry again.

9. Taste the rice to see if it is tender. If not, continue to cook, adding the remaining stock ½ cup at a time until the rice is just tender.

10. Stir in the remaining butter and the grated cheese, fluffing the rice with a fork. Serve at once.

SERVES 8

Mon Grenier

"**T**hank heaven for little girls," you cry as "Gigi," the dressmaker's dummy, is rolled to your table with the crayoned menu that announces marvelous dishes of French creation.

Ventura Boulevard is the mise-en-scène for up-and-coming restaurants and the lead has been given to Mon Grenier, under the highly personalized service of owner/chef Andre Lion and the skilled culinary baton of Robert Pichot. The melon and gold attic setting is imaginative, splendidly bathed in fresh flowers. Specialties include quail, rabbit and squab. The Plat d'Eté is almost too pretty to eat. Who can refuse cheesecake, especially when it is prepared in the old-fashioned way? Then there are Mon Grenier Strawberries Marie-Josef, Peach Cardinal and Pear Belle Hélène.

"Gigi" is fickle. She changes with the seasons—that is, her apron on which is written the menu—but there is nothing fickle about the quality of the cuisine she heralds.

18040 VENTURA BOULEVARD, ENCINO

California

Plat d'Eté
(Summer Platter)

4 avocados
Lemon juice
8 medium tomatoes
2 cups small shrimp, cooked
1 cup mayonnaise
1 teaspoon tomato puree
½ teaspoon Worcestershire sauce
Salt and pepper
2 hard-cooked eggs
Parsley
Lettuce

1. Split the avocados, remove the seed and brush with lemon juice to prevent darkening.

2. Plunge the tomatoes into boiling water for 30 seconds. Remove with a slotted spoon and peel off the skins. Cut off a slice from each tomato and scoop out the seeds. Place upside down on a drain to remove all excess juice.

3. In a bowl, mix the tomato puree with the mayonnaise, and then stir in the shrimp.

4. Season with the Worcestershire sauce and salt and pepper to taste.

5. Turn the tomatoes upright and season the interior lightly with salt and pepper.

6. Place the avocados and tomatoes alternately on a serving platter. Fill the tomatoes and avocados with the shrimp mixture. Replace the tops of the tomatoes and top each fruit with a slice of hard-boiled egg. Sprinkle with parsley. Surround the dish with finely shredded lettuce.

SERVES 8

L'Odéon

Black, gold, white—classic colors, uncompromising quality.

Peter Zane is not a stern man. He grew up in Greece, a light and lovely place. But his adult life, he says, has been lived in restaurants. First, the family restaurant in Nogales, Mexico. Then he worked for Scandia, in Los Angeles, and the Lambros and the Balalaika in San Francisco before opening his own Copenhagen in San Francisco. (It was destroyed by fire in 1963.) In 1966, he opened L'Odéon, a restaurant which works.

His chef de cuisine, Claude Troska, acquired part of his training in the kitchens of the Paris Ritz Hotel, because his father is chef there. Troska and Zane work closely together; San Franciscans are a notoriously fussy bunch. Baked Spanakopitta; Filet of Sole Véronique; a brochette of lobster tails, prawns, crab legs and scallops to tempt—and to please. On the side, a salad of fresh mushrooms with avocado or garlic-kissed cottage fried potatoes that deserve a more elegant name.

Black, gold, white; antique mirrors increasing the feeling of spaciousness; crystal chandeliers; murals of ancient Attica; soft lighting. A place that is classic, neither real nor unreal, neither French nor Greek; a place which works for Peter Zane . . . for you.

565 CLAY STREET, SAN FRANCISCO

California

Fresh Mushroom Salad

15 medium-size mushroom
    caps
½ avocado, peeled and
    mashed
1 hard-cooked egg yolk,
    mashed
1 teaspoon chopped parsley
1 teaspoon finely chopped
    onion
1 teaspoon wine vinegar
Juice of 1 lemon
2 tablespoons garlic oil
    (page 424)

Garnish:
Watercress
3 thin slices of feta cheese

1. Wash mushrooms thoroughly and cut into thin slices. Place in a large salad bowl.

2. Combine the avocado, egg yolk, parsley and onion and add to the mushrooms. Toss lightly.

3. Just before serving, add the oil, vinegar, lemon juice and garlic oil. Toss thoroughly and serve on chilled salad plates, garnished with sprigs of fresh watercress and a thin slice of feta cheese.

SERVES 3

Ondine

A 15-minute drive across the Golden Gate Bridge—or a slightly longer trip by ferry—brings San Franciscans to the Sausalito waterfront where they dine sumptuously while enjoying a sweeping view of the Bay and the city's skyline, jeweled with light as the sky darkens and night falls.

Moving spirits behind this excellent restaurant that opened 19 years ago in an extensively remodeled bay-front building are Frederico Martinez, George Gutekunst and Alfred Roblin. The latter, whose preparations are in the tradition of classic French cookery, is the chef, and a disciple of Escoffier. Boneless Squab Montmorency and Pheasant Ondine are favorites among the fowl, fish and seafood entrees Roblin regards as his specialties (with advance notice he will prepare game or fish brought in by his patrons who are successful hunters or fishermen). The desserts include soufflés of ethereal lightness.

Ondine's logo is a perky mermaid who in one hand holds a trident—symbol of Poseidon, God of the Sea—while reaching for a star with the other. A suitable device for a dining spot with an unsurpassed view of sea, sky and sparkle.

558 BRIDGEWAY, SAUSALITO

Pheasant Ondine

1 pheasant
1 onion
1 carrot
1 stalk celery
1 leek
1 bay leaf
½ teaspoon thyme
4 juniper berries
¼ cup dry sherry

1. Disjoint the bird. Break or cut the leg at the thigh joint, keeping only the thigh. Set breasts and thighs aside. Cut the carcass and leg into small pieces for stock. Chop the onion, carrot, celery and leek.

2. Make the stock: Combine pheasant bones and sherry in a covered saucepan and cook until the sherry evaporates. Add the chopped vegetables, bay leaf, thyme, juniper berries and water. Bring to a boil, skimming off any scum that rises to the surface, then

4 cups water
Salt and pepper
6 tablespoons butter
6 tablespoons flour
¼ pound butter
2 tablespoons vodka
8 mushroom caps, sliced
4 shallots, chopped
2 cups sour cream

cover, reduce heat and simmer 1½ hours. Strain and season with salt and pepper.

3. Melt the ¼ pound butter over moderate heat in a large skillet. Add the pheasant breasts and thighs, cover and cook slowly 30 minutes or until tender, turning several times. Keep the heat moderate to low so the color of the bird remains pale. Do not brown.

4. Make velouté: Melt the 6 tablespoons butter. Add the flour and beat with a wire whisk until smooth. Add 2 cups of the stock and bring to a boil. Cook about 10 minutes, until thick and creamy.

5. When pheasant breasts and thighs are done remove them to a heated platter and keep warm. In the same skillet sauté the mushrooms quickly. Add the vodka and cook until the liquid is nearly all evaporated. Add shallots and cook until transparent but not browned.

6. Add ¾ cup of the velouté to the skillet and bring to a boil, stirring gently with the wire whip. Remove from heat and stir in the sour cream. Return to moderate heat just long enough to warm the sour cream. Taste and correct seasoning as needed.

7. Pour sauce over pheasant and serve at once.

SERVES 2

L'Orangerie

If it has been said that one French restaurant looks like any other, then L'Orangerie will blow the myth to smithereens. This leading Frisco dining place has tried to be refreshingly unique and has succeeded. The attractive interior is a series of intimate salons, each individually decorated. To the right of the entrance is a library-bar, with shelves of books and tastefully hung paintings. Ahead lies the dining room, summery and gardenlike with white latticework over green walls and artificial topiary orange trees. The tables are set with refined Vannes-le-Chatel crystal and Céralene china of the "Indian Summer" pattern. The overall effect is that of a charming private house awaiting the arrival of the dining guests.

The hospitable feeling owes much to the charming French proprietor, Madame Roselyne Dupart, and the glories of the kitchen are in the capable hands of Basque chef Alphonse Achéritogaray. The two work continually on new dishes, which may take up to six months to perfect. Given a day's notice, the chef will prepare his specialties: Sole Alphonse, Homard du Maine à l'Armoricaine, Cuisseau de Veau *Lur-Saluces*. But even the everyday menu has its own quintessential flavor. The Salade d'Endives is classically simple yet tasty, the Oeufs Farcis Chimay are hard-boiled eggs stuffed with *duxelles* and capped with a béchamel glazed with cheese. The Quiche Lorraine is a quivery custard studded with bacon and baked in a tender crust of *pâté brisée*. L'Orangerie is well known for its Carré de Porc, especially since the roast loin of pork is sliced at the table and bathed in a rich orange and cognac sauce. But the real variations on the orange theme come with desserts such as the Orange Glacée masterpiece, an orange shell piled with Grand Marnier-flavored vanilla ice cream and signed with whipped cream and mint leaves.

419 O'FARRELL STREET, SAN FRANCISCO

California

Carré de Porc à L'Orangerie *(Roast Pork with Orange Sauce)*

1 rack of pork (4 pounds)
Salt and pepper
1 tablespoon sugar
1 teaspoon vinegar
1 cup fresh orange juice
2 cups veal stock or concentrated beef consommé
2 tablespoons butter
1 tablespoon cognac
3 oranges

Garnish:
Orange slices
Watercress
Celery

1. Preheat the oven to 400 degrees F.
2. Sprinkle the pork with salt and pepper. Wrap it in foil and place in a roasting pan and cook for 2 hours.
3. Make the sauce by cooking the sugar with a teaspoon of water in a heavy small skillet until it turns light brown. Add the vinegar and orange juice. Cook 10 minutes.
4. Add the veal stock and let it boil down to half its original volume. Strain.
5. Whip the butter and cognac into the sauce. Keep warm.
6. Remove the pork from the foil. Place in an open roasting pan on a rack and cover with 2 oranges, peeled and quartered. Sprinkle with a little sugar. Put back into a 500-degree oven for 10 minutes or until golden brown.
7. Place the pork on a heated platter, remove the orange quarters and garnish with fresh orange slices. Put in small bunches of watercress and 2 stalks of celery at each end of the roast.

SERVES 6

Paolo's Continental Restaurant

If you know the way to San José—and appreciate a menu of variety and excellence—Paolo's is the place. The offerings include 75 entrees and over 100 special delicacies, all cooked to order. Each of the two dining rooms has a center table laden with cheeses, pastries and an array of fresh fruit that ranges from the familiar apples and pears to fresh almonds, loquats and prickly pears. There is even variety in decor. The west dining room is airy, light and casual, while the east dining room is formally elegant.

The population of San José, located 50 miles south of San Francisco, was 60,000 in 1955; it is 600,000 today. Paolo's was opened by John and Geri Allen in 1959, and its popularity has grown, keeping pace with the growth of the city it graces.

The restaurant is cosmopolitan and eclectic, but the flourishes are predominantly Italian. There are 28 different kinds of pasta and noodles, and Paolo's makes its own Cassata, Zuppa Inglesa, Cannoli, Cassatini and Sfogliatelle. Also featured is a moist and delicately flavored cheesecake that pleases the discriminating.

520 EAST SANTA CLARA STREET, SAN JOSE

California

Paolo's Original Empress Salad

Dressing:
- ½ cup olive oil
- 5 tablespoons red wine vinegar
- Juice of 2 lemons
- ½ teaspoon Worcestershire sauce
- 1 teaspoon dry mustard
- ½ teaspoon sugar
- 1 teaspoon coarse pepper
- 2 teaspoons salt
- 2 cloves garlic, minced

Salad:
- 3 Belgian endive
- 4 handfuls fresh spinach
- 2 cups fresh mushrooms, sliced ¼ inch thick
- 1½ cups Dungeness crab legs
- 1½ cups baby shrimp
- 1 cup thin pimiento strips
- 1 cup crisp-cooked bacon pieces
- 4 hard-cooked eggs, coarsely chopped

1. Combine the ingredients for the dressing and mix well.

2. Cut end of each endive and separate the leaves. Throw the well-washed spinach into a large pan of salted boiling water for 15 seconds. Remove, drain and cool.

3. Mix the spinach, mushrooms, crab, shrimp and pimiento with ¾ of the salad dressing.

4. Place the endive in a salad bowl and mix with the remaining dressing.

5. Divide the mixture equally in mounds on 4 large cold plates.

6. Arrange the endive leaves, laying them on top of the salad like a tent. Sprinkle chopped egg and bacon on top of each salad and serve.

Note: Endive and mushrooms require a little extra salt, so taste for seasoning.

SERVES 4

Raffaello

Family tradition flowers at this restaurant.

The owner and manager is Remo d'Agliano; the head chef is his mother, Mrs. Amelia d'Agliano. The restaurant's name honors the late Raffaello d'Agliano, Remo's father and Amelia's husband, a famous chef and the son of a famous chef.

Here, then, one finds the distillation of three generations of experience in the preparation of the regional specialties of Tuscany and Piedmont. The menu lists a variety of pastas, all made from scratch under the watchful eye of Mrs. d'Agliano, along with fresh fish, chicken, veal, sweetbreads and beef entrees prepared to the diner's order. The authentically Italian desserts include zabaglione and homemade spumoni ice cream. As might be expected, the wine list offers excellent wines from Italy as well as the products of France and California. The setting is intimate, with fresh flowers and sparkling crystal on the tables; the pace is relaxed. Dinner at Raffaello's is a pleasant experience that should not be hurried.

What better end for a day on Carmel's picturesque beaches than the sun-drenched, sea-kissed cuisine of the country that might be called Europe's California?

MISSION BETWEEN OCEAN AND SEVENTH, CARMEL

Fettuccine alla Romana

Homemade pasta:

3 cups all-purpose flour
2 teaspoons salt
3 whole eggs
2 tablespoons oil

1. Pour the flour onto a working surface and fashion a well in the center. Put the salt and eggs in the well and start working the eggs into the flour until mixed.

2. Start adding the oil gradually and work until you have a firm, shiny, elastic dough.

3. Roll very thin and cut into narrow strips. Let the strips dry for 1 hour before cooking. (If you have a pasta machine it will

Sauce:
¼ pound butter, softened
 1 egg yolk
¼ cup fresh cream
½ cup freshly grated
   Parmesan cheese
Salt and pepper

do the kneading, rolling and cutting for you.)

4. Prepare the sauce: Beat the butter until it is fluffy. Still beating, add the egg yolk and then the cream. Finally beat in the cheese and season with salt and plenty of black pepper.

5. Boil the pasta in a large kettle of salted boiling water for 6 to 7 minutes or just until tender (al dente).

6. Drain the noodles thoroughly and toss with the sauce. Serve with crusty Italian bread and a green salad.

SERVES 4

The Ranch House

California

"**I** know a little garden close/set thick with lily and red rose," sings the poet. Guests have discovered that dining in a gourmet garden setting at Alan Hooker's Ranch House in the Ojai Valley is a delightful new experience. The decor here is strictly sylvan. Ensconced in bucolic surroundings beneath the branches of ancient oaks, lulled by the plashy babble of a brook in the patio (instead of an orchestral din), the world of the booming highway seems far removed. The great god Pan might be lurking behind a nearby rhododendron.

Cuisine at The Ranch House is cooked to order. The fresh herbs (80 varieties) that flavor the food are grown on the premises as are some of the vegetables. Regular trips are made to the wharves in Santa Barbara to obtain fresh fish. Six different breads are produced in the restaurant bakery and sold by the loaf to take home, if you wish.

Formerly a vegetarian guest house, the restaurant reopened with meat added to the bill of fare in the late '50s. Alan Hooker, inexperienced as a meat cook, found it necessary to experiment and in time originated a number of recipes that were finally published in three cookbooks. A sampling of meats on the menu testifies to the author's skill as a chef. During a quiet hour, try the Chicken Poached in Champagne with fresh mushrooms and sweet herbs; or Lamb Armenian with oriental rice; or Pork Hawaiian with fresh pineapple, fresh ginger and fresh coconut.

102 BESANT ROAD, OJAI

Lamb Armenian

6 eggplants
3 pounds leg of lamb, ground
4 tablespoons butter

1. Cut off ¾ inch from stem ends of the eggplants and reserve them.
2. Using a spoon, hollow out the eggplants, leaving a shell ¾ inch thick. Be careful not to puncture the skin.
3. Steam the eggplants in a large covered

3 tablespoons fresh mint
leaves, minced
¼ cup cooked rice
½ cup old-fashioned
oatmeal, uncooked
1 cup tomato sauce
1 teaspoon salt
½ teaspoon onion salt
¼ teaspoon garlic salt
2 whole eggs, beaten

kettle for 9 minutes, using very little water. Do not overcook. Remove and cool immediately, draining out any juice.

4. Preheat oven to 400 degrees F. Sauté the meat in butter just until it begins to lose its red color. Add all the remaining ingredients.

5. Stuff the mixture in the eggplant. Put tops on eggplants and set them in shallow pan. Bake uncovered at 400 degrees F. for 45 minutes.

SERVES 6

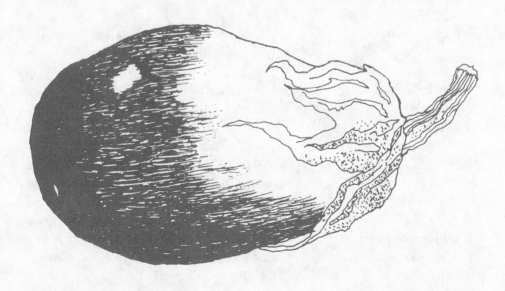

René Verdon's Le Trianon

Le Trianon brings 18th-Century reasonableness to dinner. René Verdon was White House chef during the Kennedy administration, and much of the glamour still lingers in the rose pompadour interior of his restaurant. The classical setting is yet a little frivolous, which would suggest that although Monsieur Verdon excels in the great classical dishes of French haute cuisine, one does not wear a learned scowl when eating his good food. No matter the Gallic tradition of the weighty table; no matter the stories of chefs' suicides (as that of Louis XIV's when the fish course failed to arrive on time, or in our own day, when a restaurant loses its Michelin stars); no matter the cream sauces, Le Trianon is alive with edible, gay, lightly delicious food. Mrs. Onassis, a confirmed Francophile, has said, "We envy San Francisco for having you there."

Le Trianon is expensive. But one leaves with the feeling of consciousness expanded, of possibilities examined. Free from the phoniness of many pseudo-French eating houses, the restaurant is the genuine article.

242 O'FARRELL STREET, SAN FRANCISCO

Arlequin Soufflé

Vanilla sauce:
1 cup milk
3 egg yolks
¼ cup sugar
1 teaspoon vanilla extract

Soufflé:
1 cup milk
8 egg whites
1 tablespoon sugar
6 egg yolks
¼ cup sugar

1. To make the vanilla sauce, heat milk to a boil over high heat.

2. Put the egg yolks, sugar and vanilla in a blender and turn to high speed. While blender is running, add the hot milk slowly. Chill in the refrigerator.

3. To make the soufflé: Preheat oven to 350 degrees F. Grease 6 individual soufflé dishes (3 inches in diameter) with butter and chill in the refrigerator. When they are well chilled, butter again and sprinkle with granulated sugar. Divide each dish in half with a folded piece of aluminum foil.

4. Bring milk to a boil.

¼ cup flour
2 teaspoons vanilla
  extract
½ ounce unsweetened
  chocolate

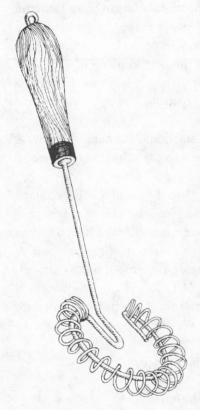

5. Put the egg whites into a large bowl and beat with an electric beater until the mixture is light and stands in soft peaks. Gradually add the 1 tablespoon of sugar and mix until blended. Set aside.

6. Beat 2 egg yolks in a small bowl until light. Add the ¼ cup of sugar and the flour and mix until it becomes a paste. Add the paste to the hot milk and whisk over high heat until it becomes thick and smooth. Add the vanilla and blend well.

7. Divide the mixture into 2 saucepans. Add chocolate and 2 egg yolks slightly beaten to 1 pan and stir over medium heat until chocolate is blended.

8. Add 2 egg yolks to the other saucepan and stir over medium heat until well mixed.

9. Fold about a third of the beaten egg whites into the vanilla mixture; fold the remaining beaten egg whites into the chocolate mixture.

10. Pour the chocolate mixture into half of each of the prepared soufflé dishes, and the vanilla into the other halves. Carefully remove the foil.

11. Place soufflé dishes on a baking sheet and bake 30 to 35 minutes or until firm.

12. Serve at once, warm, with the chilled vanilla sauce.

SERVES 6

Ristorante Chianti

Although the location is a corner store, this eating place, opened by Romeo Salta some 40 years ago, is not your regular red-candle-in-a-Chianti-bottle Italian restaurant. The decor has been described as Tuscan Art Nouveau and not Italian Funky. It is possible to order spaghetti, but Cotoletta di Vitello alla Milanese would be more appropriate.

President Laurence Mindel believes in a combination of style and quiet intimacy. The candlelight falls on white linens, the waiters in black tie stand out against the colors of the murals. Accordingly, for those whose days are spent before movie cameras and flashbulbs, the place is solace. A Burt Reynolds or a Dinah Shore may be seated in the first booth to the right of the entrance, Top figures in the contemporary American art world may be huddled there, too, discussing a new limited edition. The restaurant is not without signs of its own devotion to modern art.

Reservations are a must, since the place is small and the bar quite tiny. A banquette along the side will give you a chance to see animated Hollywood squeeze itself into a pleasant formality.

The food, you will find, is superb, the Osso Buco of chef Bernhard Koeniger being a star performer. Fork-tender veal has the spotlight in a selection of classic renderings, and you may want to try Chianti's own Italian salad, a delectable mixture of romaine, tomatoes, salami, cheese, garbanzo, mushrooms, Parmesan and the salad dressing of the house, or the Stracci-atella alla Romana. Follow with Fettuccine Alfredo and the Lombatina, a thick T-bone veal loin chop grilled in herb butter. Dessert may be just those little Amaretti cookies they pass out; or, if you must be partial to sweet things, try the Zabaglione.

7383 MELROSE AVENUE, LOS ANGELES

Stracciatella alla Romana
(Roman Egg Soup)

1½ pounds fresh spinach
3 quarts well-seasoned
  chicken broth
6 eggs, slightly beaten
¼ cup grated Parmesan
  cheese

1. Wash the spinach carefully.

2. Place in a large kettle of boiling salted water and cook until tender. Drain thoroughly. Cool and chop coarsely.

3. Bring the chicken broth to a boil and add the chopped spinach.

4. Reduce the heat and add the eggs gradually while beating with a wire whisk. Whisk rapidly so that the eggs become like thin noodles.

5. Serve the soup in heated soup plates and sprinkle each serving with grated cheese.

SERVES 6

Ristorante Orsi

"**R**eminiscente a una serata a Firenze," beams the knowledgeable traveler after dining at Ristorante Orsi, for this is one of the few fine American restaurants that specialize in the subtle cuisine of the northern Italian province of Tuscany.

A native of Tuscany, chef Oresti Orsi has pursued his calling under varied conditions. He cooked for Italian restaurants before World War II, then for an officers' mess in the Italian army. Later, captured by the Germans, he sharpened his skills in a prison camp by making the most of the meager provisions that came his way. Finally, he escaped via the Polish underground and in San Francisco joined forces with another Tuscan, Joseph Orsini. Ristorante Orsi opened in 1963 with host Orsini overseeing the dining rooms and wine cellar, and chef Orsi planning the menu and directing food preparation.

Linguine alla Vongole—pasta with tiny, extremely sweet clams steamed in white wine—is a favorite entree, as is Beef alla Orsi—a tender fillet stuffed with prosciutto and bathed in wine sauce. The cannelloni are superb.

Many deem Tuscan cooking the finest of all Italy's regional cuisines. Ristorante Orsi gives San Franciscans an opportunity to decide for themselves.

375 BUSH STREET, SAN FRANCISCO

California

Beef alla Orsi

2   pounds tenderloin of
    beef, well trimmed
¼   pound prosciutto, thinly
    sliced
4   tablespoons butter
1   5-ounce piece of
    tenderloin or sirloin
    (boneless and fat-free)
¾   cup Burgundy wine
1   tablespoon chopped
    truffles
4   tablespoons cognac

1. Preheat the oven to 400 degrees F. Butterfly the beef neatly by cutting lengthwise through the middle but not cutting through.

2. Spread a thin layer of prosciutto across the cut and close the tenderloin. Heat the butter in an overproof skillet and brown the meat on all sides. Place in the oven and roast 15 to 20 minutes according to desired doneness.

3. Sprinkle a small skillet with salt and sauté the 5 ounces of beef over high heat just until brown on both sides. Squeeze the juice through an old-fashioned orange juice press or through a clean dish towel (unless you have a duck press). You will need ½ cup of beef juice.

4. Transfer the beef tenderloins to a serving platter and keep warm.

5. Add the wine and truffles to the pan and cook over moderate heat for 10 minutes or until the sauce thickens. Stir with a fork. Add the meat juice and 2 tablespoons of the cognac and pour into a gravy boat.

6. Heat the remaining cognac. Pour over the meat and touch with a lighted match just at the time of serving.

SERVES 2 TO 4

The Sardine Factory

If it hadn't been for one man, John Steinbeck, Monterey's Old Cannery Row might now be only an empty local memory. Just before the sardines mysteriously disappeared, and the clanking canneries wheezed into silence, the novelist's hilarious *Cannery Row* created an unforgettable world of raucous fish workers and poetic bums.

Perched on a rocky prominence above The Row, surrounded by chunks of cannery machines and an actual early fishing boat, The Sardine Factory is a gourmet restaurant that has maintained the friendly atmosphere of the old days. Included on the menu are savory Italian dishes whose recipes have been handed down from the original fishing families. Proprietors Ted Balestreri (related to a Salinas lettuce pioneer) and Bert Cutino (descendant of one of the first Sicilian fishermen to colonize the area) chose to decorate their restaurant with authentic drawings and early photos of Cannery Row in its heyday. Among the memorabilia is a menu billboard that lists Soup, 10¢; Sandwich, 10¢; Chili Beans, 15¢; Pie, 10¢; Doughnut, 6¢; Coffee, free.

Though whistles no longer blow in the night to bring cannery workers down from Huckleberry Hill to cut fish, Monterey's Sardine Factory Restaurant preserves an illusion of the good old days when Steinbeck walked The Row, a hulking figure in his sheepskin coat.

701 WAVE STREET, MONTEREY

Veal Cardinal

6 6-ounce lobster tails
1¼ pounds fine white veal,
  cut in thin slices
Flour
2 tablespoons butter

1. Dip the lobster and veal in flour. Heat the butter in a skillet and sauté the lobster lightly.

2. Add the mushrooms and continue cooking until the mushrooms are tender.

3. Remove the lobster and mushrooms with a slotted spoon and set aside.

1½ pounds fresh mushrooms,
washed and sliced

½ cup dry sauterne wine

2 tablespoons fresh
chopped parsley

2 tablespoons fresh
chopped garlic

Juice of 1 lemon

Salt and pepper

4. Sauté the veal until golden brown on both sides, adding more butter if necessary. Return the lobster and mushrooms to the skillet.

5. Add the wine and touch with a lighted match.

6. When the flames have subsided, add the parsley, lemon juice and garlic. Simmer for 2 to 3 minutes, taste for seasoning and serve.

SERVES 6

18 prawns or jumbo shrimp

Beer

1½ pounds crab meat

¾ cup lemon juice

1 cup grated Parmesan
cheese

1 cup cracker meal or fine
bread crumbs

5 egg yolks

1 cup chopped parsley

6 hard-cooked eggs,
chopped

1 cup shredded Swiss
cheese

1 cup Hollandaise

1. Shell prawns and split them open, butterfly-style. Marinate them in beer (enough to cover them) at room temperature.

2. Combine all other ingredients except the Hollandaise for the stuffing.

3. Preheat the oven to 350 degrees F. Drain prawns and place them in a shallow casserole. Divide the stuffing among them and top each with 1 teaspoon of Hollandaise.

4. Bake 20 to 30 minutes. Serve 3 to a person.

SERVES 6 AS AN APPETIZER

Prawns St. James

La Scala

The *Los Angeles Magazine* aptly described Jean Leon's swinging restaurant as "va-rooming like a Maserati." The writer noted, "At times I think I'm in an Italian street opera when waiters cluster and carry on about whatever is curious of the moment . . . other times it's like a jazzy resort hideaway with leagues of leggy girls at the bar . . . other moments make me wonder if we're not all back in *haute* Hollywood when the world was golden and Lana Turner itched to rhumba and smog was unreal." It's Via Veneto in spirit, "very merry with a sort of slap-on-the-bottom attitude about life."

Gary Cooper called La Scala his second home, the Kennedy clan had their California parties catered from here, all the Hollywood somebodies come in droves. The waiters in dinner jackets and white bow ties are reminders that a reputation for dining is based on more than a fun atmosphere. The food must be well prepared. So Leon offers a Mozzarella Marinara which is golden and crusty, with a melting center of rich Teleme cheese, a clever substitute for stringy mozzarella, and delectable eggplant crêpes. There are generous prime New York cut sirloins and steaks with green peppers sautéed in cognac. For a finale, try the whipped wonders of Grand Marnier Soufflé or Crêpes Suzette.

La Scala's wine cellar is reputed as one of the best in the West. A Basque, Leon has been able to enjoy fine wine since childhood. Today, he buys wines as another man would acquire choice stocks or bonds and adds to his collection with vintages from his own vineyards in Northern Spain.

9455 SANTA MONICA BOULEVARD, BEVERLY HILLS

Melenzana Nostra (Eggplant Crêpes)

12 very thin savory crêpes (page 421)

1. Make the crêpe batter and let it stand in the refrigerator at least 30 minutes. Lightly grease a 6-inch skillet and heat it well. Pour in a large spoonful of crêpe batter and tilt the pan to coat the bottom with a thin

1½ cups Béchamel sauce
(page 416)

Spanish sauce:
2 tablespoons chopped
onion
1 clove garlic, minced
2 tablespoons butter
1 tablespoon chopped
green pepper
2 cups plum tomatoes
1 bay leaf
1 teaspoon salt
¼ teaspoon sugar
⅛ teaspoon cloves
3 tablespoons chopped
olives

Filling:
¼ cup olive oil
½ small onion, finely
chopped
1 eggplant, cut in
½-inch cubes
1 ripe tomato, peeled,
seeded and chopped
½ teaspoon oregano
12 slices Fontana cheese
(1½ inches square)
½ cup imported Parmesan
cheese

film. Cook over moderately high heat just until lightly browned on underside. Flip and cook second side just about 30 seconds. Stack finished crêpes between sheets of waxed paper.

2. Make the Béchamel sauce and set aside.

3. Make the Spanish sauce: Sauté the onion and garlic in the butter until golden. Add the other ingredients and simmer 15 minutes.

4. Prepare the filling: Heat the oil in a large skillet and sauté the onion just until golden. Add the eggplant and cook until tender, stirring occasionally. Add the tomato and spices and stir for a moment or two. Add 3 tablespoons of the cheese and ½ cup of Béchamel sauce. Mix well and spin in the blender until smooth.

5. Preheat the oven to 375 degrees F. Fill the crêpes: Lay the crêpes on a working surface and place a spoonful of mixture on each crêpe. Fold over the sides to make a square enclosing the filling.

6. Place the filled crêpes in a lightly buttered baking dish. Top each with a slice of Fontana cheese. Cover first with the remaining Béchamel sauce and then with the Spanish sauce. Sprinkle with the remaining Parmesan cheese and bake 10 minutes.

SERVES 6

Scandia

Ken Hansen, owner of one of the greatest dining places in the world, introduced the Oscar to Hollywood, to America—Veal Oscar, that is. But every night is a Night of the Oscars at Scandia. Reservations only. People book a year in advance to be seated there on Christmas Eve.

The luncheon blackboard presents constantly changing selections, from tasty bouillabaisse to wiener schnitzel. At noonday, ladies make for the big room, bright with plants. The men head for the bar where the high-back swivel chairs insure privacy and good business conversation.

Dinnertime at Scandia offers its own particular delights. There's a Smörgäsbricka of Scandinavian selections, to be washed down with ice-cold Danish aquavit or Carlsberg beer. Another favorite is Gravlaks, marinated northern salmon carved at your table and served with dill sauce.

It has been suggested that if you are in a hurry or just want a light meal—say, on your way to face a movie mogul—then Scandia is the place to feast on appetizers alone, with a cold aquavit on the side. Start with shrimps in dill, move to Baltic salmon and the herring appetizer assortment, and finish with tiny pancakes served with sour cream and Danish caviar.

9040 WEST SUNSET BOULEVARD, HOLLYWOOD

Kalvfilet Oscar (Veal Cutlet with Asparagus)

6 6-ounce veal cutlets
Salt and pepper
Flour
Béarnaise sauce (page 416)
12 tablespoons butter
24-30 asparagus tips, freshly cooked

1. Order the veal cutlets, preferably ¼-inch slices cut from the veal top sirloin. Flatten lightly with a mallet between sheets of wax paper. Season with salt and pepper. Dip into flour.

2. Make the Béarnaise sauce and keep warm.

3. Cook the asparagus tips, drain and keep warm.

4. Warm the crab legs in 4 tablespoons of butter.

30-36 cooked Dungeness
crab legs

5. Heat 3 tablespoons of butter in a large skillet and sauté the cutlets until golden brown on both sides. Remove cutlets to a heated platter and keep warm. Add 2 or 3 tablespoons of water to the skillet and stir until it boils. On each veal cutlet place 4 or 5 asparagus tips and on top of the asparagus 5 or 6 crab legs. Pour the sauce from the skillet over the cutlets and top each serving with Béarnaise sauce.

SERVES 6

Mustard Ring Mold

1 envelope (1 ounce)
plain gelatin
1 quart California white
wine
6 eggs
½ cup lemon juice
2 tablespoons sugar
2 tablespoons dry Coleman's
mustard
4 tablespoons butter
Salt and pepper
Tabasco
2 cups whipping cream

1. Dissolve gelatin in 2 cups of the wine.

2. Separate the eggs. Put the yolks in the top of a double boiler with the lemon juice, the rest of the wine, the sugar, mustard and butter. Heat over boiling water, beating constantly with a wire whisk, until mixture thickens to a creamy consistency. Remove from heat.

3. Stir in wine-gelatin mixture, salt, pepper and a dash of Tabasco. Cool and refrigerate.

4. Beat the egg whites until stiff and whip the cream. When the gelatin mixture is chilled and almost set, fold the egg whites and whipped cream into it and pour into a ring mold (1½-quart size). Refrigerate.

To serve: Turn mold out onto a platter and fill with seafood or chicken salad.

Top o' the Cove Restaurant

With a name as whimsical as a Dr. Seuss tale (Theodor Geisel is a patron), and a setting just as charming, Top o' the Cove, in a 19th-Century English cottage, overlooks the La Jolla Cove, the Riviera of America.

In earlier days Anna Helf attracted artists from all over the world to her Green Dragon Colony in this seaside village with its towering trees and gardens. Today, owner Gene Gamble has established a favorite dining spot for villagers and visitors alike. Their curries call for accolades; the Langosta con Guacamole is irresistible.

With hand-blocked linen wall coverings and Chippendale chairs, with cocktails in the terraced garden as a happy prelude to dining, and with the view of the Pacific always before you, as happy addenda to the cuisine, it is small wonder that the Johnny Carsons, Robert Stacks, and Barbra Streisands—as well as La Jollans Helen Copley, Dr. Salk, and the Christmas Grinch man—come to dine.

1216 PROSPECT STREET, LA JOLLA

Sweetbreads Kabab

Rice pilaf:
- 1 small onion, chopped
- 3 tablespoons butter
- ¾ cup rice
- 1½ cups water

- 3 pairs of sweetbreads
- 1 teaspoon lemon juice
- 6 strips bacon, halved
- 6 mushroom caps
- 1 tablespoon butter

1. Prepare rice pilaf: Preheat oven to 375 degrees F. Melt the butter and sauté the onion until soft but not browned. Add the rice. Cook over low heat until the rice becomes opaque. Add 1½ cups water and bake 20 to 25 minutes or until all water is absorbed.

2. Soak the sweetbreads in ice water for 1 hour. Place in a saucepan with simmering water. Add the lemon juice. Simmer 10 minutes. Drain and plunge into a bowl of ice water. Cool and remove all tendons and tissues. Cut in 1-inch squares.

18 1-inch squares green
pepper
12 Mandarin orange slices
¾ cup brown sauce
(page 418) or gravy
2 tablespoons sherry
4 tablespoons sour cream

3. Wrap 12 squares of sweetbread in bacon.

4. Sauté the mushroom caps in a small skillet, just until tender. Remove from heat.

5. On a skewer, place 1 mushroom cap, 1 green pepper square and 1 sweetbread square. Repeat this 3 times. Two of the sweetbread squares wrapped in bacon should be on each skewer.

6. Prepare Stroganoff sauce: Combine the brown sauce with sherry and sour cream. Heat but do not boil.

7. Place the skewers on a rack on an open broiling pan and broil until the bacon is crisp on all sides, turning frequently.

8. Serve on a bed of rice pilaf with the mushroom cap and first sweetbread square directly on the rice. Place a Mandarin orange slice on each side of the mushroom caps. Spoon a small amount of Stroganoff sauce over the sweetbreads.

SERVES 6

The Tower

Along with superlative food and impeccable service, The Tower offers a panoramic view of downtown Los Angeles. In San Francisco this would be no big deal—there are a dozen restaurants with spectacular views—but in L.A. it is something special.

"In daylight, like a mosaic," enthuses one restaurant critic, "at night a blanket of twinkling lights on alternating current, like Christmas lights." "Freeways, winding like chains of rubies and diamonds, off to the horizon—or into the smog," writes another.

Some diners come for the view, perhaps, but they return for the excellent food. Every day's menu lists five or six special items—fresh seafood flown in from the East Coast, baby veal from Wisconsin, salmon from Scotland, as well as traditional French dishes like Supreme of Fresh Crab Meat Escoffier and Noisettes of Prime Lamb à l'Estragon.

The Los Angeles Restaurant Writers Association recently voted their top awards to The Tower and guiding spirit Raymond Andrieux. A tribute from the cognoscenti!

OCCIDENTAL CENTER, 1150 SOUTH OLIVE STREET, LOS ANGELES

Suprême of Fresh Crab Meat with Caviar, Escoffier

- 2 cups prepared mayonnaise
- ¼ cup chili sauce
- ¼ cup catsup
- 1 tablespoon chopped sweet relish

1. In a large chilled salad bowl, mix all the ingredients except the crab meat and caviar. Mix thoroughly but gently, then take out ½ cup of the dressing.

2. Fold the crab meat gently into the dressing without breaking up the crab meat.

3. Fold the caviar very gently into the reserved ½ cup of dressing.

4. Line 6 stemmed sherbet glasses with lettuce leaves and divide the crab meat mix-

1 teaspoon chopped
   fresh parsley
2 tablespoons fresh
   lemon juice
1½ ounces Escoffier sauce
   (bottled)
Salt and pepper
1 pound fresh lump
   crab meat
2 ounces fresh
   Beluga caviar
Boston lettuce leaves

Garnish:
Lemon wedges
Parsley sprigs

ture between them. Top with the caviar and garnish with lemon wedges and sprigs of parsley.

SERVES 6 AS AN APPETIZER

Glazed Baked Tomatoes, Florentine

6 small tomatoes
1 pound leaf spinach
Butter
½ cup whipping cream
Salt and pepper

1. Cut the tops off the tomatoes and scoop the insides out to form a hollow shell. Season with salt and pepper, inside and out.

2. Wash spinach well and remove stems. Chop the leaves coarsely and saute in melted butter until tender. Stir in the whipping cream and season to taste with salt and pepper.

3. Preheat oven to 375 degrees F. Spoon the spinach mixture into the tomatoes and place them on a baking sheet. Bake 15 to 20 minutes and serve hot as a garnish with lamb or beef.

SERVES 6

Trader Vic's

Victor J. Bergeron is author, painter, sculptor and amateur geologist. He is also, first and foremost, restaurateur; and as Trader Vic he is well known in London, St. Louis, New York and other points east, north and south. There are today 23 Trader Vic's, but the one in San Francisco is home and headquarters. Vic is a native San Franciscan who has traveled the world over but always returns to the city by the Bay.

At Trader Vic's the decor is primarily Polynesian, running to giant tikis, outrigger canoes and giant clam shells, but the bill of fare ranges widely. There are Chinese, Hawaiian, Japanese and Tahitian dishes, some Americanized to accommodate Western tastes and some faithfully prepared to original specifications. And there are many continental specialties as well. The drinks—served in fantastic containers or garnished with fresh flowers—are events in themselves.

20 COSMO PLACE, SAN FRANCISCO

Bean Sprout Sunflower Salad

¼ cup shelled raw sunflower seeds
2 cups fresh bean sprouts
¼ cup julienned cooked white chicken
cup julienned roast pork
¼ medium Jalapeño pepper, thinly sliced
¼ cup chopped green onion
½ teaspoon Dijon mustard
⅓ cup safflower oil

1. Simmer sunflower seeds in a little water for 10 minutes, then drain and cool.
2. Blanch bean sprouts by dropping them into boiling water and letting them cook 1½ to 2 minutes. Drain and cool.
3. Combine the mustard, oil, vinegar and lemon juice with a little salt and pepper to make the dressing. Mix well and set aside.
4. Combine the bean sprouts, chicken, pork, Jalapeño pepper and green onion. Toss with the dressing. Serve on lettuce leaves on green plates, with the sunflower seeds sprinkled on top.

SERVES 4

½ tablespoon red wine vinegar
Juice of ½ lemon
Salt and crushed black pepper

1. Peel and cut the fruit into 6 slices each.

3 kiwi fruits

2. Combine the ingredients for the batter, using just enough water to give a thick consistency.

Fritter batter:
½ cup flour
⅔ cup cornstarch
½ teaspoon baking powder
¼ teaspoon sugar
Pinch of salt
Water

3. Combine the sugar and cinnamon and place in a small bowl.

4. Heat 1 inch of oil in a skillet.

5. Holding the slices with a fork, dip them in the batter and then in the oil. Fry until golden brown and drain on paper toweling. Do not fry more than 6 at a time.

6 tablespoons sugar
2 tablespoons cinnamon
6 servings vanilla ice
  cream
Oil for frying

6. Coat each piece with the sugar-cinnamon mixture.

7. Serve the ice cream and surround each portion with 3 fritters.

SERVES 6

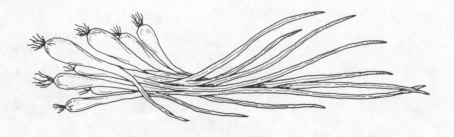

Valentino Restaurant

Rudolph Valentino was Italy's gift to the motion picture industry. It is appropriate that his name and fame were borrowed for a restaurant that serves unsurpassed Italian cuisine: Pasta alla Carrettiera (spaghetti peasant style), Muscoli alla Pescatora, Coniglio in Agro-Dolce (rabbit in a sweet-sour sauce), and Zuppa Inglese. The restaurant is a place where motion picture people come to see and be seen and trade industry gossip—and dine well.

The enormous popularity of Valentino, the actor, made him a legend in his own time. The restaurant Valentino, which has earned a legendary popularity of its own, is presided over by host and paterfamilias Piero Selvaggio. Ever cheerful and enthusiastic, he moves from table to table greeting old friends (his memory for faces—and voices on the telephone—is fantastic) and making sure the service is up to his high standards.

In charge of the kitchen is Chef Vincenzo Parrino (a Sicilian, like Selvaggio), ably assisted by Cesare D'Antonio, a master of Roman cuisine.

The menu is extensive, offering Continental fare that is not limited to Italian specialties. Seafood is important, but veal and chicken offerings are also numerous. The wine list is outstanding and there is a bar.

Writing in *Los Angeles Magazine* recently, Bruce Colen called Valentino "one of the better Italian restaurants in Southern California, and on many nights you may change that to *the* best."

3115 PICO BOULEVARD, SANTA MONICA

Steamed Mussels alla Valentino

6 dozen mussels, cleaned
  and scrubbed
1½ teaspoons minced garlic
3 tablespoons olive oil
6 medium-size fresh
  tomatoes, peeled,
  seeded and chopped
1 teaspoon oregano
1 tablespoon sweet butter
1 teaspoon black pepper
¾ cup dry white wine
1 tablespoon minced
  parsley

1. Put all the ingredients together in a large covered kettle and steam until the mussels open.

2. Serve in large bowls or soup plates with hot French bread.

SERVES 6 AS AN APPETIZER

The Windsor

The maître d' is Norwegian; the master chef, German; the waiters are from Central America, Greece, England; and the owner, Iowa-born. Blend the varied backgrounds and talents of these highly professional personalities, add a pound of regal atmosphere, and Ben Dimsdale's "perfect product" becomes a reality—The Windsor Restaurant.

The dinner menu offers the Continental range from veal to duckling to Dover sole, lobster tail, tournedos, squab, roast beef. The superb 19-page wine list boasts French, German, Italian and California wines—many from such vintage years as 1953 and 1959.

Today, the greats of politics, entertainment, sports and the arts dine at The Windsor on such favorite entrees as Filet de Boeuf Pique Forestier, Fritto Misto, Piccata Milanaise, and Grenadine of Beef Béarnaise.

As they dine, surrounded by oil paintings and stained-glass windows, solid oak-trimmed walls and red-leather booths, the loyal customers must certainly know that they are the raison d'être for Ben Dimsdale and his eye for excellence.

3198 WEST SEVENTH STREET, LOS ANGELES

Windsor Salad

Windsor dressing:
3 eggs
1 tablespoon crushed anchovies
½ tablespoon dry English mustard
1 tablespoon grated horseradish

1. Beat up eggs and add all the ingredients except the oil. Mix well.

2. Beating constantly, add the oil slowly as if making mayonnaise. Continue beating until all the oil is incorporated. Taste for seasoning. (This recipe makes about 2 quarts. Bottle and refrigerate what is not used immediately.)

3. Salad: Pull the iceberg lettuce into small pieces with your fingers. Place in a

2 tablespoons Lea &
   Perrins
4 drops of Tabasco
1 teaspoon salt
1 teaspoon white pepper
½ cup red wine
   vinegar
1 bunch chopped
   watercress
1 bunch green onions,
   chopped
½ cup lemon juice
¼ cup chili sauce
½ gallon salad oil

Salad:
Medium-size fresh iceberg
   lettuce
¾ cup thin turkey strips
½ pound shrimp, small or
   diced
4 tablespoons chopped
   green onions (scallions)

bowl and sprinkle with the turkey, shrimp and green onions. Spread generous serving of the sauce over the salad.

SALAD SERVES 2

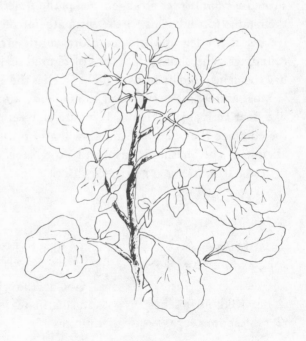

Yamato

Edward Shigematsu Ishizaki well remembered "Executive Order 9066." The time was World War II, and the directive incarcerated all Japanese-Americans and confiscated their property. The hysteria of war resulted in Ishizaki's imprisonment and the loss of his fruit market. Released in 1944, he could not manage the financing to reopen his store and instead, in 1946, founded a modest restaurant serving Japanese foods at Pacific and Powell Streets in San Francisco. The enterprise thrived and, in 1950, was moved to its present location on California Street. Other highly acclaimed restaurants followed in Los Angeles and Newport Beach. Today, with the success of the Ishizaki family, sons Koichi, Ryozo, and Kenzi have joined the business. The senior Ishizaki, nationally famous, died in 1974.

Yamato caters to the discerning Japanese and American client alike. From *ikebana* flower arrangements in the American-style dining rooms with their table-top hibachis to the intimate Japanese-style rooms with *kitatsu* (recesses) for leg and foot comfort, subtle artistic touches grace the surroundings. The sliding doors are of figured teak and bamboo. The napkins have been inspired by birds in flight (such is the art of *origami*).

Most entrees are prepared at the table by kimono-clad waitresses. Dishes like Beef Teriyaki, Sukiyaki, Tempura and Teppan Steak are elevated from the edible to the celestial. Yamato will also fulfill the more ethnic needs for aficionados of Shashimi, Sushi and Yose Nabe.

717 CALIFORNIA STREET, SAN FRANCISCO

Tatsuta-Age
(or Sesame Chicken)

¼ cup Kikkoman sauce
2 tablespoons sugar

1. Blend the soy sauce, sugar, sake and ginger.

2. Cut the chicken into 1½-inch strips and marinate in the sauce for 30 to 40 minutes.

2 tablespoons sake or dry
  sherry
½ teaspoon grated fresh
  ginger or powdered
  ginger
1 2¼-pound chicken,
  boned
¼ cup cornstarch
1 tablespoon toasted
  sesame seed
2 cups oil

3. Combine cornstarch and sesame seed. Place in a paper bag.

4. Remove the chicken from the marinade and put in the paper bag. Shake and let stand for 10 minutes.

5. Heat oil to 350 to 375 degrees F. in skillet. Fry the chicken for about 4 minutes or until golden brown.

6. Serve with white rice, with additional soy sauce and hot mustard.

SERVES 6

Sunomono
(Cucumber Salad)

2 pounds cucumbers
1 teaspoon salt
1 cup cider vinegar
¾ cup sugar
1 teaspoon monosodium
  glutamate

1. Peel cucumbers and cut into thin slices. Sprinkle with salt and let stand 1 hour at room temperature.

2. In a mixing bowl, combine the other ingredients and mix thoroughly.

3. Measure ½ cup of the vinegar dressing and pour it over the cucumber slices. Stir gently and drain.

4. Just before serving, pour the remaining dressing over the cucumber slices and transfer them to 8 individual salad bowls. If desired, garnish each with cooked crab, cooked shrimp and a tomato slice.

SERVES 8

Château Pyrénées

The mule is alive and well in Denver. That is, the mule, the "camel of the Pyrénées," is featured prominently in Floyd Hopper's lifelike mural that fills the Andorra Room of this restaurant. Nestled in the labyrinth of the Pyrénées that hump the boundaries between Spain and France is the small nation of Andorra with its population left over from the defeat of Attila the Hun some 1,500 years ago. So Hopper's scene is bucolic, the costumes colorful, much in the spirit of this unusual new château-style restaurant that has won early acclaim from gourmets and connoisseurs of bright interior design.

Director John Kauffman seats his guests in surroundings conducive to relaxation and good dining. In the dining room, the lion-legged silver roast beef server is from the estate of Baroness Consuela Von Gothard. The grand piano, which you will hear played, is of Louis XVI design (built in 1874) and considered one of the most ornate in America. Admirers of antique furniture will appreciate the Regency upholstered couches with rosewood frames inlaid in brass; they date back to 1820. A part of the Château's permanent collection of art is an original crayon and ink drawing by Marc Chagall entitled *Femme au Bouquet*.

A circular staircase leads down to the wine cellar, where the best of Spanish and French vintages preserve their delicate balance at a constant temperature of 55 degrees. After the meal, you are invited to enter the Andorra Room for a late cordial—and, perhaps, a game of backgammon.

6338 SOUTH YOSEMITE CIRCLE, ENGLEWOOD

Crêpes à la Sue

Crêpes:
½ pound butter, melted
½ cup cold water
¼ cup milk
2 eggs
¾ cup flour
1 tablespoon sugar
1 teaspoon grated orange peel
1 teaspoon vanilla extract

Filling:
8 ounces cream cheese
1 pint French vanilla ice cream
¾ cup powdered sugar
Juice and rind of ½ orange

Sauce:
1 cup heavy cream
2 tablespoons powdered sugar
2 tablespoons Grand Marnier
½ cup almonds
1 cup Swiss chocolate topping (store bought)

1. Spin all the ingredients for the crêpes in a blender until smooth. Let stand in the refrigerator for at least 30 minutes.

2. Beat the cream cheese until soft. Beat in the ice cream and the remaining filling ingredients. Blend well and freeze.

3. Whip the cream and sweeten with the powdered sugar. Fold in the Grand Marnier.

4. Toast the almonds in a 350-degree oven for 6 to 8 minutes.

5. Lightly grease a 6-inch skillet and heat it well. Pour in a large spoonful of crêpe batter and tilt the pan to coat the bottom with a thin film. Cook over moderately high heat just until lightly browned on the underside. Flip and cook the other side for about 30 seconds. Turn onto a working surface and continue until you have made 12 crêpes.

6. To serve: Fill the pancakes and roll up. Top with the chocolate sauce and pipe or spoon whipped cream over the sauce. Sprinkle with the almonds. Serve 2 to each person.

SERVES 6

Palace Arms

A writer once noted: "The story of Greece is in its temples, that of America is in its hotels." But the great institutional hotels have been falling to the wrecker's ball and sleek golden-glassed cylinders have been taking their place. Fortunately, Denver's Brown Palace Hotel has not only survived but it has expanded. "A miniature world in itself" was the appellation given the superb structure at its opening in 1888. Every care was lavished on the building of warm brown Arizona sandstone, with its 810 feet of frontage on three streets. So meticulous were the contractors that they imported fine sea sand from the coast for the mortar, in order to insure uniform thin joints.

Preserving this tradition of opulence and careful attention is the Palace Arms Dining Room with its array of draped campaign flags hanging martially aloft over banquettes upholstered in elegant Moroccan leather. (In May of 1905, President Theodore Roosevelt set up quarters in the Brown Palace— "the temporary White House"—and his flag hung opposite the President's seat in the banquet hall.) The dining room is a veritable museum of military lore. The wall decorations are all authentic objects dating from 1670 to 1825, including dispatch cases belonging to Napoleon and Maria Luisa, cartridge cases, dueling pistols, a bridle which belonged to Napoleon, breast-plates, swords and various insignia.

The present commander of the kitchen is chef Ira Dole, who preserves tight battle lines in providing the best cooking; the Steak Diane, the rainbow trout fresh from icy-cold Rocky Mountain streams. But as Lucius Beebe once remarked about dining at the Brown Palace: "None of the dishes are advertised with lyric adjectives, a circumstance which should lay up treasure for the management in heaven."

THE BROWN PALACE HOTEL, 321 SEVENTEENTH STREET, DENVER

Colorado

Broccoli Polonaise

2 pounds broccoli
Pinch of baking soda
1 tablespoon salt
12 tablespoons butter
2½ cups fresh chopped
    white bread crumbs
4 hard-cooked eggs,
    finely chopped
3 tablespoons chopped
    parsley
Salt and pepper

1. Cut off the hard stem bottoms and leaves from the broccoli. Place in a saucepan and cover with cold water, soda and salt. Bring to a boil and simmer just until tender. Drain well.

2. Heat the butter in a skillet and, when the butter is golden brown, stir in the bread crumbs. Stir until golden brown. Remove from the heat and add the chopped eggs and parsley.

3. Preheat the oven to 400 degrees F.

4. Place the broccoli in a shallow oven-proof serving dish. Cover with the bread crumb mixture. Sprinkle with salt and pepper and brown in the oven for 10 minutes.

SERVES 8

Biscuit Tortoni

1 cup whipping cream
¼ cup confectioners' sugar
1 egg white
½ cup macaroon crumbs,
    almond flavor
2 teaspoons rum

1. Whip the cream and gradually fold in the powdered sugar.

2. Whip the egg white until it stands in stiff peaks, then fold it into the whipped cream.

3. Reserve a few fine macaroon crumbs. Fold the rest of the crumbs, alternately with the rum, into the whipped cream.

4. Spoon mixture into 2 individual paper cups. Top with the reserved crumbs and place in the freezer until firm.

SERVES 2

Pierre's Quorum Restaurant

Dining can be an adventure at Pierre's Quorum. Just order the item mysteriously called "For the Trusting." It is a five-course dinner chosen for you by Pierre, or by one of his two chefs, and prepared at their discretion. The adventurous diner can count on one thing only—whatever appears on his table is bound to be delicious.

Pierre is Pierre Wolfe, a native of Alsace-Lorraine, who studied hotel and restaurant management in Switzerland and won a field commission in the British army before arriving in Colorado in 1950 to pursue his culinary art amid scenery almost as spectacular as that he knew as a boy. His restaurant is contemporary in style, with cuboid furniture, smoked glass and chrome. On the walls are original paintings, one room being devoted to the work of Marc Chagall.

The works of art that are borne proudly to the diners' tables include Stuffed Mushrooms Luxembourg, Veal Slices Pyrénéenne, Filet of Beef Marchand du Vin. Even the vegetables get the artist's touch—Pierre's Carrots with Honey Glaze and Mint deserve framing. Turn on a TV in Colorado, and you are likely to see chef Pierre working this magic, for he pursues a second career as star of his own gourmet cooking show.

233 EAST COLFAX, DENVER

Veal Slices Pyrénéenne

- 6 tablespoons butter or salad oil
- ½ pound (2 or 3 medium-size) onions, sliced
- 1 cup Béchamel Sauce (page 416)

1. Heat 2 tablespoons of butter or oil in a skillet and slowly sauté the onions until soft.

2. At the same time, make the Béchamel Sauce.

3. Combine the sauce and the onions. Remove from the heat and beat in the egg yolks which have been previously blended with the cream or milk. Season with salt and pepper.

2 egg yolks
¼ cup light cream or milk
Salt and pepper
8 thin slices veal
Flour
1 tin (4 ounces)
   imported pâté de foie
   gras
16 mushroom caps
2 sliced truffles
2 tablespoons chopped
   chives

4. Dust the veal slices with flour. In a heavy skillet melt 2 tablespoons of butter and heat until sizzling. Sauté the veal quickly until browned on both sides.

5. Slice the foie gras and make a sandwich of a slice of pâté between 2 slices of veal. Place the meat in a heatproof shallow serving dish.

6. Sauté the mushroom caps in the remaining butter until tender and arrange them around the meat.

7. Preheat the broiler. Cover the meat with the onion sauce and garnish with slices of truffle. Sprinkle with chives and brown under the broiler.

SERVES 4

Nendel's Inn

This restaurant is pure Oregonian. Just look at its background.

It was America during the Depression of the '30s. George and Margaret Nendel lived in Portland, trapped by Prohibition, unemployment, high living costs. George finally found work as a steward on the Union Pacific Railroad. Though the family had to leave the countryside for the city in order to find work, every penny was saved for the time they could return to the green fields. In 1934, the magic moment arrived; the Nendels could move ten miles outside the city limits and fill ten acres with gladiolas, tulips, roses, cedar seedlings; they had a road cut through the hills to the roadside, and Margaret was able to sell her cut flowers, bulbs and produce to passersby. Friends dropped in to savor the excellent home cooking at the farm—the chicken, baked potatoes, fresh vegetables. Inevitably, the couple decided they should start a country inn, so walls were knocked out, additions made, and Margaret brought out the four lace tablecloths from her cedar chest and draped them over the four small tables that George had constructed from wooden crates.

At the start, people paid one dollar for a full course of vegetable soup, watercress salad, fried chicken, baked potato, and fresh fruit pie. There was also a profusion of homemade breads, jellies and relishes on the tables. The water was crystal-clear drinking water from a small well on the farm. Friends were joined by a clientele of hikers who enjoyed the meandering trails that climbed over the surrounding forested hills. By the late '30s, the inn's reputation had carried throughout the northwest region of Oregon. Cars were lined up all the way down to the roadside.

The inn changed hands, finally passing to Bob and Nora Harrington. They tastefully refurbished Nendel's in early American decor, seating was expanded to 125, and Bob cooked every meal himself. Prosperity has come to Nendel's, yet Bob has not forgotten the axiom that helped him maintain a countryside tradition: "You can't cut yourself off from your customers and go sit somewhere in an office and hope things will run themselves. I enjoy my business—and the customers."

9900 S. WEST CANYON ROAD, PORTLAND

Oregon

Chicken Liver Sauté

3 pounds chicken livers
Flour
2 cups sliced
   mushrooms
1 cup thinly sliced
   onion rings
¼ pound butter
Salt and pepper

1. Clean the livers well, removing any tendons. The livers should be in bite-size pieces.

2. Season the liver with salt and pepper and toss in flour.

3. Heat 4 tablespoons of butter in each of 2 skillets.

4. Sauté the chicken livers in one skillet and the mushrooms and onions in another. The livers should be browned on the outside but still pink in the inside. The onions should be tender and very lightly browned.

5. Combine the livers with the onions and mushrooms. Season with salt and pepper.

6. Serve on toast rounds or on top of a rice pilaf (page 427).

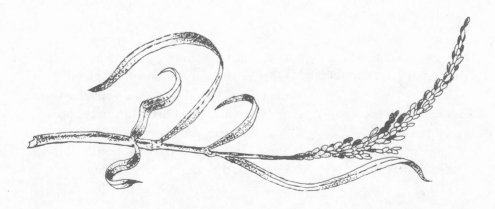

Salishan Lodge

Salishan Lodge is more than a resort. It is a guided tour of one of the world's most beautiful regions. Here are miles of wooded forests—the great expansive Northwest that we read about in travel books. A visit requires a stroll along the nature trails that wind through 700 acres of pine woods—endless, or so it seems. There is golf, tennis, swimming and one of the finest restaurants in all of Oregon.

The Gourmet Room, where dining is enhanced by the breathless view of Siletz Bay and the Pacific Ocean, has three levels. A portable dance floor, a cozy fireplace and 13 large teakwood panels, sculpted by local artist Leroy Setzoil, provide flavor for the evening before the first morsel of food has even arrived.

But it is then that the real treat begins. Swiss chef Franz Herrmann, who has manned the Salishan kitchens since the lodge opened 11 years ago, supervises the preparation of every dish that leaves the expansive kitchen. Filet of Sole Marguery, joined by little shrimp, puff pastries and mussels, is a favorite with visitors, who frequently remark that the food of this popular resort is equaled only by the beauty of the Lodge's surroundings—the virgin forests and clear blue waters of some of America's loveliest country.

SALISHAN LODGE, GLENEDEN BEACH

Dungeness Crab Pompadour en Casserole

¼ pound butter
⅔ cup flour
1½ cups light cream
1 teaspoon salt

1. Heat the butter and stir in the flour. When those ingredients are well blended, add the cream, salt, Accent and pepper. Stir and add the white wine. Bring just to the boil.

2. Preheat the oven to 425 degrees F. Sauté the mushrooms in butter and add them and the crab meat to the sauce.

1 teaspoon Accent
⅛ teaspoon white
  pepper
½ cup dry white wine
  (Riesling preferred)
¼ pound mushrooms,
  sliced
2 tablespoons butter
1¼-1½ pounds Dungeness crab
Grated sharp Cheddar cheese

3. Place the mixture in four individual ramekins. Sprinkle with a thin layer of grated cheese and bake 10 to 15 minutes.

SERVES 4

Les Huîtres
à la Normandie
(Oysters Normandy)

24-28 oysters
½ pound butter
2 teaspoons crushed
  garlic
½ teaspoon thyme
Pinch freshly ground black
  pepper
1 teaspoon chopped
  shallots
1 cup chopped parsley
½ teaspoon nutmeg
Pinch salt
Gruyere cheese

1. Dry the oysters on paper toweling and place in a heatproof baking dish.

2. Preheat the oven to 400 degrees F. Melt the butter and stir into it all the other ingredients except the cheese.

3. Pour the butter over the oysters and lay thin slices of imported Swiss Gruyère cheese over all.

4. Bake 6 to 8 minutes. Serve immediately, allowing 6 or 7 oysters per person.

SERVES 4

Canlis

The waitresses at Canlis Restaurant in Seattle wear elaborate flower-bright kimonos with obi sashes, but the menu is International. There are Chinese and Japanese specialties, but there are also lamb stews and minted salads derived from Peter Canlis' own culinary heritage (his mother was Lebanese, his father Greek), and the most popular entrees are all-American charcoal-broiled steaks and seafood.

Legend has it that tourists from Seattle who visited Canlis' restaurant in Honolulu asked Mr. C. why he didn't open a similar eating place in their hometown. "When I got to Seattle and saw this beautiful mountain with this beautiful view and no steak house, I was hooked," he says.

The setting is impressive. The restaurant's vast windows offer a sweeping view of Lake Union and, at night, the lights of the city. It is today one of four Canlis' restaurants—the third and fourth ones are in San Francisco and in Portland, Oregon.

2576 AURORA AVENUE, SEATTLE

Poached Salmon with Egg and Hollandaise Sauce

4 fresh salmon steaks
  (6 ounces each)
1 teaspoon pickling spices
1 tablespoon olive oil
1 tablespoon white wine
  vinegar

Sauce:
¼ pound butter

1. Put the steaks, spices, oil and vinegar in enough boiling water to cover the fish. Let stand 15 minutes.

2. Meanwhile, bring the butter and lemon juice to the boiling point over moderately low heat. Add the hard-cooked egg and simmer 2 minutes. Add the raw egg and pepper and whip until thickened. Season to taste with salt. Serve the sauce over the fish.

SERVES 4

Washington

4 tablespoons lemon juice
1 hard-cooked egg, chopped
1 raw egg
1 teaspoon ground pepper
Salt

Canlis Quilicene Oysters *(Pan Fry)*

Butter sauce:
1 tablespoon lemon juice
½ cup white wine (Chablis)
¼ pound butter, melted
½ teaspoon chopped parsley

2 dozen Quilicene or
   other medium-size
   oysters
½ cup milk
1 egg
Flour
Cooking oil
Salt and pepper
Accent (optional)

1. Make butter sauce: Mix lemon juice and white wine together, then whip in hot butter and finely chopped parsley.

2. Beat egg and milk together. Season with salt, pepper and Accent, if desired. Add oysters and allow them to soak for 5 minutes.

3. Heat cooking oil in a skillet to medium hot (325 degrees F.). Flour oysters lightly and fry a few at a time to golden brown, turning once. Remove oysters from oil as soon as they are done; do not overcook.

4. Pour butter sauce over the oysters and serve at once.

SERVES 4

Rosellini's Four-10

There was a family reunion *ristorante* style when the doors of the new Four-10 were first opened. Owner Victor Rosellini welcomed his extended clan home again, the former staff and familiar customers bustling happily about as if the original Four-10 had never changed locale—that homey atmosphere genuinely preserved. Right to the countdown, Rosellini was inspecting every detail, arguing passionately over the most minute problems, insisting upon the perfection that has made him famous. Faithful employees and relatives followed dutifully behind.

For Rosellini, "family" is both a literal and figurative term of endearment. Members of his immediate family have contributed dozens of recipes to the Four-10 menu: Ravioli della Mama and Veal Parmigiana alla San Francisco, served with Reggiano Parmesan, the best anywhere. Continental cuisine, featuring Roast Duckling and Châteaubriand, is as fussed over by the Four-10 chefs as the Italian dishes for which the restaurant is famous.

Rosellini—always eager to expand his family—believes in treating patrons right. "You've got to make the people feel at home," he says. Certain to prove his point: crunchy white bread to munch on when you first sit down, heavy silver-plated coffee servers, waiters literally "raised" under the strict guidance of father Rosellini to see that everyone who visits the Four-10 feels that he is surrounded with kin.

FOURTH AVENUE AT WALL STREET, SEATTLE

Washington

Frittata Rosellini
(Vegetable Omelet)

4 slices bacon, diced
1 cup chopped zucchini
1 cup chopped spinach,
   cooked and drained
¼ cup chopped onion
½ teaspoon salt
⅛ teaspoon pepper
Oregano
6 eggs, beaten until light
2 tablespoons Parmesan
   cheese

1. Cook the bacon until crisp in a 12-inch ovenproof skillet. Drain off all but about 2 tablespoons of the fat.

2. Add the vegetables. Stir and cook for 5 minutes. Season with salt, pepper and oregano.

3. Preheat the oven to 350 degrees F.

4. Combine the beaten eggs with the Parmesan cheese and blend with the vegetable mixture.

5. Return the entire mixture to the skillet and cook covered over low heat until lightly browned on the bottom. Place in the oven and bake for 10 minutes.

6. To serve: Loosen the omelet by sliding a small spatula around the edges. Turn onto a warm platter.

SERVES 4

Rosellini's Other Place

Diners at the opening of Robert Rosellini's Other Place in Seattle in 1974 may well have expected that the city's newest restaurant would be much like the famous Four-10, an elegant and well-respected spot owned and operated by Robert's father, Victor Rosellini. That alone would have been quite an accomplishment for the 30-year-old Robert. But not one to live off his father's glory, Robert compiled a host of new ideas, worked to see that they all came to life, and today he enjoys the privilege of owning one of the finest restaurants in the Northwest.

Robert has seen to it that Rosellini's Other Place lives up to its name—that it is, truly, an-Other place. He orders from a game farm fresh pheasant, quail, chukar, guinea-fowl, squab, and grouse. Three times a week he goes to trout pens, selects the finest fish, and transports them back to the kitchen. Often, he gets up before dawn to buy or gather the finest morel and chanterelle mushrooms, visiting the cold water lakes of the nearby mountains to find the freshest crayfish.

It was that kind of dedication that sent Robert to Europe several years ago, where he recruited his French-speaking kitchen staff, taking, in the end, three years to find those chefs that he liked best, and persuading them to return with him to Seattle. A chef at the Other Place never really knows what he will be called on to prepare, so uncertain is the availability of wild boar, crayfish, pheasant and many other entrees on the menu. The offerings, as one might expect, change every day.

319 UNION STREET, SEATTLE

Partridge à la Bourguignon

2 partridges (¾ pound each)

1. Preheat the oven to 400 degrees F.
2. Wipe the partridges inside and out with toweling and tie the legs and wings close to the bodies.
3. Grease a heat-proof dish with the oil

2 teaspoons vegetable oil
2 slices bacon
3 tablespoons butter
1 cup pearl onions
1 teaspoon sugar
1 cup small mushroom caps
1 cup Burgundy wine
1 cup demi-glacé sauce
  (page 422)

and place the two partridges in it. Cover the breasts with the bacon and roast 15 minutes.

4. While the partridges are in the oven melt 1½ tablespoons of butter in a small saucepan and cook the little onions until almost tender. Sprinkle with sugar and continue cooking, shaking the pan frequently, until the onions are shiny.

5. At the same time sauté the mushrooms in the remaining butter, in a separate pan, until tender.

6. Remove the partridges from the heat-proof dish and keep warm. Discard the bacon.

7. Add the wine to the heat-proof dish and cook over medium heat, scraping the pan juices from the bottom, until it is reduced to half its original quantity. Add the demi-glacé and simmer for 1 minute. Season to taste with salt and pepper. (For best results, use demi-glacé made with part of a game carcass.)

8. Return the partridges to the dish and simmer 3 minutes.

9. Serve the partridges on croutons or on a bed of wild rice, on warmed plates. Top with the glazed onions and the mushroom caps. Pour a little sauce on each bird and serve the rest in a side dish.

SERVES 2

Offshore, Over the Border

Robert Frost noted there was something that doesn't love a wall. Fortunately, good dining knows no boundaries, no checkpoints. The excellence of a chef, the hospitable service of a maître d' hôtel are international passports; the choicest aromas of the world's kitchens unite gloriously in the stratosphere.

Benignly, nature has created its own pacific barrier between Hawaii and the mainland. Eden mustn't be reached by a turn-off on the Interstate. Hawaii is a mood as much as it is a place; a sense of petals, blue waters and softly twanging music. Here you relax after mutiny from the bounty of freeways and curbside service. One whiles away the time tropically, regally, on Mai Tai cocktails, roast pig, teriyaki steak and tangy fruits.

On the other hand, the Rio Grande country, between Mexico and the United States, is forbidding—a wide grazing country, dry, blanketed by low, viciously spiked cacti. But men have learned to smile at one another across the mesquite. Lost among its mountains, Mexico early on was bountiful. The West owes this nation cocoa, vanilla, tomatoes, chili, avocados, red and green peppers. Today, Mexico dines on three leisurely meals daily. Lively conversation hovers for hours over ranch-style eggs, omelettes, thick slices of ham and plate-smothering steaks. Across the border, people are enjoying the barbecue—but that was originally Mexican too, the *barbacoa*.

Canada is tied to the American landmass; yet its ties are international. There will be more foreign news in the Vancouver press than in the San Francisco papers. Quebec and Montreal will be fighting for their French heritage while Victoria will be enjoying its afternoon, very British teatime; the Eskimo will be fighting the ruggedness of the north country, while the Cape Breton Scot sees the Highlands in the landscape before him. This is a vast country, second only to Russia, with three million square miles of outback. Little wonder that the dining pleasures of Canada are truly International, with *haute cuisine* and provincial dishes. Even the armed services send entries to the gastronomic competitions.

Canlis

The Peter Canlis restaurant operation, with a healthy $4.5 million annual gross, had its start in Honolulu, where one of his famed eating places is still situated. In 1941, when he was 29, Canlis was pushing hard goods in Hawaii's capital city. The Army-Navy YMCA at Pearl Harbor was one of his customers—in fact, Peter used to eat at the Y restaurant and thought the food was lousy. He told the manager how he felt about the food and the manager replied tartly, why didn't he open his own place. The outcome was his leasing a house in Waikiki and converting it into a restaurant (total outlay: $6,000), the beginning of his successful chain.

After decades in the business, Canlis has been able to form very definite ideas about serving the gourmet public. He is a stickler for perfection. At the start he had problems with his potato supplier. "I had to have 16- to 18-ounce Idaho bakers. But he wouldn't give me any. There's no such thing, he told me. They don't grow that big. So I went to a new man who shipped me 50 pounds of them at once to show his good faith." Canlis tries out all the recipes. His first efforts were notable in that his was the first steak and lobster restaurant in the business. Then he had seven entrees; now he has 35. He is a tough boss, yet he can count on one hand the number of people he has had to fire in his 35 years as restaurateur. He notes: "Whenever I visit one of my restaurants, the first place I go is the icebox. I stick my finger in this sauce or that to see if it's fresh. That's before I even say hello to anyone."

Asked about the plush decor of his restaurants, Canlis replies: "I build a restaurant for men that women want to go to." Such is the philosophy behind Canlis' founding restaurant in Honolulu.

2100 KALAKAUA AVENUE, HONOLULU

Canlis' Special Salad

2 heads Romaine
2 peeled tomatoes

1. Wash the lettuce, dry very well and cut into 1-inch strips.
2. In a large wooden bowl place 2 table-spoons imported olive oil, sprinkle with salt

Condiments:

¼ cup chopped green onions

½ cup freshly grated Romano cheese

½ cup finely diced cooked bacon

½ cup croutons

Dressing:

¾ cup olive oil

Juice of 2½ lemons

½ teaspoon freshly ground pepper

¼ teaspoon chopped fresh mint

¼ teaspoon oregano

1 coddled egg

and rub firmly with the cut side of a large clove of garlic.

3. Discard the garlic and place the tomatoes, cut in eighths, in the bottom of a bowl. Cover with the Romaine. You may add other salad vegetables if you like but always put the heavy vegetables on the bottom.

4. Sprinkle the green onions, cheese and bacon over the lettuce. Combine the dressing ingredients in a bowl and mix well, whipping the coddled egg vigorously into the mixture.

5. When ready to serve pour the dressing over the salad. Add the croutons and toss thoroughly.

SERVES 4 TO 6

Canlis' Shrimp

2 pounds large raw shrimp in shell

2 tablespoons olive oil

2 tablespoons butter

1 clove garlic, crushed

¼ teaspoon salt

¼ teaspoon freshly ground pepper

Juice of 2 lemons

¼ cup dry vermouth

1. Heat olive oil in a large skillet. When simmering, add shrimp and cook until golden brown.

2. Reduce heat and add butter, garlic, salt and pepper. Stir gently and toss the pan, to blend seasonings.

3. Add lemon juice and vermouth and return to high heat. Cook 1 minute, stirring or shaking continually. Serve at once, inviting guests to suck the juices from the shells as they eat.

SERVES 4 TO 6 AS AN APPETIZER

Maile Restaurant

King Kamehameha would have had an easier time of it if he had landed with his army to conquer the island of Oahu in the present and not in 1795, for near his beachhead is now situated the luxurious Kahala Hilton and its equally inviting Maile Restaurant. He could have relaxed among fountains and flowers and feasted on specialties such as Roast Duckling Waialae, served with bananas, lichees, mandarin oranges and Grand Marnier orange sauce on wild rice; Opakapaka, an island fish sautéed and served with creamed mushrooms and bananas; Mahimahi, a delicate Hawaiian fish served in a light wine sauce.

The restaurant is named after the Maile leaf, which had special significance for the ancient Hawaiians. It was one of the plants used on the altar of Laka, the goddess of the hula. Later, garlands of Maile were worn by *alii* (chiefs) on ceremonial occasions. Now Maile leis are worn for weddings and other festive events.

The menu is a table d'hôte offering of international, island and oriental favorites. Pert and pretty Charlene Goodness, the manager, greets arriving patrons and leads them past orchids and fountains to the dining delights beyond.

KAHALA HILTON HOTEL, 5000 KAHALA AVENUE, HONOLULU

Hawaii

Baked Kumu

1 whole fish
   (approximately 2
   pounds)
Salt and pepper
2½ lemons
1 bunch dried fennel
   leaves
¼ pound butter
1 onion, sliced thin
2 medium potatoes, sliced
   thin
2 fresh tomatoes, cut in
   quarters
½ cup white wine
3 tablespoons Pernod
Chopped parsley

1. Preheat oven to 375 degrees F. Season the fish inside and out with salt, pepper and juice of half a lemon. Place fennel leaves inside fish.

2. Heat the butter in a large ovenproof skillet and brown the fish on both sides. Bake in the oven for 10 minutes.

3. Place the onions around the fish. Bake 10 more minutes.

4. Add potatoes and sprinkle with salt and bake 20 more minutes.

5. Add the tomato quarters. Pour wine over the fish and sprinkle with Pernod. Bake 8 minutes.

6. To serve: Transfer the fish with 2 spatulas to a large heated platter. Arrange the vegetables around the fish. Pour the pan juices over the fish and sprinkle with parsley. Garnish with 4 lemon halves.

SERVES 2

Note: Use sea bass or red snapper if Kumu is not available.

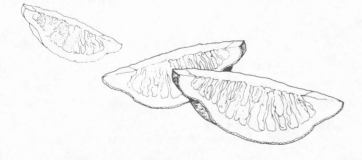

363

Michel's at the Colony Surf

Hidden away in the far reaches of Waikiki, behind doors, down steps, around corridors, is a preciously elegant French restaurant to which gourmets of the world have beaten a path. It is Michel's at the Colony Surf Hotel—a delightful discovery in elegant dining. The most frequent recipient of the *Holiday* Dining Award in Hawaii, Michel's is a composite of European opulence and the natural beauty of the islands.

Inside, crystal chandeliers, gilded mirrors, sparkling tableware and snowy linen set the scene. Outside, just an armspan away, is a sandy beach lapped by waves that glisten in the sun by day and reflect the moon's wake by night. The entire length of the restaurant is open to the magnificent seascape.

Headed by General Manager J. Hans Strasser and Executive Chef Paul O. Grutter, Michel's offers a remarkable menu and *La Grande Cuisine*. The tantalizing Canard Rôti à l'Orange is roasted to perfection with wild rice and Bigarrade sauce, and then flamed and served at diner's table. Baby Lamb Rack, grilled as you wish, is served with Old English Mint sauce and Bouquetière of Fresh Vegetables. After traveling and searching for recipes, Chef Paul created the Entrecôte Café de Paris, using only prime sirloin steak, broiled perfectly to your taste, sliced thinly and topped with a superb Café de Paris sauce—a mixture of many herbs and butter. Preface the entree of your choice with cold Vichyssoise and conclude with Soufflé Grand Marnier.

THE COLONY SURF HOTEL, 2895 KALAKAUA AVENUE, HONOLULU

Soufflé Grand Marnier

¼ pound sweet butter
2½ cups all-purpose flour
3¼ cups milk, warmed
8 egg yolks
4 whole eggs
1 cup Grand Marnier

1. Heat the butter in a saucepan over moderate heat. Add the flour and stir until well blended.

2. Add the warm milk and stir until very thick and the mixture no longer sticks to the side of the pan.

3. Remove from the heat and, beating constantly, add the egg yolks one by one.

4 egg whites
½ cup sugar

Continue beating while adding the whole eggs. Stir in the Grand Marnier.

4. Preheat the oven to 380 degrees F. Beat the egg whites very stiff. Continue beating while adding the granulated sugar very gradually until the meringue is very firm. Fold into the other mixture very gently.

5. Butter individual soufflé dishes with sweet butter and dust with flour. Fill the dishes ¾ full with the batter. Bake 18 minutes.

6. Remove from the oven, dust with powdered sugar and serve immediately.

SERVES 8

Vichyssoise

6 tablespoons butter
1½ cups chopped onions
½ cup chopped leeks (white part only)
1 bay leaf
2 tablespoons chopped ham
1 quart water
½ pint half and half cream
1½ cups Instant Mashed Potatoes
1 teaspoon chopped parsley
1 teaspoon Aromat seasoning
Chopped chives

1. Heat the butter in a 4-quart saucepan.

2. Sauté the onions and leeks just until soft. Do not brown.

3. Add the bay leaf, ham, water and simmer for 10 minutes.

4. Add the cream and simmer 5 minutes longer.

5. Mix in the potato, parsley and Aromat and simmer 5 minutes longer.

6. Pour the soup into a blender and process just long enough to make it smooth. Cool and refrigerate.

7. Serve very cold in bouillon cups, garnished with chopped chives.

SERVES 8

The Pavilion Room

When a Rockefeller goes casting about the globe for suitable places to build new vacation resorts, his eye is not likely to settle on an interstate highway exchange but on gorgeous unspoiled locations. Accordingly, in July 1960, Laurance S. Rockefeller lighted on the quiet beauty of the Kohala Coast on Hawaii's Big Island and decided to build there his Mauna Kea resort, which has since become one of the trendsetters for the resort industry. Some 650 employees, many of them local residents, pander to the wants of an elite clientele who appreciate an elegance that blends perfectly with the environment. The leisured life is spent among terraced buildings graded to the contours of a knoll and vivified with native tropical gardens. Even before the hotel opened, over half a million plants were imported for the 500-acre site and thousands more have since been propagated in the hotel's own nursery.

In such Edenic surroundings, lunch or dinner at the Pavilion can only add to one's pleasure. The structure is a long, rectangular-shaped room overlooking the Pacific Ocean. The decor is of modified Oriental design with Asian and South Pacific artifacts. Three hundred diners may be seated on three levels in this free-standing timber frame restaurant. Later additions to the dining area include the Garden Dining Pavilion and the Batik Room. Feast to the lilt of Hawaiian music on Baked Papaya Mauna Kea, Roast Loin of Pork Normandy Style and Red Indian Peach dessert.

MAUNA KEA BEACH HOTEL, KAMUELA

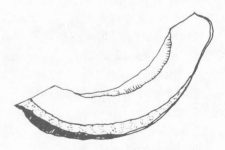

Hawaii

Baked Papaya
Mauna Kea

3 papayas (medium size)
1½ cups cottage cheese
1½ cups cream cheese (12 ounces)
1 teaspoon curry powder
2 tablespoons chopped chutney
½ cup very thinly sliced water chestnuts
2 tablespoons yellow sultana raisins
3 tablespoons sugar
1 tablespoon cinnamon
4 tablespoons melted butter

Preheat the oven to 450 degrees F.

Cut ripe papayas in half and scoop out the seeds.

Mix the cheeses, curry powder and chutney. Blend thoroughly and add the water chestnuts and raisins.

Fill the papayas with the cheese mixture.

Sprinkle with a mixture of the cinnamon and sugar and dribble with melted butter. Bake 15 minutes.

SERVES 6

The Third Floor Restaurant

"A happening" is how the Hawaiian Regent hotel's general manager Nikolaus Klotz refers to the invigorating experience awaiting guests on his third floor. The restaurant adjoins the garden-terraced swimming pool and overlooks the Spanish-style courtyard below. Interior design is the work of Richard Crowell, who combined the clean-cut lines of Scandinavia with flamboyant wickerwork from the Orient. Rippling fountains flow into a bed of river rocks below massive open-beam ceilings, like the dome of a futuristic cave. The decor is highlighted by enormous copper chandeliers and rich koa-wood wall mosaics by artist Ron Rieman. An abundant display of fresh fruits, vegetables and fish whets the appetite for the dining experience to come.

The meal begins with a relish tray of assorted Greek olives, baby corn, pickled tomatoes, celery hearts and peppers, and, as a special treat, the hotel's Indian baker, Ram Aurora, adds a slice of "naan" bread to this opener. Another special offering is the unusual Manoa lettuce, a salad delicately laced with the house vinaigrette dressing that precedes Executive Chef Fred Hellekes' incomparable entree selection of Scampi Provençale (red Spanish prawns sautéed in garlic butter with tomato concassée and saffron rice), Chicken in Champagne, Médaillons of Venison Forestière served with light cream sauce and chanterelles (a Third Floor exclusive) and the perennial favorite, Rack of Spring Lamb Provençale flanked by a variety of fresh vegetables with mint sauce.

The coffee selection is served from a hammered-brass espresso machine which serves such delicacies as Chocolaccino, Kaffe Svenska, Cappuccino l'Amour and Devil's Punch. There are 15 varieties of tea to choose from.

HAWAIIAN REGENT HOTEL, 2552 KALAKAUA AVENUE, HONOLULU

Hawaii

Chicken in Champagne

3 2½-pound chickens, split
8 tablespoons sweet butter
½ medium onion, sliced
1 medium carrot, sliced thin
1 tablespoon sugar
1 teaspoon salt
¼ teaspoon white pepper
Pinch of thyme
1 bay leaf
3 sprigs parsley
½ cup brandy
2 cups champagne
2 cups heavy cream
1 cup seedless grapes
1 cup sliced peaches
Cooked rice (page 426)

1. Preheat the oven to 400 degrees F.

2. Heat the butter in a large ovenproof skillet and sauté the onion and carrot just until the onion is soft.

3. Add the chicken halves and sauté until brown on both sides. Remove the chicken and cut each half in 2 or 3 pieces (breast, thigh and leg).

4. Put the chicken parts back in the skillet. Sprinkle with sugar, salt, pepper and herbs. Pour over the brandy and champagne. Cover and cook in the oven for 30 to 45 minutes. Prepare the rice.

5. Remove the chicken to a heated platter. Keep warm.

6. Strain the sauce from the pan and add the cream. Cook 3 minutes, blending well.

7. Pour a little of the sauce over the chicken and serve the rest in a separate dish. Garnish the platter with the grapes and peaches and serve with the rice.

SERVES 6

Le Bonaparte

The rumor in Quebec these days hints that Napoleon Bonaparte does not lie entombed within Les Invalides. To be sure, his Grande Armée was overwhelmed at Smolensk, battered at Leipzig and crushed at Waterloo, but "the little crop-head" is said to have escaped Saint Helena to found the Canadian restaurant that now bears his name. With dining halls named for Josephine, Les Incroyables and Madame Sans Gêne; a bar called Le Bivouac and a wine cellar dubbed Le Petit Caporal, Le Bonaparte Restaurant might well be host to more than speculation. After all, the wine steward does strike a rather notorious pose, fingering his cummerbund with his right hand.

But whether or not this story has any basis, the restaurant itself is quite real—something for which its many friends can be thankful. Imposing with its rough-cut gray stone exterior topped by a gabled roof, Le Bonaparte could have been snatched from early 18th-Century France. Certainly the fare follows that tradition, boasting such specialties as Le Médaillon de Veau St-Hilarie, La Brochette Filet de Boeuf des Pyramides and Les Rognons de Veau Austerlitz. The wine list is equally impressive, featuring some rather rare vintages. Just don't make your selection from 1815: It wasn't a very good year.

680 GRANDE ALLÉE EST, QUEBEC CITY, QUEBEC

Canadian Apple Pie

Pastry:
2½ cups flour
6 tablespoons sugar
Pinch of salt
7 tablespoons butter
1 egg
2-3 tablespoons ice water

Filling:
3 apples, peeled, cored
   and sliced in eights
5 tablespoons water
4½ tablespoons sugar
½ vanilla pod or
   1 teaspoon vanilla
   extract
2 apples

Topping:
½ cup apricot jam

1. Heap the flour on a working surface. Fashion a well in the center with fingertips and in the well place the sugar, salt, slightly softened butter and egg. Work the flour toward the center, gradually incorporating all the ingredients. Add just enough of the ice water to form a firm ball of dough. Work as quickly as possible so as not to "tire" the dough. Cover and let rest for at least 20 minutes.

2. Combine the apple slices, water, sugar and vanilla in a small saucepan and cook until the liquid has a jelly-like consistency. The pieces of fruit will still be whole.

3. Peel and core the remaining apples and cut them in half-apple slices.

4. Preheat the oven to 400 degrees F.

5. Roll out the pastry to a circle 1½ inches larger than a 9-inch pie tin. Line the tin with the pastry and fold under the edges, pressing them to the rim and pinching the dough between thumb and forefinger.

6. Pour in the cooked apples and cover with overlapping slices of the raw apples.

7. Bake 10 minutes. Reduce the heat to 375 and bake 20 to 25 minutes longer.

8. Remove the pie from the oven and, while it is still hot, brush the surface with the apricot jam.

SERVES 6 TO 8

The Burgundy Room

Chef Joseph Vonlanthen has perfected "the stamp of approval." A new feature of this dining room at the Constellation Hotel is The President's Table, a heavy oak table, set with hand-crocheted golden place mats, the finest Royal Doulton bone china, lead crystal glasses and gleaming silverware. Anyone wishing to make a reservation for this table must notify ten days in advance and the menu and wine selections will be arranged by the chef and Gino Clementi, the maître d'. This special menu will then be printed with the name of the host, on parchment, stamped with the official Burgundy Room crest and signed by the executives.

Another feature of the restaurant is the wine list, with its courteous words of warning. Some bottles are priced individually, so choices have to be made between a Château Lafite Rothschild 1965 at $96 and a Château Mouton Rothschild 1965 at $65. The introduction mentions the years of exceptional vintages to help your selection. There is a cavernous warning not to go too far back with the Burgundies, for "beyond 25 or 30 years the peak of quality may well have passed."

CONSTELLATION HOTEL, 900 DIXON ROAD, REXDALE, ONTARIO

Lamb Chops Vonlanthen

6 tablespoons butter
1 small onion, chopped
1 cup long-grain rice, raw
2 cups water, hot
Salt and pepper
4 center-cut 1-inch
   lamb chops
12 white seedless grapes,
    peeled

1. Prepare rice pilaf: Heat 4 tablespoons butter in a heavy saucepan and sauté the onion until soft but not brown. Add the rice and cook over moderate heat 3 to 4 minutes, stirring occasionally. Add the hot water, cover and cook over low heat or in a 350-degree oven until all the water has been absorbed (about 20 minutes). Season to taste with salt and pepper.

2. Season the lamb chops with salt and pepper. Sauté the lamb chops in 2 table-

2 ripe bananas, peeled
   and sliced
½ cup Bing cherries
4 tablespoons cognac
½ cup Champagne
2 tablespoons toasted
   almonds

spoons butter for 3 to 4 minutes on each side or to desired doneness. Add the grapes, bananas and cherries, and when they are heated, add the cognac and touch with a lighted match. Add the Champagne and simmer for 1 minute.

3. To serve: Arrange the lamb chops in the center of a ring of the rice pilaf. Top with the fruit and sprinkle with toasted, sliced almonds.

SERVES 4

Café de L'Auberge

A generation ago, Toronto had a reputation for stuffiness, some of it deserved; but all this has changed. Canadians and visitors now gravitate to the city as to a London, Paris or Rome. It has become the meeting place for the inquiring minds of the nation. It has become one of the leading theater towns in America, a home of progressive jazz and modern art. For the sophisticated, there are the nightclubs along Yonge Street and a plethora of fine restaurants—one of the leaders being Café de L'Auberge in suburban Don Mills. Here one can dance away the wee hours after a memorable meal. Or instead of joining in the party tempo, a couple can enjoy the intimate, romantic candlelight setting, while fondling a glass of wine from Canada's most impressive collection of French vintages.

Eugene Clementi and his polished staff will suggest specialties from an outstanding menu: true Dover Sole Amandine or Meunière, Chateaubriand Bouquetière, Tournedos Wellington. The pastries have won their own awards. You are reminded of Lord's Byron's dictum: "That all-softening, overpowering knell/the tocsin of the soul—the dinner bell."

INN ON THE PARK, 1100 EGLINTON AVENUE, EAST, DON MILLS, ONTARIO

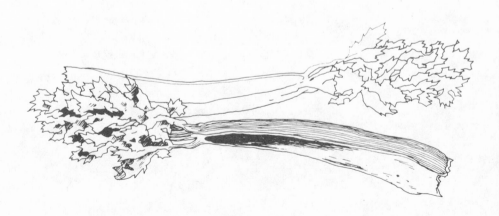

Canada

Crystal Spring Trout
Maçonnaise

1 onion, sliced thin
1 carrot, sliced thin
1 stalk of celery, sliced
   thin
Butter
2 fresh river trout
½ teaspoon thyme
1 bay leaf
3 sprigs parsley
Dry red wine
12 pearl onions
4 medium mushroom caps
2 slices white bread,
   trimmed
1 clove garlic, cut
2 tablespoons clarified
   butter (page 420)
Salt and white pepper
1 tablespoon flour

1. Preheat the oven to 400 degrees F. Sauté the vegetables lightly in butter, in a shallow oven-proof dish.

2. Season the trout inside and out with salt and pepper.

3. Place the fish on top of the vegetables; add the herbs and enough red wine so that it almost covers the trout. Bring to boil on top of the stove. Cover with brown paper and cook for 10 minutes in the oven.

4. Cook the pearl onions in 2 tablespoons of butter, 1½ teaspoons of sugar and ¼ cup of water in a small pan until glazed.

5. In another small pan sauté the mushroom caps in 1 tablespoon of butter.

6. Brown the 2 slices of bread in 1 tablespoon of the clarified butter. Rub each piece with fresh garlic and cut into small cubes.

7. Strain the cooking liquid from the trout into a small saucepan.

8. Remove the skins from both sides of the trout. Place on a serving platter and keep warm.

9. Mix the flour with 1 tablespoon of clarified butter and, when well blended, drop in small portions into the strained cooking liquid. Cook until thickened and pour over the trout. Garnish with the glazed onions and mushroom caps and croutons.

SERVES 2

Café Martin

What spectator at the battle of Hastings could have possibly foreseen that someday French customs and English tastes would coexist peacefully, much less merge harmoniously under one roof? Well, someday has arrived—at least at Le Café Martin in Montreal. Combining fine French cuisine with the warm Victorian atmosphere of an old three-story townhouse, the Cafe has catered to the whims and caprices of local clients for more than half a century. Whether they were enchanted by the small salons, charmed by the grand dining hall, taken with the Dandurand family art collection, or impressed by the fine architectural detail, gourmets—both Canadian and cosmopolitan—infallibly make a point of dining here whenever in town.

Once within the Café's elegant entranceway you cease to wonder what attracted such celebrities as Sir Anthony Eden, Ed Sullivan and Robert Kennedy. From the carved oak staircase to the 19th-Century oil originals, from the foyer's stained glass to the striking Tiffany-period lamp, this restaurant provides a welcome respite from the chaos of modernity, a return to an era when elegance and gentility were the accepted standards. Even the food serves to enhance this atmosphere of intimacy and relaxation. Indeed, who can think of mergers and lawsuits once Escalope de Veau à la Crème or le Filet Mignon Andréef has been placed before him?

2175 RUE DE LA MONTAGNE, MONTREAL, QUEBEC

Tranche Sicilienne
(Sicilian Ice Cream)

½ cup candied fruit,
  finely diced
½ cup crumbled macaroons
½ cup rum
1 pint strawberry
  ice cream

1. Mix together the candied fruit and the macaroon crumbs. Pour the rum over the mixture and set aside.

2. Line a loaf tin (8"x4"x4") with ¾ of a pint of slightly softened strawberry ice cream. Freeze 1 hour.

3. Combine the coffee ice cream which has been slightly softened with the whipped cream. Add the rum mixture and mix well.

1½ quarts coffee ice cream
2 pints heavy cream,
  whipped

4. Fill the chilled mold and freeze 1 hour.

5. Cover over with the remaining strawberry ice cream and freeze at least 4 hours before serving.

6. To serve: Place mold in a pan of hot water for 2 to 3 seconds. Unmold onto a dessert platter and garnish with fresh fruits in season (strawberry, orange or banana slices) and the remaining whipped cream. Cut into half-inch slices with a knife dipped in hot water.

SERVES 12

Baked Oysters
Café Martin

12 fresh oysters
1 tablespoon butter
1 small onion, chopped
¼ cup dry white wine
½ cup Hollandaise sauce
  (page 424)
½ cup heavy cream
½ teaspoon chopped mint
  leaves
½ teaspoon chopped
  tarragon leaves

1. Shuck oysters, saving half the shells and arranging these shells on a bed of rock salt in a large roasting pan.

2. Melt the butter in a skillet. Add the oysters, onion and white wine and cook, stirring gently just until the edges of the oysters curl. Lay the oysters back in the shells.

3. Make sauce by mixing the Hollandaise, cream, mint and tarragon. Divide the sauce among the oysters, spooning a little on each.

4. Place under the broiler just until sauce begins to brown. Serve garnished with lemon wedges and sprigs of parsley.

SERVES 2 AS AN APPETIZER

Café de Paris

The name Pierre Demers is synonymous with Canadian gastronomy. His preparation of dishes in the kitchens of the Ritz Carlton Hotel put Canada on the map as an exemplar of modernized haute cuisine. Since its renovation in the early '70s, the hotel is more regal than ever and a true setting for the lavish menus of the Café de Paris and the Maritime Bar. Today Chef Demers has as his chief assistant a fellow townsman, Paul Bergeron, whom he has expertly trained. Pierre, who had been trained in turn by legendary chef Paul Diat in the now defunct New York Ritz, tells the story of culinary dedication, of Diat's having to be torn away from his office as the bulldozers were hacking away at the building, and of his dying a few months later of a broken heart.

But Pierre Demers is not making the same mistake. As he sums up his life's work: "Cooking shouldn't dominate one's life. Make it your hobby." He has been in hotel kitchens for nearly half a century but ruefully comments, "I still can't open a bottle of ketchup properly. I usually have to give it to one of the kids to open." He's tried his hand at wine-making but even there success has escaped him: "I make wine, and let's say that I always have a supply of vinegar on hand for salads." The mark of the great modern chef is the combination of expertise with infectious humor and a child's wonder at life.

RITZ-CARLTON HOTEL, 228 SHERBROOKE STREET, MONTREAL, QUEBEC

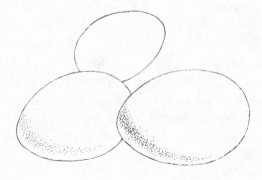

Lobster in Pernod Sauce

2 2-pound lobsters
2 tablespoons finely
    chopped carrots
2 tablespoons finely
    chopped shallots
2 teaspoons butter
4 tablespoons Pernod
4 tablespoons cognac
2 cups heavy cream
1 egg yolk, beaten
Salt and pepper

1. Cut a live lobster in pieces and remove the meat from the claws and tail. Cut the meat into large pieces.

2. Sauté the carrots and shallots in butter in a saucepan. Add the lobster pieces and cook a few minutes until firm.

3. Add the Pernod and cognac and touch with a lighted match. Spoon the sauce over the lobster until the flame subsides.

4. Add the cream and simmer until the sauce thickens slightly.

5. Add a little of the hot sauce to the beaten egg yolk. Then return the mixture to the sauce. Stir a few moments without letting the sauce boil. Remove from the heat. Add salt and pepper to taste.

6. Serve on hot plates with white rice.

SERVES 2 OR 3

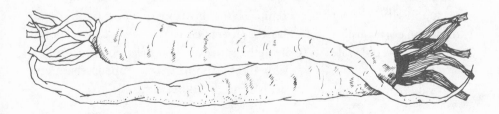

Le Castillion

Duning the '76 summer Olympics, many an athlete, ambitious for gold, went panning for refreshment and entertainment at the Hotel Bonaventure where the night life includes both dining and entertainment. The Castillion, named for the famous French pioneer Jacques de Castillion, is designed after the 17th-Century French Canadian *manoir*. Elegant gold chandeliers, glowing hues of red in the decor warm both heart and palate. You will want to linger over the rich French cuisine and extensive wine list before deciding on the perfect combination of culinary delights. Try the Chicken Castillion served with a dash of Hollandaise—an ingenious flavor discovery.

After dinner you needn't go far to find live entertainment in Bonaventure's own show bar lounge, Le Portage. You can swing to the band or relax with a romantic ballad.

BONAVENTURE HOTEL, 1 PLACE BONAVENTURE, MONTREAL, QUEBEC

Délice du Lac St.-Jean

Melba Sauce:
  2 cups of fresh raspberries
     or 1 package of frozen
     raspberries, drained
  ½ cup currant jelly
  ½ cup sugar
  ⅛ teaspoon salt
  1 teaspoon cornstarch
  2 tablespoons cold water

  ¾ pint vanilla ice cream
  ½ cup Melba sauce

1. Make the Melba sauce: Spin the raspberries in a blender. Strain to remove the seeds. Add the jelly, sugar, salt and the cornstarch mixed with the cold water. Stir and cook over moderate heat until thickened. Cool and keep in a covered jar in the refrigerator.

2. To serve: Place a scoop of vanilla ice cream at the bottom of each of 4 parfait glasses. Cover ice cream with 2 tablespoons of Melba sauce and 1 tablespoon of Curaçao. Add 4 tablespoons of whipped cream and garnish with blackberries.

SERVES 4

4 tablespoons Curaçao
½ cup heavy cream, whipped
2 tablespoons
   confectioners' sugar
1 cup blackberries

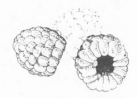

The Carpetbagger
(Tenderloin with Oysters)

2 8-ounce tenderloins
1 tablespoon olive oil
2 tablespoons Scotch
   whiskey
Salt and pepper
8 raw oysters
¼ cup demi-glacé (page 422)
3 tablespoons cream

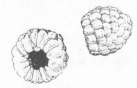

1. Have the butcher butterfly the tenderloins by cutting the meat horizontally without completely cutting through and spreading the two halves apart.

2. Heat the olive oil in a heavy skillet and cook the tenderloins to taste (rare or medium-rare). Pour the whiskey over the tenderloins and ignite with a match. When flames subside season with salt and pepper and transfer the tenderloins to a platter. Cover and keep warm.

3. Add the oysters to the skillet and allow them to simmer 1 minute.

4. Add the demi-glacé and cream to the pan and stir gently. Return the tenderloins to the pan just until reheated.

5. Place the tenderloins on hot dinner plates. Use a slotted spoon to place 4 oysters on half of each, then fold the other halves over. Spoon sauce from the pan over all. Serve at once.

SERVES 2

Le Champlain

Although it bears his name and maintains his legend, Chateau Frontenac's Le Champlain Restaurant is far removed from the early explorer and the land he colonized. Where the Iroquois nation once hunted in stealth, French-Canadian waiters now serve with grace. Where Samuel de Champlain once feasted on campfire venison and duck, the gourmet can now savor house specialties: Le Filet de Flétan Grillé aux Herbes, Le Soufflé de Homard Frontenac à la Sauce Nantua, and Les Cailles Normande Farcies au Foie Gras. And unlike the early 1600s when hostile Englishmen or Indians afoot meant certain battle, the only conflict today lurks at the well-appointed table: namely, should the diner choose a Chassagne Montrachet 1972 or a Pouilly-Fuissé to accompany his Dover sole?

No matter what the selection, however, contentment is assured. Seated in a grand hall adorned with mementos of Champlain and his exploits, the guest quickly comes to appreciate what this first governor of French Canada, and the founding father of L'Ordre de Bon Temps, meant by "camaraderie and conviviality." The restaurant—indeed, the entire establishment—exudes both. Any visit to this spectacularly situated hotel becomes an event, and dinner at Le Champlain a suitable climax.

CHATEAU FRONTENAC, QUEBEC CITY, QUEBEC

Coquilles Saint-Jacques (Seafood in Scallop Shells)

2 tablespoons butter
1 tablespoon chopped shallots
8 mushrooms, cleaned and sliced

1. Melt the butter in a saucepan. Add the shallots, mushrooms, wine and scallops. Bring the liquid to a boil and simmer 5 minutes.

2. Add the cooked shrimp; heat together for 2 minutes.

3. Remove the scallops, shrimp, mushrooms with a slotted spoon. Set aside.

4. Boil down the liquid in the pan until it

½ cup of dry white wine
2 cups Mornay sauce (page 426)
1 pound scallops
12-15 cooked shrimp
1 tablespoon chopped parsley
1 tablespoon whipped cream
Salt and white pepper

measures 3 tablespoonfuls. Add 1½ cups Mornay sauce. Mix well and strain through a fine sieve.

5. Combine the sauce with the scallops, shrimp and mushrooms. Add the parsley and season to taste.

6. Divide the mixture between 6 scallop shells or small ramekins. Add the whipped cream to the remaining Mornay sauce and spread over the shells. Brown quickly under a very hot broiler.

SERVES 6

Strawberry Cheesecake

1 pound cream cheese
½ cup sugar
2 tablespoons cornstarch
3 eggs
¼ cup light cream
½ cup strawberries, fresh or frozen
1 cup sugar
1 cup dry red wine

1. In the bowl of an electric mixer beat the cream cheese at moderate speed. Mix together the ½ cup sugar and cornstarch and add to the cream cheese. Add the eggs one at a time, beating after each addition, and finally the cream.

2. Preheat the oven to 350 degrees F. Place the cheese mixture in a heatproof glass bowl set in a pan of hot water and bake 1½ hours. Cool, then turn out on a dessert platter and refrigerate.

3. Thirty minutes before serving, combine strawberries, sugar and wine in a glass bowl and set aside. Pour over cheesecake just before serving.

SERVES 6

Chez Bardet

André Bardet is a nationalist when it comes to food; he "makes no concessions to the Americans," at least not in his kitchen. Bardet's commitment to *haute cuisine à la française* will not even permit the chefs to use a Mixmaster. But they are not complaining; what they lack in modernity is made up in their elaborate preparation of authentic French fare. Bardet is eminently serious about his establishment: "It's a love story. When you choose a profession, you marry it."

So that his customers will not have to pay outrageous prices for imported wines, Bardet travels annually to France to purchase wines for sommelier Laurent Anselini's wine cellar. Each dish has the Bardet touch. A perfect dinner might include Escargots à la Chablisienne or L'Escalope de Veau à la Crème aux Morilles and, of course. Le Soufflé au Grand Marnier. After a sumptuous repast, don't be surprised if Barden himself stops by to inquire after your enjoyment. His one goal is "to leave a happy memory."

591 HENRI BOURASSA, EAST MONTREAL, QUEBEC

Omelette Soufflée
Flambée *(Flaming
Soufflé)*

8 egg yolks
7 tablespoons sugar
1 teaspoon vanilla extract
12 egg whites
Salt
2 tablespoons Curacao or
Grand Marnier

1. Preheat the oven to 400 degrees F.
2. Beat the egg yolks with 6 tablespoons of sugar and the vanilla. Beat vigorously until the consistency is smooth and creamy.
3. In a second bowl, beat the egg whites with a pinch of salt until very stiff.
4. Fold the egg whites into the yolks, gently but completely, using a wooden spoon or rubber spatula.
5. Butter the bottom of a heat-proof shallow baking-serving dish and sprinkle it with the remaining sugar.
6. Pour in the egg mixture, smoothing the top evenly with a small spatula.
7. Put into the oven and bake 6 minutes or until nicely puffed. Meanwhile warm the liqueur in a small metal pitcher.
8. To serve: The warm liqueur can be poured over the omelet, touched with a lighted match and brought flaming to the table. Or, the omelet may be placed before the host and hostess who will pour on the liqueur at the table, ignite it and spoon the liqueur over the omelet until the flames subside.

SERVES 4

Le Neufchatel

For patrons who combine a taste for fine literature with a taste for fine dining, Le Neufchatel has a library. The management frowns upon reading while eating, but approves of browsing before dining or after. The books are real ones, with printed pages in them, and they stock the shelves of an alcove raised above the floor level of the dining room and furnished cozily with leather armchairs and tiny glowing lamps.

Le Neufchatel is the prestige dining room of Le Château Champlain, the Canadian Pacific's hotel in Montreal. Recent guests were Princess Anne and her husband, Captain Mark Phillips; like the other guests, they dined from Wedgwood china designed for an earlier visit by the princess' mother, HRH Queen Elizabeth.

Dinner music features that most elegant and artistic of instruments, the harp. What are suitable viands to consume from Wedgwood, to the accompaniment of a harpist's tinkling melodies? Try a delicate Hare Pâté With Port Jelly, a Timbale of Sole seasoned with pistachio, pernod and paprika, or a magnificent Mignon de Boeuf Chevalier.

Neufchatel gets its name from a mild white cheese made with milk, not cream; and the cheese, in turn, is named for a village in France. When in France, order Neufchatel at Neufchatel; when in Montreal, do the same.

LE CHATEAU CHAMPLAIN, PLACE DU CANADA, MONTREAL, QUEBEC

 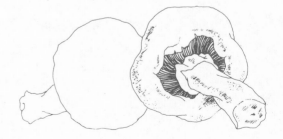

Cassoulet Quebecois
(Quebec Ramekins)

2 tablespoons butter
2 tablespoons oil
1 pound beef, cut in
  small cubes
1 pound pork, cut in
  small cubes
1 pound lamb, cut in
  small cubes
4 tablespoons flour
¼ cup finely chopped
  onion
½ dry red wine
6 cups of water
1 teaspoon salt
¼ teaspoon black pepper
2 teaspoons dried savory
½ pound pure pork
  cocktail sausages
½ cup diced mushrooms
¼ cup dry white bread
  crumbs
1 large clove garlic,
  pressed
2 tablespoons chopped
  chives
2-3 tablespoons butter,
  melted

1. In a large skillet, sauté the meat cubes in the oil and butter until browned on all sides. Add the onions and continue cooking until onions are light brown. Add the wine, 6 cups of water, salt, pepper and savory. Bring to a boil and cook over moderate heat, covered, for 2 hours.

2. Shortly before serving, pan fry the sausages and sauté the mushrooms in a little butter.

3. Mix the bread crumbs with the garlic and chives.

4. Divide the meat among 8 to 10 ramekins or shirred egg dishes. Top with sausages and mushrooms and sprinkle with the seasoned bread crumbs.

5. Dribble a few drops of melted butter on each dish and brown under a preheated broiler.

SERVES 8 TO 10

Restaurant Le St. Amable

In 1642, exactly 150 years after Columbus discovered America, Paul de Chomedey sailed up the St. Lawrence River to found Montreal. Today, in addition to his historical fame as pioneer and Montreal's first governor, de Chomedey is also celebrated for having settled the land on which Restaurant Le St. Amable stands—an accomplishment for which that establishment's devoted patrons, most of whom are cosmopolitan and all of whom are connoisseurs, are grateful. Indeed, in the opinion of more than one local gourmet, this restaurant is Montreal's finest.

Located in the city's historic quarter—a section now being zealously restored as Montreal rediscovers her glorious past—the building dates back to the early 18th Century, thereby rivaling in vintage some of the superb wines that comprise its select stock. Equally classic are the Sole Soufflé, a house specialty, and the Tournedos Opéra, a beef dish served in a delicate pastry shell with a rich glazing of foie gras, mushrooms and truffles.

188 RUE ST. AMABLE, MONTREAL, QUEBEC

Bavarois au Kirsch
(Bavarian Cream)

 1 envelope gelatin
¼ cup cold water
3½ cups milk
15 egg yolks
 2 cups confectioners'
    sugar
Kirsch
 1 quart whipping cream
½ cup diced candied fruit
Ladyfingers or spongecake

1. Soften the gelatin in the water. Scald the milk.

2. In a large saucepan, beat the egg yolks and add the confectioners' sugar. Beat until creamy. Add the hot milk slowly, while continuing to beat. Cook over low heat, stirring continuously, until the mixture coats the spoon. Remove from heat and put through a strainer. Stir in softened gelatin.

3. When cooled, stir in kirsch, and sprinkle a little more over the candied fruit. Refrigerate.

4. When the custard is chilled and begin-

ning to thicken, whip the cream and fold it into the custard.

5. Sprinkle a little of the candied fruit in the bottom of a fancy Bavarian mold. Cover with some of the custard and a layer of ladyfingers or sponge cake slices. Repeat layers until mold is filled. Refrigerate at least 3 hours.

6. Turn mold out onto dessert platter and garnish with more whipped cream and fruit, if desired.

SERVES 8

Cassolette Escargots
(Snail Ramekins)

24 snails (canned)
2 tablespoons butter
2 shallots, chopped fine
1 tablespoon cognac
4 tablespoons white wine
1 cup heavy cream
1 egg yolk, slightly beaten

1. Melt butter in a skillet and sauté the chopped shallots until golden brown.

2. Add the snails; cook for 2 to 3 minutes and add the cognac. Touch with a lighted match.

3. When the flame subsides, add the white wine and cook for 1 minute. Add the cream and let it cook down to half its original quantity, stirring continuously for 2 to 3 minutes over moderate heat. The mixture will thicken. Gradually add the egg yolk, stirring vigorously, and reheat but do not let the sauce boil.

4. Serve very hot in individual shallow ramekins, accompanied with French bread.

SERVES 4 AS AN APPETIZER

Royal Hunt Dining Room

The tastes of huntsmen have advanced considerably since the days of Squire Allworthy. Immediately after the hunt the Squire would like nothing better than to grab hold of a leg of roast chicken and withdraw to some dusty corner near the hearth. Indeed, Henry Fielding's *Tom Jones* may have captured the spirit of the rugged hunter in its rendering of Squire Allworthy, but these days hunters prefer elegance along with their rusticity.

And so they go to the Royal Hunt Room where displays of stuffed game birds and pictures of Olde English hunting scenes surround the niceties of gourmet dining. But you can still feast on roast chicken served on large brass platters. Or, perhaps, you are more inclined toward heartier fare. The Royal Hunt may be fresh out of buffalo, but the steaks and prime ribs of beef are specialties.

After dinner take a climb to the 33rd floor for cocktails and dancing at Stop 33. Nowhere in Toronto will you find a more breathtaking view.

SUTTON PLACE HOTEL, 955 BAY STREET AT WELLESLEY, TORONTO, ONTARIO

Sauce Diable

1 cup mayonnaise
1 teaspoon dry mustard
6 drops Tabasco
¼ teaspoon crushed chili peppers
1 pinch curry powder
Salt and pepper

Combine the seasonings with the mayonnaise and mix gently. Serve as a dip in a small bowl, surrounded by a selection of raw, bite-sized vegetables (carrot sticks, cauliflower florets, celery sticks, radishes, green onion, cucumber slices, cherry tomatoes, etc.) in place of a salad.

SERVES 4 AS AN APPETIZER

Scampi à la José
(Chafing Dish Shrimp)

16 cooked jumbo shrimp
    (scampi), shelled and
    deveined
 4 tablespoons butter
 2 tablespoons olive oil
 3 green onions, chopped,
    white part only
 1 clove garlic, minced
 3 tablespoons chopped
    chives or parsley
Juice of 1 lemon
 3 tablespoons Pernod
 3 tablespoons cognac
Salt and freshly ground
    black pepper

1. In a chafing dish over direct flame or in a skillet on the stove, heat the oil and butter over moderate heat. Add the onion, garlic, shrimp and lemon juice. Toss with wooden spoons or by shaking the pan to coat the shrimp with butter and cook until the shrimp are heated through.

2. Sprinkle with salt and pepper; stir gently. Add Pernod and cognac and touch with a lighted match.

3. When the flame disappears, sprinkle chives or parsley over the shrimp and stir.

4. Serve as an appetizer or, with rice, as an entree.

SERVES 4 AS AN APPETIZER, 2 AS A MAIN COURSE.

La Saulaie

A writer once penned, "The island of Montreal is set like a giant emerald in a medallion of elaborate Florentine silverwork, for there lies all about it a network of turbulent and celebrated waterways that throughout its history have been beautiful, dramatic and tragic as man attempted their conquest." No better place can be found to catch this view, this spirit, than at Edmond La Barre's French kitchen restaurant, only a half-hour drive from downtown Montreal. Terraces overlook green lawns and weeping willows, while beyond ships ply the St. Lawrence River.

Brillat-Savarin is quoted on the menu: "The discovery of a new dish does more for the happiness of man than the discovery of a new star." In such rustic surroundings, amid the country cauldrons and spits, it is easy to agree with the famed gastronome. The maître d'hôtel becomes the landlord filling the flowing bowl, triumphantly bringing to your table a flaming Steak Diane or a Steak au Poivre Lucifer et sa Sauce Divine. The pyrotechnic virtuosity continues through the Poires Flambées au Ricard or the Pêches Flambées. For a warming conclusion to the meal, Café Brésilien is suggested.

1161 MARIE VICTORIN, BOUCHERVILLE, QUEBEC

Les Crevettes Bolshoi
(Shrimps, Russian Style)

2 tablespoons mayonnaise
1 teaspoon Beluga caviar
1 tablespoon vodka
½ cucumber
10 large shrimp, cooked and peeled

Blend together the mayonnaise, caviar and vodka.

Cut the cucumber into 2 shorter pieces and set on ends. Hollow out part of the seeds to form cups and fill each with half the mayonnaise mixture.

Set each sauce-filled cucumber-cup in the center of a bed of lettuce, and surround with the shrimp, cut and spread open butterfly-style.

SERVES 2 AS AN APPETIZER

Canada

La Suprême de Volaille Rougemont *(Chicken Breasts Rougemont)*

2 chicken breasts, boned
Flour
2 tablespoons butter
1 tablespoon oil
2 teaspoons Calvados
1 cup heavy cream
1 apple

1. Preheat oven to 350 degrees F. Heat 1 tablespoon of butter and the oil on top of the stove in an oven-proof dish.

2. Dip the chicken breasts in flour and cook the chicken until golden brown on both sides. Add the Calvados and ¾ cup of cream. Cover the dish and place in the oven. Bake 17 minutes.

3. Take the dish out of the oven and remove the chicken and keep warm. If the sauce is too thick, add the rest of the cream. Simmer for 5 minutes, adding a little salt and pepper. If the sauce is too thin, thicken it with a little *beurre manié* (page 417).

4. Peel and core the apple. Cut it into 8 pieces and sauté in the remaining butter until golden.

5. To serve: Place the chicken breasts on a small platter, pour over the sauce and garnish with the apple pieces.

Note: If Calvados is not available, substitute applejack.

La Traite du Roy

Those of us who are unable to cross the Atlantic and who still hunger for the sound of spoken French, the sight of wine drinkers, the authentic taste of Pâté de Maison, the evocative scent of something like the Paris Métro, narrow and tortuous streets with fearless Gallic motorists, should visit Quebec City. You won't be swindled by the taxi driver or shopkeeper; you won't lose the shirt off your back through your wife's visits to salons of haute couture. To sense the true spirit of the amiable Quebecois, we recommend a visit to La Traite du Roy restaurant, situated in a building that was started in 1684.

The decor is so rustic, the food so plentiful and delicious that the place is haunted with the presence of past owners. When François Hazeur, a merchant, was erecting his residence nearby on Place Royale, Notre Dame des Victoires church and the Villeray-Fornel home—both still extant—were being built. When Hazeur died, ownership passed to a trader, and from him to a rich merchant, who used the basement (now a discothèque) as a wine cellar. More owners came and went. But since 1967, gourmets and music lovers have rollicked in this historical building, so filled with its original 17th-Century atmosphere.

25¼ RUE NOTRE DAME, QUEBEC CITY, QUEBEC

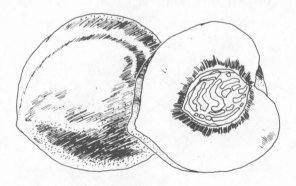

Pêches Flambées
(Flaming Peaches)

8 peaches
2 teaspoons sugar
1 tablespoon butter
2 tablespoons pear brandy
1 tablespoon Grand Marnier
  or Cointreau
Vanilla ice cream
1 tablespoon raspberry jam

1. Peel the peaches and cut into half, catching any juice.

2. Heat very slowly in a chafing dish the sugar, butter and a little of the peach juice. Stir until the sugar is dissolved into a smooth syrup.

3. Add the peaches with the rest of the juice and cook until the liquid is syrupy.

4. Pour on the liqueurs and touch with a lighted match. When the flame subsides, add the raspberry jam.

5. Serve over vanilla ice cream.

SERVES 4

Saumon Henri
(Salmon Henri)

4 tablespoons butter
4 8-ounce fillets of salmon
Flour
1 cup cream
1 pound mushrooms, sliced
2 tablespoons Porto (port
  wine)
2 tablespoons white wine
Salt and pepper

1. Melt the butter in a skillet. Coat the pieces of fish with flour and cook 5 or 6 minutes on each side. Add the mushrooms, Porto and white wine. Cover and cook 8 to 10 minutes.

2. Add cream and simmer 3 to 4 minutes. Lift salmon fillets onto a platter and keep warm. Continue cooking the sauce, stirring, until it is reduced to about half its volume. Add a little more butter if desired and pour sauce over fish. Serve with rice or boiled potatoes.

SERVES 4

Truffles

Since no method of cultivating truffles has ever been discovered, they must be harvested in their natural habitat. The French use pigs, which seem to have a knack for searching out the subterranean vegetable in the oak groves and forested areas where it thrives. A group of good, smart sows, set free in a French forest, will unearth ten to twelve pounds of truffles in a good day.

At the Truffles Restaurant in the Toronto Hyatt-Regency, Dover Sole Truffles, served in a rich Chablis and cream sauce, enhanced with crab meat, tiny shrimp, mushrooms, artichokes, fleurons and truffles, is a standard menu item.

Since truffles do not grow on this continent the restaurant imports them from France where, one must assume, some intelligent hog with a superior snout can be credited with their discovery.

The atmosphere at Truffles—walls lined with old books, original oil paintings, and a 400-year-old French tapestry—is that of a 17th-Century French chalet. Each of the two dining wings has timbered beams, gas and candlelight, wrought-iron candelabra and comfortable high-backed chairs.

If you don't want to eat truffles at Truffles, try the tomato soup which has in it, instead, gin.

HYATT-REGENCY HOTEL, 21 AVENUE ROAD, TORONTO, ONTARIO

Gordon's
Gin-Tomato Soup,
Chafing Dish Style

5 slightly over-ripe
   tomatoes
5 firm, ripe tomatoes
½ cup tomato juice
Small clove garlic
Pinch of thyme
Pinch of sweet basil
Dash of paprika
1 small bay leaf
½ teaspoon salt
Pinch of sugar
¼ teaspoon coarsely
   ground black pepper
2 tablespoons butter
2 shallots, finely chopped
6 medium mushrooms
   sliced thin
3 slices crisply cooked
   bacon
6 tablespoons Gordon's
   gin
1 cup heavy cream

1. Peel all the tomatoes. Seed the firm ones and cut one of them into thin strips. Coarsely chop the rest of the tomatoes.

2. Place all the chopped tomatoes in a saucepan and add the tomato juice, garlic, thyme, basil, paprika, bay leaf, sugar, salt and pepper. Simmer until the tomatoes are very soft. Strain through a fine sieve.

3. At the table, heat a chafing dish and add 1 tablespoon of butter. Sauté the shallots for a minute. Add the mushrooms and cook until they are tender.

4. Add the bacon, cut into fine strips, and the tomato that was cut in strips. Simmer for a few moments.

5. Warm the gin and add to the soup. Immediately touch with a lighted match.

6. Add the strained tomato liquid and simmer down to two-thirds of the original quantity.

7. Add the cream and remaining butter. Heat but do not boil.

8. Serve in warmed soup cups.

SERVES 4

Truffles

Vancouver has been called "young and brash"; but how, you may ask, can a city that is a gloved hand-wave from the Island of Victoria, where everything stops in the afternoon for tea, be so brazenly progressive? Perhaps the critics missed a saunter in lush green Stanley Park, or missed unfurling themselves among the sailboats by the waterfront—or missed a visit to Truffles, that leisured haven for the discriminating diner.

Vancouver has a moist climate—truffles like it dry. So truffles arrive at Truffles by air transport, fresh from the dry woodlands of France, to enhance the most distinguished culinary feats. One can enjoy a French repast amid lavish surroundings (Tiffany lamps, deep leather chairs). To borrow a line from Maurice Chevalier in the film *Gigi*, you will remember you dined at eight—at Truffles—you will remember it well. Those splendid Truffles en Croûte Périgourdine, that superb Bisque of Maine Lobster.

For after-dinner entertainment, downtown Vancouver is only minutes away—for pop to opera diversity.

HYATT REGENCY HOTEL, 655 BURRARD STREET, VANCOUVER, BRITISH COLUMBIA

Salmon en Croûte Regency (*Salmon in Puff Pastry*)

1 10-ounce salmon fillet
Thyme, salt and
    Worcestershire sauce
2 teaspoons lemon juice
Flour
3 tablespoons butter

1. Cut the salmon into 6 pieces, sprinkle with thyme, salt, Worcestershire sauce and lemon juice. Roll lightly in flour.

2. Heat 2 tablespoons of butter in a skillet and when it is very hot, brown the salmon on both sides, turning with a spatula. Remove the salmon from the pan to a wax-paper-lined dish. Chill in the refrigerator.

3. Prepare the dill sauce: Melt the butter over low heat. Add the flour and cook, stir-

Dill sauce:

- 2 tablespoons butter
- 2 tablespoons flour
- 1 cup milk
- ½ teaspoon salt
- ½ teaspoon crushed dill

- 1 medium onion, diced
- ½ pound puff pastry (store bought)
- 2 egg yolks, beaten

ring constantly, until the mixture is smooth and bubbly. Add milk gradually, stirring constantly until thickened. Add seasonings and simmer 2 minutes.

4. Sauté the diced onion in 1 tablespoon of butter until soft. Add to the dill sauce and cool.

5. Preheat oven to 375 degrees F.

6. Roll out the pastry into 2 10-inch rounds. Place 3 pieces of chilled salmon on one half of one round. Cover with ¼ cup of dill sauce. Paint the other half of the round with beaten egg yolks and fold over the salmon, turnover style. Paint the top with egg yolk and firmly seal the edges together with the tines of a fork. Repeat the procedure for the second turnover, using the remaining 3 pieces of salmon and ¼ cup of the remaining dill sauce.

7. Place on a cookie sheet and bake for 25 to 30 minutes or until golden brown. Serve hot accompanied by the remaining ½ cup of dill sauce, warmed.

SERVES 2

Winston's

Aboard the *Williamsburg*, FDR's private yacht, one evening Sir Winston Churchill was concentrating. If a man had consumed—as he had—an average of one quart of wine or spirits each day since his sixteenth birthday, what volume would he have quaffed in the past 65 years? Would it fill the *Williamsburg*'s salon? The answer, calculated by his close friend Lord Cherwell, was devastating. Instead of "swimming like goldfish in a bowl" as Churchill had envisioned, Presidential guests would merely be knee-deep in alcohol: two and one-half feet deep, to be precise.

Although not exactly awash with claret or Chablis, the wine cellar beneath Winston's Restaurant in Toronto could easily satisfy even Churchill. Boasting a stock that "exceeds $100,000" while featuring such gastronomical delights as Beef Wellington, Chateaubriand, Cheese Cake Soufflé and Black Forest Cake, Winston's can please just about everyone—a necessary capability, considering that its "cosmopolitan clientele" arrives from all parts of the world. Business magnates, stage and screen stars, socialites, the young and the old—all are likely to be found there.

Winston's first opened its doors in the '30s. In those early days the waiters wore white gloves, and the music was classical—the performers were off-duty instrumentalists from the Toronto Symphony. In the '40s, regular patrons were given their own keys to the front door, a gambit later copied by after-hour bistros across the border.

Winston's is not giving out keys today, but they are serving superlative food, to lucky strangers as well as to regular and favored patrons.

104 ADELAIDE STREET WEST, TORONTO, ONTARIO

Pâté Winston's

½ pound chicken livers
1 large white onion, chopped
4 tablespoons vegetable oil
½ cup chicken broth
1 bay leaf
Pinch of thyme
1 tablespoon Madras curry powder
¾ teaspoon of salt
⅛ teaspoon of pepper
3 cloves of garlic
½ pound pork fat
1 cup heavy cream
2 tablespoons brandy
4 ounces port wine

1. Sauté the chicken livers in 2 tablespoons of oil just until browned on all sides. Sauté the onions in another frying pan in 2 tablespoons of oil until transparent. Add bay leaf, thyme, curry powder, salt, pepper and garlic.

2. Put all the ingredients through a fine food chopper or spin in a food processor.

3. Put the mixture through a food chopper or food processor a second time, this time including half the pork fat.

4. Put the mixture into a large bowl and work in the cream, brandy and port.

5. Slice the remaining pork fat very thin and line the bottom and sides of a small tureen. Fill with the chicken liver mixture. Bake 40 minutes in a 450-degree oven.

6. Cool and place in refrigerator for 24 hours.

7. Serve cold as a first course with thin slices of rye bread or toast.

SERVES 8 AS AN APPETIZER

Ye Olde Steak House

The rough wooden shield that swings over the doorway could have come from the Cheshire Cheese. But it didn't. The elaborate paneling inside and the heavy wooden beams without could easily belong to Simpson's. But they don't. And the entrees, hors d'oeuvres, and garnishes; the soups, puddings and pastries could have been created at the Dorchester. But they weren't. For you're not in London visiting an Elizabethan establishment; you're in Windsor, Ontario, feasting at Ye Olde Steak House which opened in 1967.

As an echo from England's past, it is undeniably impressive—every bit as rustic and quaint as the restaurants Dr. Samuel Johnson, Jonathan Swift and Alexander Pope once frequented. All that is needed are a few patrons in ruffled shirts and buckled shoes and a snuff box or two to make the 18th-Century atmosphere complete. So while lesser restaurants might throb to the beat of rock or blues, here frills and amusements are sacrificed for quality and quiet as past and present come together.

Windsor is, of course, right across the bridge from Detroit. Convenient for auto moguls; they can flee the chrome and vinyl culture of the automobile capital for an hour or two to feast in the mellow ambience of another day when a coach and four rather than a Coupe de Ville might have waited at the door.

46 CHATHAM STREET WEST, WINDSOR, ONTARIO

Beef and Kidney Stew

1   pound veal kidneys
6   tablespoons butter
1   large onion, sliced thin
2   pounds lean beef
    (chuck or round), cut
    in 1-inch cubes
1   tablespoon flour
1   cup red wine
4   sprigs parsley
1   sprig fresh thyme or
    ¼ teaspoon powdered
    thyme
½   bay leaf
½   pound fresh mushrooms
½   cup beef stock
    (page 416), bouillon
    or water
½   teaspoon salt
¼   teaspoon freshly ground
    black pepper

1. Bring the veal kidneys to a boil in just enough water to cover. Simmer 5 minutes. Drain and pat dry with toweling. Cut into 1-inch cubes, removing any tendons or gristle.

2. Heat the butter in a heavy deep pan or Dutch oven and sauté the sliced onion until tender and golden.

3. Add the beef and brown on all sides, stirring frequently.

4. Remove the beef with a slotted spoon to another dish.

5. Add the flour and stir with a wooden spoon until brown.

6. Add the wine, parsley, thyme and bay leaf.

7. Add the mushrooms which have been washed, dried and sliced. Stir gently for a few moments.

8. Add the beef stock, bouillon or water and stir until the mixture comes to a simmer.

9. Add the beef, kidneys, salt and pepper. Bring to the boiling point again, stirring gently.

10. Cover tightly and simmer 2½ hours. Check from time to time and, if the stew becomes dry, add more beef stock or water.

11. Before serving, taste for seasoning.

12. Serve with fresh buttered peas and baby carrots.

SERVES 6

Ambassadeurs

Service at "Amba," as it is known familiarly to a third generation of an old club, is formal and efficient. Since its founding in 1944 at the hub of Mexico City by famed restaurateur Dalmau Costa, Ambassadeurs has been considered the cornerstone of classical French cuisine in Mexico, and a favorite meeting place for gourmets and Mexican businessmen who are known for their habit of turning luncheon into a banquet.

Culinary delicacies are served under expert supervision. Many of its highly coveted recipes are a legacy of Parisian chef Raymond Oliver, who performed several gastronomic exhibitions in the city. The restaurant is under the direction of Jordi Escofet and Alberto Carraminana, while the cuisine is prepared by Mexican chef Miguel Duran, a 34-year veteran of the house.

The decoration is predominantly classical French-style, with elegant wooden panels, golden velvets, chandeliers and a fine blend of iron and silver work. A beautiful garden and terrace were recently added, giving a touch of gaiety to the quiet sobriety of the main dining room. The entrance hall is decorated with photographs of some of the distinguished guests who have visited this establishment, which makes the greatness of the past endure.

PASEO DE LA REFORMA 12, MEXICO CITY 1, D.F.

Soufflé Glacé Martiniquais *(Cold Pineapple Soufflé)*

1. Remove the outer skin and the core from the pineapple and cut into very small cubes. You will need about 4 cups.

1 pineapple
¾ cup sugar
2 cups water
6 egg whites
2 cups heavy cream
6 egg yolks, well beaten

2. Take 2 cups of pineapple and spin in a blender or food processor or force it through a fine sieve. Stir in the sugar and water. Cook over moderate heat, stirring until sugar is dissolved. Continue cooking until a candy thermometer registers 180 degrees F. or until the syrup spins a fine thread when dropped from the end of a spoon.

3. Beat the 6 egg whites with the heavy cream until the meringue stands in a peak. Set aside.

4. In the top of a double boiler, beat the egg yolks well. Place over simmering water. While beating constantly, pour the hot syrup in a thin stream into the egg yolks. Continue cooking, beating constantly, until the custard thickens.

5. Pour the custard into a small bowl and place it in a large bowl filled with ice. Keep beating the custard until it cools.

6. Fold the pineapple custard into the meringue along with the remaining 2 cups of finely diced pineapple.

7. Tie a 2-inch collar of wax paper around the edge of 6 to 8 individual soufflé dishes. Fill with pineapple mixture and put in the refrigerator for at least 6 hours. Remove the paper collars before serving.

SERVES 6 TO 8

La Cava

Will Rogers was captivated by the diversity of Mexico City. He once remarked, "Say, what a city this is! She is a cross between New York, Tulsa and Hollywood, with a bit of Old San Antonio and Nogales, Arizona, thrown in." La Cava restaurant partakes of this mélange. In its new quarters, close by the university city, this 22-year-old establishment combines crisp modern decor with the glow of the past. The rush seats, stained glass and Mexican ceramics on the walls offer an indigenous flavor, while at the same time the crisp simplicity is Scandinavian Contemporary. La Cava is entirely Mexican and also entirely International. You can enjoy a local dish cooked to perfection or a Continental specialty as served in a leading U.S. restaurant. The wine cellar pours itself out with the same International flavor.

One of the innovations at the new location is a patio and garden which perfectly blend the modern and traditional. You may dine under the red brick arches of the patio or walk by the clean-cut, futuristic fountain in the center and enjoy the superb climate along with superb food. The pillars and stucco wall facings, with their sunburst reliefs, call for a subdued *Olé*.

AVENIDA INSURGENTES SUR, 2465, MEXICO CITY 20, D.F.

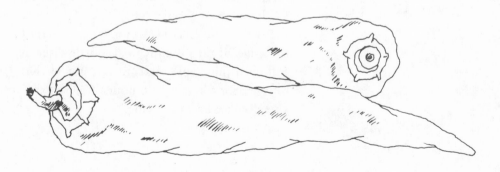

Mexico

Ceviche of Red Snapper Acapulco

2¼ pounds fresh fillet
    of red snapper
1 pint lemon juice
3 pounds (9-12) ripe
    tomatoes
½ cup chopped onion
Hot green peppers (chiles
    Serranos), minced
5 sprigs coriander,
    finely chopped
1 teaspoon marjoram,
    powdered
½ cup olive oil
20 green olives, halved
2 avocados, peeled and
    sliced in 20 long
    pieces
Salt and pepper

Cut the fish into 1-inch-square pieces. Put them into a stainless steel or glass bowl and cover with the lemon juice. Cover with a tight-fitting lid and store in the refrigerator for 1 to 2 days.

Rinse, peel and halve the tomatoes. Squeeze out the seeds and crush the tomatoes over a fine strainer so that the juice can fall into a bowl. Chop the pulp rather coarsely.

Add the onion, coriander, 15 minced green chiles, olive oil, marjoram, olives, salt and pepper. Add the strained tomato juice.

Drain the fish. Rinse in cold water. Combine with the sauce and taste for seasoning. You may want to add more hot green chiles. Serve in stemmed glasses, each garnished with 2 slices of avocado.

SERVES 10 AS AN APPETIZER

Delmonico's

"**T**he most extravagant dinner possible" was Mexico's answer to Craig Claiborne's extravaganza at the Chez Denis in Paris and the $575-a-person 15-course meal at Maxim's in Chicago. Delmonico's rose to the occasion with 16 courses and 11 wines. "A display of variety and opulence that can be achieved using our fine native products," explained owner Nick Noyes, not without a certain humor. The Blinis of Ant Roe tasted like crisp, fried bacon. The fresh Mousse of Stone Crab and Chowder of Turtle were more familiar. Then came the Cockscombs and Maguey Worms. The Iguana Tail, another first, was delicious and prepared in an Italian-style tuna sauce. The roasted peacock, borne in by two of the staff dressed as Oriental slaves, was the sensation of the evening. The bird had been prepared according to a 19th-Century recipe. Next course: a refreshing salad of rose petals, prickly cactus and giant water chestnuts. The special guests still had room for helpings of the Queen Julianne Ice Bombe and a handful of chocolate "frivolities." The accompanying liqueur was a honey and anise variety from Yucatan called Xtabentum.

Such a special-occasion menu may strain the ordinary palate but it does show the exuberance and orginality that pertain at Delmonico's restaurant, where patrons have learned to eat with mucho gusto.

LONDRES 87, MEXICO CITY 6, D.F.

Grilled Turkey Steak Delmonico's

Breast of 1 turkey, frozen

Marinade:
1 cup olive oil
4 cloves garlic, crushed

1. Have the butcher cut away the legs of a frozen turkey and then saw the breast, crossways, into 6 equal slices.

2. Combine ingredients for the marinade. Pour over the turkey slices and let stand in the refrigerator overnight.

3. Shortly before serving time lift the turkey slices out of the marinade to drain. Grill

½ onion, sliced
Dash Worcestershire sauce
½ cup dry white wine
1 stalk parsley
Salt and pepper to taste

Tiny Bay Scallops
in Lime-egg Sauce

1½ pounds bay scallops
Juice of 6 large limes
2 egg yolks
4 tablespoons prepared
mustard
1 cup olive oil
¼ cup white wine vinegar
Salt and freshly ground
pepper
Tabasco
Worcestershire sauce

medium rare under the broiler or over char-coal, outdoors. Baste lightly with a little of the marinade. Do not overcook, as the meat will be dry.

4. Serve on a large platter, surrounded by brandied peaches, half-guava shells filled with currant jelly, spiced applesauce and sliced pineapple.

SERVES 6

1. Put the scallops into a shallow bowl, sprinkle with salt and the juice of 4 limes and set aside for 1 hour. Stir occasionally.

2. In an electric mixing bowl, combine the egg yolks and mustard.

3. Slowly add the olive oil, beating continuously as if making mayonnaise. Continue adding the oil intermittently with the vinegar until the sauce is thick.

4. Add the juice of 2 limes and season to taste with salt, pepper, and a dash of Tabasco and Worcestershire sauce.

5. To serve: Place the scallops in individual hors d'oeuvre dishes. Pour the sauce over and decorate with small onion rings and black olives. Serve with Chablis or Alsatian wine.

SERVES 6 AS AN APPETIZER

Las Mañanitas

Dr. Doolittle dines at Las Mañanitas. Owner Robert Krause loves birds, as do his patrons; and so peacocks, flamingoes, cranes, egrets, macaws roam freely among the diners. But if birds are just ornery critters to you, then admire the fine collection of sculptures and paintings by Mexico's leading artists.

You can order a stuffed baby chicken—or a T-bone steak. Besides international dishes—Vichyssoise, Braised Oxtail, Osso Buco—the restaurant prides itself on authentically prepared local fare, such as Tortilla Soup, Chiles Rellenos de Queso, Enchiladas and Red Snapper Veracruzano.

Las Mañanitas has thrived on its relaxed and cordial style. In 1955, Krause, then a 27-year-old bachelor lawyer from Oregon, happened upon a charming Mexican Colonial-style house with a lovely old garden and five bedrooms. He moved into one of the servants' rooms. The bedrooms became guest rooms; into the kitchen flew Manuel Quinto, a culinary angel who had been cooking for prominent residents in the area. Over the years, terraces and additional suites were added to the structure, all fashioned with easy-going elegance. Two months after the opening, a 15-year-old boy, Ruben Cerda, came to work as an assistant busboy. Krause sent him to Europe to complete his education, and now he is the proud general manager of Las Mañanitas.

RICARDO LINARES NO. 107, CUERNAVACA, MORELOS

Mexico

Brazilian Pie

1 pound vanilla wafers,
    crushed
¼ pound butter, melted
1 can (14 ounce) sweetened
    condensed milk
3 egg yolks, slightly
    beaten
½ cup white raisins
½ cup pecans, finely
    chopped
5 egg whites
1 cup sugar
¼ teaspoon vanilla
Grated rind of 1 small
    lemon or 1 lime

1. Preheat oven to 350 degrees F. Crush the wafers with a rolling pin or pulverize them in a food processor. Mix well with the melted butter and press them well in a 9-inch pie pan.

2. Cook the condensed milk over moderate heat until it begins to thicken. Stir in the egg yolks, raisins and pecans and cook until thick and creamy. Cool and pour into the unbaked pie shell.

3. Beat egg whites until very stiff and gradually add the sugar. Continue to beat until the meringue is very stiff. Add the vanilla and most of the grated lemon or lime rind. Reserve a bit to decorate the top.

4. Bake the pie 25 minutes. Sprinkle with remaining rind. Chill in the refrigerator and serve very cold.

SERVES 6

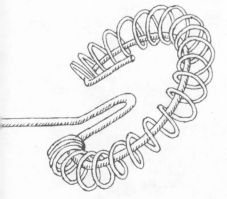

Restaurant del Lago

To understand Mexico City, you join the families enjoying themselves in Chapultepec Park. The stupendous museums and outdoor sculptures speak of Mexico's past, its long struggle for freedom; but the Mexican people, who represent the present, are here in profusion—hard-working mothers and fathers, exuberant children, chasing over the grass, paddling in gaily painted canoes. There is another side to Mexico City. It is a splendid city, where people live splendidly. You catch this feeling in the bronze and marble heroes reared heavenward, intersecting the broad avenue of the Reforma. In modern terms, the Del Lago restaurant in Chapultepec Park is the epitome of this splendid living.

Founded in 1964, a part of the new recreational area of the park, the Del Lago is a soaring structure resembling a futuristic version of a great sailboat, which stands by an artificial lake. Facing a central façade is a fountain 150 feet in diameter that sprays a large whirling jet of water. At night, bright colors shine respendently through these jets. Inside, chef René Valentin and his staff of thirty assistants offer a flawless menu of French and other international delicacies, along with Mexican favorites. The food and the setting will be long cherished—the night you glided away in a sailboat of glass panes, with a roof that opened to the sky like a giant shell.

NUEVO BOSQUE DE CHAPULTEPEC, MEXICO CITY, D.F.

Mexico

Strawberry Sherbet au Champagne

2 quarts ripe strawberries
2 cups sugar
½ cup water
2 tablespoons lemon juice
1 bottle dry champagne,
    chilled

1. Wash and hull the berries and puree them through a fine food mill or in a food processor. Save out 8 berries for garnish.

2. Place the puree in a saucepan and stir in the sugar. Cook over moderate heat, stirring with a wooden spoon until the sugar dissolves. Add the lemon juice. Cook without stirring until the mixture measures 220 degrees F. on a candy thermometer.

3. Cool the mixture and pour into ice trays. Freeze until it reaches the mushy stage and has started to harden around the edges. Beat quickly in a previously chilled electric mixing bowl until fluffy. Put back into the ice trays and freeze for 6 hours. To serve: Spoon balls of the sherbet into individual champagne glasses. Fill the glasses with cold champagne. Top each with a fresh strawberry.

SERVES 8

Sauces and Other Basics

Sauces and Other Basics

Béarnaise Sauce

2 shallots, chopped fine
1 teaspoon chopped
   tarragon
1 tablespoon chopped
   parsley
⅓ cup tarragon
   vinegar
Hollandaise sauce

Combine the shallots and half the chopped tarragon and parsley with the vinegar in a small saucepan and simmer until it measures 1½ tablespoons. Set aside.

Make the Hollandaise and add the vinegar and herbs after the butter. Stir in the rest of the herbs.

Béchamel Sauce

4 tablespoons butter
4 tablespoons flour
2 cups milk
Salt and pepper

This sauce may be halved or doubled according to the requirements of a recipe.

Heat the butter in a saucepan over moderate heat. Add the flour and whisk for about 2 minutes, without letting the mixture brown. Add the milk all at once and whisk vigorously until the mixture comes to a boil and becomes thick and smooth.

MAKES 2 CUPS.

Beef Stock

4 pounds combination
   veal and beef bones
1 cup sliced onions
1 cup sliced carrots
2 stalks celery, sliced
2 tablespoons sugar
2 large bay leaves

1. Preheat oven to 450 degrees F. Place bones and vegetables in a roasting pan and bake 30 to 40 minutes or until brown. Sprinkle with sugar and bake 15 minutes longer.

2. Transfer everything to a deep kettle. Add the herbs and spices.

3. Dissolve the tomato paste in a cup of water and pour into the roasting pan and

½ teaspoon thyme
2 teaspoons salt
10 peppercorns, crushed
2 teaspoons tomato paste
Water

bring to a boil, scraping all the brown particles from the bottom of the pan.

4. Pour into the kettle and add enough water to cover the bones. Bring to a boil.

5. Reduce the heat and simmer 2 hours, removing any scum that floats to the top.

6. Strain and cool. Chill in the refrigerator.

7. Skim off the fat that forms on the surface and store in ½-pint and 1-pint containers. This may be frozen.

Beurre Manié

2 tablespoons butter, softened
3 tablespoons flour

Beurre Manié is used for thickening sauces. Work the butter and flour together with a fork or with your fingers. Drop in small portions into the boiling liquid and whisk until the sauce thickens. The amount of paste will determine the thickness of the sauce.

Beurre Noisette

½ pound butter
4 tablespoons wine vinegar

Clarify the butter by heating it slowly until it separates. Pour off the clear yellow butter and discard the white sediment (whey). Heat the clear butter over moderate heat until it turns a golden brown—not black.

In another small saucepan boil down the vinegar to about 1 tablespoonful. Stir into the butter and season with salt and pepper.

MAKES 1 CUP

Bordelaise Sauce

4 tablespoons minced
   shallots
1 cup red Burgundy wine
⅛ teaspoon ground
   black pepper
⅛ teaspoon thyme
1 bay leaf
1 cup brown sauce or
   demi-glacé
4 ounces beef marrow
6 tablespoons butter
¼ teaspoon lemon juice

1. Put the shallots, wine, black pepper and herbs in a saucepan.
2. Boil down until the liquid measures approximately 4 tablespoonfuls.
3. Add the brown sauce or demi-glacé and simmer very gently for 30 minutes.
4. Skim from time to time.
5. Strain through a fine sieve. Set aside.
6. Dice the beef marrow and simmer for 2 minutes in boiling water.
7. When ready to serve, add the lemon juice and the beef marrow; stir in 6 tablespoons of butter. Taste for seasoning.

MAKES 2 CUPS

Brown Sauce

5 cups strong beef stock
4 tablespoons unsalted
   butter
4 tablespoons all purpose
   flour
1 clove garlic, peeled
1 bay leaf
½ teaspoon dried chopped
   thyme
1 small onion, chopped
¼ teaspoon Worcestershire
   sauce

Preheat oven to 350 degrees F. Boil stock in small heavy-bottomed saucepan. Melt butter, add flour, blend with a whisk. Cook a few minutes until mixture is slightly browned. Pour stock into casserole dish and stir in the butter-flour mixture. Simmer until the stock thickens. Add garlic, thyme, bay leaf, onion, Worcestershire sauce, and place the casserole in oven to "roast" for 1½ hours.

Strain sauce into a bowl, add wine and season to taste with salt and pepper. Store for convenience in ½-pint and 1-pint containers. Brown sauce may be frozen.

Sherry wine to taste
Salt and freshly ground
    black pepper to taste

Chicken Stock

2 pounds chicken backs
  and wings
2 quarts cold water
1 stalk celery with
  leaves
1 carrot
1 medium onion, peeled
  and quartered
4-5 sprigs parsley
1 small bay leaf
⅛ teaspoon powdered
  thyme
1 teaspoon salt
6 peppercorns

Place the chicken backs and wings in a kettle containing cold water. Bring slowly to a boil, skimming off any foamy substance that rises to the top. Add the herbs, vegetables and seasonings. Bring to a boil, cover and simmer gently for 2 hours.

Cool the stock, strain and refrigerate. Remove the fat that coagulates on the surface. Store in the refrigerator for a week or in pint containers in the freezer until needed.

MAKES 1 QUART

Chicken Velouté Sauce

4 tablespoons butter
4 tablespoons flour
1 cup rich chicken stock
  or bouillon
½ pint all-purpose cream
Salt and pepper

Heat the butter and stir in the flour. Cook without browning for 2 minutes. Add the chicken broth and whisk until smooth. Add the cream and heat just to the boiling point. Season with salt and pepper.

MAKES 2 CUPS

Clarified Butter

Put the butter into a small heavy saucepan or into the top of a double boiler. Heat very slowly until the butter melts. When the milky solids have separated from the clear butter, gently pour off the clear butter, leaving the milky sediment (the whey) behind. Discard the whey.

Crème Anglaise (Custard sauce)

4 egg yolks
2 tablespoons flour
4 tablespoons sugar
⅛ teaspoon salt
2 cups milk, scalded
1 teaspoon vanilla or other flavoring

In the top of a double boiler beat the egg yolks, flour, sugar and salt together until blended. Add the hot milk and cook over boiling water, stirring constantly until the mixture is thick enough to coat a metal spoon.

Strain and cool. Chill in the refrigerator.

Crème Chantilly (Sweetened whipped cream)

1 cup heavy cream
2 tablespoons confectioners' sugar
1 teaspoon vanilla
1 egg white (optional)

Pour the cream into a chilled electric mixer bowl and whip until it forms stiff peaks. Continue beating while adding the sugar, 1 tablespoon at a time, and the vanilla. Adding 1 egg white, beaten separately and then folded into the whipped cream, is helpful if the Crème Chantilly has to be prepared several hours before it is to be served.

Crêpes, Savory

6 tablespoons flour
¼ teaspoon salt
3 eggs slightly beaten
2 cups milk
1 teaspoon melted butter

Combine all ingredients. Beat until smooth, then let batter stand 30 minutes or longer before making crêpes.

Lightly grease a 6-inch skillet and heat it well. Pour in a large spoonful of crêpe batter and tilt pan to coat the bottom with a thin film. Cook just until lightly browned on the underside. Flip and cook the other side for about 30 seconds.

Crêpes, Dessert

1 cup skim milk
3 egg yolks
1 tablespoon sugar
1¼ cups all-purpose flour
2 tablespoons brandy
5 tablespoons butter, melted and cooled.

Combine all ingredients in a blender and spin until thoroughly blended. Store batter covered in the refrigerator for 3 hours or longer before making crêpes.

Croutons

Croutons may be either (I) large toasts on which to serve game, chicken or small steaks or (II) small squares served as a garnish for soups and salads.

Croutons I: Cut stale white bread slices ½ inch thick into ovals, rounds or squares. Brush with melted butter and bake in a 400-degree oven until golden brown.

Croutons II: Cut stale white bread, free from crusts, into small cubes. Heat butter with 1 clove of sliced garlic (optional) in a skillet. Remove the garlic with a slotted spoon and fry the croutons in the butter until light brown. Stir occasionally to brown the croutons on all sides.

Demi-Glacé
(Rich brown sauce)

¼ cup chopped mushroom
  peelings and stems
6 tablespoons dry sherry
2 cups brown sauce
1 tablespoon meat extract

Simmer the mushrooms in the sherry until the sherry measures about 3 tablespoons. Combine with the brown sauce (or canned beef gravy) and the meat extract.

Cover and simmer 20 to 25 minutes. Strain before using.

Drawn Butter

⅓ cup butter
3 tablespoons flour
½ teaspoon salt
Dash pepper
1½ cups hot fish stock
  or hot water
1 teaspoon lemon juice

Melt half the butter in a heavy saucepan. Add the flour, salt and pepper and mix until smooth. Add the hot stock or water, bring to a boil and simmer, stirring, for 5 minutes. Add the rest of the butter in small portions and finally the lemon juice.

Fish Stock

2 pounds fish trimming
(head, tail and bones)
3 quarts cold water
2 bay leaves
2 onions, each stuck with
1 clove
2 carrots, sliced in large
pieces
2 stalks celery, sliced
2 teaspoons salt
8 white peppercorns

1. Put everything in a kettle. Bring to a boil slowly, removing any scum that floats to the surface. Simmer 45 minutes.

2. Strain through a fine sieve.

3. Store in ½-pint and pint containers for convenience.

4. Fish stock may be frozen.

Fish Velouté

2½ cups fish stock or
diluted clam broth
6 tablespoons butter
12 tablespoons flour
Salt and pepper

1. Make fish stock by simmering the bones and trimmings of any white fish in water with onions, carrots, celery, bay leaf, salt and peppercorns for 45 minutes. Strain through a fine sieve.

2. Heat 6 tablespoons butter and stir in the flour. Add 2½ cups of fish stock and stir with a whisk until blended. Cover and barely simmer for 30 minutes. Season with salt and pepper.

3. This will keep 10 days in the refrigerator or may be made in large quantities and frozen in convenient amounts for future use.

Garlic Oil

1 cup olive or peanut oil
2 large cloves garlic, pressed

Put the oil and garlic into a jar. Cover and let stand for 24 hours. Strain and use as desired.

Hollandaise Sauce I

3 large egg yolks
1 tablespoon water
10 tablespoons soft butter
¾ teaspoon lemon juice
Salt and pepper

Whisk the egg yolks and water in a heavy saucepan or in the top of a double boiler until frothy. Add the butter tablespoon by tablespoon, whisking constantly until the mixture thickens. Work over moderate heat so as not to scramble the eggs. Season with lemon juice, salt, pepper and a dash of cayenne.

MAKES 1 CUP

Hollandaise Sauce II
(Blender Method)

12 tablespoons
   (1½ sticks) butter
4 egg yolks
Juice of 1 lemon
   (2 tablespoons)
½ teaspoon salt
⅛ teaspoon white pepper

Heat the butter slowly. Put the egg yolks into a blender. Add the lemon juice, salt and pepper. Spin the egg yolks over low speed, gradually adding the butter in a steady stream. (The whey should stay in the saucepan.)

Spin just until thick and smooth.

MAKES 1 CUP

Hollandaise Sauce III
(Quick)

Whisk the egg yolk and cream in a small saucepan over moderately high heat just until it starts to thicken. Remove from the heat, whisk in the lemon juice and butter and

1 egg yolk
1 tablespoon cream
2 tablespoons butter
1 teaspoon lemon juice
Salt, pepper, cayenne

return to the heat and cook just until it starts to thicken, whisking constantly and vigorously—a matter of moments.

Remove from the heat and season with salt, pepper and a dash of cayenne.

SERVES 2; THIS RECIPE CAN BE DOUBLED OR TRIPLED

Madeira Sauce

3 tablespoons butter
3 tablespoons minced
   shallots or green onions
   (scallions)
2 cups brown sauce
6 tablespoons Madeira
4 teaspoons lemon juice

Heat the butter in a small saucepan and simmer the shallots or scallions until soft. Do not brown.

Add the brown sauce, Madeira and lemon juice. Cover and simmer for 10 minutes. Taste for seasoning.

MAKES 2 CUPS

Mayonnaise

2 egg yolks
2 teaspoons Dijon mustard
½ teaspoon salt
⅛ teaspoon white pepper
4 tablespoons wine
   vinegar or lemon juice
2 cups olive oil (or 1 cup
   olive oil and 1 cup
   salad oil)

Mix the egg yolks with the mustard, salt and pepper and beat with a whisk or with a rotary beater. Gradually add the oil in a very fine stream until the mixture begins to thicken. Add the vinegar slowly and continue beating, adding the rest of the oil.

MAKES 2 CUPS

Mornay Sauce

Béchamel sauce
2 teaspoons Dijon mustard
¾ cup grated Cheddar
cheese

Make the Béchamel sauce. Add the mustard and grated cheese and stir over moderate heat until the cheese melts. Taste for seasoning.

MAKES 2 CUPS

Mousseline Sauce

3 egg yolks
½ cup cream (heavy or
all-purpose)
¼ cup fish stock
½ pound soft butter
Salt
White pepper
Lemon juice

Put the egg yolks, cream and fish stock in a mixing bowl. Set the bowl over a pan of simmering water. Beat the mixture with a wire whisk or rotary beater until thickened to a creamy consistency. Do not overheat the water or the eggs will scramble.

Remove the bowl from the pan and beat in the butter, a small piece at a time, until it is absorbed. The sauce will have the consistency of Hollandaise. Taste for seasoning and add, if necessary, salt, pepper and lemon juice, a few drops only.

Rice

1. Pour 1½ to 2 cups long-grain white rice into a large kettle of briskly boiling salted water. Stir once and bring to a rapid boil. Boil 11 minutes.

2. Drain in a colander and wash in luke-warm water to remove excess starch. Fluff the rice with a fork or with your hand.

3. Place in an ovenproof serving dish. Dot generously with butter and season with salt and pepper. Cover.

4. Before serving, place in a pan of hot water and reheat 25 to 30 minutes in a 350-degree oven, or reheat over boiling water in a double boiler.

SERVES 6 TO 8

Rice Pilaf

  6 tablespoons butter
  1 small onion, chopped
1½ cups long-grain raw rice
  3 cups water, or chicken
    or beef bouillon, heated
Salt and pepper
  ⅛ teaspoon powdered
    saffron (optional)

One cup of raw rice will yield 3 cups of cooked rice. This recipe for 6 servings can be adjusted to make the required number of servings.

Heat the butter and sauté the onion over moderate heat until softened. Add the rice and cook slowly 3 to 4 minutes or until the rice is opaque. Stir in the hot broth.

Cover tightly and cook over low heat or in a 350-degree oven until all the liquid has been absorbed. This should take about 20 minutes.

Season with salt, pepper and, if desired, saffron. Mix gently.

SERVES 6

Vinaigrette
(French Dressing)

4 tablespoons wine vinegar
2 teaspoons Dijon
   mustard
1 teaspoon salt
¼ teaspoon white pepper
1 cup olive oil, salad oil,
   peanut oil or a
   combination

Mix together the vinegar, mustard, salt and pepper. Whisk the oil in slowly, adding water if it becomes too thick.

Wild Rice

1 cup wild rice
Boiling water

1. Wash the rice and place in a saucepan. Pour in enough boiling water to cover the rice. Cover and let stand until cool. Drain completely.

2. Repeat the process 3 times.

3. The rice can be reheated in the top of a double boiler with a tablespoon of butter, or heated in an ovenproof casserole at 350 degrees F. for 25 to 30 minutes.

SERVES 6

Index

Index of Restaurants

Index of Recipes